DYNAMICS

OF THE

UNITED STATES

AUTOMOBILE INDUSTRY

DYNAMICS
OF THE
UNITED STATES
AUTOMOBILE INDUSTRY

by Charles E. Edwards

UNIVERSITY OF SOUTH CAROLINA PRESS • COLUMBIA

To

Elizabeth Orr Edwards

and

Edward Edwards

ACKNOWLEDGMENTS

MANY ACADEMIC MEN have helped me in the course of my work leading to this book. For their continuing advice and encouragement, Joe S. Floyd, Jr., of the University of North Carolina and James A. Morris and Steven J. Shaw of the University of South Carolina are due my greatest appreciation. Others to whom I owe special thanks for their encouragement and suggestions include Richard P. Calhoon, Milton S. Heath, Clifton H. Kreps, Jr., Clement S. Logsdon, Ralph W. Pfouts, Gustav T. Schwenning, and William A. Terrill of the University of North Carolina; D. Rutledge Vining of the University of Virginia; and Alpheus R. Marshall of the Georgia Institute of Technology.

Men of the automobile manufacturing industry, as well as of the closely related automobile retailing industry, have provided help in a variety of ways, including giving generously of their time to discuss problems of the automobile industry and of particular firms, and/or furnishing materials related to the industry and to specific firms. Singled out for individual recognition are Bernard A. Chapman, Edward L. Cushman, George E. Gullen, Jr., Howard E. Hallas, William W. Hotchkiss, Leonard C. Kropp, Gerald C. Myers, and Andrew F. Wilson of the American Motors Corporation; George H. Brown and Fred G. Secrest of the Ford Motor Company; Byers A. Burlingame of the Studebaker Corporation and Melvin L. Milligan, II, formerly of the Studebaker Corporation; and Paul E. Herzog of the National Automobile Dealers Association. My thanks go also to the public relations and other officials of Chrysler Corporation and General Motors Corporation, as well as of the three companies previously named, for their prompt and courteous provision of numerous publications of their companies and in several instances of suggestions regarding additional sources of company and industry information.

Among others to whom I am obligated are C. E. Logwood of the South Carolina Public Service Commission and Roger C. White of the South Carolina Automobile Dealers Association for their assistance in providing certain reference materials; Miss Margaret L. Porth for her careful work in typing the final manuscript; and my wife for her help with the earlier drafts.

Much of the work for this book was completed during the period of a grant from The Southern Fellowships Fund, when an earlier version was prepared as a doctoral dissertation accepted at the University of North Carolina. Additional work was completed during the course of a Ford Foundation Regional Seminar in Economics at the University of Virginia. Final stages of the work were assisted financially by the Committee on Faculty Research and the School of Business Administration of the University of South Carolina.

I alone, however, am responsible for any errors of fact or interpretation which may be found in this book.

Charles E. Edwards

Columbia, South Carolina
July 31, 1964

CONTENTS

ACKNOWLEDGMENTS   vii

LIST OF TABLES   xii

LIST OF CHARTS   xiii

INTRODUCTION AND BACKGROUND: THE
PROBLEMS OF BUSINESS   1

I. SETTING THE STAGE FOR MERGER   13

The Independents' Position   13
Restricted Production   16
A Major Turning Point   17
The Independents' Financial Performance   18
Net Sales and Operating Profits   18
Operating Profit Rates   22
The Change in Market Conditions   23
Setting the Stage for Merger   31

II. THE MERGERS   34

The Nash-Kelvinator-Hudson Merger   34
The Studebaker-Packard Merger   38
An End and a Beginning   44

III. AMERICAN MOTORS' RESURGENCE   47

The Lean Years   48
Product and Production Changes   48
A Decline in Market Position   52
Financial Effects of Sales Decline   54
Resurgence and Prosperity   63
The American Motors Strategy   64

IV. STUDEBAKER-PACKARD'S STRUGGLE   70

The Years of the Full Line   70
Market Position Effects of the Full Line   73
Financial Effects of the Full-Line Approach   74
Financial Influence of Reduced Defense Sales   80
Curtailment of the Full Line   81
Curtiss-Wright Agreement   83
Quasi-Reorganization   85
Product and Organizational Changes   86
Financial Effects of Curtailment of
Full Line   90

[ix]

Complete Abandonment of the Full Line   92
    Refinancing   92
    Product Programs and Policies   94
A New Look   95
The Studebaker-Packard Strategy   101

V. NONSCALAR PROBLEMS   104

Impact of Easy Selling Conditions, 1946-1952   105
Significance of Changed Market after 1952   109
Nonscalar Problems, 1953-1957   110
    Credit Restrictions   110
    Price Relationships   111
    Labor Costs   115
    Management Complacency   118
    "Orphan Car" Influence   123
    Defense Sales   124
A Summary and Comment   125

VI. THE INDEPENDENTS AND THE COMPACT   127

Success of the Compact Car   127
Trends of the 1950's   129
    A Trend toward Uniformity   133
    A Squeeze on the Middle   134
The Appeal of the Compact   135
The Impact of the Compact   138
Significance of the Compact   139

VII. THE QUESTION OF SIZE   142

The Nash-Kelvinator-Hudson Merger   143
The Studebaker-Packard Merger   144
Disparities in the Sizes of Car Producers   146
Significance of the Mergers   147
Some Questions   148

VIII. THE MANUFACTURING PROBLEM   149

Nature of Manufacturing Economies of Scale   149
Cost Differentials and Profits   152
Organization for Automobile Manufacture   153
Volume Requirements for "Low" Unit Cost   154
    Romney Statements   154
    Bain Estimates   162
    Maxcy and Silberston Estimates   163
    Reconciliation of the Estimates   164
Actual Output vs. Estimated Requirements   166
The Mergers and Manufacturing Potential   168
A Summary Comment   169

IX. THE PHYSICAL DISTRIBUTION PROBLEM   170

Physical Distribution Systems   170
Central Assembly Cost Disadvantages:
  The 1950's   172
Requirements for Low Transport Cost:
  The 1950's   177
The Piggyback Innovation: The 1960's   179
Summary   183

X. THE MARKETING PROBLEM   185

Advantages of Large Volume Operations   185
The Market Environment   188
Style and Style Change   201
  Justification of Styling Emphasis   201
  Tooling Costs of Style Change   204
  The Risks of Style Change   213
Advertising   216
Dealer Organizations   224
  Market Coverage   225
  Sales per Franchise and Dealer   227
  Requirements for Competitive Dealership
    Organization   230
Price Policies   234
  Price Leadership   234
  Cost Leadership   237
  Consumer Acceptance   239
The Marketing Problem and the Independents   243

XI. DIVERSIFICATION AND OTHER PROBLEMS   247

Financing   247
Purchasing   251
Management and Research   254
Diversification   257
Summary   260

XII. THE HISTORICAL ELEMENT   261

Cumulative Influences of History   261
The Corporation   265
The Antitrust Dilemma   266

SUMMARY AND CONCLUSION: THE TASK
OF MANAGEMENT   275

SELECTED BIBLIOGRAPHY   285

INDEX   289

TABLES

1. United States Passenger Car Production and Percentage Shares of Production of the Leading Independents, Other Independents, the Big Three, and their Totals, 1946-1963 14

2. United States New Passenger Car Registrations and Percentage Shares of Registrations of the Leading Independents, Other Domestic Independents, Foreign Producers, the Big Three, and their Totals, 1946-1963 15

3. New Passenger Car Registrations and Share of Total United States Registrations of American Motors Cars, 1946-1963 53

4. American Motors Corporation Abbreviated Comparative Income Statements for Years Ended September 30, 1954-1963 56

5. American Motors Corporation Abbreviated Comparative Balance Sheets for Years Ended September 30, 1954-1963 57

6. New Passenger Car Registrations and Share of Total United States Registrations of Studebaker-Packard Cars, 1946-1963 74

7. Studebaker (Studebaker-Packard) Corporation Abbreviated Comparative Income Statements for Years Ended December 31, 1954-1963 76

8. Studebaker (Studebaker-Packard) Corporation Abbreviated Comparative Balance Sheets for Years Ended December 31, 1954-1963 77

9. Factory Advertised Delivered Prices of the Lowest-Priced Four-Door Sedans by Make for the Leading Independents and the Big Three for 1952-1957 Models 112

10. New Passenger Car Registrations and Shares of Total Registrations in the United States of U. S.-Made Full-Sized Cars, U. S.-Made Compact Cars, and Foreign-Made Cars, 1955-1963 130

11. Suggested Factory Advertised or Port of Entry Delivered Prices of Selected Lowest-Priced Four-Door Models of Full-Sized and Compact Passenger Cars, 1950, 1952, and 1954-1963 Models 132

12. Production of Compact Cars in the United States, 1957-1963 140

13. Amortization of Special Commercial Tools, Dies, and Equipment by the Independents and the Big Three, 1946-1963 205

[xii]

14. Amortization of Special Commercial Tools, Dies, and Equipment per Car Produced by the Independents and the Big Three, 1946-1963 206
15. Passenger Car Advertising Expenditures by Manufacturer and per Car Registered, 1949-1962 . . . 219
16. Passenger Car Advertising Expenditures by Make, Total and per Car Registered, 1950, 1956, and 1962 . 220
17. Estimated Total Advertising Expenditure by Passenger Car Manufacturers in Measured and Unmeasured Media 223
18. Number of Franchises and Dealers of United States Passenger Car Manufacturers at the Beginning of 1958 and 1959 226
19. Number of Franchises of United States Passenger Car Manufacturers at the Beginning of 1950 . . 227
20. New Car Registrations per Franchise by Make of Car for the United States Passenger Car Manufacturers, 1950 and 1955-1963 228
21. Number of Franchises and Dealers of United States Passenger Car Manufacturers, January 1, 1962 . . 230
22. New Car Registrations per Franchise and Dealer of United States Passenger Car Manufacturers, 1957 and 1960 231
23. Dealer Local Advertising per Car, 1956-1963 . . 231
24. Total Finished Sheet Steel Purchases, Total Cost of Such Steel, and Average Price per Ton for the Big Three and American Motors, 1956 253

CHARTS

1. Net Sales and Operating Profits or Losses of the Leading Independents, 1946-1958 19
2. Percentage Operating Profit Rates on Net Sales, Operating Assets, and Long-term Investment for the Leading Independents, the Big Three, and All Manufacturing, 1946-1958 24

INTRODUCTION AND BACKGROUND

THE PROBLEMS OF BUSINESS

IN 1953, the four leading independent manufacturers of automobiles — Hudson Motor Car Company, Nash-Kelvinator Corporation, Packard Motor Car Company, and Studebaker Corporation—suffered sudden, serious setbacks in their positions in the United States new car market. The shares of new car registrations accounted for by their makes fell sharply from their previous levels. Concurrently, the four firms were confronted with sharp reversals in their financial performances; and in the following year, their separate corporate existences were brought to an end. On May 1, 1954, Hudson Motor Car Company merged with Nash-Kelvinator Corporation to form American Motors Corporation; and on October 1, 1954, Packard Motor Car Company and Studebaker Corporation combined to become Studebaker-Packard Corporation.

A STRUGGLE FOR SURVIVAL

The mergers, which were widely viewed as essential moves in a struggle for survival by the relatively small independent manufacturers of automobiles, did not provide immediate solutions to the problems of the companies. The course of business was not smooth for either of the new corporations. Indeed, it seemed for a long while that neither new firm would be able to survive.

From 1954 through 1957, neither of the new companies was able to report a profit. For each of its first four consecutive annual reports, American Motors recorded losses before tax adjustments varying from a low of more than $12,000,000 to a high of almost $29,000,000 per year, the firm's largest loss having occurred in 1956. So serious was the situation, officials of the company publicly acknowledged that American Motors could not long survive if such heavy losses continued.[1]

[1] George Romney, "The Future Is Here," an extemporaneous talk given at the third annual employee product review at Milwaukee Arena, September 14, 1957, published in U. S., Senate, Committee on the Judiciary, Subcommittee on Antitrust and Monopoly. *Hearings, Admin stered Prices*, 85th Congress, 2nd Session, Pursuant to S. Res. 57 and S. Res. 231 (Washington: U. S. Government Printing Office, 1958), Part 7, pp. 3814-15.

In the same years, the losses of Studebaker-Packard were even larger, ranging before tax adjustments from a low of approximately $11,000,000 to a high of more than $103,000,000. The firm's largest loss occurred in 1956 after a special charge of $60,000,000 was made to write off surplus and obsolete plant and equipment. Studebaker-Packard officials considered the possibility of liquidating the firm. They acknowledged that the company would have had to default on its bank loans had it not been able to work out an agreement with Curtiss-Wright Corporation which brought some $35,000,000 into the Studebaker-Packard treasury.[2]

Although they came close to failure in their automotive operations, both American Motors and Studebaker-Packard survived the ordeal. In fact, American Motors staged one of the most phenomenal comebacks in the history of American business, earning more than $25,000,000 before taxes in 1958, $105,000,000 in 1959, and equally astonishing profits in the following years, after having been down and almost counted out before 1958.

Studebaker-Packard was less fortunate. The company earned more than $29,000,000 before taxes in 1959, then fell back approximately to the break-even level from 1960 through 1962 and to a sizeable loss in 1963. Despite some of the largest losses ever to confront a single business enterprise, however, the company, renamed "Studebaker" in 1962, survived, though not as a participant in the United States automobile industry. It had finally decided in late 1963 to eliminate its domestic car manufacturing operations and to concentrate its remaining automobile production in Canada!

PURPOSE AND SCOPE

What happened to the leading independent automobile manufacturers after 1952? The most readily apparent answer is that they were too small to compete effectively with the well known three largest firms of the United States industry; but this is too simple an answer, for there were variations after 1952 not only in the performances of the leading Independents but also in those of the largest firms. "Size" problems have multiple aspects, and close study reveals other significant factors, too. We shall be concerned with variations in the reaction of automobile manufacturers to

[2] Studebaker-Packard Corporation, "Letter to Shareholders," September 24, 1956.

various influences, and particularly with similarities and differences in the courses of action of the Independents and the success or failure of their actions. The central issue is: What were the major requirements a firm had to meet to survive and prosper in the automobile industry? We are interested in this question for the insight it provides into the problems of modern business and its management.

Encompassing a study of the individual firm's ability to survive and prosper, this book is focused on the experiences of the leading independent automobile manufacturers as participants in the United States new passenger car market. It is a study of business enterprise in action, of success and of failure. It is largely a descriptive work, having as its general purpose an illustration of some of the problems as well as the opportunities of business enterprises in the environment of the "free-enterprise" economy in the decades following the end of World War II, with special reference to the participation of relatively small business enterprises in an industry dominated by a few large firms, an industrial structure which occurs frequently in the United States. The leading independent automobile manufacturers were such firms, and the automobile industry was such an industry.

A fundamental premise on which this study is based is the belief that the experiences of the leading Independents provide a means for discovery and description of the major influences at work upon and within the automobile industry, and perhaps of similarly structured industries. Our interest is in those underlying influences which affected the survival and prosperity of individual firms of the industry and which presumably determined the course of activity of the industry. These influences may be considered the dynamics of the automobile industry: the causes of change—the opportunities and restrictions of opportunity to which the owners and managers of the firms collectively responded and which consequently served to shape the structure of the industry.

Recommendations of correct managerial decisions are beyond the scope of this study, although owners and managers may find in it factors relevant to their making of decisions. The difficulty of the managerial process is acknowledged. Instead, we are interested primarily in the conditions which influenced those who had to make the decisions. Our viewpoint, broadly speaking, is that of the student of business, whether in or out of the academic environment, who is concerned with the nature of modern business.

Concentrating on the experiences of the four leading Independents and their two successors in the years 1946 through 1963, this study obviously is limited in scope. Both the selection of the firms and the time period for study were somewhat arbitrary, although there are reasons for both limitations. The mergers among the leading Independents and the contrasting experiences of their successors as passenger car manufacturers were principal justifications for singling out these companies for study. In addition, the reconversion following the end of World War II provided a convenient beginning point. All the firms producing cars in 1946 were in the position of having to enter or re-enter the industry after the end of the war. From 1947 through 1952, the leading independent automobile manufacturers enjoyed substantial profits; but this was followed by a sharp decline in the financial performance of the firms in 1953, the mergers in 1954, severe financial difficulties from 1954 through 1957, and later, a return to profitable operations. While long-lasting for American Motors, the return to a profit position was temporary for Studebaker and was followed eventually by the firm's withdrawal from the domestic industry. The years 1946 through 1963 thus provided relatively complete phases in the history of these firms.

This study also has been concentrated mainly on the participation of the leading Independents in the passenger car or automobile manufacturing industry—the terms are used here as synonyms—and on their experiences in the United States new car market. This was the principal market for their products in the years studied although they were engaged to some extent in international operations. Although the proportions varied from year to year, the production and sale of cars was the principal endeavor of the Independents and the dominant influence on their financial performances in the period under consideration.[3]

[3] In 1950, e.g., four smaller companies in the industry, Hudson, Kaiser-Frazer, Packard, and Studebaker, made 99.9 per cent of their total shipments in motor vehicles and related items. See U. S., Federal Trade Commission, *Industrial Concentration and Product Diversification in the 1,000 Largest Manufacturing Companies: 1950* (Washington: U. S. Government Printing Office, 1957), Table 49, p. 117. Of these firms, only Studebaker produced trucks, selling in 1950 about 50,000 trucks compared with more than 268,000 passenger cars. Automobile Manufacturers Association, *Automobile Facts and Figures*, 1958 edition (Detroit, Michigan), p. 10; and Automobile Manufacturers Association, *Motor Truck Facts*, 1959 edition (Detroit, Michigan), p. 3. Only Nash-Kelvinator, which the

While the experiences of the leading independent automobile manufacturers are the principal focus of this book, the examination of them must, of course, be conducted against the background of the actions of their competitors, especially the larger ones. Hence, the study is broader in scope than might appear at first thought. Brief references are made to the other Independents who were engaged in the domestic car industry in the selected period; but much attention is devoted to comparisons of the leading Independents' experiences and performances with those of the three largest firms of the industry. Considerable attention is also given to the rising penetration of the United States market by foreign produced cars after 1955. However, this book does not consider the influence of non-automotive firms whose products—especially consumer durable goods—are to some degree substitutes for the automobile and competing with it for consumer purchase dollars.

Even with the limitation of the study to the experiences of the leading Independents and to the period from 1946 through 1963, it is impossible, of course, to cover completely the history of these firms. This study is limited in terms of both the materials selected for inclusion as well as those excluded. Our emphasis is on the organization of the manufacturing and marketing activities of the firms as automobile producers; but we consider briefly other problems and activities of the firms, too. Despite the limitations, the experiences of the leading independent manufacturers of automobiles illustrate the nature of much that appears common to modern industrial activity.

SOME GENERAL OBSERVATIONS

Dealing with the survival and prosperity of individual firms, this study belongs primarily to the field of business history; but it is business history with policy implications. The emphasis on the individual firm does not mean that problems of social and economic policy toward industrial activity and organization are considered unimportant. Rather, just

Federal Trade Commission included among the four largest firms of the industry who, as a group, had 83.2 per cent of their total shipments in motor vehicles and related items in 1950, had a significant output of other products. In the early 1950's, sales of appliances averaged about 35 per cent of Nash-Kelvinator's total sales. W. B. Harris, "Last Stand of the Auto Independents?" *Fortune*, L (December, 1954), 206.

the opposite is the case. The problems and opportunities of the individual enterprise may be significant in the formulation and application of public policy toward industry since, whatever policy is established, it will be the attitudes and actions of owners and managers which determine the actual conduct of industrial activity within the established framework. However, no attempt is made in this study to formulate or implement a complete public policy toward industrial organization, although some of our observations relate to the existence of a dilemma for those concerned with such tasks.

So long as business enterprises or firms—the terms may be used interchangeably—are numerous and small, both in relation to one another and to the extent of the markets in which they compete, and are largely extensions of personal or family activities, easily financed, organized, and managed, there is little reason for public concern with the individual enterprise. Industries today, however, often consist of a few large enterprises rather than numerous small firms. Modern technology and the corporate form of doing business have provided a stimulus and a means for the growth of individual firms to large size. Having grown large, whether through cumulative benefits of past success "fairly won" or through predatory or monopolistic practices, individual firms have become important social and economic institutions, valued for the job and investment opportunities they provide, the tremendous quantities of goods they produce, and the competitive stimulus—actual or potential—they provide to their few remaining competitors, although the latter admittedly is difficult to evaluate.

From the viewpoint of relatively small firms—whether newly formed or already existing—the difficulties of continued participation in concentrated industries often may seem overwhelming. The dominance of an industry by a few firms may intensify the problems of those business enterprises which remain in the competing industry group. Under the conditions of limited numbers of competitors so characteristic of the modern industrial economy of the United States, the owners and managers of business enterprise can not limit the responses of their firms only to market price-cost relationships; they must also consider the actions and reactions of competitors who are aware of their moves. To managers and owners of the small firm the position of their firm may seem that of David doing battle with Goliath, and David, in this case, seldom wins; or, if the battle is won, the war is lost. Of course, not all industrial activity exhibits such characteristics, but some of it does.

Although they were relatively small compared to the Big Three of the United States industry—Chrysler Corporation, Ford Motor Company, and General Motors Corporation—the leading Independents were relatively large compared to most enterprises. They were important individually to their employees, owners, suppliers, and customers who had a direct personal interest in them. As competitors in the industry, they were important to the general public too.

New entry into the automobile industry has been considered virtually impossible. For example, D. K. Smith observed that Kaiser-Frazer had insufficient resources to enter the industry successfully,[4] and this despite the fact that the firm initially had raised approximately $55,000,000 in stockholders' money plus millions of dollars in credit to begin its operations. Joe Bain estimated the financial requirements for a new manufacturer at $250,000,000 to $500,000,000 for a one-plant operation,[5] and George Romney put the total requirement for successful entry at more than $576,000,000 for a manufacturer of 250,000 cars annually plus more than $326,000,000 supplied independently by dealers.[6] Because of the enormous capital requirements for entry, the leading Independents occupied an all the more crucial position as perhaps the last remaining domestic source of competition with the Big Three. With Kaiser's withdrawal after 1955 and excluding Checker Motors Corporation, a fringe producer of taxicabs with some limited sale to the general public, they were the last of the Independents and two of the last five United States passenger car manufacturers; the others were

[4] D. K. Smith, "The Problems of a New Firm in an Oligopolistic Industry: Kaiser-Frazer's Experience in the Motor Vehicle Industry," (unpublished Ph.D. dissertation, Harvard University, May, 1950). Henry Kaiser referred to his firm's entry into the automobile industry as "the roughest thing we ever tackled." See "Kaiser-Frazer, the Roughest Thing We Ever Tackled," *Fortune*, XLIV (July, 1951), 75. Kaiser-Frazer's successor, Willys Motors Division of Kaiser Industries, eventually withdrew from the production of automobiles, its last domestic U. S. passenger cars having been produced in 1955. See Automobile Manufacturers Association, *Automobile Facts and Figures, loc. cit.*

[5] Joe S. Bain, *Barriers to New Competition* (Cambridge, Mass.: Harvard University Press, 1956), Table XV, p. 170.

[6] U. S., Senate, Committee on the Judiciary, Subcommittee on Antitrust and Monopoly, *Report, A Study of Administered Prices in the Automobile Industry*, 85th Congress, 2nd Session, Pursuant to S. Res. 231 (Washington: U. S. Government Printing Office, 1958), pp. 16-17.

the Big Three. In fact, it was partly for this reason that the experiences of the Independents attracted the interest of agencies entrusted with the protection of the public. The Federal Trade Commission, for example, indicated:

> The Nash-Hudson, Kaiser-Willys, and Studebaker-Packard mergers have posed a dilemma for antitrust agencies, namely, is the public interest best served by permitting the independents to merge and thereby to strengthen their competitive positions, or by attempting to force them to continue to compete independently with the three dominant companies at the risk of possible eventual disappearance of at least some of them through total withdrawal or bankruptcy?[7]

The Commission further stated that "one of the principal developments to focus attention on industrial concentration has been the dwindling position of the smaller manufacturers of passenger automobiles."[8]

In the conduct of its responsibilities under the Antimerger Act of 1950, the United States Department of Justice also was interested in the problems of the smaller firms in the automobile industry, having been asked for unofficial pre-merger clearances by the leading Independents. Concluding that the mergers could do no damage to smaller firms since the merging firms were the small ones in the industry and believing that the mergers might revitalize the firms that remained, the Attorney General approved of the mergers.[9]

Other public agencies also showed an interest in the small firms of the automobile industry. The difficulties of American Motors Corporation, Studebaker-Packard, Kaiser-Willys and their predecessors figured prominently in at least two

---

[7] U. S., Federal Trade Commission, *Report on Corporate Mergers and Acquisitions*, H. Doc. 169, 84th Congress, 1st Session (Washington: U. S. Government Printing Office, 1955), p. 13.

[8] U. S., Federal Trade Commission, *Industrial Concentration . . . ,* *op. cit.,* p. 110.

[9] The attitude of the Department of Justice was indicated in U. S., Senate, Committee on the Judiciary, Subcommittee on Antitrust and Monopoly, *Hearings, A Study of the Antitrust Laws,* 84th Congress, 1st Session, Pursuant to S. Res. 61 (Washington: U. S. Government Printing Office, 1955), Part 1, p. 298. Testimony of Stanley N. Barnes, then assistant attorney general in charge of the Antitrust Division, Department of Justice.

Congressional investigations of the 1950's.[10] In addition, some independent observers have commented on the public policy implications of the problems of small firms in the industry, although, it should be added, they are far from agreement on an appropriate course of public action toward the industry.[11]

Interest in the survival of passenger car manufacturers is readily understandable since, in the words of J. M. Clark, "Competition is our main safeguard against exploitation."[12] In addition, the number of firms in an industry is widely thought to have an influence on the competition among the firms. George Stocking and Myron Watkins, for example, indicate that "the effectiveness of competition is apt to vary directly with the number of sellers up to the maximum consistent with the economies of scale."[13] Corwin Edwards states the requirements for effective competition as follows:

> There must be an appreciable number of sources of supply and an appreciable number of potential customers for substantially the same product or service. Suppliers and customers do not need to be so numerous that each trader is entirely without individual influence, but their number must be great enough that persons on the other side of the market may readily

[10] See U. S., Senate, Committee on the Judiciary, Subcommittee on Antitrust and Monopoly, *Hearings, A Study of the Antitrust Laws,* 84th Congress, 1st Session, Pursuant to S. Res. 61 (Washington: U. S. Government Printing Office, 1955); and U. S., Senate, Committee on the Judiciary, Subcommittee on Antitrust and Monopoly, *Hearings, Administered Prices,* 85th Congress, 2nd Session, Pursuant to S. Res. 57 and S. Res. 231 (Washington: U. S. Government Printing Office, 1958).

[11] Compare, e.g., the comments of Donald A. Moore, "The Automobile Industry," in *The Structure of American Industry,* Revised edition, Walter Adams, editor (New York: The Macmillan Company, 1954), pp. 274-323; Robert F. Lanzillotti, "The Automobile Industry," in *The Structure of American Industry,* Third edition, Walter Adams, editor (New York: The Macmillan Company, 1961), pp. 311-354; and Leonard W. Weiss, *Economics and American Industry* (New York: John Wiley & Sons, Inc., 1961), pp. 324-378.

[12] J. M. Clark, *The Alternative to Serfdom* (New York: Alfred A. Knopf, 1948), p. 62. Also, see J. M. Clark, *Competition as a Dynamic Process* (Washington: The Brookings Institution, 1961), esp. pp. 9-18, discussing "What is competition?"

[13] G. W. Stocking and M. W. Watkins, *Monopoly and Free Enterprise* (New York: The Twentieth Century Fund, 1951), p. 108.

turn away from any particular trader and may find a variety of other alternatives.[14]

In the United States, numerous laws, which have as their general objective the "promotion of competition in open markets,"[15] dedicate the federal government to the maintenance of competition as an appropriate goal of public policy. Even with widespread recognition of oligopoly as a dominant industrial structure [16] and extensive questioning of the efficacy of competition under the technological and organizational conditions of modern industrial activity,[17] the goal of maintaining competition remains the law of the land. Consequently, although it is not clear how many are required to constitute the "appreciable" number necessary for "effective competition," it is readily understandable why the difficulties of some of the few participants in the automobile industry should have attracted the attention which they received. They were individually important firms, both to those who had a direct personal interest in them and to the general public.

METHOD AND PLAN

Approaching from the viewpoint of the individual firm, we give attention first to a survey of relatively apparent changes in industry conditions and their impact on the financial performances of the leading Independents. Since an influence on the financial health of a firm is also an influence on its ability to survive, the financial performances of the Independents provide a convenient beginning point for the attempt to discover and describe those underlying influences which served to shape the structure of the industry and the course of its activity. The financial statements were reflec-

[14] Corwin D. Edwards, *Maintaining Competition* (New York: McGraw-Hill Book Co., 1949), p. 9. Reprinted by permission of McGraw-Hill Book Co., Inc.

[15] This is from the opening statement in the *Report of the Attorney General's National Committee to Study the Antitrust Laws*, Stanley N. Barnes and S. Chesterfield Oppenheim, co-chairmen (Washington: U. S. Government Printing Office, 1955), p. 1.

[16] See the discussion of J. K. Galbraith, "Monopoly and the Concentration of Economic Power," in *A Survey of Contemporary Economics*, Howard S. Ellis, editor (Philadelphia: The Blakiston Company, 1948), esp. pp. 101 and 107.

[17] See, e.g., Robert A. Brady, *Organization, Automation, and Society* (Berkeley, California: University of California Press, 1961); and Gardiner C. Means, *Pricing Power and the Public Interest* (New York: Harper & Brothers, 1962).

tors, though perhaps crude ones, of the impact of those influences in which we are most interested.

Complete internal cost and price data for the automobile manufacturers are not publicly available because, as in other sensitive fields, many men of business are reluctant to divulge "confidential" information. Therefore, many of our observations are qualitative in nature, being "more than" or "less than" comparisons, or expressions of tendencies toward convergence or divergence.

Even if actual cost data were available, many difficulties would remain in the analysis of the problems confronting specific firms. Actual cost data, for example, would be historical records of past commitments of funds and allocations of joint cost. Depreciation costs in particular raise problems in efforts to make interfirm cost comparisons because of variations in the timing of new plant and equipment additions in periods of rising prices like the one covered by this study. Variations in product diversity and degree of product integration also raise problems. Our most meaningful comparisons perhaps would be of anticipated costs, and such cost comparisons simply are not available from even the best of historical accounting records. Even the managers of the firms involved lacked such information for exact comparison of their performances with those of their competitors. Nevertheless, they had major responsibilities for the actions which we observe.

With the financial performances, market positions, and actions of the various firms of the automobile industry as central features, an historical survey of the experiences of the leading Independents is provided in Chapters I through IV, and VI. The emphasis in these chapters is on relatively apparent, easily observable, often recorded phenomena drawn from industry statistics, company documents, and other observations of industry and company action, including such things as the people involved, product offerings, or organizational changes, as features of the historical review. With the mergers among the Independents as a convenient point around which to study the changes that occurred, an effort is made to recapture the visions of impending difficulty as seen by the managers of the firms involved and to record the adjustments the companies made to overcome their difficulties. In the second phase of the work, consisting primarily of Chapters V, and VII through XII, an effort is made to go behind the more apparent historical phenomena to discover and describe the underlying influences on the survival and prosperity of the automobile manufacturers. The emphasis in these chapters is on the reasons for what happened to the leading Independents. Much attention is given in these chapters, as well as in some of the earlier chapters, to comparisons of the experiences and performances of the leading Independents with those of the Big Three of the industry. In the final chapter, a summary of the study is provided along with observations on its meaning for management.

CHAPTER I

SETTING THE STAGE FOR MERGER

FOLLOWING THE END of World War II, the firms of the United States automobile industry were presented with opportunities to sell all the passenger cars they could physically produce. The need for new cars was urgent; the average age of cars in use was high; used cars were in short supply; and a tremendous backlog of demand existed for new cars to replace prewar vehicles.

Despite immense problems of reorganizing automotive facilities and personnel after the end of the war, the firms of the United States industry turned in amazing performances in readjusting to peacetime passenger car production. Shortages, strikes, and other difficulties posed many obstacles. Yet, as may be seen in Table 1, total car production reached more than 2,150,000 units in 1946 and climbed each year thereafter to more than three times this number in 1950. New annual output records were set in 1949 and 1950, far surpassing the previous record of 4,455,000 units in 1929. The last prewar output level of approximately 3,780,000 units in 1941 was exceeded by 1948.[1] With the expansion in production, new car registrations, which are shown in Table 2, also mounted rapidly. From fewer than 2,000,000 units in 1946, new car sales at retail also rose to new records in 1949 and 1950 which far exceeded the last prewar sales level of approximately 3,731,000 units in 1941.[2]

THE INDEPENDENTS' POSITION

The leading Independents—Hudson, Nash-Kelvinator, Packard, and Studebaker—were among the quickest to respond to the enormous postwar demand for new automobiles. In 1946, the share of United States new car registrations accounted for by leading Independent makes surged to a level more than 50 per cent above the 9.0 per cent share held by

[1] Automobile Manufacturers Association, *Automobile Facts and Figures*, 1958 edition (Detroit, Michigan), pp. 3 and 10. The 1929 and 1941 figures are for factory sales; the other figures are for production.

[2] *Automotive News* (*1954 Almanac Issue*), April 26, 1954, p. 60, for this and subsequent comments on 1941 and earlier registrations and shares of registrations.

Table 1

UNITED STATES PASSENGER CAR PRODUCTION AND PERCENTAGE SHARES OF PRODUCTION OF THE LEADING INDEPENDENTS, OTHER INDEPENDENTS, THE BIG THREE, AND THEIR TOTALS, 1946-1963[a]

Year	Leading Independents Units (Thousands)	Leading Independents Share (Per Cent)	Other Independents Units (Thousands)	Other Independents Share (Per Cent)	Total Independents[b] Units (Thousands)	Total Independents[b] Share (Per Cent)	The Big Three Units (Thousands)	The Big Three Share (Per Cent)	Total[b] Units (Thousands)	Total[b] Share (Per Cent)
1946	313	14.5	16	0.8	330	15.3	1,825	84.7	2,155	100.0
1947	396	11.2	164	4.6	560	15.9	2,970	84.1	3,530	100.0
1948	526	13.5	224	5.7	751	19.2	3,149	80.8	3,899	100.0
1949	618	12.1	75	1.5	693	13.6	4,399	86.4	5,092	100.0
1950	672	10.1	166	2.5	838	12.6	5,799	87.4	6,636	100.0
1951	553	10.4	110	2.1	662	12.5	4,649	87.5	5,311	100.0
1952	453	10.5	113	2.6	566	13.1	3,759	86.9	4,325	100.0
1953	480	7.8	60	1.0	540	8.8	5,593	91.2	6,132	100.0
1954	208	3.8	18	.3	226	4.1	5,282	95.9	5,507	100.0
1955	343	4.3	6	.1	349	4.4	7,601	95.6	7,950	100.0
1956	201	3.5	4	.0c	205	3.5	5,602	96.5	5,807	100.0
1957	187	3.1	4	.0c	191	3.1	5,929	96.9	6,120	100.0
1958	274	6.5	3	.0c	278	6.5	3,970	93.5	4,247	100.0
1959	555	9.9	6	.1	561	10.0	5,038	90.0	5,599	100.0
1960	592	8.8	7	.1	599	8.9	6,104	91.1	6,703	100.0
1961	451	8.2	6	.1	457	8.3	5,065	91.7	5,522	100.0
1962	542	7.8	8	.1	550	7.9	6,394	92.1	6,943	100.0
1963	548	7.2	7	.1	556	7.3	7,088	92.7	7,644	100.0

[a] Source: Computations based on production data from Automobile Manufacturers Association, *Automobile Facts and Figures*, 1958-1964 editions (Detroit, Michigan).
[b] Because of rounding, the other columns may not add exactly to the totals shown.
c Less than 0.05 per cent.

TABLE 2

UNITED STATES NEW PASSENGER CAR REGISTRATIONS AND PERCENTAGE SHARES OF REGISTRATIONS OF THE LEADING INDEPENDENTS, OTHER DOMESTIC INDEPENDENTS, FOREIGN PRODUCERS, THE BIG THREE, AND THEIR TOTALS, 1946-1963[a]

Year	Leading Independents Units (Thousands)	Leading Independents Share (Per Cent)	Other Independents[b] Units (Thousands)	Other Independents[b] Share (Per Cent)	Total Independents[b] Units (Thousands)	Total Independents[b] Share (Per Cent)	Foreign Producers Units (Thousands)	Foreign Producers Share (Per Cent)	The Big Three Units (Thousands)	The Big Three Share (Per Cent)	Total[b] Units (Thousands)	Total[b] Share (Per Cent)
1946	252	13.9	11	0.6	263	14.5	—	—	1,552	85.5	1,815	100.0
1947	336	10.6	147	4.6	483	15.2	—	—	2,684	84.8	3,167	100.0
1948	435	12.5	216	6.2	651	18.6	16	0.5	2,824	80.9	3,491	100.0
1949	570	11.8	114	2.4	685	14.2	12	.3	4,142	85.6	4,838	100.0
1950	651	10.3	155	2.5	807	12.8	16	.3	5,504	87.0	6,326	100.0
1951	509	10.1	138	2.7	648	12.8	21	.4	4,393	86.8	5,061	100.0
1952	445	10.7	116	2.8	561	13.5	29	.7	3,568	85.8	4,158	100.0
1953	436	7.6	78	1.4	515	9.0	29	.5	5,195	90.5	5,739	100.0
1954	246	4.4	30	.5	276	5.0	32	.6	5,228	94.4	5,535	100.0
1955	278	3.9	8	.1	285	4.0	58	.8	6,826	95.2	7,170	100.0
1956	213	3.6	4	.1	217	3.7	98	1.6	5,640	94.7	5,955	100.0
1957	173	2.9	4	.1	178	3.0	206	3.5	5,598	93.6	5,982	100.0
1958	234	5.0	6	.1	240	5.2	378	8.1	4,036	86.7	4,655	100.0
1959	497	8.2	6	.1	502	8.3	614	10.2	4,925	81.5	6,041	100.0
1960	529	8.0	32	.5	560	8.5	499	7.6	5,517	83.9	6,577	100.0
1961	443	7.6	7	.1	450	7.7	379	6.5	5,026	85.8	5,855	100.0
1962	501	7.2	7	.1	508	7.3	339	4.9	6,091	87.8	6,939	100.0
1963	493	6.5	7	.1	500	6.6	386	5.1	6,671	88.3	7,557	100.0

[a] Source: Registration data by courtesy of R. L. Polk & Co. and computations based on these data.
[b] Because of rounding, the other columns may not add exactly to the totals shown.

the same makes in 1941; and in 1947, retail sales of leading Independent makes exceeded the 335,000 units registered for the same makes in 1941. It was not until two years later that the total industry exceeded its 1941 level. However, after the initial surge in 1946, the leading Independents as a group experienced a gradually declining market penetration. Other firms, principally the Big Three of Chrysler, Ford, and General Motors, expanded more rapidly. Still, as may be seen in Tables 1 and 2, the early postwar period from 1946 through 1950 was an attractive one for the leading Independent group. Their unit production and sales expanded each year to a postwar peak in 1950;[3] and throughout the period, the share of new car registrations held by their makes exceeded the share which they had held in 1941.

Restricted Production

After the record production and sales year of 1950, the passenger car industry found its output curtailed because of government priorities for scarce materials needed in defense production for the Korean "police action." Steel and copper were crucial items. As a result of restrictions on production which were continued through the first quarter of 1953,[4] unit production of the entire domestic car industry and registrations of all makes were reduced sharply from 1950 to 1951 and again from 1951 to 1952.

Although production levels of the leading Independents were cut along with those of other firms in the industry, the shares of production of the smaller firms increased slightly from 1950 through 1951-1952. Material allocations were made to the several car manufacturers on the basis of their outputs in 1950 with some special adjustments favoring Chrysler and the Independents.[5] Unit sales of leading Independent makes with slight variation generally followed the

---

[3] *Infra*, Tables 3 and 6, for data on sales of individual makes of the Independents.

[4] The material restrictions are discussed in *Automotive Industries*, June 1, 1951, p. 17, and June 15, 1951, p. 17. They were removed from 2nd quarter 1953 production. *Ibid.*, January 1, 1953, p. 34.

[5] Chrysler suffered a 100-day strike in 1950 and therefore received a special adjustment. "Chrysler's Hundred Days," *Fortune*, XLI (June, 1950), 70. Officials of the National Production Authority were reported to have made adjustments to provide the Independents larger shares of output to keep them at profit-making levels. "Whittling Autos' Big Three," *Business Week*, December 29, 1951, p. 27.

over-all industry decline. The leading Independents' share of sales fell from 1950 to 1951 but rose again in 1952 with the further reduction in output and sales of the entire industry. In these years the leading Independent makes were still exceeding their 1941 market penetration. However, a drastic change was imminent. The ending of the materials restrictions would remove the restraints on the supply of cars.

A Major Turning Point

A major change occurred in the market position of the leading Independents in 1953. In the seven years of 1946 through 1952, the market penetration of leading Independent makes declined gradually, resulting in a net decrease of 3.2 percentage points in their market share over the period. In the one year from 1952 to 1953, the net change in their market share was a decline of 3.1 percentage points to 7.6 per cent, a level substantially below the 9.0 per cent share held by the same makes in 1941.

In 1953, for the first time in the postwar period, an annual unit production increase of the leading Independents from the previous year was *not* accompanied by a rise in unit sales of their makes.[6] From 1952 to 1953, unit production of the leading Independents' makes rose 27,000 units; but new car registrations of their makes fell 9,000 units.

In contrast, the total industry achieved sharp increases in both production and sales. From 1952 to 1953, total industry production increased more than 1,800,000 units; and total new car sales of all makes rose almost 1,600,000 units. The increases were accounted for entirely by automobiles of the Big Three. Foreign-produced makes had not then become a significant factor in the market; and the other Independents, who had suffered a slump in market penetration after 1948, experienced a further contraction in their market share. Clearly, the leading Independents suffered a sharp setback in their market position in 1953, since they had increased their output and could have increased it more—they were operating far below their 1950 levels—only to be confronted with reduced retail sales of their makes. They entered 1953 account-

6 Compare Tables 1 and 2.

ing for more than 10 per cent of the market but ended the year with a rate below six per cent.[7]

THE INDEPENDENTS' FINANCIAL PERFORMANCE

The setback in market position of the leading Independents in 1953 was accompanied by declining financial performance, particularly in comparison with the firms' earlier performances and those of the Big Three. However, their sales of products other than cars moderated their decline in 1953.

Net Sales and Operating Profits

In the early postwar period from 1946 through 1950, as may be seen in Chart 1,[8] the dollar sales volumes of Nash-Kelvinator and Studebaker expanded rapidly, largely as a result of increased passenger car sales but with contributions from appliances for Nash-Kelvinator and trucks for Studebaker. Hudson and Packard were less fortunate. Their sales volumes peaked in 1948, then declined somewhat (with the decline for Hudson being slight and that for Packard somewhat greater) but remained comparatively high through 1950.

After 1950, the sales performances of the leading Independents continued to be mixed, with the variations among them depending largely upon their relative participations in defense production. Except for Hudson which secured its maximum postwar dollar sales volume in 1948, the year of its greatest postwar car output, the leading Independents as separate companies obtained their largest postwar dollar sales volumes in 1953. Studebaker's sales reached a total of more than $594,000,000 in 1953, and those of Nash-Kelvinator and Packard also attained very high levels. However, much of the dollar sales of the Independents in 1953 came from military and other products besides automobiles. Defense sales amounted to about 10 per cent of total Hudson sales in

---

[7] Sales of leading Independent makes reached only 182,000 units and 6.4 per cent of total United States sales in the last six months of 1953; their output was reduced to only 166,000 units and 5.8 per cent of total United States production in these same months. In the last quarter of 1953, they sold only 80,175 units for 5.9 per cent of the total new car registrations in the quarter. Computations based on monthly data on new car registrations for 1953 in *Automotive News* (*1955 Almanac Issue*), April 25, 1955, p. 42; and monthly production data for 1953 in *Automotive News* (*1954 Almanac Issue*), April 26, 1954, p. 12.

[8] Except for Nash-Kelvinator Corporation whose fiscal years ended September 30, the data for Chart 1 are on a calendar year basis.

CHART 1

NET SALES AND OPERATING PROFITS OR LOSSES OF THE LEADING INDEPENDENTS, 1946-1958

(Millions of Dollars)

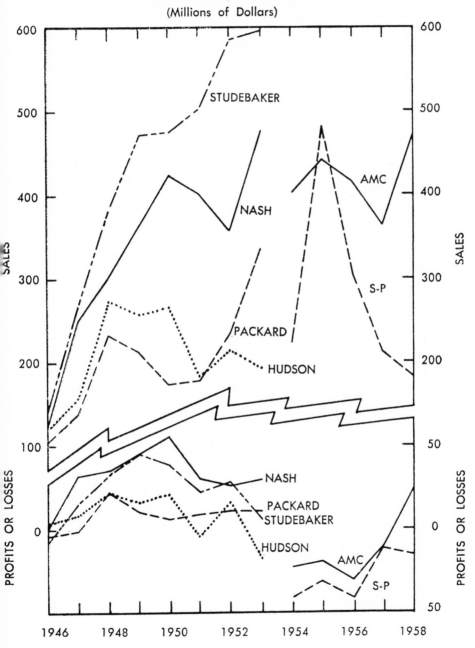

Source: Annual reports of the several companies.

1952 and 18.6 per cent in 1953.[9] In 1952, almost 30 per cent of Packard sales were of defense products; in 1953, defense sales were 42.5 per cent of the firm's total sales.[10] In 1952 and again in 1953, approximately 36 per cent of Studebaker sales were trucks and other defense products sold to the government.[11] Defense sales contributed 8.8 per cent of Nash-Kelvinator's total sales for 1953. In addition, much of the increase in sales of Nash-Kelvinator in 1953 came from a 40 per cent increase in appliance output. Nash-Kelvinator had expanded in the home laundry equipment field with the purchase of Altofer Brothers Company in 1952. Expanded car output also contributed to Nash-Kelvinator's peak 1953 sales volume; but it should be noted that its fiscal year ended September 30, 1953, which was midway in the period of declining automotive sales of the leading Independents in the last six months of 1953. Nash produced about 167,000 cars during its fiscal year 1953; but its calendar year production was only 135,000 units, thus reflecting the late 1953 curtailment of its car output. The financial impact of this last quarter reduction was not reported until the following fiscal year.[12]

The changing fortunes of the leading Independents in the postwar automotive market were shown even more clearly in their operating profits or losses, the differences between their net sales revenues and those expenses involved in generating such revenues.[13] Despite their other operations, the dominant influence on operating profitability of the Independents generally was their production and sale of passenger cars and related parts and accessories.[14]

After the reconversion year of 1946, as may also be seen

[9] Hudson Motor Car Company, *Annual Reports*, 1952 and 1953.

[10] Packard Motor Car Company, *Annual Reports*, 1952 and 1953.

[11] Studebaker Corporation, *Annual Reports*, 1952 and 1953.

[12] Nash-Kelvinator Corporation, "Proxy Statement," dated March 24, 1954, p. 10, for defense sales figure; Nash-Kelvinator Corporation, *Annual Report*, 1952, p. 5, for purchase of Altofer Bros.; and *Annual Report*, 1953, pp. 3-6, for the other items.

[13] Comparable figures were also prepared for the Big Three with whom the Independents are compared as a group in the next section. Cost of goods sold, depreciation and amortization, selling, general, and administrative, incentive compensation and bonus, and pension expenses and provisions for product warranties are included as operating expenses in computing the operating profit or loss. Other income from assets such as investments in subsidiaries or marketable securities and other expenses such as interest payments related to financial structures are excluded from these profit computations.

[14] *Supra*, pp. 4-5.

in Chart 1, the leading Independents enjoyed exceptional operating profits through 1950, with profits for each of the firms often ranging in the $20,000,000 to $50,000,000 bracket before taxes. With the curtailment of car output in 1951, Nash-Kelvinator's and Studebaker's operating profits slipped to approximately one half their earlier peak levels, and Hudson suffered a loss; but Packard's profits rose. In 1952, Nash-Kelvinator, participating relatively less than the other firms in defense business, found its operating profits slipping while Studebaker and Packard obtained increased profits; and Hudson bounced back with a substantial operating profit.

Then, in 1953, despite its peak postwar dollar sales, Studebaker's operating profit fell sharply to approximately $5,000,-000. Hudson suffered an operating loss of more than $17,000,-000. Packard's operating profits declined only $200,000; but more than 40 per cent of its sales—they rose almost 50 per cent from 1952 to 1953—were in defense products which provided a stabilizing influence. Nash-Kelvinator reported an increase in operating profit to $29,000,000 for its fiscal year 1953; however, this report did not cover the fourth quarter of the calendar year 1953 as was the case for the other firms.

The annual reports of operating profit understated the extent of the deterioration in the Independents' financial performances in 1953. Profitable operations in the first six months had offset sharp profit declines or losses on automotive operations in the last half of the year. In the fourth quarter of its fiscal year ended September 30, 1953, Nash-Kelvinator lost $3,100,000 before tax adjustments and $1,000,-000 after tax credits; and in the fourth quarter of calendar year 1953, the firm's profit after tax was below $1,000,000.[15] Packard's sales for the first six months totaled more than $222,000,000 compared with $113,500,000 for the last six months of 1953; its profits of $16,500,000 before taxes in the first six months were offset by a $4,000,000 loss in the last six months.[16] Studebaker's sales fell from approximately $349,-000,000 in the first six months to $245,000,000 in the last six months of 1953; its net profits before taxes fell from $4,400,-

[15] Nash-Kelvinator Corporation, "Proxy Statement," *loc. cit.*

[16] *The Commercial and Financial Chronicle*, Vol. 178 (September 7, 1953), p. 856, for six-month figures to June 30, 1953, which are subtracted from figures for year ended December 31, 1953, in Packard Motor Car Company, *Annual Report*, 1953, to obtain figures for the last six months of 1953.

000 for the first six months to $600,000 for the last six months. Early 1953 tooling difficulties and work stoppages, including a 10-week strike against Warner Gear, a principal supplier of transmissions to Studebaker, had limited Studebaker's first-half profits, too. In 1952, Studebaker's net profits before tax had been $29,100,000.[17] Hudson's net loss of almost $18,000,000 before tax credits fully reflected its decline in 1953.[18]

Operating Profit Rates

The turn-around in 1953 in the financial performance of the leading Independents is seen even more distinctly in an historical comparison of their percentage operating profit rates as a group with the corresponding rates for the Big Three as a group and with all manufacturing corporations.[19] The Independents' declining profits and profit rates in 1953 would not have been viewed so pessimistically if all firms

[17] *Ibid.*, Vol. 178 (September 28, 1953), p. 1165, for six-month figures to June 30, 1953, which are subtracted from figures for year ended December 31, 1953, in Studebaker Corporation, *Annual Report*, 1953, to obtain figures for the last six months of 1953.

[18] Hudson Motor Car Company, *Annual Report*, 1953, p. 10. The sharp profit declines from 1952 to 1953 by Hudson and Studebaker may be attributed partly to their accelerated writeoff of special tools, dies, and equipment used to create style characteristics. Hudson's depreciation and amortization charges rose from $3,600,000 in 1952 to $14,000,000 in 1953. Those for Studebaker increased from $3,600,000 in 1952 to $13,100,000 in 1953. See *Moody's Industrial Manual*, 1954 edition (New York: Moody's Investors Service), for these figures. Although it is possible that the accelerated writeoffs resulted from progress toward merger, it may be emphasized that the adjustments were made concurrent with observed changes in market conditions in 1953. These facilities and equipment probably should have been written off more rapidly in the past.

[19] The operating profit rates included here were computed for each year by dividing the sums of the operating profits of each group by the respective totals of their sales, their operating assets, and their long-term investment. Operating profits were described above. Net sales are self-explanatory. Operating assets are taken for convenience as the total of current assets including prepaid expenses and deferred charges plus the book value of property, plant, and equipment less accumulated depreciation reserves. Adjustments were made to secure comparability of current assets of the different firms by including as a current asset those amounts of United States government and foreign securities often reported as offsets against accrued taxes, a current liability. Long-term investment is the sum of long-term notes or bonds outstanding and total stockholder equity.

had suffered similar experiences. But as may be seen in Chart 2, all other firms did not suffer a similar decline. (General Motors' operating profits were up 10 per cent and Ford's 80 per cent, but Chrysler's were down — much like the Independents — by 20 per cent.)

After the readjustment year of 1946, the average operating profit rates, whether on sales, operating assets, or investment, for the leading Independent group compared favorably with the corresponding rates for the Big Three through about 1950, although a gap opened after 1948 between the average rates for the leading Independents and those for the Big Three. The leading Independents were still showing fairly high returns through 1952, however. Indeed, the differentials between their rates of return and those of the Big Three as a group were narrowed slightly in 1952. In 1953, however, the situation was different. The rates of return for the leading Independents as a group fell to one sixth and less of the corresponding rates for the Big Three, compared to performances ranging around one third to one half and occasionally close to equality with the Big Three in earlier years of the postwar period.

Except for Packard which benefited from its jet engine contract, the declining operating effectiveness of the leading Independents in 1953 adversely affected their net working capital, the excess of current assets over current liabilities, and cash positions. Hudson and Studebaker were especially hard hit, each suffering a decline of approximately 45 per cent in its cash from year-end 1952 to 1953. Excluding holdings of United States government securities to be applied in payment of Federal income taxes, Nash-Kelvinator's cash and marketable securities were reduced by about 30 per cent from beginning to end of its 1953 fiscal period. Although the firms still had substantial sums in cash and marketable securities at the end of their 1953 reporting periods, the squeeze was on. Substantial declines occurred in the net working capital of the firms during the year. Although Packard initially had seemed less seriously affected, the leading independent manufacturers clearly had been confronted with seriously deteriorating financial strength by the end of 1953.

THE CHANGE IN MARKET CONDITIONS

The managements of the leading Independents all concluded that a drastic change had occurred in 1953 in the

CHART 2

PERCENTAGE OPERATING PROFIT RATES ON NET SALES, OPERATING
ASSETS, AND LONG-TERM INVESTMENT FOR THE LEADING
INDEPENDENTS, THE BIG THREE, AND ALL
MANUFACTURING, 1946-1958

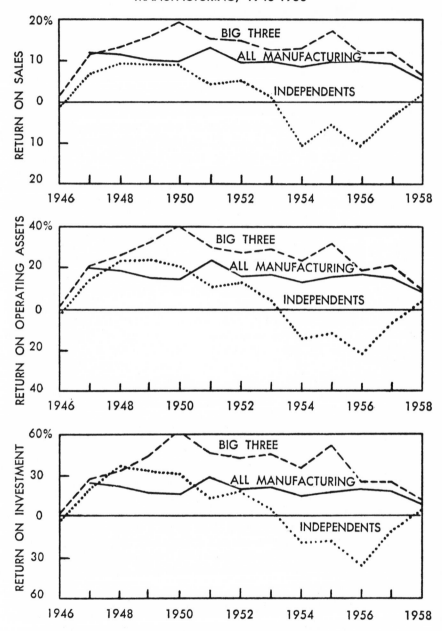

Source: Computations based on annual reports of the several
companies and Federal Trade and Securities and Exchange Commis-
sions, Quarterly Financial Report for Manufacturing Corporations (1st
quarter, 1947-1958).

market conditions confronting their firms. Packard reported that "after mid-year, with the whole automobile industry geared to heavy production, supply exceeded demand and it was necessary to drastically curtail production in order to avoid unbalanced inventories."[20] Packard limited its late 1953 production to dealer orders. Studebaker observed that there was "a softening of the retail market for cars in the last part of the year, because some manufacturers were continuing to produce and ship more cars than their dealers could sell on a normal and profitable basis."[21] Hudson attributed its difficulties to "numerous problems among which was the inability of dealers to handle the anticipated volume of cars due to a combination of wholesale credit restrictions imposed by finance companies and overstocked new and used car markets."[22] In its report which included the fourth quarter of the calendar year 1953, the successor of Nash-Kelvinator reported that Nash and Hudson had been "faced after mid-summer of 1953 with slower retail demand, and the necessity for reducing prices to meet competition."[23] In addition, it was observed that "the automobile industry operated for the first time in many years under the competitive conditions of a buyers' market."[24] And, several years later while reviewing the change in market conditions, J. J. Nance, then president of Studebaker-Packard, was to state, "In about August of 1953, when the backlog of pent-up postwar demand for automobiles was satisfied, the industry entered a market which many have said was, and still is, the most highly competitive in its history."[25]

Even General Motors, the largest of the car manufacturers, found that "there was a trend toward normal peacetime competitive markets in the United States. . . . Competition was more aggressive, and consumers were more selective in their buying."[26]

Admittedly, market conditions in 1953 were vastly differ-

20 Packard Motor Car Company, *Annual Report*, 1953, p. 5.

21 Studebaker Corporation, *Annual Report*, 1953, p. 3.

22 Hudson Motor Car Company, *Annual Report*, 1953, p. 3.

23 American Motors Corporation, *Annual Report*, 1954, p. 2.

24 *Ibid.*

25 U. S., Senate, Committee on the Judiciary, Subcommittee on Antitrust and Monopoly, *Hearings, A Study of the Antitrust Laws*, 84th Congress, 1st Session, Pursuant to S. Res. 61 (Washington: U. S. Government Printing Office, 1955), Part 2, p. 864. Testimony of J. J. Nance.

26 General Motors Corporation, *Annual Report*, 1953, p. 11.

ent from conditions in the earlier postwar years 1946 through 1952.

Beginning in 1946, shortages, strikes, and governmental controls had tended to restrict the supply of new cars. Sheet steel and nonferrous metals were in especially short supply throughout most of the period to 1953. Frequent labor difficulties resulted in considerable lost working time. The largest automobile manufacturers, in particular, and many of their suppliers experienced lengthy strikes during the period.[27] Despite these difficulties, record-breaking output levels were attained in 1949 and 1950; but, so great was the backlog of demand for cars that, with relatively minor exceptions in late 1949 and early 1950, little difficulty was experienced through 1952 in selling all cars produced. Retail sales, upon which factory sales were closely dependent, had amounted to little more than order-taking in most of this period.

From 1946 through 1952, more than 30,900,000 passenger cars were produced in the United States; approximately 28,-800,000 of these were registered in this country.[28] The latter number exceeded the total of 28,100,000 privately owned passenger cars in 1946 and almost equalled the prewar peak total registrations of approximately 29,500,000 units in 1941. With the great surge in postwar output, total registrations of privately owned cars rose to almost 43,700,000 units by 1952; and in 1953, with the industry's increased output, the total rose to more than 46,250,000.[29] Although the number was to continue to increase in later years, used cars had become relatively plentiful by 1953.[30]

From 1946 through 1952, the average age of cars in use was comparatively high. The average in July 1946 was estimated at 9.0 years. The average age of cars in use had ranged from 5.7 years in 1935 to 5.5 years in 1941. In July

[27] The annual reports of the several automobile manufacturers all made frequent references to these difficulties. Hudson and Studebaker even found it necessary to purchase steel finishing plants to secure needed materials. *The New York Times,* December 12, 1947, p. 49, and December 27, 1947, p. 19.

[28] *Supra,* Tables 1 and 2. The differences between production and registrations were accounted for principally by exports. Annual changes in dealer stocks were of little importance in the early postwar years.

[29] Registration data from U. S. Bureau of Public Roads as reported in Automobile Manufacturers Association, *Automobile Facts and Figures,* 1962 edition (Detroit, Michigan), p. 18.

[30] The number was above 55,690,000 in 1957 and 61,430,000 in 1960. *Ibid.*

1946, only six per cent of cars in use were under five years of age, 59 per cent were five through nine years old, and 35 per cent were ten or more years old. In 1941, about 51 per cent of cars in use had been under five years old, 32 per cent were five through nine years old, and only 17 per cent were ten or more years old. Even with record-breaking output and sales from 1946 through 1950, the average age of cars in use declined only to 7.8 years by July 1950. By this time, however, 45 per cent of cars in use were under five years old. By July 1953, the average age of cars in use still had fallen only to 6.5 years; but more than 55 per cent of the cars in use were under five years old.[31]

With the shortage of cars in the earlier postwar years, used car trade-ins on new cars created no selling problem for dealers. Many automobile owners retained their used cars while purchasing new ones for cash; and even when traded in, used cars created no selling problem. They were bringing exceptional prices, particularly in the earlier years through about 1950. This favorable influence was reflected in the ratio of used car sales to new car sales. In 1949, the ratio stood at 0.9 used car sold for each new car sold; in 1950, the ratio was 1.1 to one; in 1951, 1.4 to one; and in 1952, 1.6 to one, possibly signaling the end of a favorable used car market. Even with the 1,500,000 unit sales increase from 1952 to 1953, the ratio again stood at 1.6 to one demonstrating a corresponding increase in used car trading accompanying the increased sales of new cars.[32]

During the early postwar period, ready cash appeared available for car purchases. Credit may substitute for cash. The fact that cash plus a trade-in with no use of credit was available for a larger proportion of purchases in the earlier period supports the general impression that spending for automobiles was freer in the early postwar years than later. Buyers were freer to avoid credit restrictions then than they have been since 1953. In 1946, 77 per cent of new cars were sold for cash plus the trade-in, if any. In 1947, the proportion was 71 per cent; thereafter, it fell to 54 per cent in 1950, 52

31 It was not until 1956 that the average age of cars in use declined to the 1941 level of about 5.5 years; but after 1957 the average rose again, reaching almost 6.0 years in 1961. *Ibid.*, 1946-1962 editions.

32 Ratios of used car to new car sales from U. S., Department of Commerce, Business Services Administration, *Operating Ratios for Automotive Dealers: 1955* (Washington: Business Services Bulletin, no date), p. 3.

per cent in 1951, and 41 per cent in 1952, also possibly indicating the close of the favorable selling conditions. In 1953, the proportion sold for cash plus trade-in was 40 per cent.[33]

Evidence of a temporary easing of the favorable selling conditions had appeared in late 1949 and early 1950. A reporter for *Business Week* foresaw an impending end of the sellers' market for cars in 1950.[34] In early 1950, the Packard management mentioned its anticipation of a return to a buyers' market.[35] Nash-Kelvinator reported some slackening in retail demand for its cars in late 1949 and made some reductions in prices of its cars.[36] Some slackening may also have been felt by General Motors since they reduced prices of their cars twice during 1949, once in February and again in May.[37] However, the price cuts were attributed to downward adjustments of wages and salaries based on cost-of-living factors included in union agreements and to lowered material costs. After the end of the first quarter in 1949, General Motors had operated at or near capacity for the first time since reconversion to peacetime car production. The shortages and other difficulties of earlier years had been overcome. With production at record-breaking levels in 1949 and 1950, the automobile industry probably would have been faced with a widespread buyers' market in 1950, had it not been for the occurrence of a 100-day strike at Chrysler and the outbreak of the Korean conflict which served to stimulate "scarcity" buying by consumers afraid of future shortages. Then, as a result of the government materials controls during the Korean conflict, the short supply situation was continued, thus delaying the transition to a buyers' market.

With the great outpouring of cars in the years from 1946 through 1952—even with the material restrictions in 1951 and 1952, production for the two years totaled almost 10,000,-000 units—and with the declining age of cars in use along with a great increase in the total number of privately owned

[33] The proportion sold for cash plus trade-in was 38 per cent in 1954, 39 per cent in 1955, and 34 per cent in 1956 and 1957, reflecting a continued greater reliance on credit after 1951. Automobile Manufacturers Association, *op. cit.*, 1952 edition, p. 14, for the years 1946-1950; and 1958 edition, p. 32, for the years 1951-1957.

[34] "End of the Auto Boom," *Business Week*, October 28, 1950, p. 21.

[35] Packard Motor Car Company, *Annual Report*, 1949, p. 4.

[36] Nash-Kelvinator Corporation, *Annual Report*, 1949, p. 7.

[37] General Motors Corporation, *Annual Report*, 1949, pp. 14-15.

cars, the foundations were laid for a significant shift in the ease of selling cars.

Following the stabilizing of the Korean defense situation, the removal of government material controls after March 1953 permitted a struggle for volume leadership among the Big Three, stemming at least partly from a desire of the Ford management to outproduce and outsell Chevrolet. Ford's announced objective was to be first in sales.[38] The result was a period of renewed and vigorous competition in the domestic passenger car market. In 1953, the industry had the capacity to produce more than enough cars to satisfy consumer demand at prevailing price levels, and the firms were willing to use their capacity. By the middle of 1953, the supply of new cars was greatly increased. All makes were readily available. The easy retail selling conditions ended. What had been a sellers' market became a buyers' market.

The change in retail selling conditions was reflected in declining dealer profits. Average operating profits before tax of National Automobile Dealers Association member dealers fell to 2.2 per cent of sales in 1953. In 1950, their profit rate on sales had been 6.3 per cent. In 1951, it was 4.9 per cent; and in 1952, 3.6 per cent. With automobile dealers having had to bear some relatively fixed costs despite declining sales, the decline in the last two years may have been expected since the production of automobiles was curtailed by government material restrictions during the Korean "police action." In 1954, member dealers of the association were to average only 0.6 per cent profit on sales.[39]

Even General Motors dealers felt the intensifying competition. In 1953, the average after-tax profit for General Motors dealers amounted to 14.4 per cent of net worth. Earlier, their returns were 15.3 per cent in 1952 and 24.6 per cent in 1951, both of which presumably were affected by the Korean war restrictions. In 1947, General Motors dealer

[38] W. B. Harris, "Ford's Fight for First," *Fortune*, L (September, 1954), 195; and "Top Goal of Ford's New Management: To Outsell Chevrolet," *Business Week*, June 13, 1953, pp. 92-96.

[39] Their return climbed to 1.7 per cent in 1955, then declined each year to a low of 0.2 per cent in 1958, and thereafter ranged around 1.4 per cent annually through 1961. For the years 1950-1955: Table prepared by National Automobile Dealers Association and provided in a letter dated May 8, 1959, from Clark Moody, Manager, Business Management Division, NADA; for the years 1956-1961: "Operating Averages for the Automobile Retailing Industry," 1956-1961 editions, an annual publication of the National Automobile Dealers Association, Washington, D. C.

profits had soared to 98.5 per cent of net worth after allowance for taxes. In 1950, their return was 42.4 per cent of net
worth. In 1954, average profits after tax of General Motors
dealers fell to 9.0 per cent of their net worth.[40]

In comparison, Studebaker dealers suffered a loss of 1.3
per cent on net worth and 0.2 per cent on sales in 1953. In
1952, Studebaker dealers had earned before taxes about 11.4
per cent on net worth and 1.9 per cent on sales. Their 1951
profit before tax amounted to 17.5 per cent on net worth
and 3.0 per cent on sales. Their profit on sales had ranged
above 11 per cent in 1947 and 1948,[41] and their return on net
worth probably approximated that of General Motors dealers.

During 1953, the number of dealer failures increased significantly. Annual dealer failures climbed from 80 in 1951,
to 88 in 1952, and to 219 in 1953. Liabilities of failing dealers
were over $13,000,000 in 1953 compared with less than $3,-
000,000 in 1951 and about $3,500,000 in 1952. Dealer failures
in the earlier period had ranged from a low of nine in 1946 to
a high of 174 in 1949 but had declined to 110 in 1950.[42]

Clearly, there was a significant change in selling conditions confronting car dealers in 1953. It was in this period
that "bootlegging" of new cars to nonfranchised "supermarket" dealers was initiated by overloaded franchised dealers.[43] Dealers found it increasingly difficult to sell their cars;
and so did manufacturers, though it was mainly the Independents who were unable to maintain factory sales. This
was the change which resulted in the observations of the

[40] U. S., Senate, Committee on the Judiciary, Subcommittee on Antitrust and Monopoly, op. cit., Part 8, p. 4055, for the years 1947-1952,
Part 7, pp. 3503-04, for the years 1953-1954.

[41] Dealers of Studebaker-Packard returned to profitable operations
after the new company was formed. Computations for Studebaker dealers
before 1954, and Studebaker-Packard dealers from 1954 through 1957,
based on estimated figures furnished in a letter dated November 21, 1958,
from M. L. Milligan, Secretary, Studebaker-Packard Corporation. The
estimated figures were based on an 80 per cent sample of dealers.

[42] After 1953, annual dealer failures continued at high levels; they
climbed to 246 in 1954, leveled off from 1955 through 1957, but rose to a
new record postwar level of 353 in 1958. Automotive News (1959
Almanac Issue), April 27, 1959, p. 182, based on original data prepared
by Dun and Bradstreet, Inc. The number of failures included those withdrawing as a result of bankruptcy, foreclosure or attachment with loss to
creditors, voluntary withdrawal leaving unpaid obligations, voluntary
compromise with creditors, or involvement in court actions of receivership, or reorganization.

[43] "New Kind of Car Market," Fortune, XLVIII (September, 1953), 98.

leading Independents that competitive conditions had returned. Production capability was no longer a limit on sales; the willingness of consumers to buy at the prevailing prices was the principal limit after the middle of 1953. The changed market conditions were reflected in the deteriorating sales and financial performances of the leading Independents, who apparently were unable to weather the return to more "normal" competitive conditions.

SETTING THE STAGE FOR MERGER

The managements of the independent automobile firms clearly realized that a major turning point had occurred during 1953 in their post-World War II experiences in the automobile industry. They had entered the year anticipating further profits;[44] instead, they found their profits vanishing during the last half of the year. Their ability to survive was soon to be tested strenuously.

The return to "normal" competitive conditions, which had been both eventually expected and looked upon apprehensively by the Independents, was seen as a threat to the continued financial health and survival potential of the leading smaller firms, all of whom had faced serious difficulties in the depressed, intensely competitive automotive markets of the 1930's. The abrupt appearance of a buyers' market after the middle of 1953 confirmed that the anticipated threat was at hand. The recognition of these changes stimulated a movement toward merger among the leading Independents.

Merger had long been recognized by the managements of the smaller firms as a potential solution to the problems which were anticipated with the return of a buyers' market. George Mason, then president of Nash-Kelvinator, had been an early proponent of merger as a possible solution to the problems of the independent passenger car manufacturers, having discussed the possibility of merger with other companies as early as 1946.[45] Nothing resulted from these early talks.

Although the possibility of merger was widely discussed, the small firms had appeared to be in no rush to merge during the highly profitable years from 1946 through 1950 nor during

[44] See, e.g., Packard Motor Car Company, *Annual Report*, 1952, p. 7, for an expression of optimism coupled with an anticipation of increasing competition; and Nash-Kelvinator Corporation, *Annual Report*, 1952, p. 4, for an even more optimistic outlook.

[45] American Motors Corporation, *Annual Report*, 1954, p. 2.

the period which continued through 1952 with still attractive profits. As one contemporary observer of the changes was to write, the Independents were complacent in their high profits.[46] Even though the assumption by J. J. Nance of the presidency of Packard in 1952 could be considered a signal of Packard's move toward merger since he went to Packard with the stated objective of using it as a nucleus for merger,[47] the Independents still seemed in no hurry to merge until after their slump in 1953.

Since the officials of the smaller firms had discussed the possibility of merger, they had an apparently convenient solution to their anticipated problems. However, they did not seem fully to have anticipated the suddenness of the return of a buyers' market in 1953 or the harshness of its effects.

As a result of the changed market conditions and the accompanying financial consequences which became evident in the last half of 1953, a flurry of speculation and rumors arose concerning the impending disaster believed to be facing the leading independent passenger car producers. The Independents' abilities to survive were widely questioned; but merger was frequently specified as a way—perhaps the only way—for the smaller firms to overcome the threat to their survival.[48]

By the end of 1953, officials of two of the leading Independents admitted that they were engaged in merger negotiations. Early in November 1953, George Mason of Nash-Kelvinator publicly confirmed that merger discussions were being held with Hudson officials.[49] Later in the same month, A. E. Barit, then president of Hudson, admitted that conferences were in progress; but despite the fact that much had already been agreed upon, he referred to them as only "exploratory" talks.[50] Although J. J. Nance of Packard and Harold Vance, then president of Studebaker, were to deny, at least for public consumption, as late as March and April 1954 that their companies planned to merge,[51] conditions

[46] W. B. Harris, "Last Stand of the Auto Independents?" *Fortune*, L (December, 1954), 116.

[47] "Nance's Idea: Merge Packard," *Business Week*, May 17, 1952. p. 29.

[48] Business and other publications contained many such articles too numerous for listing here.

[49] *The New York Times*, November 4, 1953, p. 41.

[50] *Ibid.*, November 27, 1953, p. 37.

[51] *Ibid.*, March 15, 1954, p. 82; and April 20, 1954, p. 43.

appeared right for their merger which was finally announced in June 1954.

The events of 1953 thus set the stage for the mergers. among the leading Independents. The leading Independents had secured satisfactory earnings through 1952, especially in comparison with their own historical performance, and had seemed in no hurry to merge; but after the middle of 1953, they were confronted with drastic profit declines and a threat of future financial difficulties as independent manufacturers. The result: the leading Independents rushed toward merger.

Chapter II

THE MERGERS

WITH THE INTENSIFICATION of competitive market conditions and the sharp decline in relative market position and financial returns of the smaller firms after mid-1953, the leading Independents' movement toward merger accelerated. Kaiser-Fraser Corporation had already acquired Willys-Overland Motors, Incorporated; and before the end of 1953, the presidents of Nash-Kelvinator and Hudson confirmed that they were engaged in merger discussions.[1] The chairman of the board of directors of Studebaker acknowledged that his company had been approached concerning the possibility of merging with another.[2] It was not long after the beginning of 1954 that the first of the new combinations was formally announced; and the other was publicly acknowledged by the middle of the year.

THE NASH-KELVINATOR-HUDSON MERGER[3]

Having proposed as early as 1946 the possibility of merger among Independents as a solution to the problems anticipated with a return to competitive conditions, George Mason, who was then president of Nash-Kelvinator, was perhaps the most active proponent of merger among top officials of the Independents. He discussed merger with Hudson officials in 1946, but Hudson was not interested then.[4] Then in late 1947, Mason initiated discussions with Packard officials;[5] but noth-

[1] *The New York Times*, November 4, 1953, p. 41; and November 27, 1953, p. 37.

[2] *Ibid.*, October 30, 1953, p. 41.

[3] The material in this section is based on Hudson Motor Car Company, "Letter to Stockholders and Notice of Special Meeting of Stockholders," dated February 8, 1954; and "Proxy Statement," dated March 24, 1954; the almost identical letter and statement of Nash-Kelvinator Corporation; and interviews of American Motors Corporation officials in February, 1963; except where otherwise indicated.

[4] U. S., Senate, Committee on the Judiciary, Subcommittee on Antitrust and Monopoly, *Hearings, A Study of the Antitrust Laws*, 84th Congress, 1st Session, Pursuant to S. Res. 61 (Washington: U. S. Government Printing Office, 1955), Part 1, p. 464. Testimony of George Romney.

[5] See also "Auto Merger Rumors," *Business Week*, December 27, 1947, p. 59; and *The Wall Street Journal*, April 18, 1955, p. 15.

ing came of the effort. Mason made Packard an offer, but the Packard directors rejected it in 1948. Later, Mason discussed the possibility of a Nash-Packard merger after J. J. Nance moved to Packard in 1952; but nothing resulted from this either.[6] A major stumbling block was the desire of both Mason and Nance for the presidency of any resulting company.[7]

Once the return of a buyers' market became fully apparent after the middle of 1953, Mason was contacted by A. E. Barit, then president of Hudson Motor Car Company, a firm that had lost $3,100,000 on operations in 1951 and was again losing money heavily in 1953. The two met in June 1953 and at a luncheon meeting quickly agreed upon the major points of a Nash-Kelvinator and Hudson merger,[8] although it was to take the rest of the year to work out the legal and other details of the plan.

The directors of Nash-Kelvinator and Hudson eventually signed a formal "Agreement of Merger" on January 14, 1954, and called for special meetings of the stockholders of each company to be held in March to consider and vote upon the adoption of the merger proposal. Public announcement of the signing of the "Agreement of Merger" was made the same day.[9] The new company was to be called the American Motors Corporation.

The "Agreement of Merger" provided for the combination of the two firms through an exchange of stock. Nash-Kelvinator was to be the legal parent with its corporate charter to be changed to meet the requirements of the merger agreement. The holders of Nash-Kelvinator stock were to receive one share of the new American Motors stock for each share of their old stock; Hudson shareholders were to get two shares of American Motors stock for three shares of their old Hudson stock. Each share of Nash-Kelvinator stock thus was to be exchanged as the equivalent of one and one half shares of Hudson stock. Out of 10,000,000 shares authorized with a par value of $5.00 per share, 5,675,710 shares of

6 "Nance's Idea: Merge Packard," *Business Week*, May 17, 1952, p. 29.

7 "Linking the Last of the Independents," *Business Week*, June 26, 1954, p. 28.

8 See also *The Wall Street Journal*, April 18, 1955, p. 15, for Barit's recollections of the merger negotiations; and Tom Mahoney, *The Story of George Romney*, (New York: Harper & Brothers, 1960), pp. 169-70.

9 *The New York Times*, January 15, 1954, p. 1; and *The Wall Street Journal*, January 15, 1954, p. 16.

American Motors stock were to be outstanding after the exchange for the merger, Hudson shareholders receiving 1,334,-601 shares, and the Nash-Kelvinator shareholders 4,341,109 shares, or 76.4 per cent, of the American Motors stock. Consummation of the merger awaited only the approval of the stockholders.

In the meantime, Mason and George Romney, then executive vice-president of Nash-Kelvinator, made a further unsuccessful attempt to draw Packard into merger;[10] but Nance had other plans and was soon involved in merger negotiations with officials of the Studebaker Corporation.

Many advantages were expected to result from the integration of the extensive businesses of Nash-Kelvinator and Hudson. Although their separate corporate existences would end with the merger, it was planned for the surviving company to continue the existence of its predecessors as separate and distinct divisions: the Hudson Division, the Nash Division, and the Kelvinator Division. Separate dealer organizations of each division also were to be maintained. The new company would be a large firm. During 1953, the two companies had had an average combined employment of approximately 40,000 people. The plants of the new company would include three automobile body plants, complete engine manufacturing facilities, and automobile assembly plants. Two of the body plants were owned by Nash and the other by Hudson. Neither firm made a line of trucks; but Nash-Kelvinator also had extensive facilities devoted to appliance production plus a controlling interest in Ranco, Incorporated, a subsidiary engaged in the production of heater controls.

Full physical capacity had not been achieved by either firm in the postwar period. Hudson's peak year was 1929 when it produced almost 301,000 cars while Nash's greatest volume year was 1950 with almost 190,000 cars.[11] Each of the merging companies had sufficient capacity to produce approximately 250,000 cars per year on a straight time basis.

Major advantages of the merger were expected to be the combining of managerial talents and bigger research and engineering resources and purchasing power; opportunities for new manufacturing economies and improved methods; a reduction of overhead and administrative costs; added product diversification which tends to stabilize earnings in periods

10 See also Mahoney, *op. cit.*, pp. 170-71.
11 *Automotive News* (*1959 Almanac Issue*), April 27, 1959, p. 28.

of high and low business activity; and the spreading of special tooling costs over larger quantities with less cost per unit of output.[12] Both of the companies used the same type of construction for their cars. Although other companies were later to adopt it, the monocoque or unit body-frame type of construction was used in the United States industry at the time only by these two manufacturers.

Other anticipated advantages included the larger dealer organization capable of selling the cars of the new firm. Nash had approximately 1,600 dealers and Hudson 2,000 dealers. The financial resources of the new firm were also expected to provide greater financial strength than either could muster independently; and it was anticipated that the new firm would benefit from tax credits in a carryback of Hudson losses against previous Nash-Kelvinator profits.

A strong case thus was built in support of the merger. Indeed, it was widely believed that the firms could not long survive if they attempted to continue as Independents. Yet, the merger was not to be consummated without dissent.

The merger plans announced January 14, 1954, provided that either company would have the option of withdrawing from the merger agreement if holders of more than 40,000 shares of Hudson stock opposed the merger and demanded immediate cash payment for their stock, as was provided in the "Agreement for Merger" under the laws of Michigan to protect the interests of minority stockholders. Too great a demand for cash payment could have handicapped the new company financially. However, when holders of approximately 140,000 shares of Hudson stock actually requested cash payment,[13] Nash-Kelvinator declined to use its option and proceeded with the merger. Although a few dissented, on March 24, 1954, the stockholders of both Hudson and Nash-Kelvinator voted overwhelmingly in favor of the merger.[14] On May 1, 1954, the merger of Hudson and Nash-Kelvinator

[12] *The Wall Street Journal*, January 15, 1954, p. 16, quoting a joint statement issued by Barit and Mason upon announcement of the "Agreement of Merger."

[13] *The New York Times*, April 17, 1954, p. 20; and April 23, 1954, p. 37. Dissenting stockholders eventually received, as a result of court order, $9.8125 per share. American Motors Corporation, *Annual Report*, 1957, p. 9.

[14] *The New York Times*, March 25, 1954, p. 45.

was legally completed; and the American Motors Corporation came into existence.[15]

George Mason, continuing in the same capacities in which he had served Nash-Kelvinator, became chairman of the board and president of American Motors. A. E. Barit, president of Hudson, became a special consultant to the new firm as well as a member of its board of directors. George Romney continued in the capacity of executive vice-president with the new company; and Roy D. Chapin, Jr., assistant sales manager and member of the board of directors of Hudson, became a member of the board of directors of American Motors. The eight man board of directors of Nash-Kelvinator was expanded to ten in number to include Barit and Chapin as representatives of Hudson stockholders in the new company.

Mason's long-standing objective of merging Nash-Kelvinator with another Independent was fulfilled, though he had fallen short in his efforts to include Packard. The new company was in existence and ready to do an expanding business.[16]

THE STUDEBAKER-PACKARD MERGER[17]

Packard's move toward merger was signaled in 1952 by the assumption of the firm's presidency by J. J. Nance whose intention was to use Packard as a nucleus for merger.[18] A slump in Packard sales in 1950 and 1951 while most cars were still in short supply awakened the Packard management to their need of a better merchandising program. Packard was viewed in the industry as possessing an adequate engineering staff but an unsatisfactory selling organization; the firm traditionally had emphasized engineering quality and not sales promotion.[19] In fact, it was not until 1947 that Packard assumed most of the responsibility for direct distribution of its products to dealers as had been done for years by the

---

[15] American Motors Corporation, *Annual Report*, 1954, p. 2.

[16] *Ibid.*, pp. 5-6, for expression of optimism regarding 1955 operations.

[17] The material in this section is based on Packard Motor Car Company, "Letter to Shareholders and Notice of Special Meeting of Shareholders," dated July 9, 1954; and "Proxy Statement," dated August 17, 1954; a similar letter and statement of Studebaker Corporation; and interviews of Studebaker Corporation officials in February, 1963; except where otherwise indicated.

[18] "Nance's Idea: Merge Packard," *loc. cit.*

[19] *Ibid.;* and "Packard's Road Back," *Fortune*, XLVI (November, 1952), 118.

industry's leaders.[20] Much of its sales volume previously had been channeled through wholesalers.

When first approached by Packard's board of directors concerning the position as Packard's president, Nance was in charge of General Electric's Hotpoint Division, which he had built into the appliance industry's third largest seller. At first Nance declined the offer but later changed his mind and moved to Packard in May 1952, replacing Hugh Ferry as president. Ferry remained chairman of the Packard board of directors.

At this time the problems facing the firm were considered to be Packard's merchandising weakness, including a poor dealer organization, and an older management nearing retirement. One contemporary observer reported, "To the outsider, at least, Packard looks antiquated from one end of the operation to the other."[21]

Initially, Nance considered a merger with Nash-Kelvinator an especially attractive opportunity for forming a new company large enough to compete with the Big Three. Such a merger would have given Packard a line of appliances, a product with which Nance was quite familiar, a full line of cars, ranging from the lowest priced field to the highest, and at least a partial cure of some of Packard's problems, namely in the acquisition of new management personnel and additional and stronger dealer outlets.[22] But Nance and Mason, as noted previously, could not reach a mutually satisfactory agreement.

Meanwhile, Packard went about strengthening its organization, modernizing its production facilities, rejuvenating its management, and revamping its merchandising program. Nance brought in new management, some from his previous organization, Hotpoint, and returned Packard to a sales appeal based on quality.[23] It was thought that Packard's introduction of cheaper models in the 1930's, which continued after the war with the Packard Clipper, had weakened the reputation of the firm for a quality car. That Nance was still interested in using Packard as a partner in merger was reflected in an announcement in July 1953 that Packard had obtained a $25,-000,000 line of credit to free for civilian use a portion of its

[20] Packard Motor Car Company, *Annual Report*, 1947, p. 5.
[21] "Nance's Idea: Merge Packard," *loc. cit.*
[22] *Ibid.;* and "Linking the Last of the Independents," *loc. cit.*
[23] "Packard's Road Back," *op. cit.*, pp. 188-90.

assets which were then tied up in performance of government contracts and to "carry out certain long-range plans."[24]

Several months later in October 1953, during the time of the Nash-Kelvinator-Hudson negotiations, Paul Hoffman, then Studebaker's chairman of the board of directors, acknowledged Studebaker had been approached by a group of investment bankers. Although he contended that Studebaker was not then planning to merge with any other company, Hoffman indicated that Studebaker might sell if the price was high enough or buy if the price was right. At this time, Hoffman also reported that he was optimistic concerning the outlook for Studebaker in 1954, in spite of the Independents' slump in the last half of 1953. He expected Studebaker to sell about 4.5 per cent to 5.0 per cent of the 1954 market. (Studebaker cars actually accounted for only 1.7 per cent of total unit sales in 1954.) However, he did acknowledge that he expected some dealer attrition in 1954 because of stiffening competition.[25]

After having publicly acknowledged an interest in merger, Nance suddenly reversed his field in February 1954 when he announced that Packard was not interested in merger. Speculation had arisen concerning a Studebaker-Packard merger following the announcement of the Nash-Kelvinator-Hudson merger plans in the previous month. Pointing out that Packard was shifting its engine, transmission, and axle manufacturing operations to a newly built plant in Utica, Michigan, thereby completing much of its modernization program, Nance contended that this indicated clearly that Packard was not interested in any merger.[26]

However, this did not quiet the speculation concerning a Studebaker-Packard merger. Still, both Studebaker and Packard were publicly saying no to the merger question as late as April 1954.[27]

The sales slump that had begun in 1953 continued into 1954 for the Independents. The squeeze on the smaller firms intensified. Studebaker's net profit after taxes in 1953 had fallen 81 per cent from its 1952 level, in spite of a 1.5 per cent sales increase; and the downward trend in profits continued in 1954. Studebaker reported a first quarter loss of more than

[24] The New York Times, July 7, 1953, p. 34.

[25] Ibid., October 30, 1953, p. 41.

[26] Ibid., February 9, 1954, p. 35.

[27] Ibid., February 14, 1954, Section III, p. 6; March 15, 1954, p. 82; and April 20, 1954, p. 43; for such comments.

$8,000,000 and a second quarter loss of almost $11,000,000 resulting in a loss of more than $19,000,000 for the first six months of 1954 before recovery of approximately $10,300,000 in prior years' taxes.[28] Hoffman's optimism late in the previous year thus was not matched by results in 1954.

While Packard had suffered only a slight decline in its operating profit from 1952 to 1953, its sales having increased more than $102,000,000 from one year to the next, Packard's fate in 1954 was similar to that of Studebaker. Packard suffered a loss of approximately $1,000,000 before taxes in the first quarter of 1954; and by the end of the first six months of 1954, Packard's loss had climbed to more than $5,800,000 before a tax credit of about $3,000,000 was received. In contrast, Packard had reported a profit of almost $16,500,000 before taxes in the first six months of 1953.[29]

Some of the decline in the profitability of Studebaker and Packard was attributed to cutbacks in their defense sales in the last part of 1953 resulting from the adoption of a "narrow base" production policy by the Department of Defense under "Engine Charlie" Wilson.[30] However, much of the decline was a result of poor showing of the two companies in selling their cars. Combined new car registrations of Packard and Studebaker fell from more than 128,000 units in the first six months of 1953 to less than 71,000 units in the same period of 1954.

In April 1954, commenting on Packard's losses, Nance said that Packard would need a year to readjust to the stiffening competitive struggle and to make improvements in its plants. Although he, at least for public consumption, said that no talks were then in progress with Studebaker regarding merger, he did indicate that Packard was considering a reverse split of its stock involving the issuance of one new share for five shares of the old Packard stock.[31] In view of the appearance of such a provision in the merger agreement, progress toward merger obviously had been made by Studebaker and Packard

28 *Ibid.*, April 28, 1954, p. 45; and August 7, 1954, p. 19.
29 *Ibid.*, May 4, 1954, p. 43; August 10, 1954, p. 30; and *supra*, chapter i, for comparisons.
30 Studebaker-Packard Corporation, *Annual Report*, 1954, p. 7, refers to a loss of government contracts by the firm and its predecessors as a result of restrictions in the number of defense producers.
31 *The New York Times*, April 20, 1954, p. 43.

early in 1954. Despite the public denials, it was an "open secret" that the two firms were engaged in negotiations.[32]

Finally, on June 22, 1954, it was formally announced that the directors of Packard and Studebaker had agreed to combine the two companies, pending approval of the stockholders.[33] The announcement came as no surprise.[34] The impending merger was to be the third of the automobile industry in little more than a year. The Kaiser-Willys merger of April 1953 and the Nash-Hudson merger of May 1954 had preceded it.

Acting on the advice of the securities firm of Cyrus J. Lawrence & Sons and the investment banking companies of Glore, Forgan & Co., Kuhn, Loeb & Co., and Lehman Brothers —these same investment banking firms had been involved in the reorganization of Studebaker in 1934 — officials of Packard and Studebaker formalized their decision by signing a "Purchase Agreement" June 22, 1954, spelling out the details; but stockholder approval was still necessary before the merger could be consummated.

The "Purchase Agreement" provided for Packard to be the legal parent of the new company. With stockholder approval, the company's name was to be changed to Studebaker-Packard Corporation and the merger completed by the purchase of all Studebaker assets in exchange for Packard common stock and Packard's assumption of Studebaker liabilities.

According to the agreement, J. J. Nance was to become president and chief executive officer of the new company; Paul Hoffman, chairman of the board of directors at Studebaker was to assume the same position at Studebaker-Packard; Harold Vance, president of Studebaker, would become chairman of the executive committee of Studebaker-Packard; and Hugh Ferry planned to retire as chairman of the board of Packard but stay on as a member of the Studebaker-Packard board of directors.

The merger between Studebaker and Packard was to be accomplished by having Packard's shares of stock undergo a

[32] Involving such technicalities as "negotiations then in progress," the denials were cautiously worded. Public acknowledgment of the negotiations might have adversely affected prices of the securities and progress of the negotiations of the two companies.

[33] *The New York Times*, June 23, 1954, p. 1; and *The Wall Street Journal*, June 23, 1954, p. 8.

[34] See, e.g., the comment on the rumors concerning a Studebaker-Packard merger in *The New York Times*, June 4, 1954, p. 35; and *Ibid.*, June 19, 1954, p. 19, for a report that merger discussions were scheduled.

reverse split of five for one. Then, Packard stockholders were to acquire Studebaker-Packard shares on a one for one basis and Studebaker shareholders were to receive one and a half shares of the new Studebaker-Packard stock for each of their old shares. Thus, each share of old Studebaker stock was to be the equivalent in the exchange of seven and a half shares of the old Packard stock.

Studebaker stockholders were to receive 3,542,187 shares of the new Studebaker-Packard stock while Packard stockholders were to acquire 2,898,268 shares, giving Packard shareholders 45.8 per cent of the new stock. The new stock was to have a par value of $10 per share. Out of an authorized total of 15,000,000 shares of Studebaker-Packard stock, approximately 8,500,000 were to be left unissued but available for expansion into other fields and acquisition of other companies.

As was the case of Nash-Kelvinator and Hudson, the Studebaker and Packard officials expected merger to provide many improvements in their operating performance, largely because of an increase in the scale of their operations. The combination of the two corporations would provide the new firm two lines of cars which were complementary and could be sold jointly by dual dealerships. Studebaker covered the lower priced fields and Packard the upper priced fields. In addition, Studebaker had a line of trucks. The new firm would have a larger dealer organization; and it believed that dealers in some smaller communities could be strengthened by being offered franchises of both cars. Studebaker had approximately 2,800 dealers and Packard about 1,200.

Both firms had extensive fabrication and assembly facilities and personnel organizations. Studebaker had approximately 15,000 employees and Packard 9,000. Combining the manufacturing operations was expected to result in increased efficiency and lower unit costs by elimination of duplicated effort and by providing for the use of interchangeable parts. Other improvements were expected from consolidated research, engineering, and managerial staffs to distribute their costs over larger output volumes. However, also like American Motors, the merger plans called for the two firms to continue their separate identities as company divisions, although their separate corporate existences ended.

Additional anticipated advantages included the combination of the assets of the two firms to provide greater resources for financial needs of the present business, a better basis for future growth than either company could provide alone, and a larger share of defense business with the larger combined facilities. Also, because of its greater financial resources the new company was expected to be in "a better position to diversify its products in various ways, including the possible acquisition of other businesses."[35]

The anticipated advantages of merger being numerous and the difficulties of both firms in early 1954 being widely known, the merger was approved overwhelmingly by the stockholders of both companies on August 17, 1954.[36] The merger was formally completed October 1, 1954; and the Studebaker-Packard Corporation was in business.[37]

AN END AND A BEGINNING

The consummation of the mergers among the leading Independents ended the separate corporate existence of four of the oldest producers of passenger cars.[38]

Nash-Kelvinator Corporation had been formed in 1937 by merger between the Nash Motors Company and Kelvinator Corporation of Detroit, Michigan, a manufacturer of refrigerators. The Nash Motors Company had been established in 1916 by Charles W. Nash, a former president of General Motors Corporation, to acquire the assets of the Thomas B. Jeffery Company, Kenosha, Wisconsin, an automobile manufacturing firm originally established in 1901 to produce and sell "Rambler" automobiles. Kelvinator Corporation originally had been incorporated in 1916, too. George Mason had come to Nash from the presidency of Kelvinator upon the merger of the two in 1937.

The Hudson Motor Car Company had been incorporated in 1909. It was named for its first president, J. L. Hudson, who was the owner of a large department store in Detroit and the largest original stockholder of the automobile company,

[35] *The New York Times*, July 12, 1954, p. 27.

[36] *The New York Times*, August 18, 1954, p. 1; and "New Fields for Studebaker-Packard," *Business Week*, August 21, 1954, pp. 56-62.

[37] Studebaker-Packard Corporation, *Annual Report*, 1954, p. 5.

[38] The following material on the origins of the four companies is based on U. S., Federal Trade Commission, *Report on Motor Vehicle Industry*, 76th Congress, 1st Session, House Document No. 468 (Washington: U. S. Government Printing Office, 1939), pp. 674-77, 693, 731-34, and 795-96; and the documents of the four corporations referred to *supra*, footnotes 3 and 17.

although the chief operating officer and promoter of the company was Roy D. Chapin.

The Packard Motor Car Company was established in 1902 as the successor to the Ohio Automobile Company, Warren, Ohio, which had been incorporated in 1900. The company was named for J. W. and W. D. Packard, two brothers engaged in a successful electrical business, who had built their first car in 1899 and who had participated in the incorporation of the automobile company. In 1903, the firm's plant was moved to Detroit; and in 1909, Packard was re-incorporated as a Michigan corporation under the same name. The earlier corporations had been West Virginia corporations.

The Studebaker Corporation was incorporated in 1911 as a New Jersey corporation resulting from a merger of the Studebaker Brothers Manufacturing Company and the Everitt-Metzger-Flanders Company. The Studebaker Brothers' business dated back to the year 1852. Studebaker considered its name to be the oldest in highway transportation, having been engaged initially in the manufacture of horse-drawn wagons and carriages. Studebaker had begun the manufacture of electric runabouts and trucks in 1902 and of gasoline-propelled vehicles in 1904. The Everitt-Metzger-Flanders business had originated in 1908 as a Michigan corporation formed to manufacture motor vehicles. Hence, Studebaker's origins as an automobile producer went back to 1902. Hard hit by the depression, the Studebaker Corporation went into receivership in 1933 and into trusteeship in 1934. In the reorganization that followed, a new corporation was organized in Delaware under the same name to take over the assets of the previous Studebaker Corporation.

Thus it was that the mergers in 1954 ended the separate existence of firms which traced their origins to the earliest days of the American automobile industry.

Having recognized the threat to their continued existence after the return of the buyers' market, the leading Independents had merged to improve their positions. The stockholders of all companies involved had voted overwhelmingly for merger. Essentially the same anticipated advantages of merger appeared as the factors for which the stockholders of the several companies voted. The mergers were consistent with accepted opinion in the industry that substantial size was required for success as an automobile manufacturer.[39]

39 *Infra*, chapter vii.

The eventual decisions to merge the companies were the reaction to the Independents' drastic decline in market share and financial losses in the automobile industry after 1953.

Although the firms had the alternatives of retrenching and trying to fight it out as independent manufacturers or closing down entirely, the apparent advantages of merger were overwhelming.

Many clues to the dynamics of the automobile industry can be seen in the reasons for the mergers. Great though the advantages of merger appeared, the future for the newly formed firms was to be strewn with many obstacles. The mergers were strategic moves in a struggle for survival by the Independents, if not separately, then in combination; but the struggle had only begun.

CHAPTER III

AMERICAN MOTORS' RESURGENCE

AMERICAN MOTORS CORPORATION began business May 1, 1954, under the leadership of George Mason; but less than six months later the corporation lost the services of Mr. Mason, who died suddenly, at the age of 63, on October 8, 1954, in Harper Hospital, Detroit, Michigan. Because of Mason's foresight in providing for his successor, the selection of a new president was quickly accomplished. On October 12, 1954, George Romney, who was second in command of the firm, having entered the Nash-Kelvinator Corporation as an assistant to Mason in 1948 and risen to vice-president in 1950 and executive vice-president in 1953, was elected chairman of the board of directors, president, and general manager of American Motors Corporation.[1] All three positions had been held by Mason.

One of the first problems to face Romney was the reorganization of the top management structure of the company to reduce the number of executives reporting to him. Decentralization of authority was considered imperative following Mason's death; and changes were made by Romney, although not without some rumblings of discontent. Because of his great knowledge of the industry, Mason, in the opinion of Romney, was much like Henry Ford as an administrator and had operated a highly centralized company, having had a direct voice in most top management decisions.[2] Fortunately for the continuity of American Motors operations, the corporation had, in the opinion of Romney, many capable executives at the time of Mason's death, including, among others, such outstanding men as Roy Abernethy, a former Kaiser-Willys executive who was hired in October 1954 by Romney as vice-president in charge of sales of Nash Motors Division; Elmer Bernitt, vice-president in charge of automotive manufacturing and procurement; J. L. Brown, Jr., who was then Romney's

[1] American Motors Corporation, *Annual Report*, 1954.
[2] Transcript of press conference with George Romney, president, American Motors Corporation, at Waldorf Astoria Hotel, New York City, New York, October 28, 1954; and "In League with the Future," An address by George Romney made at Nash and Hudson dealer announcement meetings, Chicago, Illinois, September 24-25, 1956.

administrative assistant; Roy D. Chapin, Jr., who came to American Motors with Hudson and who was assistant treasurer and a director of the new company; Edward L. Cushman, a well known labor arbitrator who had been hired as director of industrial relations upon the formation of American Motors; Bernard A. Chapman, vice-president and general manager of the Kelvinator Division; Donald P. Else, comptroller of American Motors since August 1954; Joseph W. Eskridge, former Hudson official who was put in charge of the Hudson Special Products Division; William McGaughey, who joined Nash-Kelvinator in 1952 and who was appointed director of communications and management development in November 1954; and Meade F. Moore, vice-president in charge of automotive research and engineering for the company.

THE LEAN YEARS[3]

The sudden change in the presidency of the new company and the necessity for welding an effective management team and operating force from the personnel of two previously separate companies were only a few among the many problems to face the officials of American Motors, for the new company had begun business in one of the most intensely competitive periods ever to confront the firms of the automotive industry. Despite the anticipated advantages of merger and the optimism of its managers, American Motors was to face an agonizing period of reappraisal and readjustment.

Product and Production Changes

For several months after the merger, American Motors continued to produce the 1954 Hudson and Nash models introduced prior to the merger; but late in 1954, the firm introduced new 1955 Nash and Hudson models based on the former Nash body shell. The previous Hudson basic bodies were dropped entirely; and the 1955 Hudson models had slight exterior differences from the Nash lines plus the Hudson nameplate. Thus, the same basic car was being used for both the Nash and Hudson lines. Production of the two lines of cars was started in December 1954 and concentrated in the Nash auto-

[3] Unless otherwise indicated, the material in this and the following sections is based on information provided by American Motors Corporation in its annual reports and proxy statements issued in the years 1954 through 1963 and comments of company officials during personal interviews with this writer in February and December, 1963.

motive plants in Kenosha and Milwaukee, Wisconsin. The Wisconsin plants of the Nash organization were considered by American Motors officials to be among the most efficient in the industry when operating at a rate between 750 and 1,000 cars per day on a one-shift basis. This was sufficient to provide approximately 200,000 or more cars per year.

Since there was much overlap in the product lines and price ranges of Nash and Hudson, integration was viewed as both a necessity and an opportunity to eliminate duplication of coverage and competition in the same price classes by dealers of the same firm.

After the end of the 1954 Hudson model run, the Hudson plants were withdrawn from automotive production. Combined Nash and Hudson sales at the time were well below the output available from the former Nash plants. With the establishment of the Hudson Special Products Division, the Hudson facilities provided the basis for one of four decentralized profit control centers set up by Romney. The others were the automotive, appliance, and export and subsidiaries profit centers. The special products division was to concentrate upon defense production and special contract work for other American Motors divisions and outside companies; but from 1955 through 1957, the company had idle facilities in the Hudson Division. A hoped-for expansion in defense sales did not materialize. Some reduction in idle facilities resulted from the sale of the former Hudson body assembly plant in December 1955, but some of the former Hudson plants could still be seen standing idle or partially destroyed in Detroit at the end of 1958.[4] Since the firm did not meet with sufficient success in securing defense contracts to use these plants, they were largely abandoned by the end of 1957.

Production of the relatively small 1955 Rambler model, which used a basic body separate from the full-sized Nash and Hudson models, also was continued in the Nash plants. With this line plus extensively redesigned 1955 Nash Ambassador and Statesman lines and the 1955 Hudson Wasp and Hornet series using the Nash basic body, American Motors, by the statement of its officials, then was using only two basic bodies for six series of cars. In reality, however, the firm

---

[4] This situation was widely noted, as, e.g., in pictures and an article on unemployment in the *Durham Morning Herald* (Durham, North Carolina), May 17, 1959, Section D, p. 12.

offered only two distinctive series: the Ramblers and the full-sized cars, so slight was the differentiation. The Rambler series carried both Hudson and Nash nameplates and used one basic body. The full-sized car lines also had both Hudson and Nash nameplates and used another basic body. They were all produced in the Nash plants.

With the introduction of its 1956 models in December 1955, American Motors began to place greater emphasis on its Rambler series. The 1956 Rambler models were described as "completely new" and were considered the new "basic volume" car of the firm. Separate facilities were provided for assembly of Rambler at Kenosha. The Milwaukee plant was used for continued assembly of Nash and Hudson models using the full-sized body shell. Rambler had begun to show greater sales promise; but American Motors officials were undecided on returning fully to the role of a specialist producer.

This viewpoint of the company had been indicated by George Romney in a very humorous talk, illustrated with wonderfully funny cartoons, "The Dinosaur in the Driveway." Boosting his firm's small-sized Rambler models, Romney predicted, "There will be a smaller percentage of mechanized dinosaurs in the American driveways of the future. However, if you still want them, we've got them, too, built a better way—our dinosaurs are smoother, safer, and roomier!"[5]

Prior to the merger and for approximately a year thereafter, neither Hudson nor Nash offered a V-8 engine in its cars. Since the automobile industry had increased its emphasis on the V-8 engine which was widely preferred at the time by consumers, American Motors, in an effort to avoid a weakening of its sales position in this period, initially purchased V-8 engines produced by Packard in its newest plant as part of a planned (at least by officials of American Motors) program of reciprocity buying; but, when the reciprocity agreement turned out to be a one-sided arrangement,[6] American Motors rushed plans for a new V-8, taking only fifteen months to get it into production. The contract with Studebaker-Packard was cancelled; and Packard's new automated

[5] A talk by George Romney, president, American Motors Corporation, delivered before the Motor City Traffic Club of Detroit, January 27, 1955.

[6] Romney once called the arrangement "a one-way street." Transcript of press conference with George Romney, at Hotel Statler, Detroit, Michigan, April 24, 1956.

engine line later was scrapped.[7] The 1956 models of Nash and Hudson were powered by V-8 engines from Packard beginning in the spring of 1956; but American Motors began producing its own V-8 engines in time for its 1957 models.

From 1954 through 1956, primary objectives of American Motors officials following the merger had been to reduce the break-even point in its passenger car production and simultaneously to develop new lines of cars and engines. By the end of 1956, the automobile lines of the firm were reduced to three series—the separate Rambler models and the full-sized Nash and Hudson models—using only two basic bodies and two new engines, one of which was the new V-8. With the consolidation of the Hudson, Nash, and Rambler activities, American Motors reported a reduction in its break-even point for automotive production to a level below 150,000 units per year. Of course, since the former Hudson facilities had been set aside in a separate cost control center, thereby removing the heavy depreciation costs of the Hudson facilities, only the Nash plants were included for the computation of the break-even point. Nevertheless, since the firm had produced six car series using four basic bodies and four six-cylinder engines two years earlier, it is apparent that much had been done by the end of 1956 to consolidate the operations and products of the two previously separate organizations. Progress was also made by 1956 toward integration of the Hudson and Nash dealer organizations. Unfortunately for the firm, as we shall see below, the hoped-for sales increase did not materialize.

In September 1957, American Motors reported a further consolidation of its operations. The full-sized Nash and Hudson models, whose sales had been disappointing since the merger, were dropped. They were replaced by the Rambler Ambassador, which used many of the basic body parts of the regular 108-inch wheelbase Rambler line on a 117-inch wheelbase car. The smaller 100-inch wheelbase Rambler first brought out in 1950 had been dropped entirely in the 1956 and 1957 models; its substitute in these years was a completely new version using a 108-inch wheelbase first introduced on Rambler in 1954. However, the 100-inch wheelbase model was again put into production in late 1957 and reintroduced in January 1958 as Rambler American. This was probably the only time that a discontinued car was ever reintro-

---

[7] *Infra*, chapter iv.

duced. It used the basic body of the earlier 100-inch wheel-base Rambler which had been discontinued after 1955; but it had altered hood, rear deck, and fender lines. The old dies were reworked and used in production of the 1958 model Rambler American.[8] Thus, by the end of 1957 American Motors was still producing cars using two different basic bodies, but they were all known as Ramblers—Rambler, Rambler Ambassador, and Rambler American. After these changes American Motors reported that its manufacturing consolidation program was completed during 1957, three years after the merger. The firm's automotive lines had been much simplified, and company officials believed that economies had been made possible through elimination of duplicating facilities.

From 1954 through 1957, then, extensive changes were imposed on the combined Nash and Hudson organizations. The Hudson plants were largely abandoned or disposed of by sale. Operations were consolidated, first in manufacturing and later in selling. The consolidation resulted in almost complete elimination of the formerly separate Hudson dealer organization and production facilities from the new company. Although a few members of the former Hudson management, several hundred former Hudson production workers, and some former Hudson dealers were still with American Motors at the end of 1957, the net result of the Nash-Kelvinator-Hudson merger was the liquidation of the Hudson organization, both as a producing group within the new company and as a participant in the domestic passenger car market. Gone was Hudson; and gone was one of the rivals with whom Nash-Kelvinator otherwise would have had to contend.

A Decline in Market Position

Concurrent with and probably because of the integration of the Nash and Hudson car lines, the unit sales of American Motors cars declined drastically from the earlier combined totals of the firm's predecessors. The use of a common body shell for both the Hudson and Nash lines and reduction in differentiation between the lines after 1954 resulted, it appears, in a contraction of American Motors' market coverage.

As may be seen in Table 3, there was a sharp decline in unit retail sales of the American Motors group from 1953

[8] See also, "Why AMC Can Gamble on Its Small Car," *Business Week*, January 11, 1958, pp. 78-79.

to 1954; and throughout the remainder of the period through 1957, unit sales of the firm's cars continued at low levels. From their 1950 peak postwar combined sales of 310,000

TABLE 3

NEW PASSENGER CAR REGISTRATIONS AND SHARE OF TOTAL UNITED STATES REGISTRATIONS OF AMERICAN MOTORS CARS, 1946-1963 [a]
(Registrations in Thousands of Units)

Year	Hudson	Nash	Rambler [b]	AMC Total	AMC Share
1946	72	85	—	158	8.7%
1947	83	103	—	186	5.9
1948	109	104	—	214	6.1
1949	138	135	—	273	5.6
1950	134	176	—	310	4.9
1951	97	140	—	237	4.7
1952	79	143	—	221	5.3
1953	67	98	40	204	3.6
1954	35	41	36	112	2.0
1955	21	37	72	130	1.8
1956	12	25	71	108	1.8
1957	5	9	91	106	1.8
1958	—	—	186	186	4.0
1959	—	—	363	363	6.0
1960	—	—	422	422	6.4
1961	—	—	371	371	6.3
1962	—	—	423	423	6.1
1963	—	—	428	428	5.7

[a] Source: Registration data by courtesy of R. L. Polk & Co. and computations based on these data. American Motors also sold the Metropolitan—a car produced in England under contract to American Motors; Metropolitan sales annually amounted to about 7,000 units from 1954 through 1956, 12,000 units from 1957 through 1958, and 7,000 to 8,000 units thereafter through 1961.

[b] Rambler sales were not listed separately until 1953 although the car was originally introduced in 1950.

units, the retail sales of American Motors cars fell to a low of only 106,000 units in 1957. In each of the four years, 1954 through 1957, total annual sales of American Motors cars ranged around one half the combined annual sales levels of their predecessors from 1951 through 1953. The 1957 low was only about one third the 1950 peak combined sales level. The decline was so extensive that the annual unit sales of American Motors cars from 1954 through 1957 were even less than those of Nash, including Nash Rambler, from 1950 through 1953. Hudson had been eliminated entirely and Nash had been sharply reduced.

The relative market position of American Motors also declined sharply in comparison with the combined position of its predecessors. From approximately 5.3 per cent of total United States sales in 1952, the share held by the American Motors group fell to only 1.8 per cent in each year from 1955 through 1957. Clearly, the firm suffered a sharp setback in its market position during the period of consolidation and readjustment from 1954 through 1957. Yet, there was even then a reason for optimism shown in the sales statistics of the firm, namely the gradually rising sales volume of the Rambler series.

Financial Effects of Sales Decline

In spite of the improvements which consolidation appeared to hold, the years following the merger were difficult ones for American Motors. From 1954 through 1957, as shown in Tables 4 and 5, the new company experienced a generally declining dollar sales volume, a series of severe losses, and declining financial strength.

The future difficulties soon to be confronting American Motors had been forecast by the firm's sharply declining sales concurrent with the merger in 1954. Instead of finding increased volume of output through merger, the new firm actually was confronted with a fall in sales of its products. For their 1953 annual reporting periods, combined sales of Hudson and Nash-Kelvinator had totaled $671,550,000. Their drastically reduced dollar sales after the merger may be seen in Table 4, although, it should be noted, the report for 1954 is not entirely comparable to the others. All Nash-Kelvinator operations but only five months of Hudson operations were included for the 1954 report.

The competitive conditions of a "buyers' market" presented to the new company a "challenging period." Even before the merger, Nash and Hudson had been confronted with a fall in unit car sales after the middle of 1953 which placed them "at a cost disadvantage in prorating their tooling and other relatively fixed expenses against a smaller number of cars."[9] The result was an increase in their unit production costs to a level that resulted in unprofitable operations.

It had been expected that the consolidation of Hudson and Nash would result in "economies in manufacturing, tool-

[9] American Motors Corporation, *Annual Report*, 1954, p. 2.
[10] *Ibid.*

ing and overhead expenses and advantages in selling, which neither company could obtain alone."[10] However, this expectation was based on an assumption that the level of output could be maintained at levels comparable to the combined output of the two previously separate firms in order to utilize available capacity. Had this actually occurred, the use of common body tooling would have provided immediate results. Officials of the company estimated that the use of a common body shell for both Nash and Hudson in the 1955 models introduced in November 1954 saved $15,000,000 in tooling that otherwise would have been required for a separate Hudson basic body. This measure would have cut approximately in half the basic body tooling cost per car if the firm could have maintained its sales and output. Instead, however, American Motors actually faced reduced sales and consequently higher unit costs. The result was a series of heavy losses from 1954 through 1957.

The losses were attributed to the firm's automotive operations and the inability to make profitable use of the former Hudson automotive facilities. Kelvinator Division and Redisco, the firm's appliance sales financing subsidiary, remained steady earners throughout this period; but both the Automotive Division and the Hudson Special Products Division, consisting of the former Hudson automobile plants, reportedly lost heavily in these years.

Large though American Motors' reported loss was for 1954, it understated what would have been reported if the operations of both predecessor organizations had been included for the full fiscal year. Both Nash-Kelvinator and Hudson were losing money before the merger; but since Hudson had been the bigger loser, inclusion of its figures would have markedly increased the total loss.

Although American Motors got off to a poor start—its first annual report showed a heavy loss—officials of the new company were optimistic regarding the future potential of the company. The large operating loss for 1954 was attributed principally to lower selling prices, increased selling expenses, increased unit costs of automobile production because of the low rate of output, and the costs of cancelling the previously separate Hudson car lines. Hudson had already accelerated its depreciation and amortization expense in the abandonment of the Hudson Jet before the merger, but the elimination of the separate full-sized Hudson cars after the

Table 4

AMERICAN MOTORS CORPORATION
ABBREVIATED COMPARATIVE INCOME STATEMENTS FOR YEARS ENDED
SEPTEMBER 30, 1954-1963[a]
(Millions of Dollars)

	1954[b]	1955	1956	1957	1958[c]	1959	1960	1961	1962	1963
Net Sales	$400.3	$441.1	$408.4	$362.2	$470.3	$869.8	$1,057.7	$875.7	$1,056.4	$1,132.4
Cost of Products Sold[d]	374.6	406.6	388.6	331.7	402.5	707.7	887.8	762.6	910.4	981.9
Selling, Advertising and Administrative Expense	48.3	54.1	50.5	41.0	42.9	62.5	72.0	67.1	81.7	88.0
Operating Profit (Loss)	(22.6)	(19.7)	(30.7)	(10.5)	24.9	99.6	97.9	46.0	64.2	62.4
Other Income	2.9	5.7	13.0[e]	2.2	3.6	6.3	8.4	4.6	9.0	12.1
Other Expense	2.9	14.7[f]	3.5	4.1[g]	2.9[h]	.8	.9	.2	.1	—
Net Income (Loss) before Tax Adjustments	(22.7)	(28.7)	(21.2)	(12.3)	25.6	105.1	105.4	50.4	73.1	74.6
Income Tax (Credit)	(11.6)[i]	(9.7)	(1.4)	(.5)	(.5)	45.1	57.2	26.8	38.9	36.8
Net Income (Loss) after Tax Adjustments	(11.1)	(19.0)	(19.7)	(11.8)	26.1	60.0	48.2	23.6	34.2	37.8

a Source: Condensation of statements from American Motors Corporation, *Annual Reports*, 1954-1963. Because of rounding, the individual figures may not add exactly to the totals.
b Includes results of Hudson operations from date of merger May 1, 1954, but excludes them prior to that date.
c Includes dealer cooperative advertising previously billed separately but billed as a part of the sales price in 1958 and thereafter. On a comparable billing basis, sales in 1957 would have been $366,390,000.
d Includes all depreciation, amortization, and employee pension expenses and provisions for warranty on refrigerators.
e Includes $10,622,000 gain on sale of Ranco, Inc., assets.
f Includes $12,000,000 writedown of idle plant and equipment.
g Includes $1,300,000 provision for loss on sale of idle plant.
h Includes $1,600,000 provision for possible loss on sale of additional idle plant.
i After deduction of $5,700,000 credit applicable to merger charges carried to retained earnings.

TABLE 5
AMERICAN MOTORS CORPORATION
ABBREVIATED COMPARATIVE BALANCE SHEETS FOR YEARS ENDED
SEPTEMBER 30, 1954-1963[a]
(Millions of Dollars)

	1954	1955	1956	1957	1958	1959	1960	1961	1962	1963
Cash	$ 45.4	$ 37.9	$ 26.5	$ 22.6	$ 34.5	$ 28.6	$ 22.3	$ 39.6	$ 45.9	$ 47.6
Marketable Securities	—	—	—	—	10.0	31.4	21.5	30.1	41.1	47.8
Accounts Receivable [b]	38.8	33.2	26.7	24.1	31.1	34.8	40.5	40.2	50.4	53.2
Inventories	80.6	89.6	84.0	68.0	59.9	98.1	115.6	93.3	96.1	127.4
Prepaid Expenses	5.0	4.1	3.5	3.3	3.0	2.9	3.9	3.7	3.9	4.1
Total Current Assets	169.8	164.7	140.7	118.0	138.6	195.9	203.8	206.9	237.4	280.0
Investments and Other Assets [c]	14.7	19.6	10.9	12.0	16.1	30.0	39.8	40.3	48.8	54.1
Property, Plant, and Equipment	156.6	129.4	129.7	124.6	107.1	117.8	159.5	157.3	167.7	192.6
Less Accumulated Depreciation	74.4	53.4	56.4	58.7	55.6	59.1	64.7	71.5	78.9	86.4
Net Property, Plant, and Equipment	82.1	76.0	73.3	65.9	51.5	58.6	94.8	85.7	88.8	106.2
Total Assets	266.7	260.3	224.9	196.0	206.2	284.5	338.4	333.0	375.1	440.4
Total Current Liabilities [d]	87.8	102.3	86.1	71.8	58.7	85.6	107.7	103.8	121.0	161.1
Other Liabilities						1.0	3.4	3.5	4.7	6.1
Long-term Debt	16.0	14.0	14.6	13.0	10.0	7.0	4.0			
Total Stockholder Equity [e]	163.0	144.0	124.3	111.2	137.5	190.8	223.3	225.7	249.5	273.1
Total Liabilities and Equity	266.7	260.3	224.9	196.0	206.2	284.5	338.4	333.0	375.1	440.4

a Source: Condensation of balance sheets from American Motors Corporation, *Annual Reports*, 1954-1963. Because of rounding, the individual figures may not add exactly to the totals.

b Includes refundable federal income taxes of prior years of $16,853,000 in 1954 and $9,684,000 in 1955.

c No goodwill or patents were listed in any years; amounts include principally investments in subsidiaries and idle plant and equipment held for disposal.

d After applying against federal income taxes United States government securities in the following amounts: 1959, $40,009,000; 1960, $35,077,000; 1961, $9,855,000; and, 1962, $18,197,000.

e All common stock; the firm had no preferred stock issues.

merger resulted in additional accelerated amortization of tooling, obsolescence of inventories, and costs of cancellation of purchase contracts, all of which totaled approximately $14,860,000. After a $5,700,000 tax credit was applied to these costs, the balance was charged against an $11,000,000 reserve established from retained earnings to cover the costs of merger. The remainder of the reserve was then cancelled. Thus, much of the reported loss for 1954 was considered a result of a nonrecurring type of expense.

The optimistic outlook of American Motors officials seemed about to be justified in 1955. Although sales of the firm's full-sized cars continued to decline, Rambler sales were up from the previous year; and American Motors found that its operating loss for 1955 was lower than in 1954. Since about 85 per cent of the loss accumulated in the first half of the firm's fiscal year, the last six months of the year reflected an improving situation. In fact, American Motors operated at a profit during the spring selling season, April through June, its third quarter of the fiscal year.

With the introduction in December 1955 of the "completely new" 1956 Ramblers and the continued building of the larger 1956 model Nash and Hudson cars around the same basic body shell used for the 1955 models, officials of American Motors anticipated further improved financial results. Capacity for Rambler production had been increased to 800 cars per day at the Kenosha plant, permitting the concentration of all Rambler production there; and the firm's El Segundo, California, plant, where Rambler had previously been built for West Coast distribution, was sold, thereby reducing the fixed costs of the automotive division.

Observing that "the practice of building several lines of cars from a common basic body shell has been followed by the larger companies for many years at a considerable financial advantage over the smaller companies,"[11] American Motors officials expected their policy to pay off in 1956. But profits continued elusive.

American Motors suffered a sharp financial setback in 1956. Sales declined but operating expenses remained relatively fixed; and American Motors' operating loss soared to more than $30,500,000. With the accomplishment in 1956 of a reduction in the company's break-even point in its car production to approximately 150,000 units per year through the

[11] American Motors Corporation, *Annual Report*, 1955, p. 2.

consolidation of the Hudson, Nash, and Rambler lines, American Motors had appeared in a position to secure lower unit costs of production. However, while the Kelvinator division enjoyed its greatest profits since 1950, the automotive division and the Hudson Special Products Division experienced losses in 1956. The anticipated sales had not materialized.

American Motors officials considered their firm's performance to have been particularly disappointing in 1956, since they believed that much progress previously had been made toward overcoming the major obstacles which stood in the way of its success. They had brought out a new V-8 engine and had eliminated duplication in many operations. Some idle plants had been sold and others written down by some $12,000,000 to their estimated realizable value, eliminating them as a burden on future operations. It was believed that the groundwork had been laid for a favorable profit position. However, the improved car sales that American Motors enjoyed in 1955 proved to be only a temporary backwash from the greatest year the industry ever had through 1962; and American Motors' sales declined along with those of the rest of the industry in 1956.

The year 1956 constituted the period of greatest trial to American Motors. So serious was the situation that George Romney, then president, warned employees of the company in September and again in September 1957 that the management did not believe American Motors could long survive if it continued to experience heavy losses comparable to those of 1956.[12]

American Motors found it necessary to obtain a deferment of $2,569,000 of the $4,000,000 installments due in 1956 and 1957 on its indebtedness to the Prudential Insurance Company of America. The amount of the short-term revolving credit agreement which the company had with 27 banks also was reduced from $73,000,000 to $45,000,000 and extended for a two-year period through September 1958. In addition, the firm issued to the banks and the insurance company $6,000,000 of junior subordinated debentures of Refrigera-

[12] George Romney, "The Future Is Here," An extemporaneous talk by the president of American Motors before the third annual employee product review at Milwaukee Arena, September 14, 1957, reprinted in U. S., Senate, Committee on the Judiciary, Subcommittee on Antitrust and Monopoly, *Hearings, Administered Prices*, 85th Congress, 2nd Session, Pursuant to S. Res. 57 and S. Res. 231 (Washington: U. S. Government Printing Office, 1958), Part 7, p. 3814.

tion Discount Corporation, a wholly-owned subsidiary, retired $5,300,000 in preferred stock issued by the subsidiary to its parent, American Motors, and agreed not to pay any dividends during the period of these new credit agreements.

It was also in 1956 that American Motors faced a serious threat of a proxy fight for its control. Louis E. Wolfson, a well known financier who had made millions of dollars in a number of successful manipulations of other companies, advised George Romney that he had purchased more than 200,000 shares of American Motors stock. He said he and his associates were considering the possibility of buying another 1,000,000 shares, at prices up to $8 per share, to gain control of the company.[13] As American Motors' troubles had continued to accumulate, the price of its stock had fallen below $6 per share by mid-1956, against a book value then of approximately $22 per share. Clearly, American Motors was engaged in a desperate struggle for survival; but Wolfson and others were persuaded to give their continued support to the existing management of the firm.

Although they were deeply disheartened by American Motors' poor financial performance in 1956, officials of the company, under the enthusiastic leadership of Romney, retained an optimistic outlook for the future. The firm had experienced heavy cash drains for new facilities in 1956— $9,488,000 was paid for plant additions and $12,024,000 for new tooling, mainly for the new V-8 engine. But, American Motors officials felt that they had greatly improved their automotive product and production potential. They attributed the adverse operating results in 1956 in part to the general 1956 decline in car sales. Other unfavorable factors were said to be: the excessive cost of using a V-8 engine and transmission made by another company, and price reductions involved in liquidating year-end inventories of the full-sized Nash and Hudson models for 1955 and 1956, plus the added expenses of introducing the 1956 Rambler a year ahead of the original schedule. It was estimated that the added expense of early introduction of the new Rambler models was $5,400,000 and the excess cost of using an outsider's V-8 engine and transmission amounted to $5,300,000. Price reductions in liquidation of 1955 and 1956 models amounted to $2,700,000 and the accelerated amortization of tooling be-

---

[13] See Tom Mahoney, *The Story of George Romney* (New York: Harper & Brothers, 1960), pp. 28-47, for a fascinating discussion of Wolfson's dealings with Romney and American Motors.

cause of liquidation of prior year models was reported at $1,600,000. The total of these charges, which the firm's managers considered to be unusual, amounted to approximately one half the operating loss for 1956. Nevertheless, the company was to suffer another trying year.

During 1957, dollar sales of the corporation continued to decline; but the operating loss of the firm was reduced to about $10,000,000. A reduction in costs, particularly in selling, advertising, and general expense which was cut by $8,500,000, had accompanied the decline in sales. Still, because of the loss there was a continued and startling contraction through 1957 in the assets of the company and the equity of its stockholders, as may be seen in Table 5.

In contrast, the combined last annual reported holdings of American Motors' two predecessors were much higher at the end of their respective 1953 fiscal years, the last period prior to the merger. Combined stockholder equity was approximately $193,847,000; combined total assets, net of depreciation, were $340,633,000; combined cash totaled $47,481,-000 and was supplemented by marketable securities of $3,129,000 not including holdings of treasury tax anticipation notes; net property, plant, and equipment had reached a combined total of $97,507,000; and net working capital was a combined total of $100,097,000. At the end of their 1950 fiscal reporting periods and excluding their holdings of U. S. government securities to be applied in payment of Federal income taxes, the cash and marketable securities holdings alone of Nash and Hudson had reached a combined total of $115,222,000. Even from the disastrous period of declining sales levels in 1953 when Hudson experienced its largest postwar loss as an independent firm, the new corporation experienced a steady downward trend in financial strength from 1954 through 1957. The losses in values were indeed great. American Motors faced continued threats to its survival from the heavy losses which it was experiencing. Although officials of the company were voicing their optimism, it seemed doubtful to many observers that American Motors would be able to survive; but there were mitigating influences.

Although the operating losses of American Motors were very large, their impact was partly relieved by tax credits which the firm received from carrybacks of its losses to earlier years in which it had earned profits. From 1954 through 1957, the firm reported receiving tax credits approximating $28,940,000 of which about $920,000 resulted from offsets of American Motors losses against current profits of its Redisco, Incorporated, subsidiary. As a result of the tax credits and excluding the expenses from writedowns of idle plant, the net losses of the firm were less than its operating losses, substantially less in 1954 and 1955, and slightly less in 1956 and 1957 when the two-year carryback feature had been exhausted.

Other factors also helped. Diversification was an important factor for American Motors, which was a relatively large company compared to most firms even without its domestic automotive operations. The Appliance Division, which under the direction of Bernard A. Chapman did a brisk business throughout the United States and abroad selling Kelvinator, Leonard, and A.B.C. consumer and commercial products, was reported to have been a relatively steady earner during the years from 1954 through 1957. The payment of dividends by American Motors' subsidiaries also provided substantial amounts of cash to the parent company. The retirement of preferred stock by Refrigeration Discount Corporation, a subsidiary of American Motors, contributed cash of $1,200,000 in 1955 and $5,300,000 in 1956. Sales of idle plant and equipment contributed to the working capital of the company. Liquidation of the El Segundo, California, and the Hudson Gratiot Avenue plants provided $5,320,000 in 1956. The sale of ice cream cabinet leases provided $1,650,-000 in 1956. And finally, "gambling" on its automotive operations, American Motors obtained $10,945,000 on the sale of its investment in its Ranco Incorporated subsidiary, a leading producer of plastic parts and heater controls. Net gain on the sale totaled $10,662,000. The willingness of the firm's creditors to negotiate new credit agreements, of course, had also helped.

Had it not been for the mitigating influences, the corporation would have found itself unable to meet its current obligations at some time during the period. As it was, the company was steadily approaching its $55,000,000 minimum working capital requirement in 1956; but through the renegotiation of its credit agreements, this requirement was reduced to $42,000,000 in August. The new requirement was met, though the firm's net working capital was to fall to about $54,644,000 in September 1956 and $46,239,000 by September 1957. The years from 1954 through 1957, then, confronted American Motors with a serious threat to its survival. For its first four annual reports, the new company could show only losses; and it found its financial strength being steadily drained. But, survive it did!

RESURGENCE AND PROSPERITY[14]

American Motors finally turned the corner toward profitable operations. In 1958 the company was able to show its first annual profits. It was the only domestic automobile manufacturer to improve its position in 1958. Factory sales of its cars rose almost 60 per cent; and dollar sales of the firm rose more than $108,000,000 above the low level of 1957. An operating profit of $25,590,000 was obtained. Net income amounted to more than $26,085,000 after tax credits. Cash climbed to $34,539,000 and was supplemented by $9,995,000 in marketable securities. Net working capital rose sharply to $79,915,000 with a current ratio of 2.4. Property, plant, and equipment of the firm continued the decline of the four preceding years. Because of the complete elimination of the full-sized Nash and Hudson models for 1958, retirements, writeoffs, and amortization of special tools exceeded property acquisitions in 1958 and resulted in a continued reduction in book value of fixed assets. However, total assets increased to $206,185,000 and stockholders' equity climbed to $137,514,-000. The firm's remaining $27,000,000 in short-term bank debt was entirely paid off in July; and the long-term note to the insurance company was reduced to $10,000,000 by the end of the fiscal year.

American Motors became a pacesetter of the industry, leading the way with its compact car and enjoying exceptional profitability ratios. Its unit car sales increased greatly, and the share of new car registrations held by its makes expanded to more than three times the 1957 level. American Motors' Kenosha plant became the most intensely used assembly plant in the industry. And, although the other domestic firms followed its product leadership into the compact car class, confronting the firm with more direct competition after 1959, American Motors' sales remained at high levels.

The resurgence of American Motors in 1958, as may be

[14] An improved position for American Motors after its years of decline was aptly described by its executive vice-president, Roy D. Chapin, Jr., as "The Resurgence of American Motors," A speech before the Harvard Business School Club of Detroit, April, 1958. The heading for this section is derived in part from the title of the speech.

seen in Tables 4 and 5, was followed by even greater financial success. The firm's sales almost doubled from 1958 to 1959, increasing almost $400,000,000; and its profits before taxes climbed above $105,000,000 in each of the years 1959 and 1960. Dividend payments were resumed with almost $7,123,000 being paid in 1959. In the next three fiscal years, the firm paid out cash dividends of more than $56,000,000. Without incurring additional bank debt, although a $50,000,-000 line of credit from 24 banks was available to the company, the assets of the firm increased greatly, almost doubling the 1957 level by the end of September 1962. Its net working capital increased to a record level of more than $116,000,000 at the end of the firm's fiscal year 1962, being approximately two and a half times the level existing at the end of the corresponding period in 1957; and despite payment of the millions of dollars in dividends, the book value of stockholder equity in the company had more than doubled the 1957 level.

The improvement in American Motors' performance was mirrored in the market price of its stock. In 1954 American Motors stock had sold in a range from $9.75 to $14.75 per share; but its price fell to a low of $5.25 in 1956 and 1957. With the resurgence in 1958, the price of American Motors stock rose rapidly. It closed at $8.625 per share on January 2, 1958, climbed to a high of $41.50 during the year, and closed at $39.375 on December 31, 1958. The latter prices were well above the postwar high prices of the old Hudson and Nash-Kelvinator stocks exchanged for American Motors shares; Hudson had peaked at $34.50 per share and Nash-Kelvinator at $25.75. The rise in price in 1958, however, was only the beginning of a fabulous increase, for American Motors shares increased to a price of $96.875 in 1959 before being split three-for-one on February 10, 1960. Millions of dollars were made by traders in the American Motors stock, which had finally paid off for its faithful holders.

THE AMERICAN MOTORS STRATEGY

The approach of American Motors in concentrating on the Rambler and abandoning the broader line, which it initially had sought through merger, was to base its strategy for survival and prosperity in the automobile industry "on cars that are distinctive and unique—cars that do not compete head on with automobiles of the Big Three."[15]

The improvement in American Motors' sales potential directly resulted from the rising popularity of Rambler. As may be seen in Table 3, Rambler sales gained persistently after 1954 while those of the larger Nash and Hudson models declined. An initial upsurge followed the introduction of a 108-inch wheelbase four-door Rambler. The new car outsold the earlier 100-inch wheelbase Rambler, which was a two-door model. In December, 1955, the smaller Rambler was dropped, and a completely new-styled 108-inch wheelbase 1956 model Rambler was adopted as the "basic volume" car of the firm. Rambler, by 1957, was the only American produced car with a wheelbase shorter than 116 inches, a fact which gave it a unique position in the United States market. With increasing evidence of a preference for smaller cars on the part of many consumers, as reflected in both the growing popularity of small foreign cars after 1955 and the rising sales of Rambler, American Motors was able to reintroduce its 100-inch wheelbase model as the Rambler American in January 1958.

Beginning in 1955, American Motors promoted its newer Rambler series more boldly. After receiving the go-ahead order from Mason, Rambler had been engineered and developed under the direction of Meade F. Moore, vice-president in charge of automotive research and engineering, and was first introduced as a sports-type model in 1950. Although the line was broadened in 1954, Rambler still occupied a secondary position to the full-sized Nash and Hudson models until December 1955 and the introduction of the newly designed 1956 model Ramblers. In January 1955, Romney clearly promoted the Rambler as the car of the future compared to the outmoded "dinosaurs" of the Big Three in his speech "The Dinosaur in the Driveway," a title which had been suggested by Howard Hallas, director of public relations for American Motors. The promotional idea was carried through; and Rambler sales began to pick up. The race was on.

American Motors' advertising emphasized the Rambler's distinctiveness and boldly compared its features point by point with those of the Big Three cars. The Rambler was a type and

[15] U. S., Senate, Committee on the Judiciary, Subcommittee on Antitrust and Monopoly, *Hearings, A Study of the Antitrust Laws*, 84th Congress, 1st Session, Pursuant to S. Res. 61 (Washington: U. S. Government Printing Office, 1955), Part 1, p. 461. Testimony of George Romney.

size of vehicle, which under the stimulus of the firm's sales promotion efforts, eventually came to be known as the "compact car." At first, the company had been undecided in its product policies, keeping a foot in both camps with its full-sized Nash and Hudson models being continued, too; but the poor sales showing of Nash and Hudson lines led to their abandonment in September of 1957. Rambler, subsequently, was the firm's only make. American Motors had returned fully to the role of a specialist producer, as Nash-Kelvinator had been before the merger.

The increasing consumer acceptance of Rambler was an essential ingredient in the firm's comeback. Nevertheless, credit must be given to American Motors officials for laying in the firm's earlier period of adversity the foundations for taking advantage of larger volume operations.

Despite the problems of their company, the morale of American Motors officials had remained high. Although many company officials had favorable offers at higher pay from other companies, the management of the firm stayed with it. The five highest paid officers even accepted a voluntary reduction in salary averaging 25.9 per cent in 1957 to tide the company over. An important factor was a plan for the accrual for future payment of an executive bonus; but their staying reflected their confidence in American Motors' future.

The management of the company stuck with it; and when George Romney resigned in 1962 to become governor of Michigan, American Motors' directors chose from among their number Roy Abernethy to be president of the company. Richard E. Cross, legal counsel for the firm and a director since 1954, became chairman of the board.

In the early years after the merger, American Motors' labor costs had been higher than those of the Big Three. The difference was more in lax work standards and costly fringe benefits than in wage rate differentials. Even such seemingly insignificant factors as the elimination of a five-minute washup period before lunch could save a company the size of American Motors $1,000,000 or more per year. The firm's worst problems, though, were reported to be in the Detroit Kelvinator plant, which was organized by the Mechanics Educational Society of America. This, of course, was not an automobile plant.

In 1955, under the able direction of Romney and Edward L. Cushman, then director of industrial relations for the company, a new basis was established for improved labor relations. New agreements with both the Mechanics Educational Society of America and the United Automobile Workers of America brought American Motors labor costs more in line with those of the Big Three, saving the company millions of dollars that otherwise would have been paid out. These changes broke for the first time the Independents' postwar pattern of following basically the Big Three union agreements with higher wage rates and fringe benefits. Successful efforts also were made to tighten work standards to reduce labor costs. Despite the firm's success in breaking the previous pattern of bargaining, American Motors still paid somewhat higher wage rates and fringe benefits than the Big Three after the 1955 agreement; but in subsequent negotiations, according to officials of the company, the major inequities were eliminated.[16]

Reflecting the management philosophy of Romney and his associates, the breaking of the firm's prior pattern of bargaining was an important step. American Motors' newly found boldness in labor relations was continued into the future. In the summer of 1961, a precedent-breaking contract calling for a form of profit-sharing with hourly employees was agreed to by union and company officials.[17] The new contract provided a Progress Sharing Plan designed to distribute the returns to the company equitably among its stockholders and employees by establishing a relationship between employee benefits and company profits. The plan was implemented with the establishment of a fund representing the hourly employees' share of company profits as spelled out in the union agreement. One third of this fund was allocated to a stock purchase plan for employees, while the remainder was for a variety of employee benefits including pensions, medical care, and insurance and the reserves for them. The program required a contribution to the fund of 15 per cent of company profits on United States manufacturing operations, before taxes and before the cost of contribution to the fund, in excess of an amount equal to a 10 per cent

---

[16] These developments were widely commented upon by company officials including, among others, George Romney, in "In League with the Future," op. cit.; Roy D. Chapin, Jr., executive vice-president, in "The Resurgence of American Motors," op. cit.; and Romney in his testimony before U. S., Senate, Committee on the Judiciary, op. cit., pp. 457-59.

[17] American Motors Corporation – United Automobile Workers of America, "Agreement," September 6, 1961, pp. 129-35.

return on net worth of the company to the stockholders. One of the more important features of the plan was the making of fringe benefits to hourly employees largely a variable cost. A similar plan was provided for salaried employees, too.

Although the consolidation of American Motors' manufacturing operations had been a difficult task, the welding of its dealer organization was an even more difficult problem. For nearly two years after the merger, American Motors maintained two separate dealer groups and two advertising and merchandising programs. Occasionally, Nash and Hudson dealers found themselves located across the street from one another and selling essentially the same product. Although they were identical cars except for the nameplates, the resale value of the Hudson Rambler fell below that of the Nash Rambler, illustrating one of the peculiarities of the market for passenger cars.

American Motors' varying fortunes were reflected in its changing dealer strength. After the merger, American Motors' dealer body was strong in numbers but weak in sales volume. The Hudson dealer organization was found to possess less strength than had been anticipated. Many unproductive dealers were being maintained. The task of rebuilding the sales organization fell to Roy Abernethy, who came to American Motors in October 1954 from a position as vice-president and general manager of Kaiser-Willys Sales Division. The weaker dealers were eliminated; and dealer strength improved. Even in American Motors' two worst years, its dealers earned $15,037,000 on a net worth of $91,421,000 in 1956 and $23,184,000 on net worth of $104,093,000 in 1957.[18] With the improving and expanding sales position of the Rambler, whose proportionate resale value had begun exceeding those of low-priced Big Three makes, the American Motors franchise came into wider demand. From 2,904 in September 1955, the number of American Motors' dealers had fallen below 2,000 in late 1956 before climbing back to 2,211 in September 1957. American Motors' unique position with its Rambler was reflected in an increased number of dealers handling other makes of cars who sought Rambler franchises. Breaking previous industry patterns of opposition to intercorporate dual franchise arrangements, except in very small markets, many new dealers, including some

18 Chapin, *op. cit.*

Big Three dealers, were signed up for Rambler franchises.[19] By September 1958, the dealer body numbered 2,636; and in the years that followed, the number was maintained at about 3,000.

American Motors' strategy in emphasizing specialized vehicles not in direct competition with Big Three makes may have been viewed, in part, as a gamble to stay in business. If so, it was a successful gamble! The Ramblers, perhaps more than any other single factor, made American Motors a profitable company. They won acclaim from many sources including, among others, selection as a "best buy" by *Consumer Reports*,[20] a publication of the nonprofit Consumers Union of America organization, and as "car of the year" by *Motor Trend*,[21] a popular magazine for automobile enthusiasts. But even more important was the acclaim they received from consumers who bought them in much increased numbers. The years of economic adversity were followed by years of exceptional profits. For a company which earlier had been down and almost counted out, it was a tremendous comeback!

[19] Opposition to intercorporate dual franchise arrangements, reportedly, eased somewhat after 1956 following Congressional hearings on the industry. See, e.g., John L. Hess, "American Cars: A Narrowing Choice," *Atlantic Monthly*, CCI (February, 1958), 47; and "New System for Selling Cars," *Business Week*, August 24, 1957, p. 105, in which it was observed that the Big Three seemed tacitly to be accepting dual franchise arrangements. A broad range of merchandise was considered essential to strengthen dealers because of a price-conscious public. American Motors' dual franchise arrangements rose from 5 per cent of total Rambler franchises in 1957 to approximately 30 per cent of total in 1958. *Ibid.*; and George Melloan, "The Little Two," *The Wall Street Journal*, March 23, 1959, p. 1. About the same proportion of Studebaker dealers also handled other makes.

[20] See *Consumer Reports*, April 1959, p. 186; and April 1960, p. 191.

[21] For the 1963 models introduced in late 1962. *Motor Trend*, February 1963, p. 22.

Chapter IV

STUDEBAKER-PACKARD'S STRUGGLE

WHEREAS AMERICAN MOTORS CORPORATION favored the strategy of being able to offer essentially the same basic car with appearance and minor mechanical variations through the separate Nash and Hudson dealer organizations, Studebaker-Packard Corporation took an opposite tack.

The cars of Studebaker and Packard did not overlap significantly in price. Combining their products enabled the surviving company to offer a full line of cars, which opportunity was thought to be one of the major advantages of the Big Three.

Differing from American Motors in original merger objectives, the courses of action of Studebaker-Packard were quite different from those of American Motors; and as things turned out, Studebaker-Packard's experiences in the automobile industry were in marked contrast, also.

THE YEARS OF THE FULL LINE[1]

Under the hard-driving direction of its president, J. J. Nance, who was assisted by eleven vice-presidents drawn from the combining companies, the firm began business on October 1, 1954, as the fourth largest United States passenger car manufacturer. Combined unit sales of Studebaker and Packard cars had exceeded those of Hudson and Nash each year since 1948.

One of the firm's earliest moves after the merger was to offer dealers in smaller market areas a dual franchise arrangement for both the Packard and Studebaker lines of cars. "Important steps," it was also reported just five months after the merger, "have been initiated to effect operating economies in the consolidation of administrative, engineering and financial functions, the elimination of duplicate warehouse facilities and the consolidation of Canadian and export

[1] Unless otherwise indicated, the material for this and the following sections is based on information provided by Studebaker (Studebaker-Packard) Corporation in its annual reports, proxy statements, and prospectuses issued in the years 1954 through 1963 and comments of company officials during personal interviews with this writer in February, 1963.

operations."[2] There was, however, no rush to integrate product lines as in the Nash-Hudson combination. The product lines of the two previously separate organizations were considered to be complementary rather than directly competing. The Studebaker and Packard cars provided a full line for entry into each of four price classes. Studebaker had participated predominantly in the low and low middle classes while the Packard entries were in the upper middle and high price classes. In addition, the new firm produced a line of trucks covering about 85 per cent of the market and numerous defense products, at least initially.

In response to the highly competitive conditions they considered then to be existing in 1954, Studebaker-Packard officials concluded that the continued provision of a full line of cars was the soundest course for the corporation to follow, this being the pattern followed by the three largest firms in the industry. An easier course of action, they believed, would have been for the firm immediately to consolidate its production and sales activities around one basic car. Such a course of action would have resulted in immediate cost savings through product integration; but company officials believed it also would have brought a further shrinkage in the market position of Studebaker-Packard. Consequently, the course adopted for the 1955 models introduced in late 1954 was the continuation of the full-line approach.

Studebaker-Packard, at this time, planned eventually to integrate production of the firm's cars, the objective being to secure the cost savings of design and common tooling for Studebaker and Packard cars. But this was for the future.

In the early months after the merger, the Packard operations underwent many changes. The 1955 model Studebaker retained the previous year's basic body shell and had only exterior changes; but the new Packard and Clipper models, although they also retained the 1954 model's basic body shell, introduced a new exterior look and the "most modern and powerful V-8 engine of any American car of 1955, with torsion bar suspension providing a luxury ride far advanced of the industry."[3] This type of suspension was later adopted

[2] Studebaker-Packard Corporation, *Annual Report*, 1954, p. 5.
[3] *Ibid.*, p. 6.

by a member of the Big Three.[4] Studebaker-Packard officials believed their new models were priced competitively with comparable cars of other makes in the four price classes.

For the Packard contribution to the full line, new facilities were put into operation in 1954 at Utica, Michigan, to handle engine and transmission work. Being highly automated, Packard's new engine and transmission lines were among the most modern in the industry. Since work on this plant had started in 1953 with completion scheduled for introduction of 1955 models in late 1954, the new facilities represented a continuation of plans formulated long before the merger.

Packard also provided for its own body production in 1954, using a plant obtained from Chrysler under a five-year lease with option to purchase. This plant, the Conner Plant in Detroit, was completely reworked to provide an integrated, one-floor, final assembly operation which company officials expected to be one of the most modern in the industry. The purchase by Chrysler in December 1953 of the Briggs body plants from which Packard had secured its bodies had left Packard with the problem of producing its own bodies.[5] Packard had last produced its own automobile bodies in 1941. Arrangements for use of the Conner Plant also were made well before the merger. Unfortunately, Packard was to face many production difficulties in setting up and operating the plant, not having anticipated fully certain difficulties in the flow of the work.

Since Studebaker had its automotive operations largely concentrated in South Bend and had ample facilities, the Studebaker plants were continued in operation with little change except to accommodate the new styles.

Studebaker-Packard continued the full-line approach with the introduction of 1956 models in late 1955. Some style changes were made in the 1956 model Studebaker which retained the previous year's basic body and again featured a combination of sports-car styling with family comfort and convenience. Separate Packard and Clipper models for 1956 were also introduced. These featured "two new engineering firsts—the non-slip differential and electronic push-button

---

[4] Chrysler reported the introduction on its 1957 models of a similar suspension system which it called "Torsion-Aire." Such systems had previously been used most widely on sports-type vehicles of foreign manufacture. Chrysler Corporation, *Annual Report*, 1956, pp. 7-9.

[5] Packard Motor Car Company, *Annual Report*, 1953, p. 6.

driving."[6] The then widely preferred V-8 engine to which the industry had shifted its emphasis was also offered, having been introduced on the 1955 model Packard cars.

At this time Studebaker-Packard considered its objective to be the provision of "cars that, without being radical, are distinctive."[7] Officials of the company believed the firm had acquired "a group of the industry's most brilliant young stylists."[8] Their talents were displayed in the broad 1956 line of Studebaker and Packard cars which were produced through most of 1956. Despite the notable mechanical innovation and styling efforts of the people of Studebaker-Packard, the continuation of the full line, however attractive an opportunity it may have seemed at the time, imposed heavy operating burdens on Studebaker-Packard.

Market Position Effects of the Full Line

Although the full-line approach was continued through the 1956 models in hopes of retaining broader market coverage, Studebaker-Packard officials were to be sadly disappointed by the results of this policy. As may be seen in Table 6, the anticipated sales did not materialize, and the firm was forced to operate at drastically reduced levels.

During 1953, unit sales of Studebaker and Packard makes had not increased as rapidly as those of other makes and the share of sales held by their cars fell. In 1954, concurrent with the speculation and agreement regarding merger, unit sales of the two makes declined drastically and there was an accompanying fall in their market share.

Despite their efforts to maintain sales through broad market coverage, Studebaker-Packard subsequently found the share of the market held by its cars continuing to decline from earlier levels. The full-line policy was not sufficient.

In comparison, American Motors also experienced a loss of market position although it followed a different policy after merger, having consolidated its two lines of cars into essentially one line using the same basic body. Studebaker-Packard had not rushed into immediate consolidation. However, the sales of Studebaker-Packard cars ultimately fell farther relative to their earlier combined volume than did the sales of American Motors. From their combined postwar

[6] Studebaker-Packard Corporation, *Annual Report*, 1955, p. 4.
[7] *Ibid.*, p. 12.
[8] *Ibid.*

TABLE 6

NEW PASSENGER CAR REGISTRATIONS AND SHARE OF
TOTAL UNITED STATES REGISTRATIONS OF
STUDEBAKER-PACKARD CARS, 1946-1963[a]
(Registrations in Thousands of Units)

Year	Packard	Studebaker	S-P Total	S-P Share
1946	36	58	94	5.2%
1947	48	102	150	4.7
1948	78	143	221	6.3
1949	98	199	297	6.1
1950	73	268	341	5.4
1951	67	206	273	5.4
1952	66	158	224	5.4
1953	71	161	232	4.1
1954	38	96	134	2.4
1955	52	96	148	2.1
1956	28	76	105	1.8
1957	5	63	68	1.1
1958	—	48	48	1.0
1959	—	133	133	2.2
1960	—	106	106	1.6
1961	—	72	72	1.2
1962	—	78	78	1.1
1963	—	65	65	.9

[a] Source: Registration data by courtesy of R. L. Polk & Co. and computations based on these data.

peak year 1950 through 1955, the combined market share held by the Studebaker-Packard cars exceeded the combined share held by the American Motors cars. In 1956, Studebaker-Packard unit sales fell slightly below those of American Motors and in succeeding years, much below.

The full-line approach thus served to slow the initial sales decline of Studebaker-Packard cars relative to that of American Motors cars, but both automotive groups were reduced to much lower unit sales levels than they held before 1954. Studebaker-Packard's decline in market position, unfortunately for the company and those who had an interest in it, was to be both more severe and longer lasting than that of American Motors.

Financial Effects of the Full-Line Approach

For five annual reporting periods following its formation, that is, from 1954 through 1958, Studebaker-Packard experienced continually declining dollar sales and staggering operating losses; but the heaviest losses of the firm came during the period of its efforts to maintain a full line, as may be seen in Tables 7 and 8.

In 1953, Studebaker sales reached approximately $594,-250,000 while Packard sales amounted to $335,820,000. The dollar sales reported for 1954 for the combined firm amounted to $222,310,000, a total which was less than that for either of the two previously separate companies in 1953. However, these total sales figures were not entirely comparable.

The Studebaker-Packard abbreviated profit and loss statement shown for 1954 included all Packard operations for the year but only the Studebaker operations for the last quarter. Because of this, the first annual profit and loss statement, large though the reported loss was, failed to show fully the severity of the losses of Studebaker and Packard in 1954. The Studebaker losses of the first nine months were charged against Studebaker accounts before the merger, but the end results of these Studebaker operations were shown in the balance sheets, which are comparable to those of the firm's predecessors. Even after prior offsets resulting from tax credits, a reduction of approximately $42,760,000 in the stockholders' equity of the new firm at the end of 1954 from the combined equity reported at the end of 1953 for its predecessors resulted. This may be compared with the $26,180,000 net loss after tax credits reported for 1954 to gain an indication of the prior losses of Studebaker, except for $944,000 accounted for by Studebaker's payment of a cash dividend early in 1954. The results of operations for 1954 thus were severely damaging to the financial health of Studebaker and Packard.

Studebaker-Packard officials attributed the heavy losses in 1954 to a decline in car sales as a result of reduced retail demand coupled with consequent high unit production costs caused by low production levels. The continuation of separate lines of cars resulted in accompanying heavy financial burdens. When the anticipated sales failed to materialize, the firm found itself with excess capacity and continuing large overhead charges.

Operating losses were augmented by initial starting costs of producing the newly styled Packard and Clipper lines of cars and the amortization of some Studebaker tooling applicable to prior years' cars. Large nonrecurring expenses also

TABLE 7
STUDEBAKER (STUDEBAKER-PACKARD) CORPORATION
ABBREVIATED COMPARATIVE INCOME STATEMENTS FOR YEARS ENDED
DECEMBER 31, 1954-1963[a]
(Millions of Dollars)

	1954[b]	1955	1956	1957	1958	1959	1960	1961	1962	1963
Net Sales	$222.3	$480.0	$303.0	$213.2	$180.7	$387.4	$323.2	$298.5	$365.5	$403.3
Cost of Products Sold	241.0	470.4	301.5	198.1	169.3	323.3	281.7	256.0	314.6	359.2
Selling, Administrative, and General Expense	22.9	40.9	44.1	26.8	25.6	36.6[c]	43.1	45.1	49.2	56.4
Operating Profit (Loss)	(41.6)	(31.2)	(42.5)	(11.7)	(14.3)	27.4	(1.6)	(2.7)	1.6	(12.3)
Other Income	.6	.9	1.3	2.7	3.0	3.5	4.3	3.9	4.2	4.7
Other Expense	.7	1.4	2.0	2.2	2.1	1.5	1.9	4.1	5.2	9.3
Net Income (Loss) Before Tax and Adjustments	(41.7)	(31.7)	(43.2)	(11.1)	(13.4)	29.3	.9	(2.9)	.7	(16.9)
Income Tax Credit	15.6	1.2	.5	—	—	—	—	—	—	—
Income Tax [d]	—	.5	.5	—	—	.8	.2	.3	.2	—
Special Adjustments	—	1.3[e]	(60.0)[f]	—	11.2[g]	—	—	5.7[h]	2.1[i]	(64.0)[j]
Net Income (Loss) After Tax and Adjustments	(26.2)	(29.7)	(103.3)	(11.1)	(2.2)	28.5	.7	2.5	2.6	(80.9)

[a] Source: Condensation of statements from Studebaker-Packard Corporation, *Annual Reports*, 1954-1961, and Studebaker Corporation, *Annual Reports*, 1962-1963. Because of rounding, individual figures may not add exactly to totals.
[b] Includes results of Studebaker operations from date of merger October 1, 1954, but excludes them prior to that date.
[c] Includes $1,248,000 in incentive compensation awards.
[d] On income of foreign subsidiaries.
[e] Net gain on sale of excess idle property, plant, and equipment.
[f] Special charges for inventory and general obsolescence, cancellation costs, and possible loss on disposal of high operating cost and surplus property, plants, and equipment.
[g] Net gain, including deferred rental income, on sale of Utica plant to Curtiss-Wright.
[h] Net gain on sale of Gering Plastics Division.
[i] Net gain on sale of property.
[j] Special charges to provide for anticipated loss on liquidation of South Bend automotive facilities and operations.

TABLE 8
STUDEBAKER (STUDEBAKER-PACKARD) CORPORATION
ABBREVIATED COMPARATIVE BALANCE SHEETS FOR YEARS ENDED DECEMBER 31, 1954-1963 [a]
(Millions of Dollars)

	1954	1955	1956	1957	1958	1959	1960	1961	1962	1963
Cash	$ 36.0	$ 26.6	$ 12.7	$ 12.7	$ 13.3	$ 17.5	$ 9.4	$ 15.1	$ 23.3	$ 8.3
Marketable Securities	13.4	1.8	25.3	8.0	22.0	44.7	20.5	35.1	.8	.6
Accounts Receivable	32.5b	29.8	23.4	16.8	12.0	13.1	15.4	15.1	28.0	27.5
Inventories	52.8	80.2	43.4	49.3	35.0	46.7	59.4	58.5	91.1	70.7
Prepaid Expenses	1.7	1.7	.8	.7	.8	.6	.9	.8	1.9	2.8
Total Current Assets	136.5	140.2	105.7	87.6	83.2	122.5	105.6	124.6	145.0	110.0
Other Assets	4.1	2.1	.9	1.0	1.9	6.1	9.2	6.2	8.1	5.3
Property, Plant, and Equipment	159.5	141.0	124.8	97.6	71.0	75.8	89.8	85.2	115.7	117.3
Less Accumulated Depreciation c	54.2	53.4	85.4	69.7	40.8	42.2	40.8	41.6	42.3	61.4
Net Property, Plant, and Equipment	105.2	87.6	39.4	27.9	30.2	33.6	48.9	43.6	73.4	55.9
Total Assets	245.8	229.8	146.0	116.5	115.3	162.3	163.7	174.3	226.5	171.2
Total Current Liabilities	71.6	85.4	51.1	35.3	38.4	48.9	38.3	50.1	60.1	76.7
Other Liabilities	.6	.5	24.6d	22.0d	—	.9	.7	.5	.8	7.7
Long-term Debt	25.0	25.0	54.7	54.7	16.5	22.8	25.8	20.1	47.8	50.0
Total Stockholder Equity e	148.6	118.9	15.6	4.5	60.4f	89.6	99.0	103.7	117.8	36.7
Total Liabilities and Equity	245.8	229.8	146.0	116.5	115.3	162.3	163.7	174.3	226.5	171.2

a Source: Condensation of balance sheets from Studebaker-Packard Corporation, *Annual Reports*, 1954-1961, and Studebaker Corporation, *Annual Reports*, 1962-1963. Because of rounding, figures may not add exactly to totals.

b Includes $8,884,000 refundable taxes on income in prior years.

c Includes allowance for reserve for possible loss on anticipated disposal of high operating cost and surplus property, plants, and equipment in the following amounts: 1956, $31,518,000; 1957, $21,273,000; 1958, $21,100,000; 1959, $2,100,-000; 1960, $1,743,000; and 1963, $20,000,000.

d Deferred rental income from agreement with Curtiss-Wright Corporation.

e Common stock only from 1954 through 1957. Other years' figures include $5 Convertible Preferred Stock of $16,500,000 in 1958, 1959, and 1960, $973,000 in 1961, $771,000 in 1962, and $701,000 in 1963; and 5% Convertible Second Preferred Stock, Series A, of $3,000,000 in 1960 through 1963.

f Includes $21,600,000 refinancing excess from the exchange of 5% secured notes and convertible preferred stock for long-term debt, $19,430,000 credited to capital surplus as excess portion of reserve established before quasi-reorganization of 1956 for general obsolescence and possible loss on disposal of high operating cost and surplus property, plants, and equipment, plus $449,000 refund of income taxes paid prior to quasi-reorganization.

were entailed in the transfer of engine and transmission operations to the new Utica plant and the difficulties of establishing the new body operations of Packard and Clipper in facilities leased from Chrysler. The Utica plant, completed and put into operation in 1954, involved expenditures of more than $26,500,000; and the $13,000,000 expenditure incurred in setting up and transferring body and assembly operations to the former Briggs plant, which was leased from Chrysler, imposed an added financial burden on the new company.

Despite the terrible setback suffered by Studebaker and Packard in 1954, Studebaker-Packard officials believed that they had established a basis for improvement in 1955. They considered the combined dealer organization of Studebaker-Packard holding more than 4,000 Studebaker and Packard franchises—with some dealers in small markets holding both franchises—stronger than the separate groups of its predecessors. The development after 1952 of the intense competition for volume leadership among the industry as a whole and the pressures that this put on dealers served, in their opinion, to point up the advantages of operation as a full-line producer and revealed the soundness of their course of action. However, they were to be sadly disappointed.

Studebaker-Packard officials considered the year 1955 a very difficult one. Studebaker and Packard shared only slightly in the enormous increase in total car sales from 1954 to 1955. The firm faced a serious labor problem in its South Bend Studebaker plants, a task of consolidating two previously separate organizations, and a loss from idle facilities because of a cutback in defense work. The efforts of the corporation to maintain and enlarge its dealer organization were frustrated by the intense competition at the dealer level, and the market penetration of Studebaker and Packard cars declined even below their sharply reduced share in 1954.

During 1955, Studebaker-Packard disposed of a portion of its properties, thereby reducing its fixed expenses as well as obtaining a net gain of $1,304,000 on the sales. The main dispositions were the Detroit forge and foundry operation and the New Brunswick, New Jersey, Studebaker plant. The latter was built originally in 1950-1951 with capacity for Studebaker assembly at the rate of 85,000 units per year,[9] but it was used for defense production during the Korean

---

[9] *Automotive Industries*, July 1, 1950, p. 23.

conflict. With the cancellation of the Studebaker defense contracts and reduced car sales, the plant was no longer needed. However, the firm still had excess capacity.

The labor difficulties in South Bend involved extensive negotiations during which the firm suffered from work stoppages and slow-downs in 1955; but with the signing of a more competitive labor contract in January 1956, a substantial improvement was expected in the South Bend operations. With the settlement of this labor dispute—new work standards had already been set in Packard's Detroit plants in 1955 —and the resulting anticipated manufacturing cost improvements, plus the continuation of the policy of broad market coverage in the 1956 models using two separate basic bodies, the management of Studebaker-Packard expressed qualified optimism. Improvement was again expected—provided sufficient sales materialized.

In early 1956, however, Studebaker-Packard found its factory sales declining again. Dealers, stocked with record inventories of cars accumulated during the 1955 battle for volume leadership, were cutting their purchases. Although these developments were a great disappointment to Studebaker-Packard officials, they still planned to continue the full line in an effort to increase sales to levels sufficient to achieve lower unit costs, despite the cash drains that this involved.

Much of the financing of the Studebaker-Packard full line was provided by increased debt. Upon its formation on October 1, 1954, Studebaker-Packard had secured a new credit agreement for $45,000,000 from several banks. This agreement replaced previous agreements of $25,000,000 for Studebaker and $20,000,000 for Packard as individual companies. Also effective on October 1, 1954, the new company had negotiated with three insurance companies a $25,000,000 four per cent term loan repayable in $1,400,000 annual installments with the balance due October 1, 1974. This loan was used to pay off Studebaker's previous indebtedness of $7,500,-000 on September 30, 1954, with the balance being used to finance the Packard modernization program.

Studebaker-Packard also benefited from the mitigating influence of $15,560,000 in tax refunds in 1954 and $1,180,-000 in 1955 and the cash obtained from the disposition of idle plants in 1955.

Late in 1955 the firm borrowed $9,900,000 against its

$45,000,000 line of credit. An additional borrowing of $9,900,-000 was necessary in February 1956 to maintain working capital. Another $9,900,000 was obtained in the second quarter of 1956 raising the total notes payable to banks under the line of credit to $29,700,000 on June 30, 1956. In addition, on this same date, the $25,000,000 term loan was still outstanding. Although the loans provided funds for continuing the full line of cars, these loans increased Studebaker-Packard's interest payments and indirectly contributed to its financial difficulties. When Studebaker-Packard later was unable to meet the working capital restrictions of its debts obligations, it was threatened with insolvency. However, the borrowings at the time kept Studebaker-Packard and its product programs going.

In addition, the continuation of the full line had resulted in a reduction in the cash account of the firm from over $36,000,000 at the end of 1954 to about $18,800,000 by mid-1956. Had the firm been able to generate a return to the combining firms' pre-1954 sales levels, Studebaker-Packard unquestionably would have found many advantages in the merger and the preservation of the full line of cars. Unfortunately, the sales did not materialize; and in 1956, Studebaker-Packard found itself in far greater financial difficulty than American Motors which had quickly cut its product offerings.

Financial Influence of Reduced Defense Sales

Although much of Studebaker-Packard's difficulty was the result of declining car output, other factors were also important. At the beginning of 1954, both Studebaker and Packard were adversely affected by a government policy of restricting the number of defense producers. Studebaker had been a large producer of jet engines and trucks for the government. Its contracts for these items were cancelled with production virtually coming to an end in January 1954 except for production of spare parts. Studebaker's defense contracts had amounted to about $202,000,000 for 35 per cent of its sales in 1953. In addition, Packard, manufacturing jet engines for the Air Force and specially engineered, light-weight diesel engines for the Navy, found its contracts cancelled to the point where only pilot line operations remained. These contracts had amounted to about $196,000,000 per year. The cancellations severely affected the company's operations, and officials of the company made immediate attempts to secure additional defense business, but to no avail.

In 1954, in an effort to increase its defense work Studebaker-Packard acquired, as a wholly owned subsidiary, the Aerophysics Development Corporation of Los Angeles, California. This company was engaged in development contract work for the Government in guided missile research and had a staff of about 200, mostly scientists and engineers.

Unfortunately, Studebaker-Packard was able to report only that it was unsuccessful in its bid to secure added defense work. No new major contracts were secured. Thus much of the 1954 and subsequent dollar sales declines of the firm may be attributed to reduced defense output. However, if the firm had been able to reconvert these facilities to car production as they had done in the earlier postwar years, there would have been no problem. It was, at least in part, their slump in passenger car sales that left these facilities idle. Compared to combined Studebaker and Packard sales of $930,070,000 in 1953, as may be seen in Table 7, even $400,000,000 in defense sales would have left Studebaker-Packard far short of its predecessors' combined 1953 total.

CURTAILMENT OF THE FULL LINE[10]

In January 1956, the auto industry had the greatest inventory of cars for that time of year in its history. In spite of the full line, the sales of Studebaker-Packard cars continued at disappointingly low levels in 1956. The problems of the firm were "made more difficult by public uncertainty as to the survival of the enterprise, and the 'orphan car' argument against the purchase of its products."[11] The corporation was on the verge of disintegrating.

During the six months ended June 30, 1956, Studebaker-Packard lost before tax credits and special charges over $35,465,000. After a special charge of $28,000,000 to provide for estimated cancellation costs, inventory obsolescence, and

[10] In addition to reliance on the annual reports and other statements of Studebaker-Packard, the material in this section is based mainly on information provided in Studebaker-Packard Corporation, "Letter to Shareholders," September 24, 1956, and the attached "Notice of Special Meeting of Shareholders to be held October 31, 1956," and "Proxy Statement," also dated September 24, 1956, which were concerned principally with an agreement with Curtiss-Wright Corporation.

[11] Studebaker-Packard Corporation, "Letter to Shareholders," September 24, 1956.

other costs, and the establishment by the board of directors of a $32,000,000 provision for general loss and possible loss on disposal of high cost and surplus plants, property and equipment, there resulted a deficit in the corporation's earned surplus account of over $35,511,000.

The corporation had outstanding debts to both banks and insurance companies against which it had agreed to maintain working capital of at least $40,000,000. As a result of the continuation of heavy losses into 1956, it became apparent to the management of the company that the firm's net working capital would soon decline below the required $40,000,000 level at which the banks and insurance companies would have the right to declare approximately $55,-000,000 immediately due and payable. At the end of 1955, Studebaker-Packard's net working capital had amounted to about $55,000,000. By the end of June 1956, the firm's current assets had fallen to $90,660,000 while its current liabilities had risen to $85,870,000. Net working capital had fallen to less than $5,000,000, and Studebaker-Packard officials feared they would be unable to meet cash obligations. The continuation of a full line in the face of reduced sales had exacted a heavy toll, and Studebaker-Packard faced an immediate financial crisis.

The board of directors of Studebaker-Packard appointed a special finance committee of directors to work out a solution to the problems of the firm. Under the intense competitive circumstances facing the industry and the company at the time, it was concluded that the firm could *not* obtain additional funds on any practicable basis from lending institutions or from any general offering of securities to the public. The special committee worked to find other solutions. A merger or other arrangement which would be in the interest of the stockholders was sought, both within the industry and outside. But these efforts were unsuccessful.

Officials of the company considered the possibility of complete liquidation and asked two independent consulting groups to establish the probable results of complete liquidation. These groups—the firm of Ernst and Ernst, Accountants, and the firm of Robert Heller and Associates, Management Consultants—concluded that the losses would be so great that the stockholders probably would have little hope for any recovery. Almost any course of action that might net some gain, however slight, appeared to be a better alternative than dissolution.

Curtiss-Wright Agreement

After an extended period of negotiation, Studebaker-Packard reached an agreement with Curtiss-Wright Corporation which immediately brought some $35,000,000 in cash into the business and rescued Studebaker-Packard from the brink of bankruptcy. The agreement, which called for operation of Studebaker-Packard under an advisory management program with Curtiss-Wright, took effect August 6, 1956, and was to run until July 26, 1959. Curtiss-Wright was a Delaware corporation, operating under the leadership of Roy T. Hurley, its chairman and president, and engaging in a broad range of activities related to aircraft industries with emphasis on defense work. As a result of the agreement, Roy Hurley in effect became the chief executive officer of Studebaker-Packard. Although many sacrifices were required of Studebaker-Packard and its stockholders, these were not unreasonable in view of the condition of the firm. So poor was Studebaker-Packard's financial condition, the owners of the firm had little to lose.

The agreement with Curtiss-Wright Corporation was a desperation move by Studebaker-Packard to remain in business even on a reduced scale; and the directors of Studebaker-Packard believed that the agreement was the best obtainable under the circumstances. The advantages of the agreement to Studebaker-Packard were summarized as follows:

1. The Program permits the continuation of the business on a reorganized basis. It contemplates the concentration of manufacturing operations at South Bend, the orderly liquidation of high operating cost and surplus plants, properties and equipment and drastic reduction in costs.
2. It brings new cash into the business of close to $35,000,000.
3. It provides new management for the Corporation and, in addition, secures the advisory management services of Curtiss-Wright.
4. It was acceptable to the banks and insurance companies, who agreed on the basis of the Program to eliminate the above-mentioned $40,000,-000 working capital requirement and make other favorable revisions in the borrowing arrange-

ments with them. These changes avoided default by the Corporation on its bank and insurance company loans, and the receivership that could have resulted from such default.

5. Although there is no representation as to whether and when Curtiss-Wright will exercise the option called for by the Program, if and when it should do so up to $25,000,000 additional cash would be added.

6. The Program permits the continuation of the automobile business on a selective basis, with a line of new and improved cars of high quality and styling.

7. The Program affords the possibility of securing or developing new lines of products for diversification and increased earnings.

8. The continuation of the business preserves the large accumulated loss which can be carried forward for tax purposes.[12]

The directors and officers of Studebaker-Packard recommended that the stockholders vote in favor of the Curtiss-Wright agreement as being in their best interest. If the stockholders failed to approve the agreement, Curtiss-Wright had the option of withdrawing, and the banks and insurance companies had the right to declare immediately due and payable the $55,000,000 owed them. To approve the agreement, a favorable vote of two thirds of the stock was required. When the stockholders voted, more than 75 per cent of the shares were voted for the agreement.

The cash paid Studebaker-Packard by Curtiss-Wright was allocated as follows. For $25,000,000 the Utica and Chippewa plants of Studebaker-Packard were leased to Curtiss-Wright for 12 years in exchange for the entire rental payment being cash in advance. For about $8,000,000 Curtiss-Wright received the assignment of certain Studebaker-Packard defense contracts plus certain inventories, receivables, and unbilled costs and other property already accumulated under these contracts. Curtiss-Wright also acquired the Aerophysics Development Corporation for a cash payment of about $1,770,-000.

Curtiss-Wright received other benefits from the agreement. In exchange for its advisory management services, Curtiss-Wright was to receive reimbursement equal to the

[12] *Ibid.*

cost of such services plus 10 per cent of the costs. It was estimated that these expenses initially would run about $65,000 a month. Curtiss-Wright also received an option to purchase up to 5,000,000 Studebaker-Packard shares at $5 per share within a period of two years. The advisory management agreement was to run for a three-year period. Under the advisory management agreement Studebaker-Packard agreed to reimburse Curtiss-Wright for expenses of negotiating the agreement up to the amount of $100,000.

The leased properties included the Chippewa property on about 446 acres of land in South Bend, Indiana, with a main plant building of over 1,250,000 square feet. The Utica plant occupied about 55.5 acres near Utica, Michigan, on which the main features were a warehouse with about 414,000 square feet and a plant with about 667,000 square feet of usable manufacturing space originally constructed for assembling, testing, and inspection of jet engines. The Utica proving ground was included in the lease. The Utica facilities had been the newest and most modern major plants of Studebaker-Packard.

The properties included in the agreement were leased to a subsidiary of Curtiss-Wright, the Utica-Bend Corporation, which was established for the purpose of the leasing arrangement. In addition, Curtiss-Wright through Utica-Bend secured an option to purchase the leased property by agreement with Studebaker-Packard at its then fair market value or through an appraisal procedure set up by the agreement. Utica-Bend assumed the cost of taxes, insurance, and utilities for the leased property.

Quasi-Reorganization

Following stockholder approval of the advisory management agreement with Curtiss-Wright and an accompanying proposal for quasi-reorganization, the Studebaker-Packard Corporation charter was amended to provide for a change in the par value of the firm's common stock from $10 per share to $1 per share, a total difference on the outstanding shares of $58,880,000 being applied to capital surplus. After this change plus the application of the firm's losses and special charges for anticipated loss on disposal of idle facilities, balances were left at the end of 1956 of about $6,440,000 in common stock, $8,274,000 in capital surplus, and $896,000 in earned surplus. Based on the outlook for the firm by the end of 1956, these changes represented a more realistic evaluation of the residual ownership values in the firm. Total stockholder equity listed on the books fell from $118,928,000 at the end of 1955 to $15,610,000 at the end of 1956.

In addition to other benefits from the Curtiss-Wright agreement, Studebaker-Packard received agreement by its creditors postponing payments on its debts. The $29,700,000 credit outstanding with the banks was converted in the same amount to three and one half per cent six-month notes renewable through July 1959 if no events of default occurred. The $25,000,000 in four per cent long-term notes to insurance companies was continued with postponement for two years to October 1959 of the first annual repayment of $1,400,000. The maturity date was still October 1974 but with final payment of $4,000,000 compared to $1,200,000 under the earlier agreement.

The advisory management agreement with Curtiss-Wright was signed in August 1956 and the full program adopted within just a few months. By the end of 1956 the Studebaker-Packard management was able to report that it considered the new agreement as already having had a beneficial effect. As a minimum, the agreement alleviated the immediate threat of bankruptcy which Studebaker-Packard surely would have faced without it; but it also brought a drastic shake-up of the firm.

Product and Organizational Changes

In the reorganization that followed the agreement with Curtiss-Wright, Studebaker-Packard concentrated all of its domestic car and truck manufacturing in South Bend, Indiana. The Los Angeles assembly operation of Studebaker was moved to South Bend as was the Detroit Packard Clipper operation on a drastically revised basis. The lease of the Los Angeles plant was terminated, and the former Packard facilities in the Detroit area were set aside for disposal as quickly as possible. Packard's almost new Utica plant, which with the automated engine and transmission facilities had cost over $26,500,000 to set up for 1954, was, of course, no longer available for car production. Separate Packard operations were discontinued. The Conner Avenue body plant leased from Chrysler was vacated; and the separate Packard body and V-8 engines were abandoned. The expensive tooling in these plants was to wind up as scrap. All of the departments of the firm were streamlined by consolidation of the Studebaker and Packard operations into one division. With the Packard program largely eliminated, the two major warehouse facilities of the firm also were consolidated into one facility in South Bend.

The best of the Packard facilities thus were no longer available to the firm, and the rest was not usable. Even several years later some of the old Packard plants in Detroit still stood idle.[13] The disposal of facilities and the write-downs of idle facilities, however, reduced the fixed costs of the firm and in this sense were favorable.

The failure to achieve success with the full line also took its toll among the Studebaker-Packard management. In its first year, the operations of Studebaker-Packard had been directed by James J. Nance, who was president and general manager of the firm and had formerly served in the same capacity with Packard; Paul G. Hoffman, who was chairman of the board of the firm and had previously held the same office with Studebaker; Harold S. Vance, who was chairman of the executive committee of the firm and formerly president of Studebaker; and A. H. Behnke, R. E. Bremer, C. E. Briggs, G. H. Brodie, H. E. Churchill, W. R. Grant, W. H. Graves, R. A. Hutchinson, E. C. Mendler, R. P. Powers, and C. D. Scribner, who were all vice-presidents of the firm, seven of whom previously had been senior officers of Packard. Following the Curtiss-Wright agreement and the subsequent reorganization, only two of these men remained as officers of Studebaker-Packard.

Under the terms of an agreement of July 27, 1956, the Studebaker-Packard board of directors accepted the resignation of J. J. Nance as president, general manager, and a director of the corporation, Nance's resignation being effective August 6, 1956, the date of the agreement with Curtiss-Wright.[14] Paul Hoffman retired as an employee of Studebaker-Packard on May 1, 1956, but agreed to remain as chairman of the board until conclusion of the agreement with Curtiss-Wright, at which time his resignation as a director

13 *Durham Morning Herald* (Durham, North Carolina), May 17, 1959, Section D, p. 12, shows pictures of old plants standing idle.

14 In settling with Nance under the terms of his employment contract, Studebaker-Packard terminated his employment at a cost of some $286,000 paid into a trust fund, the principal and income thereupon to be paid in deferred installments to Nance and his beneficiaries, plus the payment of Nance's regular salary of $12,500 per month through January 31, 1957.

and chairman of the board became effective. Harold S. Vance earlier had resigned as a director and officer of Studebaker-Packard on October 31, 1955, to accept an appointment to the United States Atomic Energy Commission.

Walter Grant, who had come to Packard with Nance, had resigned in 1955 to become vice-president in charge of finance for the New York Central Railroad. C. E. Briggs, vice-president in charge of sales for Packard and later for Studebaker-Packard, also left in 1955 to assume a comparable position at Chrysler. The rest of the group along with R. P. Laughna and W. M. Schmidt, new additions to the vice-presidential staff following the resignations of Grant and Briggs, were caught in the staff reduction resulting from the reorganization.

Of the eleven vice-presidents of Studebaker-Packard, only Harold E. Churchill, who was formerly an officer of Studebaker and who became manager of the Studebaker Division of Studebaker-Packard, and R. A. Hutchinson, who also was previously an officer of Studebaker and who continued as manager of export operations of Studebaker-Packard, were left. Churchill became president and a director of Studebaker-Packard following Nance's resignation, and Hutchinson continued as vice-president in charge of export operations.

Armando J. Porta, a former executive of Studebaker who became comptroller of Studebaker-Packard at its founding, was elected vice-president in charge of finance and appointed a director of Studebaker-Packard to fill the vacancy created by Hoffman's resignation. Sydney A. Skillman, former general sales manager of Studebaker, became vice-president in charge of sales of Studebaker-Packard; and Arthur Gotsch, also a former Studebaker man, became treasurer. Paul M. Clark, a former Studebaker officer who became secretary of Studebaker-Packard at its founding, continued as secretary of the firm after the reorganization; but he was later succeeded by Melvin L. Milligan II, who was employed by Studebaker-Packard in January 1957 and elected secretary in August of the same year.

The difficulties of Studebaker-Packard and its reorganization thus brought many changes in management. Most of the former officials were gone, and the operating staff was drastically reduced in number. The eleven positions of operating vice-president were reduced to only three after the reorganization. The Packard men were gone. Studebaker men were left in control of the operations of Studebaker-Packard. They were, however, operating with the advice and under the general direction of Roy T. Hurley and other officials of Curtiss-Wright Corporation.

In November 1956, the 1957 Studebaker lines were introduced, the first products offered under the Curtiss-Wright direction and the new Studebaker-Packard top management. Studebaker sedans, station wagons, and hardtops were introduced, but Packard and Clipper models were absent. In January 1957, a new line of Packard Clipper models was introduced in an effort to retain a middle-priced line; but the new Clipper models were essentially Studebaker cars with minor sheet metal changes and the Packard nameplate. This move was comparable to the use of one basic body for two lines of cars by American Motors two years earlier for the 1955 models. The previously separate lines of Packard and Packard Clipper were discontinued.[15] The firm no longer provided a full line of cars, but it was attempting to offer a partial substitute for the lines which had been discontinued.

Three-way arrangements among Curtiss-Wright, Daimler-Benz, and Studebaker-Packard became effective in April 1957, giving Studebaker-Packard the exclusive right to import the Mercedes-Benz line of cars and trucks for sale in the United States. To some extent the Mercedes-Benz took the place of the Packards in the middle- and high-priced fields; however, they were foreign produced cars for which Studebaker-Packard obtained the selling rights. Studebaker-Packard did not produce them. Daimler-Benz A. G., a German corporation, manufactured them. Certain manufacturing rights also were included in the agreement giving Studebaker-Packard the privilege of using important development, engineering, and manufacturing methods of Mercedes-Benz for a period of 15 years.

During 1957, Studebaker-Packard continued the programs initiated in 1956. The agreement with Curtiss-Wright remained in effect. The firm concentrated its attenton on a further reduction in operating costs, the disposal of the Detroit and other surplus properties, the establishment of a Mercedes-Benz marketing organization, improvement of the dealer organization to increase the sales of the corporation, and the further development of the firm's products to fit

15 Because of the Curtiss-Wright lease, the firm no longer had the facilities for separate Packard production.

selective or less competitive markets. The latter was representative of the shift in policy following the agreement with Curtiss-Wright.

The 1957 styling and basic features were continued for the 1958 models introduced in late 1957. This was essentially the styling first introduced in the 1953 Studebaker models. The Packard and Studebaker lines were continued for 1958, both being essentially the same except for the nameplates and minor exterior differences; but the number of models was reduced from twenty-three in 1957 to seventeen in 1958, thirteen Studebakers and four Packards, all built on the former Studebaker basic body shell and operating gear.

Officials of Studebaker-Packard, like those of American Motors, believed that an increase in the size and cost of most domestic American cars in 1957 and 1958 had resulted in a failure to satisfy customers who desired basic, low-cost transportation. In May 1957, Studebaker-Packard introduced its Scotsman series in an attempt to fill this gap with a stripped, lower-priced car which was still considered by the firm to be full-sized although it was somewhat smaller than the lowest-priced Big Three models. From the time of its introduction through the end of the year the Scotsman models accounted for 25 per cent of Studebaker-Packard sales. Many of the cars traded on Scotsman models were competitive makes, indicating that the car was reaching a broadening market; yet, total retail sales of Studebaker and Packard cars fell to only 68,000 units in 1957. The readjustments in Studebaker-Packard's product offerings had failed to halt its sales decline.

Financial Effects of Curtailment of Full Line

Dollar sales of Studebaker-Packard declined further from 1956 to 1957 by about $90,000,000, almost a third; but the company's operating loss was greatly reduced by the closing of the Packard operations and through the subsequent disposal of high cost and surplus plants, property, and equipment. Early in 1958 it was obvious that the automobile industry was experiencing the impact of a business recession; and Studebaker-Packard officials attributed a portion of their firm's decline in sales and loss in 1957 to this recession which began in the fourth quarter of 1957. The recession adversely affected Studebaker-Packard sales along with those of the Big Three. Among the domestic firms, only American Motors found its sales rising from 1957 to 1958. Studebaker-Packard had yet to earn its first profit since its formation in 1954. But because of contraction of its operations and huge writeoffs in the previous year, the firm's financial losses in 1957 were reduced substantially from the staggering levels of the corporation's first three years. In spite of the continued sales decline, Studebaker-Packard's loss was cut to less than $12,000,000 in 1957. The ambitious full-line selling programs of the previous years had been curtailed and selling, general and administrative expenses were reduced approximately $17,000,000 from 1956 to 1957, accounting for much of the firms improved showing and giving promise of possible further improvement in 1958. Nevertheless, with the continued losses Studebaker-Packard found its financial strength continuing to deteriorate.

The heavy losses from 1954 through 1957, as may be seen in Tables 7 and 8, resulted in a very sharp attrition in both the firm's assets and the stockholders' equity in the firm.

In contrast, at the end of 1953 the combined cash and securities of Studebaker and Packard had amounted to $59,473,000; total assets net of depreciation reserves had been $293,796,000; combined stockholder equity was $191,-401,000; and net working capital had totaled $91,703,000. In 1950, the cash and marketable securities alone, excluding treasury tax anticipation notes, had reached a combined total of $86,001,000 for the two predecessor companies.

By the end of 1957, the cash and marketable securities of Studebaker-Packard had fallen below $21,000,000, despite the additional cash provided by the Curtiss-Wright agreement of 1956. After the special charges of $60,000,000 in the previous year to provide for possible loss on disposal of property and plant following the integration of the Packard and Studebaker lines in the South Bend plants, stockholder equity declined to a low figure of $4,475,000, an almost negligible amount. A steady decline also occurred in net property, plant, and equipment of the firm. By the end of 1957, the total assets of Studebaker-Packard were less than either Studebaker or Packard had had at the end of 1953 as separate firms; and the same was true of cash and stockholder equity. The only increase, and that being to the disadvantage of common stockholders, was an increase in long-term debt.

The pumping of additional cash into Studebaker-Packard

and the redirection of Studebaker-Packard's activities under the Curtiss-Wright program slowed Studebaker-Packard's financial deterioration and gave the firm a new lease on life. The curtailment of the ambitious full-line approach helped reduce the losses of the firm, but the losses continued. Vital though the Curtiss-Wright program was in keeping Studebaker-Packard alive, it was not enough. Studebaker-Packard had still to face another hurdle.

COMPLETE ABANDONMENT OF THE FULL LINE

Studebaker-Packard continued to suffer heavy losses in spite of the shrinkage in its size and the writedown of its assets. The Scotsman and Mercedes-Benz selling programs had not been enough to overcome the falling sales levels of its other products, and the firm's losses continued through 1957 and into 1958. In the first nine months of 1958, sales of the firm fell to only a little more than $92,000,000 and resulted in a loss of $22,533,000. Further adjustments were required if the firm was to survive; and they came in the form of a refinancing agreement which involved many apparent sacrifices by all parties.

Refinancing[16]

With the agreement of its 20 bank and three insurance company creditors, and of Curtiss-Wright and Daimler-Benz A. G., Studebaker-Packard in August 1958 carried out a program of refinancing which the Studebaker-Packard board of directors, after extensive search for alternative solutions to their firm's problems, considered the only feasible course of action for the company and its only hope for future improvement. Except for a compromise in the refinancing program by the holders of its long-term debt obligations, it it doubtful that Studebaker-Packard could have survived the year 1958. The compromise represented a significant sacrifice in face values of secured obligations by the banks and insurance companies from whom Studebaker-Packard had obtained credit. Creditors of the firm, however, evidently concluded that their chances of collecting something from reduced obligations in a going concern were greater than

[16] See esp. Studebaker-Packard Corporation, "Notice of Special Meeting of Shareholders to be Held October 15, 1958," dated September 4, 1958, and the accompanying "Proxy Statement"; and Studebaker-Packard Corporation, *Annual Report*, 1958.

from continued holding of existing secured notes in a liquidated firm.

The refinancing plan, which was approved by the Studebaker-Packard board of directors on August 6, 1958, was agreed to by the banks, insurance companies, and other parties on August 19, 1958, and approved by the Studebaker-Packard stockholders on October 15, 1958. Through it, a total of $54,700,000 in notes outstanding at the end of 1957 was cancelled in exchange for five per cent secured notes totaling $16,500,000 and 165,000 shares of $5 convertible preferred stock with a par value of $100 per share, or $16,500,000 face value. The banks and insurance companies thus gave up $21,-700,000 in face values of secured instruments. This difference, which was credited to surplus, along with the newly issued preferred stock had the effect of increasing stockholder equity substantially. The five per cent notes, which were payable in annual installments of $1,650,000 beginning in 1964, were secured by essentially all the Studebaker properties at South Bend plus additional collateral in the Canadian subsidiary of the firm and the Mercedes-Benz Sales, Incorporated, subsidiary set up to handle the firm's sales of foreign cars. In addition, Studebaker-Packard agreed to maintain at least $25,000,000 in net consolidated current assets as working capital.

The refinancing compromise, although it enabled Studebaker-Packard to continue in business, was not without its costs to Studebaker-Packard stockholders. Because of the creation of the convertible preferred issue, the then existing common stockholders faced a great dilution in their holdings. The convertible preferred, if fully converted, would result in the creation of an additional 5,500,000 shares of common on or after January 1, 1961. Common shares outstanding at the end of 1958 totaled 6,449,455. Either way the common stockholders faced dilution. If Studebaker-Packard did well in the future, common holders would suffer extensive attenuation of their residual ownership interest. If the firm did poorly, the preferred dividends would continue as a senior claim and burden for the common stockholders. However, since the current value of their residual ownership interest was so low at the time of the refinancing, the existing stockholders had relatively little to lose from the arrangement.

Also, as agreed in the refinancing plan, Curtiss-Wright terminated its management agreement with Studebaker-

Packard, purchased for an additional $2,000,000 the leased Utica-Bend plants on which it already had paid $25,000,000 in advance, and relinquished its option to purchase up to 5,000,000 common shares of Studebaker-Packard at $5 per share. Curtiss-Wright had helped Studebaker-Packard over one big hurdle, but another was too much.

Product Programs and Policies

With the end of the Curtiss-Wright advisory agreement, Studebaker-Packard continued under the direction of Harold Churchill, A. J. Porta, and Sydney Skillman, respectively president, executive vice-president, and vice-president in charge of sales. Other principal officers of the corporation at this time included R. A. Hutchinson, M. L. Milligan, Arthur Gotsch, and Byers A. Burlingame, respectively vice-president for export operations, secretary, treasurer, and comptroller.

Studebaker-Packard officials, observing the rising sales of foreign cars and the compact Ramblers, carried forward plans for a specialized car to compete in the lower-priced compact car segment of the market left open by the Big Three. These plans were a required component of the refinancing program. In the 1958 models, Studebaker-Packard had continued the Studebaker and Packard lines, using the same basic body for both lines with minor exterior and trim variations; but officials of the company at the time acknowledged that its current plans involved the "development of our products to fit selective or less competitive markets."[17]

In November 1958, the 1959 models showed complete abandonment of the previous full-line objective, as Studebaker-Packard introduced a smaller, less expensive car—the Studebaker Lark. The modified Packard line of the previous year was dropped completely in 1958 following a poor sales record. The Studebaker Hawk was continued on a limited production basis. Also, the Mercedes-Benz agreement was continued, but this was for foreign cars not produced by Studebaker-Packard. Emphasis was concentrated on the smaller car. All pretense of continuing a full-line approach was dropped.[18] Studebaker-Packard gambled its remaining resources on the compact car.

[17] Studebaker-Packard Corporation, *Annual Report*, 1957, p. 2.

[18] For most practical purposes it had been abandoned the previous year with the dropping of the separate body and chassis for Packard and the use of Studebaker basic bodies for all models; the Packard series using essentially the Studebaker basic body was dropped soon after this.

A NEW LOOK

The gamble paid off for both Studebaker-Packard and its creditors. It enabled the firm to present a new face to the public and led eventually to a change in the firm's name.

Following the introduction of the Lark in November 1958, factory sales increased so much for the rest of the year that Studebaker-Packard was able to report an operating profit of $3,681,000 for the fourth quarter of 1958, the first earnings for the company since its formation. Dealer and consumer response to the new car was very good. In the fourth quarter, the number of Larks sold to dealers topped combined unit sales of Studebaker and Packard in the first nine months of 1958. Combined retail sales of Studebaker and Packard had ranged between 2,600 and 3,000 units per month in the first ten months of 1958; but with public introduction of the Lark, unit sales rose above 5,000 in November and almost to 10,000 in December.[19]

The introduction of the Lark, however, came too late in the year to overcome the low sales of Studebaker and Packard in the first nine months. Including retail sales of Lark in November and December, total registrations of Studebaker-Packard cars fell to only 48,000 units in 1958, the lowest level in the firm's post-merger experience.

Dollar sales and total assets of Studebaker-Packard, as may be seen in Tables 7 and 8, also reached their nadir in 1958; but stockholders' equity was increased substantially by the refinancing program, the profit on sale of the Utica and Chippewa properties to Curtiss-Wright, and the cancellation of the remaining portion of the reserve established in 1956 for possible loss on plant disposal. Thus, 1958 provided Studebaker-Packard with the low point of its post-merger experience; but the rising sales of the Lark in the last quarter of the year also provided what later proved to be a significant turning point in the experience of the corporation. Dollar sales of Studebaker-Packard had fallen to a level of $92,-006,000 for the first nine months of 1958, resulting in a loss of $22,533,000; but in the fourth quarter alone, sales of the firm totaled $88,652,000 to provide the profit of $3,681,000.

[19] Studebaker-Packard's production in the fourth quarter of 1958 was approximately 33,000 units compared to 24,000 units for the first nine months of the year. *Automotive News* (*1959 Almanac Issue*), April 27, 1959, pp. 19 and 34, respectively for monthly production and registration data.

Reflecting the improved financial position of the firm, the price of Studebaker-Packard common stock rose to a high of $16.00 per share toward the end of 1958 compared to a low point of $2.625 per share a year earlier.

The improved performance of Studebaker-Packard in late 1958 continued in 1959; and Studebaker-Packard found its profit after all expenses and taxes rising to $28,544,000 on sales of $387,372,000, more than double the sales of 1958. The firm's net working capital rose substantially to $73,659,-000, of which cash and marketable securities comprised $62,-164,000 for a vastly improved position compared to the low levels of 1957 and 1958. The market price of its stock rose to a post-merger peak of $29.25 in 1959. The convertible preferred rose to a high of $618.00 in 1959, providing the banks and insurance companies an opportunity to recoup their investments in Studebaker-Packard and much more besides.

At last, everything clicked for Studebaker-Packard in 1959. Having accumulated a stockpile of needed raw materials, Studebaker-Packard did not lose any Lark production during the long steel strike of 1959. Although the firm found it necessary to delay introduction of its 1960 model trucks to conserve steel for passenger car production, it had obtained its first annual profit after five long years of huge losses. A good profit it was, too.

The year 1959, which was Studebaker-Packard's first full year with the Lark, the firm's compact car, also proved to be a profitable one for Studebaker dealers, whose net profits after taxes amounted to $15,523,000 in 1959 compared to $3,863,000 in 1958. The dealers' net worth rose to $139,-498,000 in 1959 from $106,040,000 in 1958. From June 1958 to June 1959, Studebaker-Packard enjoyed a net gain of 508 automobile dealers giving a total dealer body of 2,575 in 1959. Approximately one third of the dealers, 840 of them, also held franchises with other domestic automobile manufacturers.

Great though Studebaker-Packard's success was with the Lark, it was to prove only temporary. As may be seen in Tables 6 through 8, the firm's market position and financial performance declined after 1959. The automotive division operated at a loss after 1959; and total sales of the firm fell almost to the break-even level for the consolidated corporation. Profits for the total corporation were meager from 1960 through 1962; and in 1963, the losses from the automotive division more than offset the profits from other divisions. Competition in the compact car market segment had increased with the entry of the Big Three into the field in October 1959, and Lark sales fell off thereafter. But although it proved to be only temporary, Studebaker-Packard's comeback with the Lark in 1959 provided a much-needed basis for getting its long desired diversification program moving.

One of the things helping to keep Studebaker-Packard alive before 1959 despite its many setbacks was an accumulated tax loss, as of June 30, 1958, of approximately $121,000,-000, which could be carried forward to offset taxes on its future earnings or those of firms which it might acquire or with which it might merge.[20] Diversification into other industries was a key element in the refinancing plan of 1958. Accordingly, the Studebaker-Packard board of directors established an acquisitions committee and selected as head of the committee A. M. Sonnabend who had had considerable experience in diversifying Botany Mills, Inc., of which he had also been president and chairman of the board. On October 30, 1958, in addition to an annual salary of $25,000, Sonnabend was given an option to purchase up to 500,000 shares of Studebaker-Packard at $12.82 per share, a price which was not less than 95 per cent of the market price at the time the option was granted. The extent to which the option could be exercised was dependent on the earnings before federal income taxes of businesses acquired by Studebaker-Packard in its diversification program. For each $1,000,000 of earnings from acquired business through December 31, 1963, up to $50,000,000, Sonnabend was to be entitled to purchase 7,500 shares; for each $1,000,000 of earnings in excess of $50,000,000, he was to be permitted to purchase 2,500 shares. The option was to terminate on December 31, 1965, to the extent that it had not been exercised.

Before the comeback with the Lark in 1959, Studebaker-Packard had found the acquisition of other businesses virtually impossible, particularly for exchanges of stock or other securities. The success of the Lark and return to profitable operations changed this situation. On May 29, 1959, Studebaker-Packard acquired the assets of Gering Products, Inc., of Kenilworth, New Jersey, for $2,350,000 cash plus a non-

20 See also "New Try for S-P," *Business Week*, August 9, 1958, p. 32; "Sonnabend To Be S-P's Doctor," *Business Week*, August 23, 1958, p. 28; and, "Studebaker-Packard Bets Its All," *Business Week*, September 6, 1958, pp. 148-52.

interest-bearing note of the corporation for $7,650,000 due in installments to 1974. Although Gering was later sold for cash to Monsanto Chemical Company in December 1961 at a profit of $5,669,000, it was the first of many acquisitions by Studebaker-Packard.

Following the addition to the Studebaker-Packard staff in July 1959 of W. D. Mewhort, who had previously been executive vice-president of Revlon, Inc. and became the vice-president of Studebaker-Packard for diversification, Studebaker-Packard began a steady succession of acquisitions. For various combinations of cash, securities, and contingent obligations, Studebaker-Packard acquired C. T. L., Inc., in August 195%; Gravely Tractors, Inc., in May 1960; Clarke Floor Machine Company in September 1960; D. W. Onan and Sons, Inc., in October 1960; Chemical Compounds, Inc., in March 1961; both Schaefer, Inc., and Paxton Products, in March 1962; and Trans International Airlines, Inc., in October 1962. Each of these companies became a division of Studebaker-Packard. Their products covered a wide range and included such things as plastics and plastic products, hand tractors and gardening implements, floor cleaning equipment, electric generating equipment, oil additives, refrigeration cabinets for commercial uses, automotive superchargers, and airline services. In acquiring these eight businesses, the firm paid approximately $28,500,000 in cash, issued 30,000 shares of series A second preferred stock and 551,958 shares of common stock, agreed to issue 121,212 more shares of common stock, and obligated itself to make contingent cash payments of up to $4,535,000 from future earnings of two acquired companies plus an undetermined amount from future earnings of one of them and contingent payments of up to 484,848 shares of common stock for another. All or almost all the liabilities of seven of the eight companies were also assumed.

During the progress of its diversification program, Studebaker-Packard underwent further changes in management. In most cases the chief executive officers of the acquired companies continued as presidents of their respective organizations as divisions of Studebaker-Packard, becoming also vice-presidents of the acquiring company. In addition, the top management of Studebaker-Packard turned over.

The acquisition program had begun under Churchill as president of Studebaker-Packard and Sonnabend as head of the special acquisitions committee of the board of directors, but it was completed by a new management. Effective February 1, 1961, Sherwood H. Egbert, a young aggressive executive who had been executive vice-president of McCulloch Corporation, a manufacturer of chain saws, outboard motors, and other products, was elected president and chief executive officer and a director. Clarence Francis, who had been elected chairman of the Studebaker-Packard board in 1960, continued as chairman. Francis had first been elected to the board in 1958, having been formerly board chairman of General Foods Corporation. Sonnabend resigned as a director and employee of Studebaker-Packard and agreed to the cancellation of his option to purchase up to 500,000 shares of Studebaker-Packard common stock. Churchill and Porta, under whose direction the compact Lark program had been carried out, resigned their positions and terminated their employment with Studebaker-Packard with arrangements for eventual retirement under Studebaker-Packard's pension plan. Churchill continued as a director and effective March 1, 1961, was retained as a consultant by the corporation, serving in a capacity similar to that which Hugh Ferry, former president and chairman of Packard, had held through 1959. Porta became a vice-president of Associates Investment Company, South Bend, Indiana. Skillman also left in 1961, to join Ford Motor Company as market representation manager.

Five acquisitions were completed prior to Egbert's arrival at Studebaker-Packard. Egbert continued the diversification program, and five more diversified businesses were purchased, four of which were the last named above, having been bought in 1961 and 1962.

In November 1962, the acquisition program was climaxed by the purchase of the Franklin Manufacturing Company, a producer of household freezers and refrigerators and automatic washers and dryers for sale under the private brand names of major mail-order and retail businesses. The price was $29,000,000 in cash plus Franklin's unpaid 1962 income tax, 1,333,333 shares of common stock, and the assumption of most of the liabilities of Franklin. Franklin was by far the largest of the businesses acquired by the firm, its sales having reached about $69,000,000 and its earnings before taxes about $7,240,000 in its fiscal year ended March 31, 1962.

Belatedly reflecting the changes in the operations of Studebaker-Packard, the Packard portion of the corporation's name was dropped in 1962. The change in name, which took effect July 2, 1962, was somewhat of an anomaly since Packard was the legal parent of the corporation under a Michigan charter. With the elimination of the Packard operations and the termination of Hugh Ferry's membership on the board of directors in 1959, virtually all traces of the Packard connection were gone.

By 1962, the firm, now named Studebaker Corporation, was much changed. Except for its automotive operations and some of the central staff officers, principally Byers Burlingame and M. L. Milligan, the Studebaker Corporation of 1962 was virtually a new company compared even with the period just three years earlier. Operating officials of the firm in 1962 included Clarence Francis, chairman of the board; Sherwood Egbert, president and chief executive officer; B. A. Burlingame, vice-president in charge of financial matters; C. M. MacMillan, vice-president—industrial relations; Donald E. Kidder, vice-president—government relations; M. L. Milligan, secretary and general counsel; William W. Cox, comptroller; and C. G. Bunting, treasurer. In the Automotive Division many former employees still performed; but the top officials of the Division, including Lewis E. Minkel, John Soelch, and A. D. Whitmer, all of whom were vice-presidents of the Automotive Division, had not obtained these senior positions as vice-president until 1960. In addition, each of the operating divisions or subsidiaries was headed by a president. The men and their division or subsidiary were C. D. Liggett, Chemical Compounds Division; Ernest Cooper, Clarke Floor Machine Company Division; E. P. Warnken, C. T. L. Division; J. C. Hammond, Franklin Division; Kenneth Thomas, Gravely Tractors Division; L. A. Fleener, Mercedes-Benz Sales, Inc.; C. Warren Onan, Onan Division; Anthony Granatelli, Paxton Products Division; B. W. Hanson, Schaefer Division; G. E. Grundy, Studebaker of Canada, Limited; A. R. Gale, Studebaker International S. A. and Studebaker Universal S. A.; and Kirk Kerkorian, Trans International Airlines, Inc.

From 1960 through 1962 the dollar volumes of Studebaker's sales were far above the dismal levels of 1957 and 1958. Although not so large as in 1959, the firm's automotive sales were above those of the two years before 1959; and the acquisition program had provided healthy additions to sales. The automotive division still operated at a loss; but the return on the firm's investment in its acquired divisions was averaging around 14 per cent. Two contracts received in 1962 from the government calling for $53,600,000 in orders for trucks with delivery to be completed by June 1964 also contributed to increased total sales. The financial condition of Studebaker had improved; and stockholders' equity on the books continued to rise during the year, largely because of the exchanges of stock for acquired companies. The market price of Studebaker common stock ranged between $6.00 and $10.75 per share in 1962, considerably below the high of $29.25 in 1959, the best year of the Lark, but substantially higher than the miserable low of $2.625 in 1957. In contrast to almost total dependence on automotive products before 1959, Studebaker had become a diversified corporation. It had survived, and its diversified operations held promise of future improvement.

Despite extensive restyling of the Studebaker cars in 1962 for the 1963 models and again in 1963 for the 1964 models, the cars of Studebaker failed to win increased consumer acceptance; and in December 1963, after having lost $40,000,000 more in its automobile division since 1959 in trying to remain in the automobile business, Studebaker finally discontinued the manufacture of automobiles in the United States, concentrating its remaining automobile production in its much smaller Canadian plant. In the process of this change, a further turnover in top management also occurred. Sherwood Egbert resigned as president of the firm. Byers Burlingame, formerly vice-president in charge of finance, was appointed president of the corporation, while Gordon E. Grundy, president of the firm's Studebaker of Canada subsidiary, was given responsibility for all the firm's remaining automobile production. Randolph H. Guthrie, partner in a New York law firm, had replaced Clarence Francis as chairman of the board of directors six months earlier.[21] Thus ended more than 60 years of building automobiles in South Bend, the last ten of which had been a loss operation with the exception of one year, 1959.

THE STUDEBAKER-PACKARD STRATEGY

The abandonment of the full-line approach returned Studebaker-Packard to a market policy similar to that which

[21] See *The Wall Street Journal*, November 26, 1963, p. 2; December 10, 1963, pp. 3-4; and December 11, 1963, p. 4.

had been followed by the Independents before World War II when their objective had been one of attempting to provide for specialized market segments products not in direct competition with cars of the Big Three.[22] The shift in Studebaker-Packard objective thus was a return to an earlier policy which had been abandoned in favor of the full line. The change did not mean that the arguments favoring a full-line policy were invalid. It meant only that Studebaker-Packard, under the circumstances then existing, had failed to secure the benefits of the full line.

In the redirection of its efforts, Studebaker-Packard found the basis for its corporate survival, although not immediately. Unit sales of the firm fell after the dropping of the separate Packard line; and the austere Scotsman, a stripped, economy model, was not outstanding for its sales performance. Subsequently, however, the firm found a larger place in the market. With the compact Lark, Studebaker-Packard came back strong in 1959; but it was a temporary comeback. Although the Lark was further improved in quality in subsequent years, winning in 1961 a *Consumer Reports* rating as "best buy" in the V-8 engine, luxury compact car category,[23] annual sales of the Lark in subsequent years fell below the 1959 level. Studebaker-Packard's initial success with the Lark and return to profitable operations, however, provided the basis for implementation of another program for corporate survival, namely, diversification.

Diversification had been featured in the plans for the merger of Studebaker and Packard;[24] but the acquisition of other businesses was not feasible for Studebaker-Packard prior to its temporary comeback with the Lark, so great were its cash drains from the full-line approach and so poor its earlier financial condition. After 1958, with the success of the program of diversification, especially with the later and more important acquisitions, a broader basis was provided for the survival and prosperity of Studebaker-Packard. By comparison with the original full-line approach, the evolution of Studebaker-Packard's market policy was indicated in a program which was initiated by Egbert in 1961 and which then had the full support of the corporation's board of direc-

[22] See W. B. Harris, "Last Stand of the Auto Independents?" *Fortune,* L (December, 1954), 114.

[23] *Consumer Reports,* April, 1961, p. 193.

[24] *Supra,* chapter ii; also, Packard Motor Car Company, "Proxy Statement for Special Meeting of Shareholders August 17, 1954," p. 2.

tors. Major points of this program included efforts to expand the Studebaker automotive business by new approaches, to increase military sales, to set up and increase emphasis on international operations, and to continue diversification through acquisitions.[25] In a sense, the last three items represented only one element — diversification, the conversion of the firm's resources to fields other than the domestic automobile industry. Although the firm's dependence on automotive operations was substantially reduced by the diversification program, the domestic automobile business was not abandoned at that time. Further costly efforts were made to stay in the business. Representative of the automotive policy of the firm at this time was the introduction of the Studebaker Avanti, a fast, speed-record breaking, plastic-bodied, sports car which had been designed by Raymond Loewy from an initial sketch by Egbert and introduced in 1962. The firm's objective was to offer distinctive products appealing to specialized market segments. Thus the strategy eventually evolved at Studebaker-Packard was essentially that of a specialist role as an automobile producer with diversification in other fields as a counterweight for the uncertainties of continued participation in the automobile business. However, after the tremendous losses of earlier years, even this was not enough, for the sales of Studebaker failed to increase and led the firm to withdraw from the domestic car industry.

For a company which had faced repeated sales difficulties and almost insurmountable financial obstacles, Studebaker-Packard had demonstrated amazing resiliency, but the firm's survival had not seemed assured until the implementation of the diversification program. Although it had had to undergo drastic changes in its product programs and organizational structure, the Studebaker Corporation, having become essentially a new company with its many new people and widely varied operations, had survived as a corporate entity, though not as a participant in the domestic automobile manufacturing industry.

[25] See Studebaker Corporation, *Annual Report*, 1962, p. 2, for these four points. This is also based on a transcript of the remarks of Sherwood H. Egbert, then President of Studebaker Corporation, before the New York Society of Security Analysts, August, 14, 1962. Also, see Richard Hammer, "Welcome, Sherwood Egbert," *Fortune*, LXIV (December, 1961), 94-97 and 152-63, for a review of the changing scene at Studebaker.

CHAPTER V

NONSCALAR PROBLEMS

DURING THE EARLY post-World War II period, as we have seen in preceding chapters, the leading Independent manufacturers of passenger cars enjoyed relatively satisfactory financial returns, both in relation to their own historical performance and to the performance of the largest firms in the automobile industry. Unlike the Big Three, however, their positions in the market and their financial performances deteriorated rapidly after the middle of 1953. The firms merged in 1954 and were engaged in a struggle to survive through 1957. It was not until after 1957 that the continued survival of the two remaining Independents seemed assured.

What had happened to the four leading Independents? Why did they and their two successors experience such great difficulty in the period from 1953 through 1957? What was the nature of their problems? How did they manage to survive? What actions proved most successful? What were the requirements that they had to meet for survival and success? These are the questions with which we are concerned in this chapter and the following ones.

Perhaps the most obvious answers to questions on the nature of the problems of the Independents rest on the possible disadvantages of their small scale operations, particularly in comparison with the Big Three of the industry. Such answers, however, would represent an oversimplification of the nature of the Independents' problems, for these firms suffered from a number of influences which were not directly related to, or at most were only loosely or indirectly connected with, the scale of the firms' operations.

In this and the following chapter, we consider the nature of nonscalar influences on the performance of the leading Independents. In this chapter, emphasis is placed on the nature of the nonscalar problems of the firms during the period of their greatest difficulties from 1953 through 1957. In the following chapter, attention is directed primarily to the effect of the Independents' leadership with compact cars on themselves as well as the rest of the industry after 1957. In succeeding chapters, we turn to the influences of size on the market and financial performance of the leading Independents.

IMPACT OF EASY SELLING CONDITIONS, 1946-1952

In the years from 1946 through 1952, as we saw in Chapter I, the sellers' market conditions presented the United States automobile industry with an extraordinary opportunity. With the possible exception of a brief period from late 1949 through early 1950, cars were in short supply. The demand for cars far exceeded the available supply at the prevailing prices. Readjustment to full peacetime production was accompanied by material shortages, government controls, and strikes which limited the supply of cars for most of the period through 1952. Sales of new cars during the period may thus be considered to have been limited mainly by supply; and the major limitation in passenger car sales of the individual firms was their ability to produce them. Within the price ranges then prevailing, almost any car that could be produced could be sold easily.

If it is correct that production was the major limit on sales in the period from 1946 through 1952, the Independents apparently adjusted more rapidly than the Big Three and thereby secured greater sales volume relative to their last prewar position. Then, with the aid of the government restrictions in the last two years, their expanded market share was held through 1952. Was this actually the case?

It may be suggested that the Independents had a less extensive job of conversion from war production than the Big Three in 1945.[1] Being smaller, the Independents had a less complex problem of readjustment. They were highly centralized and had fewer levels of management and fewer activities for coordination. The Big Three, manufacturing a great diversity of products many of which were far removed from automotive processes, had a more difficult task of reconversion. However, all the previously existing firms — large and small — rather quickly returned to car production after the end of the war, using principally prewar tools and equipment to produce essentially the last prewar models in 1946.

Although all of the firms seem to have readjusted rapidly

---

[1] This suggestion was made to the author, in an interview, by E. C. Andrews, Automotive Specialist, Automotive and Transportation Equipment Division, Business and Defense Services Administration, U. S. Department of Commerce, March, 1959.

to peacetime car production, the cars of the leading Independents secured their greatest market share of the postwar period with 13.9 per cent in 1946. The Nash and Hudson performances were especially outstanding for quickness of readjustment. The expanded position of the leading Independents was accomplished even though Studebaker, after only three months production of warmed-over 1946 models, shut down its plants for a changeover to its first completely new postwar car.

The 1947 model Studebaker resulting from this change was the first completely new postwar car. It established the major postwar styling trend with its smooth contours and large glass areas. In addition to the benefits of their rapid readjustment, the leading Independents also benefited indirectly from a strike at General Motors which lasted from November 21, 1945, until March 13, 1946. Because of local labor difficulties in some plants, it was not until May 13, 1946, that all General Motors plants were operating again.[2]

By approximately the time of introduction of the first completely new Big Three postwar car—the 1949 Ford, introduced in late 1948—all of the leading Independents had brought out new models.[3] Although they experienced the downtime required for changeover and presumably lost the production that otherwise could have been accomplished, their makes still maintained a larger share of new car sales than they had before the war though their share did decline to 12.5 per cent in 1948 from their peak penetration of 13.9 per cent in 1946. With the production bottleneck largely broken in 1949, the market share of the leading Independent makes declined further, falling to 10.3 per cent in 1950 although unit sales of their makes expanded substantially. Still they managed to retain a larger share of the market than they had held in 1941.

It is possible that the material shortages affected the larger firms more than they did the smaller firms, particularly from 1946 through 1948. However, there appears little reason to believe that suppliers of the car manufacturers favored the Independents and slighted their larger customers. If anything, it would appear more reasonable to expect the contrary.

All of the firms in the industry reported having been con-

---

[2] General Motors Corporation, *Annual Report*, 1946, p. 13.

[3] See W. B. Harris, "Last Stand of the Auto Independents?" *Fortune*, L (December, 1954), 115-116, for timing of introductions of new models.

fronted with material shortages. Sheet steel appeared most difficult to obtain, although nonferrous metals were also in short supply. Government controls and labor difficulties in the supplier industries were reported to have contributed to the problems of the automobile industry.

The independent passenger car manufacturers, as well as the Big Three, were hard pressed by steel shortages.[4] The plants supplying more than 60 per cent of Packard's steel requirements were sold on short notice, and Packard reported that it had a difficult time finding new sources. Both Hudson and Studebaker found it necessary to enter the steel finishing industry through the purchase of finishing mills to obtain larger supplies of finished sheet steel. Nash-Kelvinator also reported having been confronted with major difficulties caused by material shortages, particularly of sheet steel. Because of these problems the smaller firms were all producing at far less than their estimated capacity levels, even though it was thought that all cars they could produce could easily have been sold. However, the Independents seemed no more hampered by the shortages than the Big Three, as is shown by the fact that the Independents were able to expand their market share above the 1941 level.

A major factor enabling the Independents to secure a relative production gain and in turn a relative sales gain compared to the Big Three during the years from 1946 through 1950 was their willingness to concede to union demands which the Big Three resisted.[5] General Motors, for example, was shut down for more than five months by the strike which covered the crucial first quarter and more of 1946; Ford suffered a lengthy series of labor disputes and a major strike in 1949; and Chrysler was closed for a 100-day period in 1950 by a strike. In contrast, the Independents generally conceded to the unions, following the pattern established by the union agreements with the Big Three but with

[4] See, e.g., the comments in Packard Motor Car Company, *Annual Report*, 1947, p. 4; *The New York Times*, December 12, 1947, p. 49; *Ibid.*, December 27, 1947, p. 19; and Nash-Kelvinator, *Annual Report*, 1946, pp. 3-7; and *Annual Report*, 1947, p. 5. It may be noted also that General Motors found it desirable to enter supply agreements with steel companies in exchange for G.M. financing of their expansion programs. *Business Week*, May 19, 1951, p. 26.

[5] W. B. Harris, *op. cit.*, p. 204; and W. B. Harris, "Breakdown of Studebaker-Packard," *Fortune*, LIV (October, 1956), 222.

somewhat more liberal wage and fringe benefit provisions.[6]

Although they were shut down at times by strikes or shortages in suppliers' plants, the leading Independents lost little time from difficulties in their own plants. Packard reported losing only seven days from labor striking its own plants in 1946 although it was shut down for 67 days because of strikes in suppliers' plants.[7] In 1948, Packard lost only one and one half days from strikes in its own plants.[8] The other leading Independents had similar experiences.[9]

In late 1949 and early 1950, the increasing supply of cars seemed about to erase the backlog of demand. General Motors reported that they had broken the three-year bottleneck of shortages. They achieved capacity operations in the second quarter of 1949 for the first time since their postwar readjustment to car production.[10] However, a 100-day strike against Chrysler and the outbreak of the Korean conflict eased the pressure on the smaller firms.[11] Steel and coal industry strikes in the fall of 1949 also served to limit production.[12] Yet the industry reached a new postwar peak in production and sales in 1950, with the leading Independents still retaining a share of new car registrations larger than their last prewar share of the market.

Finally, during the years 1951 and 1952, government material restrictions sharply reduced the volume of car production. With production allocated among the different firms on the basis of their production records in 1950 and some minor adjustments in favor of the Independents, the expanded

[6] This was commented on, e.g., in U. S., Senate, Committee on the Judiciary, Subcommittee on Antitrust and Monopoly, *Hearings, A Study of the Antitrust Laws*, 84th Congress, 1st Session, Pursuant to S. Res. 61 (Washington: U. S. Government Printing Office, 1955), Part 1, p. 457, hereafter referred to as the Testimony of George Romney; Harris, "Last Stand of the Auto Independents?" *op. cit.*; Harris, "Breakdown of Studebaker-Packard," *op. cit.*; and Roy D. Chapin, "The Resurgence of American Motors," A speech before the Harvard Business School Club of Detroit, April, 1958.

[7] Packard Motor Car Company, *Annual Report*, 1946, p. 9.

[8] Packard Motor Car Company, *Annual Report*, 1948, p. 3.

[9] Harris, "Last Stand of the Auto Independents?" *op. cit.* Also, the other leading Independents reported on favorable relations with their employees and union from time to time in their annual reports.

[10] General Motors Corporation, *Annual Report*, 1949, p. 9.

[11] "Chrysler's Hundred Days," *Fortune*, XLI (June, 1950), 70; "End of the Auto Boom," *Business Week*, October 28, 1950, p. 21; and "Whittling Autos' Big Three," *Business Week*, December 29, 1951, p. 27.

[12] General Motors Corporation, *op. cit.*

market share and favorable financial performance which the leading Independents had won in the earlier postwar years through 1950 was continued.

It appears, therefore, that a major factor—perhaps *the* major factor — promoting the expanded market position of the leading Independents in the early postwar period was a relative gain in production time and in turn a relative gain in sales obtained during an unusually favorable period of short supply. This gain had resulted largely from a combination of the rapidity of the Independents' readjustment to peacetime car production and their concessions to union demands to avoid strikes and related difficulties which affected the Big Three. Although their concessions to the unions were later to be found a major problem adversely affecting their performance after 1952, the leading Independents made the most of the extraordinarily favorable conditions of the early postwar years and enlarged their market position. However, the fact that the leading Independents had obtained a larger position in the market during the "abnormal" early postwar years made their decline after the return of more "normal" competitive conditions seem all the more precipitous.

SIGNIFICANCE OF CHANGED MARKET AFTER 1952

Production may have limited sales in the earlier postwar period before 1953, but this was clearly not the case after the middle of 1953, particularly for the Independents. Since the leading Independents had produced approximately 672,000 cars in 1950 compared with 480,000 in 1953 and only 208,000 in 1954, the physical capacity of the smaller firms to produce cars was clearly above the levels current in 1953 and 1954 (and indeed the levels attained through 1957).

There was, as we saw in Chapter I, a basic shift in the nature of the market for passenger cars after midsummer 1953 from a sellers' to a buyers' market. The sudden change resulted in part from satisfaction of the backlog of postwar replacement demand, a production and sales race among the Big Three which greatly increased the supply of cars, and an imposition of stricter credit regulations on the sale of cars at both retail and wholesale levels which tended to limit the number of persons who could buy cars at the prevailing prices. The shift in market conditions brought forth the competitive weaknesses of the Independents, and their sales and profits declined sharply. Although Ford's desire to be first in sales may be considered a contributing causative factor in the shift in conditions, all domestic manufacturers and their dealers were confronted with this change in 1953. The change was general to the industry; it was not a particular problem of the smaller firms and their dealers. Therefore, it is not sufficient merely to attribute the decline of the leading Independents to the changed market environment, however great the change may have been. The answers that we seek lie elsewhere.

NONSCALAR PROBLEMS, 1953-1957

Numerous influences which had relatively little relation to the size of the firm served to compound the problems of the Independents and affected their market and financial performances during their struggles for survival from 1953 through 1957. Although some of these influences may have been transitory in terms of the duration of their existence, their impact both on the immediate and subsequent operations of the firms may have been serious. Some of the more important of these influences, which presumably could have been overcome through determined action of management without increasing the scale of the firms' operations, are discussed in the following paragraphs.

Credit Restrictions

Concurrent with the increase in the supply of passenger cars, tighter restrictions on credit adversely influenced the dealers of the Independent manufacturers of cars in 1953 and 1954.[13] Much of the sales slump of Nash and Hudson was attributed to the failure of many of their dealers in 1953 and 1954.[14] Since Nash had followed a policy of limiting the number of its dealers in the early postwar period in order to maintain average dealer volumes at satisfactory levels, the dealer failures seriously reduced Nash's coverage of the market and created a serious sales problem for Nash. The credit restrictions, which were self-imposed by many finance

[13] These restrictions were imposed voluntarily by many finance companies who feared a glutting of the automobile market; they imposed controls aimed particularly at the financing of older models. *The New York Times*, July 12, 1953, III, p. 1. Regulation W had been suspended by the Federal Reserve Board over a year earlier. *Ibid.*, May 8, 1952, p. 1.

[14] Testimony of George Romney, *op. cit.*, p. 446.

companies, were applied to both retail and wholesale installment paper. The restrictions limited the number of cars a
dealer could carry in inventory. Because of the restrictions
and the "excessive" supply of cars held by dealers, many
Nash dealers went out of business when faced with the
greater sales difficulties after 1952, thereby sharply cutting
the sales of Nash cars. Both before and after its merger with
Nash-Kelvinator, Hudson experienced a similar problem;[15]
and it has been acknowledged that Studebaker and Packard
also faced this problem.[16]

Price Relationships

With the return of a buyers' market in 1953, relative
prices of the different makes of cars again became an important influence on sales. Using Table 9 for a comparison
of prices for the model years 1952-1957, we see that from
1952 through 1954 the lowest-priced four-door sedans of the
Big Three were substantially lower in price than those of
the lowest-priced Independent makes. Since the prices of
other models generally move in the same direction as those
of four-door sedans, the prices of four-door sedans may be
taken to reflect movements in price of all models.

It may be recalled (see Chapter I) that the cars of the
leading Independents had held their market share in 1952,
largely, it seems, because of the government restrictions on
production and the continuation of the sellers' market. The
same makes, however, slumped badly in 1953-1954 with approximately the same relative prices. How then could price
have adversely influenced the sales of leading Independent
makes of cars?

From 1952 through 1954, the prices of the leading Independent makes of lowest-priced four-door sedans had not
been increased disproportionately to others of the industry.
Between 1952 and 1953 the prices of all the leading Independent makes remained steady with the exception of a $50
increase on the lowest-priced model of Packard and the introduction of the "Jet" model by Hudson which was lower in
price than other Hudson models.

In the 1952 and 1953 models, Chevrolet continued its low-

[15] *Ibid.*; and Hudson Motor Car Company, *Annual Report*, 1953, p. 3.
[16] U. S., Senate, Committee on the Judiciary, Subcommittee on Antitrust and Monopoly, *op. cit.*, Part 2, p. 864, hereafter referred to as the
Testimony of J. J. Nance.

est-priced models with the same price; Ford increased its by $12; but Plymouth gave the appearance of a decrease with the introduction of a four-door sedan in 1953. Plymouth's

TABLE 9

FACTORY ADVERTISED DELIVERED PRICES OF THE
LOWEST-PRICED FOUR-DOOR SEDANS BY MAKE
FOR THE LEADING INDEPENDENTS AND
THE BIG THREE FOR 1952-1957 MODELS [a]

	1952	1953	1954	1955	1956	1957
Independents:						
Hudson	$2,311	$2,311	$2,256	$2,290	$2,420	$2,821
Hudson Jet	—	1,858	1,858	—	—	—
Nash	2,178	2,178	2,158	2,215	2,385	2,821
Rambler [b]	2,003	2,003	1,795	1,695	1,829	1,961
Packard	2,548	3,244	3,344	3,890	3,465	3,212
Packard Clipper	—	2,598	2,594	2,586	2,731	—
Studebaker	1,769	1,767	1,801	1,783	1,996	1,826[d]
Chrysler:						
Chrysler	2,518	2,492	2,562	2,660	2,870	3,088
DeSoto	2,353	2,386	2,386	2,498	2,678	2,777
Dodge	2,052[c]	2,025	2,025	2,093	2,267	2,451
Imperial	3,864	4,260	4,260	4,483	4,832	4,838
Plymouth	1,768[c]	1,765	1,765	1,781	1,926	2,055
Ford:						
Ford	1,678	1,690	1,701	1,753	1,895	2,042
Mercury	2,249	2,251	2,251	2,277	2,313	2,645
Lincoln	3,517	3,522	3,522	3,563	4,212	4,794
General Motors:						
Buick Special	2,209	2,255	2,265	2,291	2,416	2,660
Buick Super	2,563	2,696	2,711	2,876	3,250	3,681
Cadillac	3,684	3,666	3,933	3,977	4,296	4,781
Chevrolet	1,670	1,670	1,680	1,728	1,869	2,048
Pontiac	2,015	2,015	2,027	2,164	2,298	2,527
Oldsmobile	2,327	2,327	2,337	2,362	2,487	2,798

[a] Source: Suggested factory advertised delivered prices including Federal excise taxes and handling charges.

[b] No four-door Rambler was offered in the 1952 and 1953 models; price shown is for the lowest-priced model, a two-door station wagon. Other prices are for lowest-priced Rambler four-door models.

[c] A four-door model was not offered; price shown is that for the lowest-priced two-door model.

[d] This was the Scotsman, the stripped economy model. The next lowest-priced four-door model Studebaker, which was more comparable to the lowest-priced Ford, Chevrolet, and Plymouth cars, was listed at $2,049.

lowest-priced line previously had not included a four-door model. From 1952 to 1953, the prices of some of the Big Three makes were increased while others were held steady. There were relatively modest decreases by Plymouth and by Dodge with the prices of most makes remaining unchanged or increasing slightly. Thus, except for Packard, there was no increase but rather the effect of a decrease in prices of Independent makes relative to Big Three makes from 1952 to 1953. Yet, the share of sales of the Independent makes declined sharply in comparison with the expanding position of the Big Three from 1952 to 1953.

From 1953 to 1954, the suggested prices of the Independent makes were cut or held constant except for Studebaker which was raised $34 and the larger Packard which was increased $100 in Nance's program of "quality" emphasis. The Packard Clipper was reduced $4, Hudson was lowered $55, and the Nash was lowered $20. Rambler introduced a new four-door sedan at $1,795 in comparison with the previous lowest-priced Rambler, a two-door station wagon at $2,003. The Hudson Jet was continued at $1,858.

In contrast, from 1953 to 1954, General Motors increased the price of its four-door sedans by $10 to $12 except for a $267 increase on Cadillac; Ford increased its price on four-door sedans by $11 while Mercury and Lincoln were continued unchanged; and Chrysler continued its prices unchanged except for a $70 increase on the Chrysler line. Thus, between 1953 and 1954, there were no decreases in suggested prices by the Big Three while there were some increases.

Among the Independent makes the pattern was mixed with some reductions, some held steady, and some increases. It appears, therefore, that suggested list price *changes* had little to do with the sales slump of Independent makes in 1953 and 1954.

It may be suggested that a major influence in the sales slump of the Independents in 1953 and 1954 was the "overpricing" of their models.[17] If we review the specifications of the leading Independents' lowest-priced cars in 1952-1954, we find that they were roughly comparable to but often somewhat smaller in over-all dimensions and less powerful than even the lowest-priced Big Three models. Attention may be directed to the Studebaker, which was the largest volume

[17] See Harris, "Last Stand of the Auto Independents?" *op. cit.*, pp. 116, 204.

seller among the leading Independent makes at the time. Although Studebaker's lowest-priced line, the Champion, was entered in the low-priced field, the lowest-priced four-door Studebaker sedans in the 1952-1954 models were approximately $90 to $120 higher than the corresponding Ford or Chevrolet models, the largest volume makes in this market segment. However, they were priced only slightly higher than Plymouth—by $2 in 1953 and by $36 in 1954. The Studebaker was somewhat smaller and less powerful than its nearest Big Three counterparts, and the same was true of most other Independent makes relative to comparably priced Big Three cars.

The Independents were attempting to compete by offering, at higher prices, differentiated cars having special features. The sporty Rambler first introduced in 1950, in particular, was such a specialized smaller car. The Hudson Jet introduced as a low-priced entry in 1953 was also much smaller although its price tag was $188 higher than the lowest-priced four-door Chevrolet sedan. Although the desirability of a car does not depend solely on its size—the upsurge in sales of compact cars after 1955 was evidence of this fact—it seems clear that the leading Independents suffered a comparative price disadvantage at the time of the change in market conditions. Larger, more luxurious, and more powerful competing Big Three models were available at lower prices than the less powerful cars of the Independents.

Since with few exceptions many of the models of the Independents were smaller in over-all dimensions and less powerful than comparably priced models of the Big Three, it seems that they were overpriced in the buyers' market of 1953 and 1954. Because of the overpricing, many consumers who might otherwise have bought an Independent make turned to the relatively less expensive models of the Big Three.

The leading Independents eventually did reduce their prices in 1954 to counteract their sales slump by offering promotional discounts to dealers, who presumably passed them along to consumers.[18] Nash, in early 1954, was reported to have first cut prices on 1954 models from $20 to $65 per car.[19] Packard, in a move to stimulate spring sales in 1954, cut prices by offering bonuses to dealers of $100 to $300 for

[18] *Ibid.*, p. 204.
[19] *Automotive Industries*, February 15, 1954, p. 21.

every car sold by October 1, 1954, the date set for the Stude-baker-Packard merger.[20] Studebaker cut prices to dealers in the summer of 1954 by providing $50 to $150 per car promotional allowances.[21] Similar promotional price cuts to dealers spread to the other manufacturers except General Motors.[22]

While the "overpricing" policy of the Independents appears to have been a major factor in the sales slump of their makes after 1952, the actual differentials paid by purchasers of Independent makes at retail may not have been as great as was indicated by the spread in advertised factory delivered prices. Bargaining between dealers and purchasers may have reduced the price differentials; however, if carried to extremes, this would have left the Independent dealers in weakened financial positions compared to Big Three dealers. Either alternative would have worked to the detriment of the Independents. It seems unlikely that dealers of the Independents could have fully eliminated the differentials through retail price concessions, thus leaving the Independent makes still generally higher-priced at the time of the 1953-1954 slump. Hence, the higher prices for their makes contributed to the sharp decline in the market position of the leading Independents after 1952.

Subsequently, with the rise in prices of Big Three models after 1954, the suggested list price disadvantage of the leading Independent makes narrowed and eventually became price advantages for Rambler and Studebaker; but this is a matter for later discussion.[23]

Labor Costs

A further complication for the leading Independents was a limitation imposed by high labor costs. Although they may have gained in relative market position in the early postwar period, the concessions of the Independents to the

[20] *Automotive Industries*, September 1, 1954, p. 34.
[21] Harris, "Last Stand of the Auto Independents?" *op. cit.*, p. 204.
[22] *Ibid.*
[23] In the 1958-1959 models, the lowest-priced Big Three cars were substantially higher in list price than the surviving lowest-priced Independent makes. Although the larger cars at a lower price may not always be preferred by consumers, it may be noted that the resurgence in sales of the two remaining Independent makes in 1958-1959 was concurrent not only with their emphasis on smaller, more compact cars which the Big Three had largely abandoned but also with their relatively lower list prices at the time. But this is getting ahead of the story.

unions representing their employees—most importantly the United Automobile Workers Union—were not without costs. Even before the sharp decline in 1953 by the Independents, a divergence had appeared in the operating performances of the Independent and Big Three groups of firms with the smaller firms falling behind after 1948. The responsibility for this situation rested with top management of the Independents in the early postwar years.[24]

Studebaker, in South Bend especially, had had high wage rates and loose work standards. Even after being reduced through extended negotiations with the union following the merger in 1954, Studebaker wage rates were still two to three cents per hour higher than those in Detroit for comparable jobs;[25] but the firm's worst labor cost problem was excessively liberal work standards, in large part because of a loosely established piecework system with a plant-wide seniority system. The latter was especially troublesome in maintaining worker efficiency during periods of declining employment. Any laid-off employee could displace any other employee with lower seniority, thus causing high turnover on jobs even with minor cutbacks in the work force and creating serious managerial problems in efforts to achieve efficient use of either personnel or facilities. Walter Grant, then Packard's chief financial officer, it has been reported, estimated that Studebaker's labor costs were about double the industry average because of loose work standards.[26] Later efforts to revise the work standards met with a great deal of union and employee resistance. However, negotiations and bargaining during a series of work changes by the company and strikes and slow-downs by the union were reported to have brought Studebaker's labor costs more in line with industry averages with the signing of a new contract in January 1956. Even after this, Studebaker's labor costs evidently were higher than the industry average. Packard labor costs, it was also reported, had been brought in line prior to the merger.[27] The strikes and slow-downs during 1955, it may be noted, were especially serious in their impact on Studebaker-Pack-

[24] Robert M. Macdonald, *Collective Bargaining in the Automobile Industry* (New Haven, Connecticut, and London, England: Yale University Press 1963), esp. chapters vi and vii.

[25] Harris, "Last Stand of the Auto Independents?" *op. cit.*, p. 204.

[26] Harris, "The Breakdown of Studebaker-Packard," *op. cit.*, p. 224.

[27] *Ibid.*, pp. 222 and 224.

ard, for the firm was thus handicapped during much of a booming sales year.

American Motors' greatest labor cost problems were in its Detroit Kelvinator plants, but its passenger car production costs also were out of line.[28] However, under the direction of George Romney and Edward L. Cushman, then vice-president in charge of industrial relations for American Motors, both the appliance and automotive labor costs of the firm were brought more in line with the rest of the industry by early 1956.

Thus, by 1955 or 1956, officials of the Nance and Romney eras at Studebaker-Packard and American Motors, through the adoption of more determined bargaining positions in contrast to the more complacent attitudes which had been brought to the bargaining tables by their predecessors in the early postwar years, did eventually secure concessions from the union, thereby bringing their firms' labor costs more in line with those of the Big Three. The union was in a position of having to concede to preserve at least some of the jobs of its members or risking the loss of jobs with the failure of the two remaining Independents because of their excessive labor costs. Even after these changes, wage rates and fringe benefits of the two remaining Independents were somewhat higher than those of the Big Three.[29]

By 1958, the wage rates of American Motors compared favorably with those of the Big Three. Some rates were higher and some were lower.[30] If Studebaker-Packard officials attained their objectives, their wage rates were comparable. However, labor cost differentials between the Independents, particularly Studebaker, and the Big Three still may have existed because of different work standards. In-

---

[28] Chapin, *op. cit.*

[29] See Chapin, *ibid.*; Harris, "Last Stand of the Auto Independents?" *op. cit.*, p. 204; and Harris, "Breakdown of Studebaker-Packard," *op. cit.*, pp. 222 and 224.

[30] Wage rates of American Motors and the Big Three were furnished for Congressional hearings. Some rates for American Motors, including welding, assembly, painting and others, were somewhat higher than those of the Big Three; many other rates of American Motors were somewhat lower. U. S., Senate, Committee on the Judiciary, Subcommittee on Antitrust and Monopoly, *Hearings, Administered Prices*, 85th Congress, 2nd Session, Pursuant to S. Res. 57 and S. Res. 231 (Washington: U. S. Government Printing Office, 1958), Part 7, p. 4122; information submitted by Walter Reuther, president, United Automobile Workers of America.

deed, although interfirm comparisons are difficult, this evidently was a factor from which Studebaker never fully recovered even to the time of its eventual termination of car production in South Bend.

Had the Independents not conceded to the union in the earlier postwar years, they might have lost some sales at the time; but they might also have been in better cost positions to meet the change in market conditions in 1953 and 1954. It was not until after conditions had changed greatly and the immediate threat to survival of the two remaining firms was readily apparent that agreements actually were reached reducing the labor cost differentials of the two surviving Independents. It is clear that the historical pattern of labor negotiations in the industry before 1953, a primary responsibility of top management of the four Independents during the early postwar years, worked to the disadvantage of the Independents in 1953 and 1954 and thereafter.

Management Complacency

Criticism has been directed toward the managers of the Independents as being responsible for many of the difficulties of the firms at the time of the slump in 1953 and again in 1954.[31] Nance's move to the firm in 1952 called attention to Packard's managerial problems. At this time Packard appeared antiquated. Many Packard employees were old, having stayed on the job because of Packard's lack of a retirement program. Top management was aging, and it was recognized that Packard's management needed rejuvenating, particularly in the sales division. The production and engineering staffs seem to have been capable.[32]

W. B. Harris has contended that the managers of the smaller firms had failed to keep up with the Big Three in the modernization of their products and production facilities, that they had failed to reduce their prices quickly to competitive levels with the change to a buyers' market in 1953, and that they had followed a "short sighted" policy in their negotiations with the union during the "abnormal years." He criticized the managements of the Independents for complac-

[31] Harris, "Last Stand of the Auto Independents?" *op. cit.*, pp. 116 and 204; Harris, "Breakdown of Studebaker-Packard," *op. cit.*, pp. 141 and 222-224; and Testimony of J. J. Nance, *op. cit.*, pp. 861 and 869.

[32] "Nance's Idea: Merge Packard," *Business Week*, May 17, 1952, p. 29.

ency.[33] According to Harris, the cars of the Independents were "overpriced" in comparison with those of the Big Three. Although Hudson had won numerous stock car races, he considered Hudson to have been producing quite ordinary cars for the medium-priced ranges which were outflanked by competitive makes offering more car at lower prices. Studebaker's objective of offering lighter, cheaper cars with advanced styling failed to work with the introduction of its sports-type, European looking 1953 models which were considerably higher-priced than the lowest-priced cars of the Big Three, although roughly comparable in size and power. The Studebaker styling was considered by Harris as too advanced for the 1953 market. Inadequate consumer research was partly blamed for the car's lack of appeal to consumers. Packard, which had confused its quality picture with its lower-priced Clipper models, had not had sufficient time to return to a quality emphasis under Nance.[34] At the time of the slump in 1953 and 1954, Packard was in the midst of a program of modernizing its facilities, updating its product with a new V-8 engine, and improving its selling organization.[35]

Harris' charge of management complacency was supported by the testimony of J. J. Nance before a Congressional Committee. Discussing the position of the Independents, he stated:

> These companies in general did not, during the period of the seller's market, fortify themselves by modernizing their product and their facilities and generally strengthening their organizations, both internally and externally. As a consequence, they were not relatively as well equipped to hold their historical percentages of the market as were the larger volume competitors.[36]

Nance, who considered the resurgence of Ford a vital competitive force that contributed to the high degree of competition in the industry after 1952, pointed out that Ford had used the period of the sellers' market to strengthen its competitive position. Ford modernized its facilities and its product, improved its management, and strengthened its

[33] Harris, "Last Stand of the Auto Independents?" op. cit., pp. 114-117 and 204-208.

[34] This and the preceding statements were based on comments by Harris in "Last Stand of the Auto Independents?" op. cit., pp. 116 and 204; and "Breakdown of Studebaker-Packard," op. cit., p. 141.

[35] Testimony of J. J. Nance, op. cit., p. 865.

[36] Ibid., p. 861.

dealer organization. In comparison, Nance contended that the smaller firms had lagged and that they were unprepared for the shift to a buyers' market. Although Nance did not comment directly on the quality of the previous Packard management, he seems to have considered it laggard in updating the Packard products and facilities.[37]

However, the charges of complacency may be overstated. It is not clear that the managements of the smaller firms were as complacent before 1953 as the critics would imply. The leading Independents also had introduced new models with postwar styling and product features such as automatic and overdrive transmissions prior to 1953, although only Studebaker had introduced the V-8 engine which had come to be preferred by many consumers.[38] The V-8 engine was coming to be the preferred engine by 1953 and 1954.[39] However, even Pontiac and Chevrolet of the General Motors lines and Plymouth of the Chrysler lines did not introduce V-8 engines until the 1955 models appeared late in 1954; the rest of the General Motors and Chrysler lines had V-8's earlier. Ford, of course, had pioneered in the use of V-8 engines.[40]

By the time of its merger with Studebaker, even Packard, the smallest of the leading Independents in terms of assets, had made many improvements. Management had been shaken up considerably. Practically half the top managers were new, having been brought in by Nance; the other half were drawn from the Packard engineering and production personnel who had been considered a capable group.[41] It was in the sales programs that Nance wrought the greatest change. Further modernization of facilities was also pushed. Yet, the modernization program was incomplete at the time of the slump in 1953.[42]

[37] *Ibid.*, pp. 860, 861, and 869.

[38] Studebaker had introduced a V-8 engine in 1950 on its 1951 models several years before Chevrolet and Plymouth brought out similar engines for their 1955 models; Ford had long used the V-8 type engine. *Red Book National Used Car Market Report*, Vol. 47, No. 228, Region B, July 1 through August 14, 1958 (Chicago: National Market Reports, Inc., 1958) was used as the source for this comparison of specifications of cars.

[39] Testimony of J. J. Nance, *op. cit.*, p. 866.

[40] "V-eight Engine Makes the Grade," *Business Week*, December 13, 1953, pp. 84-86; also "The Whys of the Power Race," *Business Week*, December 4, 1954, pp. 70-74.

[41] *Automotive Industries*, May 15, 1953, p. 17.

[42] Packard Motor Car Company, *Annual Report*, 1952, pp. 6-7, and *Annual Report*, 1953, pp. 5-6; and Testimony of J. J. Nance, *op. cit.*, pp. 865-66.

The independent manufacturers had shared in the modernizing of the industry after the end of the war. If changes in the value of a firm's net property, plant, and equipment may be taken as a crude measure of the physical expansion and modernization of a firm, it appears clear that the smaller firms had not lagged seriously, if at all, in improving and expanding their plants. Of course, they may have started from a relatively weaker base; but they too had participated in the facilities expansions of World War II. From the end of 1946 through the end of 1952, Packard increased the value of its net property, plant, and equipment 164.3 per cent; Studebaker, 252.7 per cent; Nash, 286.0 per cent; and Hudson, 209.5 per cent—an average increase for the leading Independents of 228.5 per cent. In comparison during the same period, General Motors increased the value of its net property, plant, and equipment 207.7 per cent; Chrysler, 362.0 per cent; and Ford, 252.4 per cent—an average increase for the Big Three of 234.8 per cent.[43] Thus, relative to their beginning investment the smaller firms had invested approximately as much in this period in expansion and modernization as had the Big Three.

Much time is required for the development of innovations and the introduction of new models and equipment options in the passenger car industry.[44] Studebaker certainly had aggressively pushed its advanced styling. Although it may be contended that the Studebaker style was too advanced — a management error.— a program of continuing styling changes certainly did not reflect complacency with product programs.

Nance perhaps was grossly affected by the difficulties at Packard while Harris may have overstated his criticism of the managers of the Independents. Hudson had made efforts to improve its position through the introduction of the smaller

[43] Computations based on the annual reports of the several companies.
[44] This fact is illustrated by the statement of Theodore Yntema, vice-president of Ford Motor Company, that in February, 1958, Ford was engaged in production of current models; testing, establishing facilities, and tooling for 1959 models; engineering, testing, tooling, and planning facilities for 1960 models; styling, engineering, and planning facilities for 1961 models; and making market studies and developing styles for 1962 models. Other long-range programs in engineering research were also being conducted for new developments to be incorporated in 1963-1965 models. Yntema considered the development of a new car to be a four-year project excluding the engineering research. U. S., Senate, Committee on the Judiciary, Subcommittee on Antitrust and Monopoly, *Hearings, Administered Prices, op. cit.,* Part 6, p. 2731.

Hudson Jet in 1952,[45] but it did seem poorly styled and over-priced. Also, Hudson made little effort to change its larger cars after their 1948 model introduction. Both Nash and Hudson, however, had pioneered in the use of unit body-frame construction in their postwar cars.[46] Nash pioneered in the small car field in the postwar period with the introduction of its Rambler in 1950.[47] Both the type of car and its construction were later followed by the Big Three.

Furthermore, the early postwar concessions to the union may have been partly the result of size disadvantages and not simply short sight on the part of management. Strikes against the smaller firms might have resulted in their ready displacement from the market by the high volume Big Three makes. In strikes against the Big Three, the Independents, because of their more limited capacity, would still be far short of being able to displace the Big Three makes. The hesitancy in reducing prices also may have been a factor related to size of the firm and not management complacency. The managers of the smaller firms may have feared that extensive price reductions by them would have been met by greater reductions by the Big Three. As observed above, price reductions in 1954 by the leading Independents evidently had little effect on their sales. Two of the Big Three also provided price concessions.

Still, there was truth in the criticism. The managers of the Independent companies rather clearly could have done more than they did, especially in handling internal organizational problems in the early postwar years; and to some extent, they did bring their problems on themselves by a failure to move ahead as aggressively as they might have in their product design and sales activities. Their difficulties after the return of competitive conditions were anticipated by officials of the firms, but the suddenness of the change in the market in 1953 did seem not to have been anticipated. Shortcomings of management of the firms possibly could have been corrected without change in the size of the firms; however, the mergers served to provide new blood for the firms through integration of their managements and an opportunity for selection of the best managerial and engineering talent from each of the combining firms.

[45] Hudson Motor Car Company, *Annual Report*, 1952, p. 12.
[46] Testimony of George Romney, *op. cit.*, pp. 448 and 452-54.
[47] Nash-Kelvinator Corporation, *Annual Report*, 1950, p. 4.

"Orphan Car" Influence

A further factor adversely influencing the sales of the leading Independents was the fear by consumers of purchase of an orphan car — one that is no longer backed by a manufacturer and dealer organization. Much of the sales difficulty of Hudson and Nash during the period from 1953 through 1957 was attributed by Independent officials to this cause. According to Roy Chapin, public acceptance of American Motors' compact car "was agonizingly delayed by fear on the part of potential buyers that they would be buying an orphan. . . . The owning of a car whose maker no longer is around puts the purchaser at a decided disadvantage in seeking parts and service, as well as when trading in the orphan on another make."[48]

Studebaker-Packard also acknowledged the influence of the orphan car argument on the sales of its products in 1956.[49] In addition to the higher prices of the smaller firms' cars, therefore, the prospect of buying an orphan car appears to have been one of the most important influences on the sales of the Independents after the return of the buyers' market in 1953. Stimulated in part by the rumors and announcements regarding mergers among the Independents, there had been widespread speculation regarding the probabilities of the continued existence of the domestic Independents with the return of competitive conditions.[50] Since acts of merger were widely interpreted as signs of weakness, the Independents thus contributed to their own sales problems.

Arthur Pound, a number of years ago, observed the possibility of the orphan car influence:

> The automobile buyer, more definitely than the consumer in other lines of merchandise in general use, seeks reassurance of the manufacturer's stability, because the service he receives and the resale value of his car alike depend unmistakably upon the continuance of the manufacturer in business.[51]

[48] Chapin, *op. cit.*

[49] Studebaker-Packard Corporation, "Letter to Shareholders," September 24, 1956.

[50] These numerous observations should be familiar to many readers of business publications of the period from about 1948 through 1955.

[51] Arthur Pound, *The Turning Wheel* (Garden City, New York: Doubleday, Doran & Company, Inc., 1934), p. 136.

Roy Chapin, vice-president of American Motors, sum-marized the effect on his company of the hesitancy to pur-chase a candidate for the orphan category as follows:

> The demise of Kaiser-Frazer was fresh in the public's mind. The prevailing view of the remaining automotive Independents, Studebaker and Packard, as well as Nash and Hudson, was that they **had** to get together or get out of the business. All these siftings and murmurings of opinion, of course, had a direct and tangible effect on sales. . . . Not until 1957 did the Rambler car program really begin to roll the way we always felt it would and should. And what helped get it over the hump was the fact that AM had survived, had turned the corner and was going to survive.[52]

There seems little question, as Studebaker-Packard re-ported, that a similar influence was reflected in the sharp and continuing decline of Studebaker and Packard sales from 1954 through 1957 in spite of company efforts to maintain sales by offering a full line.

Defense Sales

A further influence of importance to at least two of the leading Independents was the loss of government contracts. Studebaker and Packard were both affected severely by drastic curtailment of their defense contracts. Dollar sales of both had reached postwar peaks in 1953, largely as a result of sizable defense contracts. Packard's jet engine pro-duction which had been scheduled to run through the middle of 1954 at a rate of approximately $196,000,000 per year was reduced to only $15,000,000 during 1953. Studebaker had de-fense contracts calling for about $202,000,000 sales in 1953 and 1954; these were reduced substantially and terminated in early 1954 even before the merger with Packard.[53] Approxi-mately 42 per cent of Packard's 1953 sales were defense products as were 36 per cent of Studebaker's. These reduc-tions in defense production severely reduced the sales of the two firms and left them with idle plant capacity. Studebaker's New Jersey plant, originally planned as an assembly plant and completed in 1951, had been a major center for its defense

[52] Chapin, *op. cit.*
[53] See Packard Motor Car Company, "Proxy Statement," dated August 17, 1954, pp. 13 and 18-19; and Testimony of J. J. Nance, *op. cit.*, pp. 864-65.

work; but it was subsequently sold by Studebaker-Packard when additional contracts could not be secured to utilize the plant,[54] since the firm's automotive sales were not sufficient to justify its use.

Hudson and Nash also were unsuccessful in securing additional defense contracts after 1952 to utilize their idle facilities, but they had not relied so heavily on defense sales. Approximately 19 per cent of Hudson's 1953 sales were to the government. Nash-Kelvinator was also engaged in defense production in 1953, but the amount was less than 9 per cent of 1953 sales.[55] Limited defense sales also adversely affected American Motors since the firm had continued idle capacity in the Hudson Special Products Division which it had planned for use in defense production.[56]

Thus, the sharp reductions in defense contracts of at least two of the leading Independents contributed to their difficulties in 1953 and 1954; and the inability of the successor to the other two to expand its defense sales as planned resulted in continued idle capacity in its defense products division—the former Hudson facilities.

A SUMMARY AND COMMENT

There were numerous influences of a relatively temporary nature adversely affecting the performance of the leading Independents after 1952. Many of these at least could have been partially overcome without changes in the size of the firms. The relatively high prices of Independent makes, the consumer fear of a prospective "orphan car," the loss of defense contracts, the high labor costs, and management complacency and perhaps poor managerial judgment, especially in an early postwar laxity in dealing with unions, were all significant, possibly nonscalar influences in explaining much of the past difficulty of the Independents. However, they may have been less significant than the underlying factor of scale of operations as an influence on the long-term survival potential and prosperity of the leading Independents. Determined action by management might have and did overcome some of these influences; and the elapse of time and changing

[54] *Automotive Industries*, July 1, 1950, p. 23, for completion; and Studebaker-Packard Corporation, *Annual Report*, 1955, p. 4, for disposal.

[55] *Supra*, chapter i.

[56] *Supra*, chapter iii.

consumer preferences would and did act to remove others as significant influences.

Although they were of some importance as a transitory influence, the tighter credit restrictions in themselves seem to have been of little significance as an underlying influence adversely affecting the Independents alone. The dealers of other firms presumably faced tighter restrictions, too. Size relationships seem to have been important in combination with the credit restrictions, to the extent that the tightest restrictions were imposed on dealers of the Independents, possibly because of the smaller size of their dealerships or because the financing of Independent makes was adjudged at higher risks than that of Big Three makes. Of course, from the viewpoint of the Independents themselves the tightening of credit was quite important.

CHAPTER VI

THE INDEPENDENTS AND THE COMPACT

IN PRECEDING CHAPTERS we have seen that the return to profitability of American Motors and Studebaker-Packard after their difficulties of the middle 1950's coincided with their emphasis on the type of vehicle that came to be known as the "compact car." Although American Motors had first introduced its compact Rambler in 1950, its compact car sales were not especially outstanding before 1958. And this was also true of other makes which in the early 1950's were somewhat smaller than the conventional lowest-priced cars of the Big Three, namely, the Chevrolets, Fords, and Plymouths of the time. Yet, despite its earlier lack of outstanding sales performance, the type of vehicle known as the compact car turned into a best seller after 1957. The compact ushered in perhaps the most sweeping readjustments in automotive product policies and programs in recent history and set the pattern for much that is basic to the competitive struggle in the United States automobile industry.

SUCCESS OF THE COMPACT CAR

During the years 1957 through 1959, much criticism was directed toward the three largest firms in the United States automobile industry because of their apparent reluctance to introduce vehicles of the type popularly known as "compact cars."[1] Rising sales of relatively small, less expensive cars,

[1] See, e.g., Henry Dreyfuss, "The Car Detroit Should Be Building," *Consumer Reports*, July, 1958, pp. 351-55; S. I. Hayakawa, "Why the Edsel Laid an Egg: Motivational Research vs. the Reality Principle," *ETC: A Review of General Semantics*, XV (Spring, 1958), 217-21, also reprinted as "Semanticist Hayakawa Blames Motivationists for Ills of Automobile Makers," *Advertising Age*, May 12, 1958, "Feature section," for two of the better known criticisms of the industry; and John Keats, *The Insolent Chariots* (Philadelphia: J. B. Lippincott Co., 1958), for a critical but amusing diatribe on the automobile industry. Criticism also was widespread in popular periodicals too numerous for listing here. Observations of the Big Three's apparent reluctance to change extended even to the foreign press. See, e. g., "Motors in the Lead," a supplement to *The Economist*, October 25, 1958, pp. 16-23.

which were produced in the United States, first by American Motors and later by Studebaker-Packard, too, and also in other countries, had served to reveal a gap in the coverage of the United States market by the Big Three.

Observing the rising sales of their competitors' compact cars, the Big Three finally introduced 1960 model compacts in October 1959. The new cars — Chrysler's Valiant, Ford's Falcon, and General Motors' Corvair — all achieved substantial sales volumes. Retail sales of the Ford Falcon reached a total of almost 515,000 units in the first 14 months following its introduction; combined sales of the other two reached approximately this same total. Following these models, the Big Three introduced in 1960 a second generation of compact cars which were somewhat larger and more expensive but still distinctively smaller and lower-priced than their full-sized makes. In 1961, three more completely new cars were introduced for the 1962 model year. One of these — the Chevy II — clearly fell in the compact car group; the other two — Ford Fairlane and Mercury Meteor — were manufactured from the same basic body shell and engine and fell in a size category between the earlier compact car group and the full-sized makes of their manufacturer, the Ford Motor Company.[2] Subsequently, these were followed in 1962 and 1963 by the introduction of additional intermediate-sized cars: Dodge Dart and Chevrolet Chevelle for the 1963 and 1964 models respectively.

The expanding sales of the compact cars of the Big Three did not immediately dim the sales prospects of the leading domestic and foreign compact cars — Rambler and Volkswagen. However, they did cut into the sales of most other compact makes after 1960. New car sales of Rambler had gradually increased to a level of 91,000 units in 1957, then had approximately doubled this figure in 1958, and quadrupled it in 1959. In 1956, Rambler, which was then the only domestic compact car, had accounted for slightly less than 1.2 per cent of the total United States sales. By 1958, the domestic compact cars, which then included Rambler and the new

[2] The Fairlane and the Meteor were advertised initially by their manufacturer as the new standard size for their respective makes. They, along with Chevrolet's Chevelle, were intermediate in size and power between the earlier compact and full-sized cars. Although one may consider them as demonstrating a movement away from the compact car class, they are considered here as compact cars; they were, after all, considerably smaller and less powerful than the standard full-sized models which they displaced. The Meteor was discontinued in 1963.

Studebaker Lark models introduced in November 1958, had acquired 4.3 per cent of the market; and in 1959, their combined share totaled 8.2 per cent. Following the introduction of the Big Three compacts in late 1959, the share held by Rambler and Lark declined to 8.0 per cent in 1960, 7.6 per cent in 1961, and 7.2 per cent in 1962;[3] but, as may be seen in Table 10, the total sales and share of sales held by the compact cars rose rapidly after 1958.

Foreign produced makes contributed to the growth in compact car sales. From less than 1 per cent in 1955, the share of United States sales held by the foreign makes doubled each year through 1958. (Also see Chapter I, Table 2.) Most of the foreign car sales were of vehicles which fell in the compact car category.[4] After the introduction of the Big Three compacts in 1959, the share held by the foreign makes declined as had the share of the Studebaker Lark, although Volkswagen, the volume leader of the foreign makes, continued to enjoy rising sales.[5] Much of their decline resulted from the withdrawal of foreign makes produced by Big Three subsidiaries after the Big Three started their domestic compact car production; but, in any event, the foreign makes were partly displaced by the new domestic compact cars.

TRENDS OF THE 1950's

The 1950's witnessed several major trends in the product offerings of the domestic producers of passenger cars. One of the trends was a persistent rise in the suggested factory advertised delivered prices of most domestic makes except during

[3] Compare Tables 3 and 6, *supra*, for the variations in market share between Rambler and Lark.

[4] Although a complete breakdown by foreign car make is not available, it appears that more than 70 per cent of foreign registrations were of vehicles in the compact car class; the rest were special, sport, or luxury vehicles.

[5] Volkswagen new car sales in the U. S. rose steadily from fewer than 29,000 units in 1955 to more than 120,000 in 1959 and continued to rise to almost 160,000 in 1960, more than 177,000 in 1961, almost 193,000 in 1962 and more than 240,000 in 1963. Renault, second most popular in U. S. sales among the foreign makes, sold over 91,000 cars in 1959 but suffered a decline to 44,000 units in 1961 and fewer than 30,000 units in 1962 and 1963. Most other foreign makes fell in sales too. These changes may be seen in more detail for individual makes in *Automotive Industries* (Annual Statistical Issues), March 15, 1956-1964.

TABLE 10

NEW PASSENGER CAR REGISTRATIONS AND SHARES OF TOTAL REGISTRATIONS IN THE UNITED STATES OF U.S.-MADE FULL-SIZED CARS, U.S.-MADE COMPACT CARS, AND FOREIGN-MADE CARS, 1955-1963 [a]

(Units in Thousands)

	1955	1956	1957	1958	1959	1960	1961	1962	1963
Full-Sized Car									
Units	7,039	5,786	5,684	4,076	4,815	4,456	3,534	3,969	4,502
Share of Total	98.2%	97.2%	95.0%	87.6%	79.7%	67.8%	60.4%	57.2%	59.6%
Compact Car [b]									
Units	72	71	91	200[c]	612	1,622	1,943	2,630	2,669
Share of Total	1.0%	1.2%	1.5%	4.3%	10.1%	24.7%	33.2%	37.9%	35.3%
Foreign Car									
Units	58	98	207	379	614	499	379	339	386
Share of Total	.9%	1.7%	3.5%	8.1%	10.2%	7.6%	6.5%	4.9%	5.1%
Total Registrations	7,170	5,955	5,982	4,655	6,041	6,577	5,855	6,939	7,557

[a] Source: Registration data by courtesy of R. L. Polk & Co. Computations are based on these data and rounded.

[b] The registration figures included here are those for Rambler alone for 1955-1957; Rambler and Lark for 1958; and Rambler, Lark, Corvair, Falcon, and Valiant for 1959. Beginning in 1960, Mercury Comet, Buick Special, Oldsmobile F-85, and Pontiac Tempest are added to the foregoing; beginning in 1961 with the 1962 models, Chevy II, Ford Fairlane and Mercury Meteor are added; beginning in 1962 with the 1963 model, Dodge Dart is added; and in 1963, Chevrolet's Chevelle is also added.

[c] Studebaker Lark was not reported separately for 1958, having been introduced only in November of that year; however, this figure includes 14,000 units, which were Studebaker's November and December 1958 sales, as an estimate of sales of the compact Lark.

a brief period following the end of the Korean "police action."[6] Although the rise in suggested prices shown in Table 11 for selected representative makes may overstate the final price rise at the retail level — discounts from suggested prices and increasing trade-in allowances were customary, particularly after 1952 — the price of car ownership increased throughout the 1950's.

The over-all rising trend in the price of cars perhaps is best observed in the changes in the average factory wholesale price of all makes sold to dealers since dealers generally may be presumed reluctant to provide discounts which reduce retail prices below their invoiced cost. Except for a decline from 1952 to 1953, there was a rise in each year of the 1950's in the average factory price to dealers. In 1950, the average wholesale price amounted to $1,270 per car; it reached $1,494 in 1952 after which it declined slightly in 1953 to $1,472. It increased to $1,572 in 1955 and climbed steadily each year to $1,881 in 1958. The rise was slowed in 1959 when only a $3 increase was noted.[7]

Concurrent with the upward price movement, there was an effort to expand the market coverage of many domestic makes of cars. Broader market coverage for individual makes was viewed as desirable by many dealers and manufacturers since dealers could persuade those customers who wanted something more than basic transportation to "trade up" to higher-priced models. This improved dealers' chances of mak-

[6] Inflation, of course, provides a part of the explanation for the rise; but it is the phenomenon of the rise in dollar prices and the relative prices of different makes of car, and not prices relative to other goods, in which we are primarily interested.

[7] In 1960, the first full year after the introduction of the Big Three compacts, the average factory wholesale price fell to $1,822. The average rose to $1,862 in 1961, largely because of the inclusion of heaters as standard factory-installed equipment on more makes, $1,886 in 1962, and $1,889 in 1963. These average factory wholesale prices of all domestic U. S. makes include standard factory-installed equipment and are based on data in Automobile Manufacturers Association, *Automobile Facts and Figures*, 1964 edition (Detroit, Michigan), p. 3.

A breakdown of some of the causes of the price rise may be found in an article by Franklin M. Fisher, Zvi Griliches, and Carl Kaysen, "The Costs of Automobile Model Changes Since 1949," *American Economic Review, Papers and Proceedings*, LII, No. 2 (May, 1962), 259-61, which provides estimates of the portions of the price increase to be attributed to frequent model changes in a trend toward increased power and size, additional optional equipment, and additional advertising.

TABLE 11

SUGGESTED FACTORY ADVERTISED OR PORT OF ENTRY DELIVERED PRICES OF SELECTED LOWEST-PRICED FOUR-DOOR MODELS OF FULLSIZED AND COMPACT PASSENGER CARS, 1950, 1952, AND 1954-1963 MODELS[a]

	1950	1952	1954	1955	1956	1957	1958	1959	1960	1961	1962	1963
Full-Sized Cars												
Chevrolet	$1,450	$1,670	$1,680	$1,728	$1,869	$2,048	$2,155	$2,301	$2,316	$2,316	$2,378	$2,376
Ford	1,472	1,678	1,701	1,753	1,895	2,042	2,109	2,273	2,311	2,315 i	2,507 i	2,507
Plymouth	1,492 c	1,768 e	1,765	1,781	1,926	2,055	2,169	2,283	2,310	2,310	2,262 k	2,262
Buick LeSabre b	1,909	2,209	2,291	2,291	2,416	2,660	2,700	2,804	2,870	3,107	3,227	3,004
Buick Electra b	2,139	2,563	2,711	2,876	3,250	3,681	3,789	3,856	3,856	3,825	4,051	4,051
Dodge	1,848 e	2,052 e	2,025	2,093	2,267	2,451	2,530	2,587	2,330	2,330	2,297 k	2,301
Mercury	2,031	2,249	2,251	2,277	2,313	2,645	2,617	2,832	2,730	2,587 dj	2,835 j	2,887
Pontiac	1,724	2,015	2,027	2,164	2,298	2,527	2,638	2,704	2,702	2,702	2,796	2,795
Cadillac	2,866	3,684	3,933	3,977	4,296	4,781	4,891	5,080	5,080	5,080	5,213	5,214
Compact Cars												
Rambler e	—	—	1,795	1,695	1,829	1,961	2,047	2,098	2,098	2,098	2,050	2,105
Rambler American f	—	2,003	1,800	1,695	—	—	1,789	1,835	1,844	1,894	1,895	1,895
Hudson Jet	—	—	1,858	—	—	—	—	—	—	—	—	—
Studebaker Lark	—	—	—	—	—	—	—	1,995	2,046	2,005	2,040	2,040
Volkswagen g	—	1,595	1,495	1,495	1,495	1,495	1,545	1,545	1,565	1,595	1,595	1,595
Renault Dauphine h	—	—	—	—	1,595	1,645	1,645	1,645	1,645	1,385	1,395	1,495
Chevrolet Corvair	—	—	—	—	—	—	—	—	2,038	1,974	2,111 l	2,110
Ford Falcon	—	—	—	—	—	—	—	—	2,053	1,974	2,047	2,017
Plymouth Valiant	—	—	—	—	—	—	—	—	—	2,014	1,991	1,973
Buick Special	—	—	—	—	—	—	—	—	—	2,384	2,358 m	2,363
Mercury Comet	—	—	—	—	—	—	—	—	—	2,053	2,139	2,139
Dodge Lancer (Dart) n	—	—	—	—	—	—	—	—	—	2,069	2,011	2,041
Oldsmobile, F-85	—	—	—	—	—	—	—	—	—	2,384	2,457	2,457
Pontiac Tempest	—	—	—	—	—	—	—	—	—	2,167	2,240	2,241
Chevy II	—	—	—	—	—	—	—	—	—	—	2,041	2,040
Ford Fairlane	—	—	—	—	—	—	—	—	—	—	2,216	2,216
Mercury Meteor	—	—	—	—	—	—	—	—	—	—	2,340	2,340

a Factory advertised or port of entry East Coast delivered prices including excise taxes and handling charges. Fleet specials are excluded.

b Names of Buick series were changed in 1959 models; for the earlier years, prices are for the Special and Super, respectively.

c Prices of two-door sedans; four-door sedans were not included in the lowest-priced series in these years.

d Price of 8-cylinder models; a 6-cylinder model also was offered for the first time in 1961 by Mercury at $2,471.

e Prices of 108-inch wheelbase sedan first offered in the 1954 model, except for the 1963 model for which the wheelbase was 112 inches.

f Rambler American with 100-inch wheelbase: stationwagon prices before 1955, two-door sedan in 1958-1959, and four-door sedan in other years.

g Prices are for two-door sedan; a four-door sedan was not offered.

h Not available before 1956 model.

i Prices not entirely comparable. The Fairlane series was dropped in 1962 as a full-sized car and reintroduced as a smaller model at a lower price. The 1962 price is for the Galaxie series which was the remaining full-sized Ford; the comparable 1961 Galaxie was priced at $2,590.

j Prices not entirely comparable. The Meteor series was dropped in 1962 as a full-sized car and reintroduced as a smaller model at a lower price. The 1962 price is for the Monterey series which was the remaining full-sized Mercury; the comparable 1961 Monterey was priced at $2,869.

k To compete with the newer compact cars, these Chrysler Corporation cars were reduced somewhat in wheelbase and external dimensions beginning with the 1962 models.

l Price is for Series 700. Previous year's price was for Series 500 which was discontinued in the four-door model.

m Price is for the car with the V-6 engine.

n Lancer, 1961-1962; Dart, 1963.

ing sales and keeping customers satisfied with the makes of one manufacturer.

The traditional low-priced volume leaders — Chevrolet, Ford, and Plymouth — pushed vigorously to expand the market coverage of their makes. They introduced more luxurious prestige models which, with their many optional features, extended well into the price ranges covered by the traditional middle-priced group of makes well known to most consumers. Seeing in the mid-1950's that some of the best selling models were the more expensive models of the traditional low-priced group and that the traditional middle-priced group was accounting for about 40 per cent of the market, the domestic manufacturers directed their greatest selling effort at this large, no longer well-defined middle-priced market segment.

A Trend Toward Uniformity

In the effort to expand their market potentials, the low-priced, large-volume Big Three makes were increased in size, weight, and power. The wheelbase of the lowest-priced four-door Ford sedan, for example, was gradually increased from 114 inches in the 1950-1951 models to 119 inches in the 1960-1961 models. Chevrolet and Plymouth followed similar patterns of increasing size. In contrast, the traditional middle-priced group, with the major exception of Mercury, increased wheelbase dimensions relatively little, in most cases only one or two inches, if at all. Changes in weight, over-all body dimensions, and engine power of the Big Three makes followed patterns similar to those of wheelbase dimensions. Since manufacturers had standardized on fewer basic body shells, the low-priced makes became increasingly similar to the traditional middle-priced makes, particularly after 1955.

The trend toward uniformity culminated in late 1958 when General Motors — the industry's largest producer — used the same basic body shell for all of its five volume-produced 1959 makes.[8] Chrysler already had adopted this practice. Only Ford among the Big Three still used more than one basic body shell for its several makes.[9] Although considerable variation could be achieved around one basic body shell by providing different styling features along with different engines and

[8] This includes Buick, Cadillac, Chevrolet, Oldsmobile and Pontiac. Only the Corvette, a plastic-bodied sports car, had a separate basic body shell.

[9] *Consumer Reports*, April, 1959, pp. 166-67.

running gear, a high degree of uniformity was readily apparent to buyers of new cars. The styles of the 1950's were largely continuations of basic patterns established before 1950 in the initial post-World War II change to lower, longer, sleeklooking cars with large glass areas. Adaptations of the more successful features contributed to the styling uniformity. Most domestic makes, especially after 1955, were designed as large, all-purpose vehicles with a wide range of optional equipment to appeal to an amorphous, predominantly middlepriced market.

A Squeeze on the Middle

The upward movement of the Chevrolet-Ford-Plymouth group exerted a squeeze on sales of the traditional middlepriced makes after 1955. In 1955, the traditional middle-priced group — led by Buick with almost 738,000 new registrations and more than 10 per cent of total sales — accounted for more than 40 per cent of total United States new car sales.[10] The share of new car registrations held by the group fell to approximately 30 per cent in 1957 and was down to about 25 per cent in 1960. In the process, a number of long established middle-priced makes vanished from the automotive scene; Hudson, Nash, Packard, and DeSoto were dropped. Edsel, Ford's new entry for the middle-priced market, also was dropped after a poor reception.[11]

Major casualties of the trends of the 1950's were the traditional price class grouping of cars and the low-priced car. By the mid-1950's, market price classes were no longer so well defined by make as they had been earlier. The top models of the traditional low-priced makes with their ex-

[10] Until the middle 1950's, the different U. S.-made cars had been maintained in a pattern of relative price groupings for so long a time that American consumers customarily identified them as being in recognizable price classes. Chevrolet, Ford, and Plymouth were considered as the lowest-priced class; Cadillac, Lincoln, and Chrysler's Imperial dominated the highest-priced class; most other makes fell in a middle-priced group although some attempts were made by these makes to penetrate the lowest- or highest-priced groups. In addition to those named in this paragraph, the middle-priced group included such makes as Oldsmobile, Pontiac, Dodge, Chrysler, and Mercury. With the changes occurring in the 1950's, the traditional classifications, of course, became less distinct.

[11] Edsel's demise evidently was as much a result of the competition it experienced from the upward push of Ford as from its unfortunate introduction at the beginning of the 1957-58 recession in the U. S. and the beginning of increased consumer interest in compact cars.

tensive offerings of optional equipment and features had themselves become prestige models, and they penetrated well into the price ranges of traditional middle-priced makes. The traditional low-priced cars were large, powerful, luxurious, and similar in styling to the higher-priced makes, though still offered at somewhat lower total prices when comparably equipped. Few consumers complained of these trends before 1957. But then in the succeeding period, the relatively small, less expensive, domestic and foreign compact cars began their rapid growth in market penetration.

THE APPEAL OF THE COMPACT

The compact car could satisfy a variety of consumer needs and desires. Many consumers purchased the small automobiles as a second car, but many others who purchased them owned only the one car.[12] Many consumers purchased the small car because it was a more convenient vehicle for use in congested urban and suburban areas. And there were other reasons.

Although it may not have been the most important factor, price seems to have been a significant influence in the upsurge in domestic and foreign compact car sales, especially when coupled with the initial stimulus of a "recession psychology" which influenced many consumers from late 1957 through much of 1958. The Rambler and Volkswagen, for example, had been relatively high in list price in the early and mid-1950's compared with the popular Chevrolet-Ford-Plymouth group. However, by late 1957, substantial gaps had been opened between the list prices of Rambler, especially Rambler American, and Volkswagen and the current lowest-priced full-sized makes of the domestic firms. Renault enjoyed a similar advantage. The pattern of price relationships

12 In a telephone survey of 153 buyers of small foreign cars, it was found that the primary reason given for purchase of a foreign compact car was economy of operation by 49 per cent of the interviewees, ease of handling by 20 per cent, low initial cost by 19 per cent, different from U. S. cars by 3 per cent, and other reasons by the rest. Of those interviewed 58 per cent owned another car and 42 per cent owned only the foreign car. See Robert Sheehan, "A Big Year for Small Cars," *Fortune*, LVI (August, 1957), 196. Some of the same reasons for purchase apparently applied to Rambler, particularly Rambler American, since Rambler's size and weight were in between those of the small foreign cars and the standard full-sized American cars.

among the different makes had changed with the elapse of time.

Before 1955 the compact cars, which had then included Rambler, Hudson Jet, and Volkswagen, were not outstanding sales successes. Their suggested list prices, and their actual retail prices, were comparatively high in relation to those of the popular Chevrolet-Ford-Plymouth group. With the rise in prices of the traditional low-priced cars of the Big Three in the latter 1950's, the compact cars became more competitive, securing advantages in some cases. The initial upsurge was most apparent in rising foreign car sales but was accompanied by increased Rambler sales. Compact car sales climbed slowly at first but then rose rapidly after 1956 and in a sense displaced some of the sales volume that otherwise would have gone to full-sized makes.

The retail price gap, of course, may have been somewhat less than that indicated by suggested list price differences. Volkswagen, for example, generally sold at its suggested list price while most domestic makes were discounted from list price after 1952, thus tending to close at retail the gap indicated by suggested list prices. Also, although Rambler's 1958 and 1959 models and Studebaker's 1959 model carried list prices somewhat below those of Chevrolet, Ford, and Plymouth, they were at the time selling at prices approximately equal to or slightly lower than those of the traditionally low-priced three.[13] Relative to their suggested list prices, Rambler and Lark dealers were maintaining better margins. The point, however, is that with the general rise

[13] A comparison of average retail prices of "used" 1958 model cars in July 1958, e.g., indicates that the 108-inch wheelbase Rambler was sold at average retail and wholesale prices competitive with the nearest comparable Chevrolet, Ford, and Plymouth cars. Some Rambler retail prices were lower and some were higher than those of the other makes, although the Rambler factory advertised delivered prices generally were below those of the nearest comparable other makes. The Rambler American was somewhat lower in both list and average retail price. "New" car prices probably were comparable. See *N. A. D. A. Official Used Car Guide,* Southern edition, Vol. 25, No. 7 (July, 1958). In Chicago in August 1959, Allen Jung, a close observer of the automotive scene, found that Rambler, excluding the smaller and less expensive Rambler American, and Studebaker Lark were selling at slightly lower retail prices than the nearest comparable standard-sized Chevrolet or Ford after allowance for a differential for V-8 engines in Chevrolet and Ford. See Allen F. Jung, "Compact and Foreign-Car Price Comparisons," *Journal of Retailing,* XXXVI (Fall, 1960), 155; and Jung, "Impact of the Compact Cars on New-Car Prices," *Journal of Business,* XXXIV (April, 1961), 171.

in prices of most domestic makes the compact cars of both the domestic Independents and the foreign producers became competitive and often lower in price than the traditional low-priced three. This was an important change in price relationships among the different makes. Prices being competitive or lower, many consumers took the opportunity to choose alternative features; and many chose the compact car.

In 1958, American Motors Corporation reported:

> Rambler's sales potential appears to be expanding appreciably. Basic economic and social trends continue to focus more attention on low-cost transportation units. There is an increasing demand from widely varying income groups for cars that are more economical, maneuverable and easier to park. Appeal of the compact and small cars has been heightened, too, by the greater length, width and weight of nearly all other U. S. cars—a persistent trend which is accentuated in 1959 competitive models.[14]

Studebaker-Packard jumped on the compact band wagon in 1958 with its 1959 model Lark; and it, too, enjoyed the benefits of offering compact cars not in direct competition with Big Three makes for a time.

The rising unit sales and market penetration of compact cars had provided evidence of a substantial consumer preference for such vehicles, and the Big Three followed in late 1959 with their own relatively less expensive 1960 model compacts. Then followed a proliferation of the lower-priced models as additional compacts were introduced.

It was not long before some of the best selling models were the top models of the compact lines sold with much or all of the available optional equipment, especially with the introduction of a second generation of compact cars. During the early months of 1961, for example, about 65 per cent of Ford's Falcon buyers ordered a deluxe trim kit which included more luxurious interior appointments at a $78 list price; 50 per cent of the Falcon buyers also ordered the automatic transmission. In the same period, approximately 50 per cent of the Corvair sales were the more expensive Monza model which had an exterior roof line distinguishing it from other Corvair models; and 60 per cent of Valiant's purchasers ordered the more expensive model.[15]

[14] American Motors Corporation, *Annual Report*, 1958, p. 2.
[15] *The Wall Street Journal*, March 27, 1961, p. 1.

This phenomenon was summarized in a popular magazine —perhaps facetiously—as an expression of a desire for "economy at any cost."[16] However, a more appropriate view is that the compact car was an acceptable compromise between economy and convenience, and conspicuous consumption.[17] The domestic compact models were different; they were easily distinguished from full-sized cars; and they were somewhat less expensive to own and operate than the then current full-sized models.[18]

THE IMPACT OF THE COMPACT

The emphasis on compact cars may have resulted from changed consumer preferences, an opportunity to buy a car convenient and economical to operate and often having at the same time a lower initial price, a return to coverage of a market segment largely abandoned in the latter 1950's, or a combination of these or other influences. At any rate three major changes were to follow: (1) a halt in the rising average cost of obtaining passenger car ownership, (2) a reversal, at least temporarily, of the trend toward increasing size and power, and (3) a significant expansion in the variety of domestic passenger cars.

As may be seen in Table 10, two principal shifts in relative market penetration resulted from the changed emphasis of the domestic manufacturers: (1) the invasion of the United States market by foreign produced cars was turned back, and (2) the rising volume of domestic compacts displaced much of the volume and market share previously held by the full-sized domestic makes.

That there was a decided reversal in the product programs of the three largest firms in the industry was evident in their introduction of compact cars. In addition, the second

[16] *Time*, March 24, 1961, p. 79.

[17] Jung in "Compact and Foreign-Car Price Comparisons," *op. cit.*, 155, concluded on the basis of his study of the Chicago automobile market in August 1959 that compact car buyers instead of looking for low initial cost were "evidently looking for a new concept in motoring or other nonprice advantages."

[18] Even when loaded with extras, the highest-priced compact models, the "prestige" cars, were lower-priced than comparably equipped full-sized cars of their make. Consumers having a preference for Buick, a traditionally middle-priced make, e.g., could obtain the Buick Special compact at considerably lower initial cost than was available in the case of the lowest-priced full-sized Buick.

generation of compact cars revealed a downward adjustment in prices of models carrying traditional middle-priced nameplates. For example, the compact Buick Special introduced for 1961 carried a list price considerably lower than that on the lowest-priced Buick available the previous year. This and similar price comparisons of compacts carrying nameplates of the traditional middle-priced makes may be made using Table 11. The third new group for 1962, including the new "in-between" size Ford Fairlane and Mercury Meteor, continued the expansion in the number of lower-priced models.

With the introduction of compact cars by the Big Three, the upward price spiral was halted at least temporarily. The average wholesale price did rise in 1962 but much of the increase was the result of adding heaters as standard equipment on more makes.

In many respects the compact cars were comparable to offerings of the low-priced group in the early 1950's. Although their exterior and wheelbase dimensions were somewhat smaller than those of the earlier Chevrolets, Fords, and Plymouths, their interior dimensions and power ratings were quite close to those of earlier models. The Chevrolets, Fords, and Plymouths of the early 1950's had in a sense been the equivalent of compact cars in their day. Since some of the new 1962 compact cars were even closer in dimensions and power to models of the early 1950's, the product offerings of the domestic industry thus appeared to have come full circle.

SIGNIFICANCE OF THE COMPACT

Finally and perhaps most significantly, in the sequence of events by which the compact car achieved its popularity, we see relatively small firms, domestic as well as foreign, cast in a role of product leadership. American Motors, Studebaker-Packard, and the numerous European manufacturers who entered the United States market were all relatively small firms compared to the Big Three of the United States industry. With American Motors leading and Studebaker-Packard following, it was the smaller firms who discovered, developed, and enlarged the market demand for the type of vehicle which became known as the compact car. It was their compact cars that first enjoyed success in filling a market void, thus providing a competitive stimulus to the Big Three.

It was the compact car that proved so important an element in both the tremendous comeback of American Motors and the survival of Studebaker-Packard. Then as accumulating sales evidence revealed a substantial market for compact cars, the three largest firms of the United States industry entered what was seen to be a mass market. The resulting readjustment of the production of the domestic industry may be seen in Table 12, which also includes the output of the

TABLE 12

PRODUCTION OF COMPACT CARS
IN THE UNITED STATES, 1957-1963 [a]
(Units in Thousands)

	1957	1958	1959	1960	1961	1962	1963
Independent Makes:							
Rambler	109	217	401	486	372	455	480
Studebaker Lark [b]	—	33	154	106	79	87	68
Big Three Makes:							
Chevrolet Corvair	—	—	79	259	317	297	252
Ford Falcon	—	—	101	507	486	382	342
Plymouth Valiant	—	—	20	232	122	153	222
Buick Special	—	—	—	37	100	159	152
Mercury Comet	—	—	—	198	186	145	151
Dodge Lancer, Dart [c]	—	—	—	49	55	—	175
Oldsmobile, F-85	—	—	—	40	68	102	134
Pontiac Tempest	—	—	—	32	116	146	144
Chevy II	—	—	—	—	86	369	312
Ford Fairlane	—	—	—	—	60	386	318
Mercury Meteor	—	—	—	—	16	81	23
Chevrolet Chevelle	—	—	—	—	—	—	114
Total Compact Car Output	109	250	755	1,946	2,063	2,762	2,885
Total U. S. Production	6,120	4,247	5,599	6,703	5,522	6,943	7,644
Compact Car Share of Total	1.8%	5.9%	13.5%	29.0%	37.4%	39.8%	37.8%

[a] Source: United States production by makes from *Automotive Industries*, March 15, 1962, p. 79; and Automobile Manufacturers Association, *Automobile Facts and Figures*, 1964 edition (Detroit, Michigan), p. 8; except for Studebaker Lark which is fourth quarter output for Studebaker for the year 1958 as shown in *Automotive News (1959 Almanac Issue)*, April 27, 1959, p. 19.

[b] The figures for Studebaker include some limited outputs of the Studebaker Hawk and Avanti which were not shown separately.

[c] Lancer, 1960-1961; Dart, 1963.

later intermediate-sized cars. It was a case of the tail—the Independents along with the foreign producers—wagging the dog. And it was a lesson in the interplay of competitive actions among the large and small firms participating in the Unted States market.

Striving to avoid direct competition with the Big Three, American Motors and Studebaker-Packard with their compact cars had successfully differentiated their automobiles from those of the Big Three. For American Motors, as we have seen, it was a tremendous comeback. Yet, it must also be acknowledged that the Independents had gained their opportunity for product leadership in part from the capriciousness of consumer demand and the difficulties of predicting demand as well as from the default of the Big Three, who had responded to the evidence in the early and middle 1950's of consumer preference for more luxurious, all-purpose, prestige cars. The general rise in prices of most domestic cars and the standardization on the larger basic body shells of the Big Three opened the way for other firms to enter with distinctive, competitively priced and often lower-priced vehicles. And this is exactly what the Independents did.

The compact car was a vital element in returning American Motors and Studebaker-Packard to profitable positions, though only temporarily for the latter, thereby promoting their continued survival; but the compact car by itself was not enough, for its eventual imitation by the Big Three again returned the Independents to more direct competition with the larger firms after 1959. American Motors weathered the intensified competition in the compact car segment of the market; Studebaker-Packard did not. Important though it was, the compact car alone was not sufficient to assure the continued survival of either firm in the automobile industry. In the longer run, other factors also were essential to the existence and prosperity of these firms as automobile producers.

CHAPTER VII

THE QUESTION OF SIZE

THERE WAS A widespread belief that a firm of substantial size was a necessity for participation in the American passenger car industry in the post-World War II period. A former president of Chrysler Corporation, for example, stated this belief concisely:

> The making and selling of automobiles as we know it in the United States is a large-scale undertaking. To build and equip modern factories geared to assembly-line production requires extensive capital outlays that place this industry automatically outside the category of small business. . . . Equally important is selling those products. And here the fact of first importance is that we sell automobiles in a national market.[1]

An independent observer, writing in *Fortune*, indicated the significance of firm size even more succinctly:

> To be a successful automobile manufacturer requires only three simple conditions: (1) a gigantic, smooth-running organization, of both men and facilities, to build a car; (2) a car worth building; and (3) a second and equally gigantic organization to sell and service it.[2]

Were the leading independent automotive firms in fact too small to meet the scalar requirements for efficient and effective production and sale of automobiles? Let us consider, as a beginning point, the comments of officials of the leading Independents on the scalar problems of their firms, particularly in regard to the anticipated benefits of an increase in the size of their firms gained through merger.[3]

[1] U. S., Senate, Committee on the Judiciary, Subcommittee on Antitrust and Monopoly, *Hearings, A Study of the Antitrust Laws*, 84th Congress, 1st Session, Pursuant to S. Res. 61 (Washington: U. S. Government Printing Office, 1955), Part 1, p. 344. Testimony of L. L. Colbert, then president of Chrysler Corporation.

[2] "Lincoln-Mercury Moves Up," *Fortune*, XLV (March, 1952), 97.

[3] We are not at the moment concerned with the frequently made distinctions between plant and firm size, simply including both under a general heading of "firm size."

THE NASH-KELVINATOR-HUDSON MERGER

Advantages expected from the merger of Nash and Hudson included "the pooling of executive abilities, research and engineering resources, and purchasing power; opportunities for new manufacturing economies and improved methods; reduction of individual overhead and administrative charges; a diversification of products which tends to stabilize earnings in periods of high and low business activities, and a spreading of tooling costs over more units with less cost per unit."[4] Other advantages were believed to be the greater financial resources of the combined firms and their larger combined dealer organization. In fact, one of the most important gains by Nash in the merger was anticipated to be access to the Hudson dealer organization.[5]

"The merger was consummated to achieve economies in manufacturing, tooling and overhead expenses, and advantages in selling, which neither company could obtain alone."[6] Additional savings were expected through elimination of duplicating managerial functions, accounting, automotive research, engineering, purchasing, and parts warehousing. Soon after the merger, the integration of the Nash and Hudson lines of cars, for instance, eliminated the tooling for a separate basic body for Hudson, saving American Motors millions of dollars that otherwise would have been required. The use of common tooling for several lines was considered one of the major advantages of larger automotive firms. Also, within a year after the merger, the warehouses of American Motors were reduced in number from 34 to 18 and zone sales offices were consolidated to handle both makes.

The objective of obtaining the advantages of larger size through merger was further supported by George Romney, then president of American Motors, in his Congressional testimony. Although they thought that many influences other than those of size had adversely influenced Nash and Hudson, officials of American Motors believed that their major competitors "had been aided in their drives for a larger share of the automotive market by competitive ad-

[4] *The Wall Street Journal*, January 15, 1954, p. 16, quoting a joint statement issued by A. E. Barit and George Mason.

[5] *Ibid.*; also, see U. S., Senate, Committee on the Judiciary, Subcommittee on Antitrust and Monopoly, *op. cit.*, pp. 446-65. Testimony of George Romney.

[6] American Motors Corporation, *Annual Report*, 1954, p. 1.

vantages resulting from their comparatively greater size and volume operations."[7] In their opinion, the most outstanding example of the advantage of larger size to a car producer was in the cost of tooling for the basic body of a car. Observing that there was a trend toward more frequent and complete styling changes in the automobile industry after 1950, Romney contended that the merger put Nash and Hudson in a better cost position to participate in style competition. Changing the style of new cars may add to their cost, but it also helps to sell them. A rise in the costs of style change to four or five times the prewar level, according to American Motors officials, was an impelling reason for the merger between Nash and Hudson, since the companies were at the time the only domestic firms using the unit body-frame type of construction. For single plant production at the time, it was reported, the tooling for a separate car cost approximately $15,000,000 to $20,000,000.[8]

American Motors officials believed that the combined Nash and Hudson advertising expenditures would provide greater impact on the public at lower unit cost, that larger volume would result in greater consumer acceptance of their firm's products, and that their innovations as a large firm were more likely to be accepted as the latest and best styles than equally good or better innovations by them as separate small firms. Romney doubted, for instance, that the wraparound windshield would have been widely accepted if it had been introduced by a small volume seller.[9]

In addition, Romney contended that the Independents were hampered in their bargaining with the union by their smaller size. He admitted that managers of the small firms had been partly at fault in readily conceding to the unions in the early postwar years. However, he also contended that this was partly a matter of the relative bargaining strength of the large union against the small company.[10]

THE STUDEBAKER-PACKARD MERGER

Studebaker and Packard officials also expected to secure improvements in operating performance from an increase in the scale of their operations from combination. The pooling

[7] Testimony of George Romney, *op. cit.*, p. 447.
[8] *Ibid.*, pp. 447-50.
[9] *Ibid.*, pp. 450-52, 455-56, and 471, for this paragraph.
[10] *Ibid.*, pp. 457 and 459.

of manufacturing facilities was expected to result in increased efficiency and lower unit costs in an elimination of duplication and a provision for use of interchangeable parts. The combining of research and engineering staffs was expected to provide an opportunity for a better use of facilities, reduction of duplicated effort in engineering and design, possibly better research, and lower research costs per unit.[11] Because of its anticipated greater financial resources, it also was believed that the new company would be in a better position for future growth and able "to diversify its products in various ways, including the possible acquisition of other businesses."[12]

The merger offered "wider coverage of the market, economies in manufacturing and other operating areas, research advantages and an opportunity for savings in tooling costs on new designs through the use of interchangeable parts," and it permitted "dealer franchising fitted to each community."[13] A larger and stronger dealer organization was expected to be available.

The asserted advantages of merger also were supported in the Congressional testimony of J. J. Nance, then president of Studebaker-Packard.[14] While acknowledging that the small firms in the car industry were small only in relation to the Big Three, Nance considered the decline of the Independents to be the result of "some very fundamental forces at work within the industry."[15] The shift from a sellers' market to a buyers' market after mid-1953 brought out many competitive weaknesses of the smaller firms. The size of a firm, according to Nance, while not the exclusive factor, had without doubt been a significant influence on the performance of the Independents under the changed conditions. The mergers were the result of the desire of the leading Independents to survive as participants in the passenger car industry, largely through increasing their scale of operations.[16]

[11] *The Wall Street Journal*, June 23, 1954, p. 8, an article by staff reporter John D. Williams on the plans for combining Studebaker and Packard; and *The New York Times*, June 23, 1954, pp. 1 and 37, reporting on a joint statement issued by officials of Studebaker and Packard.

[12] *The New York Times*, July 12, 1954, p. 27.

[13] Studebaker-Packard Corporation, *Annual Report*, 1954, p. 5.

[14] See U. S., Senate, Committee on the Judiciary, Subcommittee on Antitrust and Monopoly, *op. cit.*, pp. 858-80. Testimony of J. J. Nance.

[15] *Ibid.*, p. 860.

[16] See *ibid.*, esp. pp. 864, 869, 873, and 875.

A postwar movement toward broader coverage of the market by the major makes of cars contributed to selling problems at the dealer level for the Independents whose cars had been relatively specialized in their market appeals and coverage. This development tended to eliminate sharp price classes. In the prewar period, each make had aimed at a certain market price class; but these distinctions largely disappeared in the postwar market with each make seeking ever larger shares. It was believed that dealers of the multiple line producers secured an advantage in appealing to broader market groups through dualing several makes in smaller communities. Studebaker and Packard dealer volumes and strength were expected to be maintained in the same way. Studebaker covered the low and lower middle price classes while Packard covered the upper middle and highest price classes.[17] Such broad coverage was the pattern followed by the largest and most successful of the car manufacturers.[18]

Nance said that since total tooling costs for new models had increased 200 per cent above prewar levels, a principal desire of Packard in the merger was to obtain the economies of larger volume in spreading tooling expenses.[19]

DISPARITIES IN THE SIZES OF CAR PRODUCERS

Even before the mergers in 1954, the leading independent automobile manufacturers were relatively large firms compared to most business enterprises. Having many thousands of employees, dealers, suppliers, and creditors, hundreds of thousands of past and prospective customers, assets valued in hundreds of millions of dollars, and sales volumes of even greater magnitudes, the leading Independents were important enterprises with extensive operations. In 1950, all four of the leading Independents were ranked among the 200 largest industrial corporations of the United States.[20] Their assets ranged from almost $100,000,000 for Packard, the smallest, to more than $189,000,000 for Nash-Kelvinator, the largest. Following the two mergers among the leading Independents, which were among the largest ever to occur in the history

[17] *Ibid.*, pp. 863-64.

[18] Studebaker-Packard Corporation, *Annual Report*, 1954, p. 5.

[19] Testimony of J. J. Nance, *op. cit.*, pp. 862 and 866.

[20] U. S., Federal Trade Commission, *Industrial Concentration and Product Diversification in the 1,000 Largest Manufacturing Companies: 1950* (Washington: U. S. Government Printing Office, 1957), pp. 650-51.

of business in the United States, American Motors Corporation was 87th in assets and 81st in sales, and Studebaker-Packard Corporation was 109th in assets and 75th in sales among the 500 largest industrial companies listed by *Fortune* in 1955.[21]

It was only in comparison with the Big Three of the automobile industry that the leading Independents were relatively small. In 1950, the assets of the Big Three ranged from approximately $744,000,000 for Chrysler, the smallest, to more than $3,444,000,000 for General Motors, the largest. The Big Three usually have been at the top of the *Fortune* list, General Motors, for example, having been second in assets, Ford fifth, and Chrysler 14th in 1955. In the same year, General Motors was first in sales, Ford third, and Chrysler fifth.

So great was the dominance of the automobile industry by the Big Three that in no single year from 1946 through 1963 was the share of new passenger car registrations of all Independents greater than the share held by the cars of Chrysler Corporation, the smallest of the Big Three. Thus, while the leading Independents were large compared with most corporations, they were small compared with their principal competitors.

SIGNIFICANCE OF THE MERGERS

It seems clear that a principal objective of the leading Independents was the acquisition of anticipated advantages of larger volume operations. The mergers represented a striving for larger size to improve the Independents' competitive positions relative to the much larger Big Three firms. Officials of the Independents publicly emphasized the importance of this objective; and the fact that the two remaining firms struggled to maintain their several automotive product programs in the face of heavy losses supports the argument that the mergers were not accomplished as the least painful way of going out of business, although the net effect four years after the mergers was the complete elimination of Hudson and Packard. Merger had appeared to offer a means first of survival and second of prosperity.

Although only a few firms were in the domestic passenger car industry, it generally has been considered that a high degree of competition, at least of a qualitative type, existed

21 "The Fortune Directory," A supplement to *Fortune*, LIII (July, 1956), 3.

among the members of the industry. The Federal Trade Commission reached such a conclusion in the late 1930's;[22] and many observers considered the period beginning in 1953 to be the industry's most highly competitive.[23] If this was the case, the ability of the Independents to achieve the scale of output needed to produce the desired products at low unit cost appeared essential to remaining in business. Of course unit cost disadvantages of small volume might have been partially overcome through superior product differentiation, an alternative course of action but one which may be difficult to sustain because of imitation.

While size was not the exclusive factor accounting for the difficulties of the Independents after 1952, it was clearly considered a most significant factor by officials of the independent firms. If the Independents did indeed suffer from their small size, as their officials frequently asserted, their potential for survival and prosperity could be increased by becoming larger. Fundamental economic adjustments were required to overcome the disadvantages of insufficient size; mere replacement of existing factors of production was insufficient. Actual increases in factor use and volume of output were necessary. In essence the mergers were considered urgent responses to alleviate problems of small firm size.

SOME QUESTIONS

Was the emphasis of the Independents' officials misplaced? Were the leading Independents indeed so small as to suffer significant disadvantages because of their smallness? Or, were the frequently alleged problems of their relatively small size merely rationalizations for otherwise inefficient and ineffectual organizations? As we have seen, factors other than size were important. Which were the more important? The observations of the Independents' officials in support of the mergers provide suggestions for further study.

---

[22] U. S., Federal Trade Commission, *Report on Motor Vehicle Industry*, 76th Congress, 1st Session, House Document No. 468 (Washington: U. S. Government Printing Office, 1939), pp. 1073-74.

[23] Testimony of J. J. Nance, *op. cit.*, p. 864, for opinion of industry observers as reported by Nance.

Chapter VIII

THE MANUFACTURING PROBLEM

A MONG THE MANY possible influences on a firm's financial performance is the accomplishment of sufficient volume to permit acquisition of manufacturing economies of scale— the unit cost savings arising from increased outputs which permit the firm to make more efficient use of fixed productive resources as it grows in size. The unit cost savings arise from changes in technological efficiency as output is increased; and they may provide the large firm unit cost advantages over its smaller competitors, if it is actually able to expand to the output levels required for low unit cost operation.

As we have seen, the leading Independents considered their financial difficulties to be traceable mainly to their relatively small sizes. But were they in fact too small as separate firms to accomplish low unit costs of automobile manufacture?

NATURE OF MANUFACTURING ECONOMIES OF SCALE

At any given time, certain factors of production are fixed relative to a firm's volume of output; they are indivisible units. Once a firm commits itself to the use of those productive factors which are technologically available at any particular time, it has committed itself to the bearing of certain fixed total charges. Spreading such charges over a larger number of units will reduce unit costs if variable charges per unit—mainly direct labor and material costs that change with total output—are not increased. Indeed, "from a formal viewpoint almost all deviations from constant returns can be subsumed under indivisibilities."[1]

How do "indivisibilities" of productive factors arise and how does overcoming them lead to lower unit cost operatons? An answer to this question was provided long ago.[2] The

[1] George J. Stigler, *The Theory of Price* (New York: The Macmillan Company, 1946), p. 134.

[2] Adam Smith, *An Inquiry into the Nature and Causes of the Wealth of Nations*, edited by Edwin Cannan (New York: The Modern Library reprint published by Random House, Inc.), Book I, Chapter I, pp. 3-12.

division of labor, specialization, and standardization accompanying an increase in the scale of a firm permit more efficient operation. The more extensive division of labor leads to an increase in the skill of the worker, to the elimination of time lost in going from one type of work to another, and to the development of specialized machinery to facilitate the work being performed. Specialization of the worker on a job permits him to become an expert in its performance. Standardization of processes provides opportunities for development of machinery to replace human effort. And once a specific process is selected, the specialized mechanical and human factors become fixed in relation to volume of output. Superior techniques are developed and utilized. Their integration provides a more efficient flow of work and lower unit costs than can be obtained without the division of labor and use of specialized machinery.

The influence of scale on efficiency may be illustrated in the process of integration required to achieve the most favorable cost position by a firm using indivisible productive factors. Under the existing technology and with other factors held constant, let us assume that a firm uses three types of equipment in the production of a certain product and that these items are integrated into a continuous process. If the first type of equipment has a capacity of 50,000 units per year, the second a capacity of 75,000 units per year, and the third a capacity of 100,000 units per year, all on a straight time basis of 2,000 hours per year, the annual output on a straight time basis which would provide the most effective utilization of the three types of equipment requires the lowest multiple of output into which the capacity of each type is fully divisible, or 300,000 units per year. On a straight time basis, this would require six units of the first type, four of the second type, and three of the third type to utilize fully all of the available capacity provided by the use of any of the equipment.

If more than one shift were used, it would be possible to work out other combinations. For example, three units of the third type could be used on a one-shift operation with two of the second type operating on two shifts and two of the first type on three shifts. Still, if the most efficient technical use of indivisible equipment is desired, some multiples of the capacities must be used, leading to larger scale for the firm organizing production using such fixed equipment.

The accompaniment of more extensive use of the division of labor, standardization, and specialization—whether of human or mechanical factors—is a pressure to increase the scale of a firm's operations to permit full utilization of fixed factors of production in order to obtain the lowest unit cost. The development of highly specialized and often very expensive equipment requires an organization of substantial size to utilize the equipment fully. Technology, of course, is not constant. Refinements in processes are continually being made; and occasionally major innovations are introduced. With the elapse of time, technological innovation may lead to the replacement of older equipment and processes with new equipment and processes which serve to reintroduce elements of divisibility in productive factors; choices of equipment and process alternatives can sometimes be made for lower rather than higher capacity with little or no sacrifice in unit cost. However, at any given time when a decision must be made selecting an actual production process, the factors of production chosen to some extent will be indivisible. Unit cost savings will accrue to the scale of output at which all fixed factors integrated in productive processes are being fully utilized with no waste of productive potential; and, when a firm is thus able to use its productive resources most fully as a result of increased volume of output, it is securing maximum benefits of economies of scale. Total costs may have increased, but unit costs are lowered.

Given the state of the productive art, the nature of the specialized machinery and equipment, and the human resources available to the firms of an industry, there is probably some minimum level of output which the firm must achieve in order to approximate the position of minimum unit cost in manufacturing. It is conceivable also for approximately the same unit cost to prevail over a considerable range of outputs; but if productive factors are duplicated beyond the first most efficient combination of fixed factors, there probably will be variations in unit cost as output is gradually increased. The change is not continuous. "Indivisible services, by their very nature, lead to alternating stages of increasing and decreasing returns to scale of plant."[3] Beyond the first most efficient combination of productive factors in a plant, the firm may increase its scale by complete duplication of existing facilities with little change in unit

[3] Stigler, *op. cit.*, p. 134.

manufacturing costs, assuming that the firm is not so large in the market in which it is buying that its expansion causes an increase in the costs of obtaining productive factors. For intermediate ranges of output between duplication of complete plants, costs would first rise and then fall.

When a firm is large enough to achieve the first most efficient, integrated one-plant combination for full utilization of fixed productive factors, it may be in a position to produce at as low a unit cost as a larger multiplant firm, if its variable costs per unit are comparable to those of the larger firms. However, in order to achieve the benefits of economies of scale, a necessary accompaniment of an increase in the extent of the firm's commitment to fixed manufacturing investment is that the actual level of output be maintained at the volume required to approximate or equal that for the best use of the fixed productive factors. This will be the minimum unit cost range of output of the firm, assuming that direct material and labor costs per unit are constant. The actual prediction of a best output level may be more complicated than this, since direct material and labor costs per unit often vary; and the same may be true of selling prices of the goods produced. Still, the major implication is, of course, that the firm must be able to sell the larger volume of goods in order to realize the full advantages of economies of scale in manufacturing. Otherwise, there will be a failure to secure the savings which are potentially available because idle capacity will exist and must be amortized over the actual volume of output. In such a case, a level of output smaller than the minimum unit cost output volume is required to bear the fixed costs of the entire facility; and the result is a higher unit cost than would prevail at full capacity operations.

COST DIFFERENTIALS AND PROFITS

Even seemingly small cost differentials may have substantial influence on the financial returns of a firm. If they are not offset by other cost rises and are transferred intact to the profit residual of the firm, manufacturing cost savings may greatly increase the rate of return of a firm. If manufacturing costs equalled 90 cents, selling and administrative costs five cents, and profit five cents on each $1.00 of sales, a 10 per cent reduction in manufacturing cost to 81 cents would enlarge the profit residual to 14 cents, thus providing a 280 per cent profit increase. In spite of the obvious over-simplification, it appears that even slight manufacturing cost differentials may exert extensive influence on the financial statements of a firm.

ORGANIZATION FOR AUTOMOBILE MANUFACTURE

The nature of productive processes in the passenger car manufacturing industry has been such that cost differentials were expected with variations in the scale of operations of the firm. Building on the accumulated technological knowledge of previous years, enormously complex, integrated, and highly mechanized productive processes were developed by the firms of the industry. Extensive use was made of highly specialized material and human resources whose potential capacities could be most fully utilized in firms of substantial size.

The process of manufacturing passenger cars generally was carried out in a number of stages. The basic materials involved were primarily metal products although much use was made of fabrics and plastics. Sheet metals, metal castings, and other metal products were the basic materials making up most of the weight of a passenger car. Many parts were combined into component groups, such as axles, transmissions, engines, or carburetors, before being brought together at a later assembly stage with all the other parts and components required for assembly of the completed car. Many of the parts and components used in final assembly were produced by the car manufacturers; but many customarily also were purchased from outside suppliers. Usually the major parts, components, and bodies were produced by the car manufacturers themselves, although they may not have produced all of their requirements.

Lewis D. Crusoe, then vice-president of Ford Motor Company, described the organization of production in the car industry as follows:

> Automobile facilities are usually provided in basic complements of facilities. In other words, if you are going to put together a shop to make engines, you put together a line, let us say, to make a thousand engines a day, and if you wanted 2,000 you would put in another complete line, a balanced line. It grows in those kinds of multiples. That is the way

the industry is tooled, and that is the way the machine tools are built, all related to a given volume.[4]

The existence of "indivisible" factors in the passenger car manufacturing industry thus occurred in "plant complexes" and not in single plants.[5] Along with the specialized facilities and equipment used in operating, whole plants were specialized. Some plants made engines, others made bodies, others made only door handles and body trim. The organization of their work required an integrated "plant complex" comparable to the "plant" as it is usually conceived. In all of these plant complexes, extensive use was made of expensive "indivisible" equipment including foundries, mechanized conveyor systems, lathes, presses, assembly lines, and machines, often automatically controlled, in enormous variety and complexity.

VOLUME REQUIREMENTS FOR "LOW" UNIT COST

Although dollar cost figures are not publicly obtainable, industry officials have made available information on the minimum level of output which had to be achieved in passenger car manufacturing operations to approximate the range of lowest unit cost using the technology prevailing in the 1950's. Since the exchange of production technology has been common in the automobile industry, these observations, which were based on engineering relationships for effective utilization of fixed or "indivisible" productive factors, seem fairly representative of industry opinion on the minimum levels of output required for low unit manufacturing cost.

Romney Statements

One of the most detailed statements on volume-cost relationships in passenger car production was presented by George Romney, then president of American Motors Cor-

[4] U. S., Senate, Committee on the Judiciary, Subcommittee on Antitrust and Monopoly, *Hearings, A Study of the Antitrust Laws*, 84th Congress, 1st Session, Pursuant to S. Res. 61 (Washington: U. S. Government Printing Office, 1955), Part 2, p. 662.

[5] Joe S. Bain, *Barriers to New Competition* (Cambridge, Mass.: Harvard University Press, 1956), p. 244. Bain refers to an automobile plant as a related complex of facilities which are used in manufacturing components normally integrated by the assembler and in the subsequent assembly operation. He considers this related complex of facilities as comparable to the usual economic concept of the plant.

poration, to the Kefauver committee, the Subcommittee on Antitrust and Monopoly of the Senate Committee on the Judiciary, on February 7, 1958. Romney indicated the following conditions held in the fabrication and assembly of cars:[6]

Our studies, based on our own experience and that of our competitors, [show] that optimum manufacturing conditions are achieved with a production rate of 62.5 cars per hour per assembly line. To absorb the desired machine-line and press-line rate, two final assembly lines would be required. Of course, your press line and your machine line are the principal lines on which you depend for work leading up to subassemblies and the ultimate production of the car itself on the assembly line. This would result in production of 1,000 cars per shift.

A company that can build between 180,000 and 220,000 cars a year on a one-shift basis can make a very good profit and not take a back seat to anyone in the industry in production efficiency. On a two-shift basis, annual production of 360,000 to 440,000 cars will achieve additional small economies but beyond that volume only theoretical and insignificant reductions in manufacturing costs are possible. It is possible to be one of the best without being the biggest.[7]

Earlier, in 1955, Harlow Curtice, then president of General Motors Corporation, had indicated that a firm producing only 30 cars per hour would be large enough to secure the benefits of economies of scale in manufacturing operations.[8]

[6] Some years later, after American Motors Corporation had actually worked on a two-shift basis, Bernard A. Chapman, currently executive vice-president of American Motors, expressed the opinion that the Romney statements were an accurate representation of volume-cost relationships in the automobile industry except for the economies of operation on a two-shift basis. Chapman considered the unit cost savings of two-shift operation "substantial" rather than "small." Although premium wage payments were necessary for a second shift, the savings from more intensive use of fixed investment resulted in substantial benefits. Personal interview of Bernard A. Chapman, February 19, 1963.

[7] U. S., Senate, Committee on the Judiciary, Subcommittee on Antitrust and Monopoly, *Hearings, Administered Prices*, 85th Congress, 2nd Session, Pursuant to S. Res. 57 and S. Res. 231 (Washington: U. S. Government Printing Office, 1958), Part 6, p. 2851. Testimony of George Romney.

[8] U. S., Senate, Committee on the Judiciary, Subcommittee on Antitrust and Monopoly, *Hearings, A Study of the Antitrust Laws, op. cit.*, Part 8, pp. 4044 and 4048.

Recalling the earlier comments of Curtice, Romney further said:

> I would like to remind committee members that the testimony I am giving is not at variance basically with what Mr. Curtice has stated previously in hearings held here in Washington. . . .

> Well, I think 30 cars an hour is a little low. I think 62—it used to be 30. Pre-World War II you could do it with 30. You cannot do it with 30 today because cost factors have increased so it is about double where it used to be. But my point is that his figure was lower than the figure I am using, and also my point is that when you get up to 180,000 to 200,000 cars a year, the cost reduction flattens out, from a manufacturing cost standpoint, and from 360,000 to 400,000 on up it is a negligible thing.[9]

Romney also compared the position of the smaller firms with the organization of production by the Big Three.

> Now the thing you have to keep in mind is that the 1½ million Chevrolets or Fords that are produced a year . . . are not all produced in one plant. They are produced at plants scattered all over the United States, from an assembly standpoint and a good deal of the other processes are scattered.[10]

[9] U. S., Senate, Committee on the Judiciary, Subcommittee on Antitrust and Monopoly, *Hearings, Administered Prices, loc. cit.* Attention also may be directed to a prewar study of the automobile industry in which it was reported that the average unit manufacturing cost of Plymouth was $503 in 1937 with an output of less than 459,000 units in comparison with an average unit manufacturing cost of $502 for Chevrolet in the same year at an output of almost 906,000 units. Unit distribution and administrative costs averaged $21 for Plymouth and $25 for Chevrolet in 1937, resulting in a $3 lower total unit cost for Plymouth. Yet Plymouth averaged about $17 more per unit in average sales price at $573. Similar patterns were also apparent in earlier years. U. S., Federal Trade Commission, *Report on Motor Vehicle Industry*, 76th Congress, 1st Session, House Document No. 468 (Washington: U. S. Government Printing Office, 1939), pp. 538 and 603.

[10] U. S., Senate, Committee on the Judiciary, Subcommittee on Antitrust and Monopoly, *Hearings, Administered Prices, op. cit.*, pp. 2851-52. In 1958, for example, the Ford car was assembled in 15 different plants scattered throughout the country and Chevrolet in 10. Smaller volume makes were assembled in correspondingly fewer plants and some, such as Lincoln and Cadillac as well as the cars of the Independents, were each assembled in only one plant. The transportation factor, of course, was an important element in the dispersion of assembly plants when sufficient volume existed to permit regional assembly. *Infra*, chapter ix.

Confirmation of other industry spokesmen.—Observations of other industry officials have been consistent with the volume-cost estimates presented by Romney. Edgar F. Kaiser, at the time president of Kaiser Motors Corporation, also testifying before the same Subcommittee, stated that an integrated firm the size of Kaiser Motors could acquire good cost results at outputs from 250 cars on up per day. He further said, "When you again get up to this 800 or a thousand or over, then you can improve your competitive position by starting to make some of your own parts."[11] At smaller volumes it would be cheaper to buy from outside suppliers. The higher output figures specified by Kaiser approximate the Romney estimates.

At the same hearings, J. J. Nance, then president of Studebaker-Packard Corporation, refused to comment on the level of output required to achieve the benefits of larger scale in manufacturing, contending that the question was only academic since his firm then had substantial unused capacity.[12] However, Nance did indicate that his firm had carried out cost studies of manufacturing passenger cars and that these studies showed the required level to be within the capacity of Studebaker-Packard.[13] At this time the firm had the capacity to produce approximately 470,000 cars per year.[14]

With its contributions to increased machine utilization

[11] U. S., Senate, Committee on the Judiciary, Subcommittee on Antitrust and Monopoly, *Hearings, A Study of the Antitrust Laws, op. cit.,* Part 2, p. 545.

[12] *Ibid.,* p. 873.

[13] *Ibid.,* p. 867.

[14] In 1950, Studebaker actually produced over 268,000 units. Automobile Manufacturers Association, *Automobile Facts and Figures,* 1958 edition (Detroit, Michigan), p. 10. Packard actually produced about 105,000 units in 1949. *Ibid.* Earlier Packard had reported that some parts of its plant were equipped for 200,000 units per year and that it planned to bring the rest up to that level. The main bottleneck was in foundry, transmission, and axle production. Packard Motor Car Company, *Annual Report,* 1946, p. 9. The new Utica plant completed in 1954 was devoted principally to these items, presumably overcoming the bottleneck. Packard Motor Car Company, *Annual Report,* 1954, pp. 6 and 13. In 1955, Studebaker-Packard's physical capacity was "some 470,000 units" per year. U. S., Congress, Joint Committee on the Economic Report, Subcommittee on Economic Stabilization, *Hearings, Automation and Technological Change,* 84th Congress, 1st Session, Pursuant to Sec. 5 (a) of P. L. 304, 79th Congress (Washington: U. S. Government Printing Office, 1955), p. 416. Statement of Studebaker-Packard Corporation.

and to savings in labor cost, automation—a word coined by
Del S. Harder who was at the time a vice-president of Ford
Motor Company—was an important feature in the design of
automobile manufacturing facilities during the 1950's despite
its attendant requirements for greater fixed investment,
pressures for increased output to obtain low capital costs
per unit of output, and reductions in flexibility of operations
and model changes.[15] It is interesting to note that the actual
physical capacities resulting from automation of engine machine lines, in which automation perhaps had its greatest refinement, ranged up to outputs of approximately 500,000
or more units per year on a two-shift basis, a level roughly
consistent with the Romney estimates. Although higher
outputs may have been feasible engineering choices, actual
capacities extended over a rather wide range, resulting in the
early 1950's, for example, in 60 engines per hour for DeSoto,
90 for Oldsmobile, 98 for Ford for V-8 engines, and 144 for
Ford for six-cylinder engines. Plymouth's V-8 engine plant
completed in 1955 was designed for an output of 150 engines
per hour from two block lines and four head lines in an integrated process including automated assembly. Attention also
may be called to Lewis Crusoe's previously quoted comments
on engine facilities.

Automated processes were also features of the engine
lines of several of the Independents. Following Ford's lead,
Studebaker was among the first to install an automated line
for machining engine blocks in 1950; and Packard's Utica
plant included an automated engine line completed in 1954.
Packard's line for production of its new V-8 engine for the
1955 models had a capacity of about 160,000 units per year.

[15] See, e.g., Rupert LeGrand, "Ford Handles by Automation," *American
Machinist*, October 21, 1948, pp. 107-22; LeGrand, "How Ford Automates
Production Lines," *American Machinist*, March 17, 1952, pp. 135-50;
"Automation: A Factory Runs Itself," *Business Week*, March 29, 1952,
pp. 146-48; Organization for European Economic Co-operation, *Some
Aspects of the Motor Vehicle Industry in the U. S. A.* (Paris: 1953),
Technical Assistance Mission No. 92, pp. 17-18; U. S., Congress, Joint
Committee on the Economic Report, *op. cit.*, esp. pp. 51-69, Statement of
D. J. Davis, vice-president, Ford Motor Company; *ibid.*, pp. 416-18, State-
ment of Studebaker-Packard Corp.; James R. Bright, *Automation and
Management* (Boston: Graduate School of Business Administration, Har-
vard University, 1958), esp. pp. 4-5, 59-64, 84-85, 113-15, and 118; George
DeGroat, "Plymouth Puts 'Forward Look' into V-8 Production," *American
Machinist*, August 15, 1955, Special Report No. 400, pp. 88 A-P; and
DeGroat, "Rebuilding Building Block Machines,"*American Machinist*,
October 5, 1959, pp. 81-83.

However, the basic production cycle for the line was fitted to the slowest single machine operation rather than having multiple work stations—and higher capacity—to accommodate the faster operations as was the case for automated lines of some other manufacturers.[16] Thus, the over-all efficiency in machine utilization of the Packard line probably was somewhat lower than the best in the industry. Packard, however, had the plant in operation so short a time before giving it up to Curtiss-Wright that it probably did not even get the "bugs" out of the operation.

It is interesting to observe also that the Big Three often set volume targets of approximately 200,000 units per year in introduction of new models. Ford's plans for the ill-fated Edsel included a target of about 200,000 units per year.[17] Furthermore, the Big Three were reluctant to introduce their "compact" models until sufficient sales volumes could be anticipated to provide 200,000 or so units for each make.[18] These were the Corvair, Falcon, and Valiant models first introduced in 1959. Targets of 200,000 units per year were consistent with a belief that minimum unit manufacturing costs were obtained at such levels of output.

Inclusion of tooling costs.—The Romney estimates placing the output level for low unit cost at a minimum of about 180,000 to 220,000 cars per year included tooling costs, at least for the special tooling as such which may include thousands of dies and a wide variety of other special jigs and equipment for a specific model. Expenditures on design and planning of tooling requirements for model changeovers apparently were not included. In the opinion of American Motors' officials at the time of Romney's testimony, it was not necessary to achieve a larger volume for unit tooling costs to remain relatively constant:

> Now I have been discussing the manufacturing cost aspects of the automobile business in relationship to volume. There are other aspects of it, but I think I have said enough to indicate that the huge volumes that the Big Three have are not necessary to get efficient and minimum manufacturing costs.

[16] "Automation Works for Limited Volume, Too," *Steel*, December 27, 1954, pp. 41-42.

[17] *Business Week*, January 25, 1958, p. 120.

[18] Ford planned to bring out a compact car only when the total market for such cars reached about 500,000 units per year. *Business Week*, March 29, 1958, p. 27.

Now let's take tooling. There are all sorts of tooling, and when you provide tooling for high volume, you provide more expensive tooling and it costs more, and beyond these areas I am talking about you get into duplications, and if you take the most modern tooling on a 440,000 basis or a 360,000 basis, which is that required for most highly efficient manufacturing results, then you have got about double the cost for that tooling as compared to tooling for 180,-000 to 220,000 units, and if you will take the two sets of costs and divide them by volume per unit, it happens that the cost per unit comes out right on the button.

So all this talk about the disadvantage of lack of volume in relationship to tooling costs is grossly exaggerated. What I am saying is that if you have got 180,000 to 220,000 volume a year, you can compete effectively and efficiently in the automobile industry. . . .[19]

Thus, according to the Romney statement, a firm which was able to achieve an annual volume of about 200,000 units on a one-shift basis or 400,000 units on two shifts could be expected to secure most of the economies of scale available from the manufacturing technology of the 1950's. Although this was a substantial volume of cars, it was still a relatively small portion of a market for 6,000,000 cars per year and a relatively small output compared to those of the Big Three.

The problem of special tooling.—On an historical basis, a comparison of the actual special tooling costs of the leading Independents with those of the Big Three seems to support the Romney observations on volume-cost relationships. For only a few years, particularly in the period of rapid writeoff of obsolete, surplus, or inadequate equipment because of the mergers, were the actual accounting costs for amortization of special tooling per car greater for the leading Independents than for the Big Three.[20] However, the historical accounting costs do not tell the whole story.

Major economic discrepancies may have existed in the variations between the large and small firms in intensity of use of the special tooling—whether used on a one-, two-, or three-shift basis—and in the question of whether the smaller firms could amortize their tooling over longer periods of time

---

[19] U. S., Senate, Committee on the Judiciary, Subcommittee on Antitrust and Monopoly, *Hearings, Administered Prices, op. cit.*, pp. 2852-53.
[20] *Infra*, Tables 13 and 14.

and still have adequate sales. The actual choices made by management determined the historical accounting costs that eventually were reported. If the Independents could have used their tooling over longer periods of time, as they had tried to do in the past, and could have avoided low sales levels, a feat which they did not accomplish from 1953 through 1957, they presumably could have obtained unit tooling costs comparable to those of the Big Three for equivalent changes, according to Romney. But this was a big "if" since the ultimate tooling costs were a result of both the extent of the style change and the frequency of change, both of which conceivably influenced the level of sales of the firms. This problem is discussed further in a later chapter.

The Independents achieved their lower special tooling expenses by making less frequent major and less extensive minor style changes. They generally amortized their tooling over longer periods of time.[21] They have thus achieved relatively low historical tooling costs, although this may often have been accomplished at the expense of diminished sales since it was believed that style changes stimulated sales of the individual firm.[22] Nevertheless, according to Romney, the unit costs of special tooling of the Independents would have approximated those of the Big Three for comparable changes, if the Independents had maintained minimum outputs of about 200,000 units per year on a one-shift basis.

Apparent contradiction in statements.—The careful reader may conclude that a contradiction exists in Romney's contention that the Independents were not at a disadvantage in tooling for model changes and the comments that increasing tooling costs were a fundamental reason for the mergers. Romney indicated that the Independents had the potential to achieve optimum unit tooling costs at output levels of 200,000 to 400,000 units per year. Prior to the mergers, only Studebaker among the leading Independents had exceeded 200,000 units in the postwar period and then only in the three years 1949-1951 with outputs ranging from 222,000 to 268,000 units. After the mergers among the leading Independents, each of the new combinations would have

---

[21] See, e.g., Bain, *op. cit.*, p. 299, for comments on this point.

[22] Theodore Yntema, vice-president of Ford Motor Company, for example, indicated that his firm changed its cars frequently "because that is the only way we can sell cars." U. S., Senate, Committee on the Judiciary, Subcommittee on Antitrust and Monopoly, *Hearings, Administered Prices, op. cit.*, p. 2658.

achieved outputs well in excess of 200,000 units *if* the volumes attained by each of the merging companies in the period from 1947 through 1953 could have been continued. An apparent contradiction would have resulted from comparison of actual outputs with potential production levels. The firms had sufficient physical productive capacity to achieve the necessary levels for low unit cost, possibly before and certainly after the mergers; but they generally had not actually achieved even the one-shift minimum of 200,000 units per year of one body shell required for low tooling costs except in the few years cited for Studebaker.

Bain Estimates

Information on the existence of economies of scale in the production of passenger cars around 1950 has been provided by Joe Bain. The estimates of Professor Bain were based on survey questionnaire responses from officials of the firms engaged in the automobile industry.[23]

Although considerable overlap occurs in the estimates, Professor Bain's estimates of the minimum volume needed to achieve low unit cost were approximately 50 per cent higher than those of Romney, the discrepancy perhaps being partly a result of the time interval between Bain's and Romney's estimates. On the basis of his study of the industry, Professor Bain concluded:

> In general, 300,000 units per annum is a low estimate of what is needed for productive efficiency in any one line; there are probable added advantages to 600,000 units.
>
> These estimates refer to production costs alone and not to advantages of large-scale sales promotion and distributive systems. . . . As regards the shape of the plant scale curve at smaller outputs, the trend of the estimates is that costs would be "moderately" higher at 150,000 units, . . . substantially higher at 60,000 units, and uneconomical at smaller scales. But it has been impossible to obtain quantitative estimates of what a "moderate" cost disadvantage is; the firms of the automobile industry seem generally uninterested in publicizing their plant and firm scale curves.[24]

Bain also indicated that the necessity for integration of en-

---

[23] Bain, *op. cit.*, pp. 49-51.
[24] *Ibid.*, p. 245. Reprinted by permission of Harvard University Press.

gine and body subassemblies in the final assembly process required that the integrated operation be larger than that required for assembly alone.

The critical stage in plant economies is evidently found in the production of components and not in assembly. In assembly alone, from 60,000 to 180,000 units per annum is considered optimal, with advantages to a multiplant decentralized development as the critical figure is passed. There are some components which are typically either integrated by the assembler or otherwise manufactured to special designs so as not to be generally interchangeable with those used by other firms, however, and economies of large plant in the production of these are such as to require, for best over-all efficiency, a larger integrated plant complex than required for efficient assembly alone. The most important components of this sort under traditional automobile-industry practice (as oriented to securing distinctiveness of product) are bodies and engines, which together make up enough of the cost of an automobile to dominate the scale-economy picture.[25]

Maxcy and Silberston Estimates

During 1959, the publication of a study of the British motor car industry by Maxcy and Silberston provided a third major set of observations regarding the influence of size on the unit cost of manufacturing passenger cars.[26] This study contains numerous references to passenger car manufacturing in the United States. Although most of their conclusions agree with the observations of Romney and Bain, one area of conflict with earlier statements appears.

Relying on numerous observations and comments of industry officials, Maxcy and Silberston considered the final assembly of cars to be "a *relatively* small scale operation."[27] They concluded:

The efficient use of the best assembly techniques calls for a volume of roughly 60,000 units per annum, which need not be all of one model . . . but the

[25] *Ibid.*
[26] George Maxcy and Aubrey Silberston, *The Motor Industry* (London: George Allen & Unwin Ltd., 1959).
[27] *Ibid.*, p. 77.

significant economies in car assembly appear to be exhausted at about a volume of 100,000 units.[28] In the case of engine machine lines, Maxcy and Silberston, observing that Ford Motor Company had an automated line capable of producing 140 six-cylinder engine blocks per hour at 80 per cent efficiency, concluded that on a two-shift basis "such an output implies an optimum of over half a million units per annum."[29]

Finally, Maxcy and Silberston suggested that "it is the press shop which sets the over-all optimum for car production —probably in the region of 1,000,000 per annum."[30] Their suggestion was based on an observation that some presses used in stamping out body panels were capable of as many as 4,000 pressings per day.[31] Continuous operation was required to minimize the costs of using the expensive presses and dies. Changing dies was a time-consuming and fairly costly process, since about eight hours was often required to change a large die.[32]

Reconciliation of the Estimates

It is in regard to their estimates of the level of output required in the press shops to minimize unit costs that the conclusions of Maxcy and Silberston disagree somewhat with the statements of Romney and Bain. Although additional cost reductions are theoretically possible at outputs approaching or in excess of 1,000,000 units per year, the savings may be relatively small. Romney, perhaps swayed by his zeal for American Motors, a small company, seemed quite emphatic in his statement that "annual production of 360,-000 to 440,000 cars will achieve additional small economies, but beyond that volume only theoretical and insignificant reductions in manufacturing costs are possible," and that from these levels on up the cost savings were "a negligible thing."[33] It is possible that this apparent conflict is the result of the rather frequent disparity between the "practical" and

[28] *Ibid.*, p. 79.

[29] *Ibid.*, p. 80.

[30] *Ibid.*, p. 82.

[31] Their information was from Organization for European Economic Co-operation, *op. cit.*, p. 18.

[32] Maxcy and Silberston, *op. cit.*, p. 82.

[33] *Supra*, pp. 155-56.

the "theoretical,"[34] especially in relation to the volumes that the companies could expect to sell of any one make, except in the case of the tremendous sales of General Motors Corporation.

The Maxcy and Silberston conclusion was based on the physical output to obtain the lowest fixed investment cost per unit using the best equipment available; but, as a practical matter, the full capacity use of fixed assets may not result in the lowest manufacturing cost per unit. Their conclusion represented the theoretical, the "best" or "optimum," level of output to which Romney alluded; but since total manufacturing costs per unit were a result of a complex interrelationship of fixed and variable (principally labor and material) costs per unit, increased maintenance costs and differential labor costs with overtime or even a third shift to use fixed assets more intensely would tend to offset reductions in fixed costs per unit of output, and this explains the discrepancies in the several estimates. Also, if the customary working day in the passenger car manufacturing industry consisted of no more than two eight-hour shifts, as was fairly widespread practice in fabrication operations, an opportunity for changing dies, maintenance, and other adjustments would have been provided during the customary downtime of the equipment.

The huge presses used in stamping operations could be utilized fairly effectively through cycling of the dies. The dies would create the major problem, since those not in use still would have imposed a fixed cost on the firm. However, very large volumes were required if cycling of dies was to be avoided entirely, volumes in many cases being beyond the customary sales of all but a few makes of the Big Three. While the added handling costs of cycling the dies and the overhead costs of idle dies would be incurred, there would be no loss of customary working time if the dies were changed during other than the usual working hours. Costs of inventory accumulation may also have been somewhat higher with

[34] In commenting to the writer on the organization for automotive production, one industry official indicated that his company could build an integrated operation to fabricate and assemble a vehicle, using only one productive unit of some types of equipment for outputs to 1,000,000 or more units annually *if* the market would absorb the resulting product. However, he declined to estimate the resulting unit cost savings. Considering the historical development of the industry and market realities, the question was considered too theoretical.

intermittent use rather than continuous use of dies and presses; but these probably were small compared to those inventories customarily carried.

In any event, regardless of the observations used, it is clear that a substantial volume was required for the attainment of minimum unit cost levels of output in the manufacturing of passenger cars, and that 200,000 units per year were about the absolute minimum requirement for reasonable unit cost and that 400,000 units were somewhat better to permit two-shift operation and some further unit cost savings.

ACTUAL OUTPUT VS. ESTIMATED REQUIREMENTS

Except for the observations on press shop operations, the estimates of Romney, Bain, and Maxcy and Silberston regarding the minimum level of output needed to achieve low unit manufacturing cost were of approximately the same magnitude. All were below the physical capacities of the Big Three. Whether unit costs rise beyond the theoretical minimum unit cost level of output is not in question; however, the comment by Romney that duplication of facilities was a consequence of one-shift operation beyond about the 200,000 unit level and the decentralization of the Big Three suggest that manufacturing cost per unit could be held relatively constant if the large firms expanded their outputs in multiples of the most efficient one-plant-complex manufacturing unit.

Until American Motors' tremendous comeback with its compact car after 1957, an inability to reach and maintain the minimum level of output required for effective use of fixed productive factors was a major problem of the leading Independents. If the Bain and Romney estimates regarding manufacturing scale economies were even approximately correct, the leading Independents were generally unable to achieve the minimum volumes needed to secure the full unit cost benefits of manufacturing economies of scale. In the postwar period prior to the mergers among the Independents in 1954, only Nash in 1950 and Studebaker for the years 1949-1951 and 1953 exceeded the 180,000 minimum requirement specified by Romney.[35] Only Studebaker exceeded the 220,000 unit level

[35] These and the following comparisons are based on production figures in Automobile Manufacturers Association, *Automobile Facts and Figures*, 1958 edition, p. 10, for the years 1946-1957; and *ibid.*, 1959-1960 edition, p. 10, for the year 1958.

in the three years 1949-1951. From 1946 through 1953, Hudson's production ranged from a low of 76,000 to a high of 155,000 units per year; Nash's ranged from 99,000 to 190,000; Packard's from 42,000 to 105,000, and Studebaker's from 78,-000 to 268,000. In 1954, their outputs fell respectively to 28,000, 67,000, 27,000, and 86,000. In no year from 1946 through 1958 did any of the leading Independents reach the 300,000 minimum estimated by Bain. In no year did any of the Independents even approach the level of output which Maxcy and Silberston considered essential for lowest unit cost in press shop operations.

For the years prior to the mergers in 1954, Studebaker output was often in the range of the Romney minimum and occasionally approached the Bain minimum level; Nash and Hudson approached the Romney minimum but were in the range of "moderately" higher costs according to the Bain estimates; and Packard was in a range for most years corresponding to the "substantially higher" cost estimate of Bain with operation at about half the minimum estimate of Romney. Thus, the Independents were operating at levels of output somewhat lower than those required to achieve the benefits of economies of scale in the manufacture of passenger cars.

In the case of Packard, however, there was a possible moderating influence for the years 1946 through 1953 since Packard purchased body assemblies from Briggs—a firm which also produced Chrysler bodies. Packard may have operated within the lower requirement for efficient assembly operations, for which the minimum was 60,000 cars per year. However, Packard had to bear the expense of the special tooling for style changes.

A comparison of the combined total outputs of the merged companies with the estimated minimum volumes for low unit costs shows clearly why great importance was attached to the accomplishment of larger volume through merger. In each of the years from 1947 through 1953, the combined output of the subsequently merged leading Independents approximated or exceeded the Romney estimated minimum levels and approached or exceeded the Bain estimated minimum levels required to secure low unit manufacturing costs. In this period, the combined Nash and Hudson production ranged from 212,000 to 332,000 units per year, while the combined

Studebaker and Packard output ranged from 179,000 to 340,-000 units. Peak combined output for both combinations was in 1950. Had the firms in those years each been producing lines of cars using only one basic body, unit cost savings of larger manufacturing scale would have been available to them.

It is not surprising then that the Independents faced financial difficulties after the return to a buyers' market in 1953 when prices *and* costs again became significant factors.

Furthermore, after the mergers in 1954, the inability of the Independents to maintain sales at levels sufficient to continue production at the combined levels attained prior to 1953 explains much of their poor financial performance. It was not until 1958 that American Motors with production of 217,000 units again attained a production level equal to the Romney-estimated minimum for good cost results. With two-shift operation in the following years, American Motors' profits surged to record levels. However, Studebaker-Packard, and later Studebaker, never even came close to achieving the combined output levels of their predecessors.

Clearly, the financial returns of the leading Independents were limited generally by their lower volumes and higher unit costs. If the Bain, Romney, and Maxcy and Silberston estimates were even approximately correct, the financial performances of the two remaining Independents as automobile manufacturers depended to a considerable degree on their ability to achieve and maintain minimum levels of output of 200,000 to 300,000 units per year on a one-shift basis; and there probably would have been additional benefits at even higher levels.

THE MERGERS AND MANUFACTURING POTENTIAL

Although the leading Independents expected to improve their manufacturing efficiency by increased volume through merger, the firms individually had the physical capacity to produce at higher levels than they actually achieved prior to the mergers. Studebaker may have been approaching its annual capacity in several years; but, with yearly outputs above 220,000 units from 1949 through 1951, it was already approximating the levels required to secure the benefits of scale economies according to the Romney and Bain estimates and should have been in a favorable manufacturing cost position. Hudson had physical capacity for 250,000 cars on a straight time basis in 1953;[36] and, Nash-Kelvinator had approximately the same capacity.[37] Some operations of Packard were tooled for 200,000 units per year before 1954; and the firm had planned expansion of its other operations.[38]

This volume would have put Hudson and Nash as separate firms in the range above the Romney minimum and approaching the Bain minimum for achieving the volume required for low unit cost operation. In comparison with their estimated physical capacities of 250,000 units, Hudson actually produced only 77,000 cars and Nash only 135,000 in 1953. Packard production for 1953 was 88,000 units. Studebaker production in 1953 reached 187,000 units, far below its earlier peak of 268,000 in 1950.

A SUMMARY COMMENT

Although a failure actually to achieve the output levels required for best unit cost results may have adversely influenced the financial performances of the Independents, their principal difficulty, it may be suggested, was not a lack of manufacturing capacity sufficient to achieve low unit cost; their major problem was an inability to utilize effectively the physical capacity which they had. Foremost among their problems was the circle of interdependence of their selling and manufacturing activities. The Independents' inability to generate sufficient sales to make effective utilization of their capacity was an especially acute problem from 1953 through 1957.

The achievement of minimum unit manufacturing cost levels of output may result in an organization of substantial size, but the accomplishment of effective marketing activities at low unit cost conceivably may require an organization of even greater size.

[36] Hudson Motor Car Company, "Proxy Statement," March 24, 1954, p. 15.

[37] *Ibid.*, p. 6; also, after the merger, American Motors reported that its Wisconsin Nash plants alone had sufficient capacity to produce 1,000 cars per day; these were the former automobile plants of Nash-Kelvinator. American Motors Corporation, *Annual Report*, 1954, pp. 2-3.

[38] Packard Motor Car Company, *Annual Report*, 1946, p. 9.

CHAPTER IX

THE PHYSICAL DISTRIBUTION PROBLEM

LARGE THOUGH THE ESTIMATED volume requirements were for full use of a balanced one-plant facility or complex to obtain low unit costs in the manufacture of automobiles, there may have been other necessary activities of the firms in which even larger volumes provided additional unit cost savings. These also contributed to the discrepancies in financial performance among the large and small firms of the passenger car industry and raised barriers which the Independents had to offset to survive. One of these activities was that which we may call the physical distribution problem, a marketing problem closely related to and strongly influencing the organization and location of automobile manufacturing operations.

Because of the size and weight of automobiles, transportation costs generally were an important part of the delivered prices of passenger cars: the cost of moving cars from manufacturing facilities to the local markets frequently accounted for as much as $100 and more of the final delivered price of cars. Since much of the physical movement of passenger cars to points of final sale often was completed prior to finishing of manufacturing processes, the distribution function was complex in the passenger car industry. Nevertheless, the general pattern of relationships among the large and small firms was relatively clear.

PHYSICAL DISTRIBUTION SYSTEMS

Although the domestic passenger car manufacturers may be viewed as competing in a nationwide market, the United States market also may be viewed as made up of many local or regional markets in which, when they were sufficiently large, the firms enjoying large sales volumes found it advantageous to establish branch assembly plants. The transportation of parts and components to these plants was a marketing arrangement alternative to movement of completed cars and resulted in generally different patterns of distribution among the large and small manufacturers of cars.

The small firms generally followed a process of inward

shipment of raw materials, parts, and components to their centralized fabricating and assembly plants. Many of the parts and components were produced by these firms themselves, but many were also secured from suppliers. After assembly, completed cars were shipped to dealers in the many local markets for final sale to consumers. Rail freight, haulaway truck, or barge was used in this movement. The large firms interposed an additional step. Raw materials were sent to centralized fabricating plants for manufacture of many parts and components. Many parts and components also were purchased from suppliers. After fabrication, the parts and components, whether from the firm's own plants or from a supplier's plants, were then shipped to branch assembly plants for final assembly, except for a few Big Three makes which were each assembled in only one central location. Subsequently, final shipment of completed cars was made to dealers for sale to final purchasers. The decentralized operations thus involved three steps: the movement of raw materials to fabrication plants; the movement of parts and components to outlying assembly plants; and finally, the movement of completed cars to dealers.

The major difference in the centralized and decentralized operations was the shipment of parts and components by the larger firms to their outlying assembly plants for assembly and final shipment to dealers rather than shipment of completed cars over the entire distance. The movement of parts and components to outlying assembly plants substituted for some of the movement of completed cars which otherwise would have been required.

Throughout most of the early postwar period, this difference in assembly organization and transportation pattern existed between the leading Independents and the Big Three, except for limited West Coast assembly operations conducted by Nash-Kelvinator and Studebaker before the mergers in 1954. As noted previously, volumes of 60,000 or more units per year were estimated to be required to support an efficient regional assembly plant.[1] Thus, the levels required to support an extensive regional assembly system were beyond the actual sales accomplishments of the Independents in most of the postwar period. Hence, any transportation cost disadvantage experienced by the Independents lay in their inability to ship parts and components over much of the distance

---

[1] *Supra*, chapter viii.

which had to be covered in getting a completed car to a final purchaser, if the cost of moving parts and components was lower than that for moving completed automobiles.

CENTRAL ASSEMBLY COST DISADVANTAGES: THE 1950's[2]

During the 1950's, the automobile manufacturers generally found it substantially cheaper to ship parts and components rather than completed cars except to the extent that the transportation cost savings were offset by backtracking over distances already covered or by added handling costs. A freight car, for example, held only four completed passenger cars, but the equivalent of ten to eleven finished full-sized cars could be shipped in one freight car as parts and components for assembly in a regional plant.[3]

Parts and components customarily were moved by rail. If all parts and components were centrally fabricated and if the only method of transporting completed cars were also by rail, the transportation savings would be computed simply by comparing the costs of shipping over comparable distances the completed car and its equivalent in parts and components. The comparison is not so simple, however, since alternative transportation methods were available and since parts and components moved under numerous and diverse rates including incentive commodity rates to some locations for heavier car loadings. Also, the use of haulaway trucks, for instance, was usually a somewhat less expensive method of transporting completed cars than rail. Approximately 80 per cent of the shipments of completed new cars were by haulaway trucks in the 1950's; railroads and boats were seldom used except for very long hauls.[4] Generally, however, truck freight charges in the 1950's approximated the rail freight pattern but at somewhat lower rates. Also, parts and components, as is well

[2] The material in this section is based generally on testimony at the Congressional hearings printed in U. S., Senate, Committee on Interstate and Foreign Commerce, Subcommittee on Automobile Marketing Practices, *Hearings, Automobile Marketing Practices*, 84th Congress, 2nd Session, Pursuant to S. Res. 13 Continued by S. Res. 163 (Washington: U. S. Government Printing Office, 1956), Part 1.

[3] *Ibid.*, pp. 896-97. Statement by Frederic G. Donner, then vice-president of General Motors in charge of financial staff.

[4] Shipments by highway ranged from 72 per cent in 1950 to a high of 90 per cent in 1959 but fell thereafter to 74 per cent in 1962. Automobile Manufacturers Association, *Motor Truck Facts*, 1963 edition (Detroit, Michigan), p. 45.

known, were not all centrally fabricated, the practice of the industry having been to rely heavily on suppliers.

Although the costs of transporting parts and components usually were lower than the costs of shipping a completed car over comparable distances, there were added costs of handling, packaging, loading, unloading, and unpackaging the parts and components shipped to outlying plants for assembly which tended to offset the transportation savings. Other costs of a branch assembly method not borne by a centralized fabrication and assembly process may have been in higher costs of establishing such plants and managing them. Such differentials would be quite difficult to derive and are not attempted here; however, it is not logically conclusive that such plants were more expensive to establish and maintain than centralized plants, particularly if the firm involved was so large as to exert great influence on the availability of land and labor in a centralized plant community by engaging in further centralized expansion.

It is neither feasible nor necessary to determine precisely the extent of physical distribution cost differentials among the large and small firms in the 1950's. Complications of backhauls, varying distances, differing transportation methods, and regional sales distribution would influence their overall average costs. Nevertheless, some limited illustrations provide insight into the cost differentials of the two alternative methods of reaching selected local markets; and from these, it is clear that the Independents suffered unit cost transportation disadvantages which contributed to their difficulties after 1952.

In 1955, the financial vice-president of General Motors acknowledged that his firm secured lower transportation costs from the use of branch assembly plants than would have resulted if his firm produced all cars centrally for outshipment.[5] The average amount of the savings was not revealed, but added costs which partially offset any transportation savings of branch plant operation were estimated to average at least $10.00 to $15.00 per car for added handling of parts and higher costs of establishing and maintaining separate branch facilities. The minimum allowance for handling alone was estimated to be at least $6.00 per car.[6] These costs would not have been incurred if the production were all centralized.

[5] U. S., Senate, Committee on Interstate and Foreign Commerce, Subcommittee on Automobile Marketing Practices, *op. cit.*, pp. 766-70.
[6] *Ibid.*, pp. 768-69, 782, and 788.

Also in 1955, the executive vice-president of Ford Motor Company indicated that Ford's savings in transportation costs were only incidental to Ford's operation of branch assembly plants.[7] Savings in transportation costs were not a principal feature of the early establishment of branch plants by Ford. In the early days of the industry, no savings were obtained. Other reasons for use of branch assembly plants were deemed more important than transportation cost savings. Among these were the desire to avoid damage which might otherwise result in transportation of completed cars; to secure added flexibility in operations; to service local dealers more quickly; to gain local support from operations in the local community; and to avoid the problems of increasing size in central locations. However, it was acknowledged that long-run savings did accrue as improved methods of handling and shipping materials were developed, although it was also indicated that Ford would actually pay out more for transportation in 1955 than it would take in.[8]

Chrysler's president stated that Chrysler in 1955 suffered a transportation cost disadvantage when compared with its principal competitors, since Chrysler did not operate an extensive branch plant system.[9] Acting on the belief that there were savings to be secured, Chrysler planned to, and did, establish additional branch plants.[10]

If Chrysler officials felt that their company was handicapped by a lack of branch plants, then the small firms must have been even further handicapped. Two of the Independents, for a while, operated branch plants on the West Coast; but their output and sales generally were too low to justify extensive branch plant operations in the 1950's, at least before American Motors' comeback.

When the firm had a plant in Los Angeles, Studebaker-Packard had some experience in use of regional assembly plants. In 1955, Studebaker-Packard's average cost of shipping completed Studebaker cars from the firm's central fabrication and assembly plant in South Bend to dealers in the

---

[7] *Ibid.*, pp. 1011-13.

[8] Some transportation costs were not passed on to dealers and consumers, principally because of maximum freight charges established for the West Coast. *Ibid.*, p. 1014.

[9] *Ibid.*, p. 408.

[10] *Ibid.*, p. 411. Within the next two years Chrysler expanded its assembly plant system to provide plants in Delaware and St. Louis. Chrysler Corporation, *Annual Report*, 1957, p. 18.

Los Angeles assembly plant market area was $271 per car. After providing for an added cost of approximately $11 per car for crating and loading of parts and components for shipment to Los Angeles for assembly plus the average cost of sending the completed car from the assembly plant to dealers in the area, Studebaker obtained average transportation and handling savings of about $96 per car through use of the branch assembly plant, the total average transportation and handling cost per car having been reduced to $175.[11]

Comparable savings were shown in the estimated costs of moving a Dodge to the market through Chrysler's Los Angeles assembly plant. For a completed car the cost was estimated to be about $277 per car by truck and $299 by rail from Detroit to Los Angeles.[12] The estimated cost of shipping a Dodge from Detroit to Los Angeles in the form of components was about $124.[13] Added handling costs and average out-shipment costs from the assembly plant probably approximated those for the Studebaker.

Because of its low level of output after 1952, Studebaker-Packard subsequently disposed of its Los Angeles plant, leaving it at a substantial transportation cost disadvantage since all of its three largest competitors had plants in the area. Similarly, American Motors had a plant in Los Angeles but also later disposed of it when its sales fell sharply.[14]

The fact that the small firms' actual transportation costs to the western area were higher than those of the Big Three did not mean that consumers actually paid more in transportation costs for their cars than they paid for the larger volume cars of the Big Three. The Independents followed the freight cost billing pattern of the Big Three and established maximum freight charges to dealers on the West Coast.[15]

[11] U. S., Senate, Committee on Interstate and Foreign Commerce, Subcommittee on Automobile Marketing Practices, op. cit., p. 372, for these figures. These figures were for the first 11 months of 1955. The total freight charged the dealers in this area averaged $146, an amount less than the average freight charge since the company placed a ceiling on its freight charges to this area.

[12] Ibid., p. 420, for approximate rates on which figures were based for a car of about 3,500 pounds.

[13] Ibid., p. 150, for estimated cost, including 3 per cent transportation tax in effect in 1955.

[14] Supra, chapters iii and iv.

[15] U. S., Senate, Committee on Interstate and Foreign Commerce, Subcommittee on Automobile Marketing Practices, op. cit., pp. 70, 73, and 371, for comments by Romney and Nance respectively.

American Motors charged actual freight in all areas except the seven most western states where a ceiling had been placed on the freight charge to remain competitive. Studebaker-Packard followed a similar policy. The actual cost differences thus were absorbed by the small firms in order to remain competitive; however, their profit margins in this distant western market area, at least under the conditions existing in the 1950's, were lower than those they would have obtained if they could have recovered their full freight costs.

In the shipment of cars to the far western states, then, the two Independents for a considerable time operated with substantial freight cost disadvantages. They paid more freight than they collected. If they had collected the actual freight without the cost savings of having assembly plants located there, they would have suffered substantial delivered price disadvantages in the area.

Between centralized and regional assembly, transportation cost differentials also existed for shorter distances. The cost of shipping a Studebaker car from South Bend to New York City by truck convoy was about $90 in 1955. Freight on a Studebaker from South Bend to Philadelphia was about $83 per car.[16] In contrast, the estimated cost of shipping a Chevrolet in the form of equivalent parts and components from Detroit to an assembly plant in Tarrytown, a suburb of New York City, was approximately $28.[17] Even with a $15 charge

[16] Ibid., p. 373, truck convoy costs presented by Nance.

[17] Ibid., pp. 136 and 150, Charts 2 and 3, for this and the following estimates. Paul Herzog of the National Automobile Dealers Association, assuming that all parts and components of a car moved in rate class 45, provided these charts as illustrations of a practice of charging dealers "phantom freight," a freight charge in excess of actual freight cost. Illustrations have been drawn from these charts to show comparisons of estimated actual freight costs of shipping cars under different systems—either direct from central assembly plants or through regional plants to the same area. "Phantom freight" charges to dealers are not considered here. These estimates include a 3 per cent transportation tax in force in 1955 and are based on 1955 rail and truck rates.

In still another case, a completed 3,450 pound Studebaker was shipped to Enid, Oklahoma, from South Bend, Indiana, at an estimated cost of $124. For a 3,300 pound car, Chevrolet shipped the parts and components first to its Kansas City, Missouri, plant and a completed car on to Enid, Oklahoma, for an estimated total cost of $82 per car. Even a $15 added handling charge raises the total Chevrolet cost to only $97, still well below the total Studebaker charge. Approximate agreement with these estimates is also found in data prepared by Ford. It was estimated that the average cost of transporting a low-priced $2,500 car to dealers was

for handling components, Chevrolet with its branch assembly operation had a freight cost advantage of about $40 per car to this area.

In another case, the transportation charge estimated for selected shipments during 1955 was about $105 for moving a Ford from Detroit through the Norfolk, Virginia, assembly plant and on to Columbia, South Carolina. For an equivalent car going through Atlanta, Georgia assembly processes, the estimated charge was about $87 per car from Detroit to Columbia. In comparison, the estimated cost was $114 for sending a completed Nash from Kenosha, Wisconsin, to Columbia, South Carolina. With an additional charge of $10 to $15 for handling parts and components for the Fords, the Nash transportation cost would have been approximately equal to the cost of moving the Ford from Detroit through either Norfolk or Atlanta plants to Columbia. To the Columbia area, then, the charges for this Independent make were roughly comparable to those for the Big Three make. It should be noted, however, that the two cars were not exactly the same weight. The Nash was approximately 300 pounds lighter than the Ford.

REQUIREMENTS FOR LOW TRANSPORT COST: THE 1950's

If the illustrations may be used even as approximate guides, it appears quite certain that the Independents experienced substantial disadvantages in transportation costs in the 1950's, although to some market areas they may have had some advantage. Their disadvantage was greatest in serving those areas most distant from their centralized plants and especially pronounced in the communities in which Big Three assembly plants were located.

There were probably a few locations, mainly those immediately surrounding their centralized plants, in which the Independents secured transportation cost advantages. Elsewhere their transportation costs as a very rough estimate may have ranged from zero to perhaps sixty per cent more than those of the Big Three. In the areas close to their central plants the Independents probably experienced little or no dis-

$100 per unit, or 4 per cent of retail price. Figures appeared in a table used with "The Economic Outlook for 1959 and Its Impact on Auto Sales," A talk before an Educational Round Table, Louisville, Kentucky, December 9, 1958, by R. J. Eggert, Marketing Research Manager, Ford Motor Company.

advantage. In more remote regions — the Northeast, Southeast, Southwest, and West Coast — their cost disadvantage was probably substantial. Perhaps partly for this reason the Independents' shares of the markets in some of the states more distant from the Midwest were lower than in their home and nearby states.[18]

Theoretically, transportation cost savings may be considered as accruing continuously to a large firm serving a national market when the volume required to maintain the regional assembly plants is met or exceeded by the large firm. The lowest possible transportation cost in moving a car to the point of final sale to a consumer would have been the shipment of parts and components from central fabricating plants to the point of final sale, assembly of the completed car, and delivery to the consumer on the spot. There were, however, limits to the opportunity for wide dispersion of final assembly points imposed by plant and equipment requirements for accomplishing final assembly plus the added charges for handling parts and components. Since the minimum level required for low unit cost branch assembly operation was about 60,000 or more sales per year in a given region, there was a substantial volume requirement for establishment of branch assembly plants. This introduced an element of indivisibility in the organizational structure of the firm. Because General Motors and Ford produced and sold greater volumes, they had greater opportunity for use of numerous widely dispersed regional assembly plants. It was this which gave them their advantage. Obviously, the Independents with smaller volumes were unable to take advantage of this opportunity unless they could have expanded their sales levels sufficiently to maintain an efficient regional assembly plant system, a feat which they were unable to accomplish. The same was also true of the smaller volume cars of the Big Three, such as Cadillac, Lincoln, and Imperial which were each assembled in one central location; but it was the large volume Big Three makes which made existence so difficult for the Independents.

In 1958, for example, Ford and General Motors each had over 20 assembly plants widely distributed throughout the country. In addition to its Detroit area plants, Chrysler had

[18] *Automotive News* (*1959 Almanac Issue*), April 27, 1959, p. 39, shows percentage sales shares by states.

branch assembly plants in three areas. The two leading Independents had one assembly plant each with all output centralized in their home locations. The regional assembly
method was used most widely for the Ford and General
Motors' Chevrolet, Buick, Oldsmobile, and Pontiac makes, the
last three of which were assembled in the same plants in
most cases. Chevrolet alone was assembled in ten plants, Ford
in 15, and the Buick-Oldsmobile-Pontiac group in eight each.
Mercury and Plymouth were each assembled in four plants
and the other Big Three makes were assembled in from one to
three plants. Rambler and Studebaker, of course, were assembled in only one plant each.[19]

To obtain unit physical distribution costs in the 1950's
comparable to the best available to the Big Three, outputs
of approximately 1,000,000 or more units per year, all of one
basic vehicle to be assembled in regional plants located in the
largest markets, probably were required to permit the extensive regional assembly organization for lowest unit cost.
The limit of course was the ability to sell such large volumes
of a relatively standardized vehicle. Only the Big Three sold
such volumes. So long as the transportation methods, freight
rate patterns, and organizational structures of the 1950's
prevailed, the Independents suffered substantial unit cost disadvantages in physical distribution. Regional assembly plants
thus offered an opportunity for lower physical distribution
costs if sufficient sales could be generated to justify their
use. In the 1960's, however, the distribution cost pattern
was to be altered considerably by innovation in the railroad
industry.

THE PIGGYBACK INNOVATION: THE 1960's

One of the most interesting technological innovations of
the late 1950's was the development and introduction of the
"piggyback" and "rack car" method of shipping automobiles.
Oversized flatcars were a basis of the change. By 1960, this
specialized equipment had been introduced on a widespread
and rapidly increasing scale, since many railroad tunnels and

[19] Figures based on plant locations shown in *Red Book National Used
Car Market Report*, XLVII, No. 228, July 1 through August 14, 1958,
(Chicago: National Market Reports, Inc., 1958).

other facilities had been modified to permit its use.[20] The new equipment became an important facet of railroad transportation and won back for the railroads much of the transportation of completed automobiles.

The "piggyback" developments had extensive ramifications.[21] They created considerable concern and consternation on the part of people with a diversity of interests. Representatives of trucking firms complained bitterly of the loss of automobile hauling volume to the railroads.[22] Employees of these firms, many of whom found themselves unemployed as a result of the change, and their union representatives also protested heatedly. Railroad officials, on the other hand, were pleased to obtain the additional business. Much controversy arose over the setting of "piggyback" rates. Such were the problems of technological progress. Our principal interest in the innovation, however, is with its influence on the physical distribution costs of the remaining Independents —American Motors and Studebaker.

The introduction of the oversized piggyback railway flatcars and rack cars brought many changes in the pattern of physical distribution costs among the firms of the United States automobile industry.

Early in 1962, for instance, the cost of transporting a completed Rambler Classic from Kenosha, Wisconsin, to Los Angeles, California, by truck was approximately $227; and the cost of moving a completed Studebaker Lark from South Bend, Indiana, to the same destination by truck was $255.[23] Since these vehicles were somewhat lighter than those referred to previously, the costs of moving them were roughly

[20] The Milwaukee Road, which served American Motors, e.g., started transcontinental piggybacking of automobiles in early 1960 and expanded it greatly during the year. See Chicago, Milwaukee, St. Paul, and Pacific Railroad Company, *Annual Report*, 1960.

[21] "Piggyback" technically referred to automobile as well as other product shipments in truck trailers placed upon railroad flatcars rather than the direct loading of automobiles in the bi- or tri-level rack cars. The term is used loosely here for its descriptive virtues in helping one visualize also the rack car shipments.

[22] See U. S., Senate, Committee on Interstate and Foreign Commerce, Subcommittee on Surface Transportation, *Hearings, Piggyback Transportation*, 87th Congress, 1st Session (Washington: U. S. Government Printing Office, 1962).

[23] NATA Tariff 116-J, MF-ICC 468, for the Rambler with six vehicles per truckload; and NATA Tariff 118-I, MF-ICC 465, for the Studebaker also with six vehicles per truckload.

comparable to the corresponding costs of truck movements between the same locations in the middle 1950's, at which time rail shipment of equivalent parts and components had been considerably cheaper. In contrast, with the adoption of the new railway technology, the costs of moving completed cars were greatly reduced. By tri-level railway rack cars, with 15 automobiles of the Rambler or Studebaker Lark dimensions per rack car, the cost of moving the completed Rambler was approximately $127 and of the Studebaker $134 from the above same origins to Los Angeles.[24] Bi-level rack car shipments cost somewhat more, but they were still lower in cost than haulaway truck shipment. A further comparison of these costs can also be made with the estimated cost of moving equivalent parts for a Ford Fairlane, a car of approximately equal weight and dimensions—all of the cars were compacts weighing approximately 2,800 to 2,900 pounds.

The cost of transporting from Detroit, Michigan, to Los Angeles a completed Ford Fairlane (1962 model) was about $274 by truck and $140 by tri-level rack car.[25] Using the commodity rates under which most of the heavier automobile parts and components moved on an incentive basis, we estimate that freight costs for the equivalent parts and components of the Fairlane could have been as low as about $66 per automobile at the rate available for the heaviest loading of a freight car to as high as about $132 for the highest rate corresponding to the minimum freight car loading weight.[26] Because of the variety in composition of shipments plus the necessity also for moving packaging materials, in many cases, the actual equivalent cost lay somewhere between the estimated extremes. With an average freight car loading of 30,000 pounds, for example, the freight for the equivalent parts would have been approximately $106. Thus, with the added costs involved in handling parts and components, which may have been offset to some extent by the costs of loading and unloading completed cars, the advent of

[24] TCFB Tariff 1-J, ICC 1651, Supplement 107, cost per automobile shipped with 15 per tri-level rack car. Full-sized automobiles moved with 12 per tri-level rack car.

[25] NATA Tariff 62-T, MF-ICC 453, rate for 5 automobiles per truck; and TCFB Tariff 1-J, ICC 1651, Supplement 107, rate for tri-level rack car shipment.

[26] TCFB Tariff, 1-J, ICC 1651, Supplement 95, commodity rates ranging in 10 steps from minimum car loadings of 20,000 pounds to maximum loading of 120,000 pounds.

the rack car mode of transporting completed automobiles narrowed substantially the cost savings of regional assembly relative to centralized assembly, at least between these points. However, it probably did not eliminate the average differential entirely.

To some distribution points in the California area other than the assembly plant points, the piggyback method of shipment of a car may have been lower in cost than movement of an equivalent car through the appropriate regional assembly plant because of the additional cost of moving the completed car from the assembly point to the point of delivery to a dealer located at a point served directly by rack car shipments. Since the assembly points of the Big Three were in the most densely populated areas, the regional assembly method evidently still provided some average unit cost advantage, particularly in view of the fact that some of the parts and components used in the assembly plants originated in the California area rather than in central fabrication shops of the Detroit area.

Although the pattern of movements was very complicated since numerous combinations of shipment had been arranged including motor-rail-motor, rail-motor, and sometimes barge-motor shipments, plus cross-hauling arrangements for shipments between assembly plants as distribution points,[27] the piggyback innovation was spread throughout the country with results similar to those of the Detroit-to-Los Angeles shipments.[28] To some areas the piggyback methods evidently provided lower transport and handling costs; to

[27] Special rates were available between Atlanta, Georgia, and Norfolk, Virginia. Ford, e.g., could ship Fairlanes and Falcons built at its Atlanta plant by rack cars to Norfolk where its Galaxies were built and return shipments of Galaxies from Norfolk to Atlanta at special reduced rates provided the rack cars were reloaded within 48 hours. Similar opportunities were also available between General Motors plants. See SFTB Tariff 221-L, ICC S-180, esp. Supplement 35.

[28] From Detroit to Atlanta, early in 1962, provided shipments moved at class 45 rates in which most automotive parts and components moved and a 30,000 pound car loading, estimated costs of moving equivalent parts and components for a Ford Fairlane totaled about $51 compared to tri-level shipment of $43 for a completed car. Effective July 15, 1962, incentive commodity car loading rates with ten steps ranging from minimums of 15,000 pounds to maximums of 100,000 pounds provided regional assemblers an opportunity to bring freight costs for parts and components in line with costs of shipping completed cars. Cf. TLTTB Tariff E/S-1008, ICC A-946 (Boin Series); and TL-CTRB Tariff E/S-745, ICC C-305 (Hinsch Series).

other areas the costs of the regional assembly system and direct shipment seem to have been approximately equal; and to still other areas, particularly those population centers immediately adjacent to regional assembly plants, the use of the regional assembly plant system still apparently provided some physical distribution cost savings although the savings were relatively small compared with the differentials existing in the 1950's. Thus, the piggyback innovation benefited the leading Independents, since it eliminated much of their disadvantage from lack of extensive regional assembly systems.

By 1960, centralized assembly was no longer the competitive handicap that it was earlier. The Big Three, of course, had other reasons for continued use of regional plants,[29] including their existing commitments of funds to them and stimulation of local community interest from local operations; and quite appropriately, piggyback was also available to them from both their central and regional assembly locations. Also, to the extent that parts and components came from the vicinity of a regional plant rather than central fabrication operations, and provided that other costs were comparable, the regional assemblers' cost of putting a car down in the market of the assembly point was lower than might have been estimated. Despite the difficulties of comparison, so diverse were the origin, destination, and composition of shipments, it is clear that the physical distribution cost positions of the Independents improved considerably with the advent of piggyback. Whatever the differentials, they were narrowed substantially by the reduced costs of moving completed automobiles.

SUMMARY

The existence of substantial unit cost savings in the physical distribution of automobiles through regional assembly plant systems provided the Big Three significant advantages over the smaller firms through the 1950's and thus contributed to the Independents' competitive difficulties. The piggyback innovation at the end of the decade improved the physical distribution cost position of the centralized producer,

[29] See also N. P. Hurley, "The Automotive Industry: A Study in Industrial Location," *Land Economics*, XXXV (February, 1959), 1-14.

putting the one-plant complex in a better competitive position, although regional assembly evidently still provided some unit cost advantage, particularly to the extent that parts and components could be obtained in the area of the assembly plant.

Chapter X

THE MARKETING PROBLEM

INCLUDING RESPONSIBILITY FOR CHOICES of kinds and qualities of products to be produced and their prices, channels of distribution, and methods of sales promotion, marketing is a function of broad scope. The economic process of marketing is not actually complete until the goods involved are delivered finally into the hands of the consumer.[1] From the viewpoint of the firm, the ability to manufacture goods is not enough by itself. The goods produced must also be sold. Volume of sales achieved may be an important determinant of the unit cost of the marketing process, as well as of the manufacturing process, and in turn of the total unit cost of providing a product to the consumer; but the marketing process may have other dimensions, too, depending on the environmental conditions shaping the opportunities and activities of a firm and including possible strategies to counteract the advantages of large volume operations to a firm's larger competitors.

ADVANTAGES OF LARGE VOLUME OPERATIONS

Just as variations in the unit cost of manufacturing operations may be expected with changes in the scale of a firm's operations, so also variations in the unit cost of effective marketing activities may be expected with changes in scale.

In general, if indivisibilities occur in the means customarily used by a competing industry group to carry out the marketing process, a large volume seller may expect to experience lower marketing costs per unit than a small seller. So long as relatively fixed total expenditures must be made for any use, however small, of the means of carrying out the marketing functions of physically reaching, communicating with, and influencing prospective buyers of a product, large volume may be necessary to make a full and efficient use of

---

[1] In a short statement covering a large array of activities, the American Marketing Association Committee on Definitions defined marketing as "the performance of business activities that direct the flow of goods and services from producer to consumer or user." R. S. Alexander, chairman, "Report of the Definitions Committee," *Journal of Marketing*, XIII (October, 1948), 209.

the fixed factors so as to achieve low marketing costs per unit. Volume of sales in part also may influence the selection of the means by which the marketing functions are conducted. As was the case with fixed factors in manufacturing operations, the unit costs of using the fixed factors, because of their indivisibility, can be expected to fall as output is increased.

The condition of indivisibility in the means used to perform marketing functions is one which might be expected in the case of a mass market comprised on the demand side of a large number of prospective buyers whose preferences as individuals are not identifiable with certainty. In such a market, communication to inform consumers of product quality and availability, for example, perhaps may best be accomplished through a large-scale advertising campaign using mass media, such as national magazines or television, for which large and small firms alike presumably pay the same price for comparable time, space, or frequency of coverage regardless of the number of sales actually generated by the advertising. With unit costs equal to or even lower than those of a small producer, the large volume seller may achieve greater total market impact in terms of market saturation with its advertising; or, for the same degree of saturation the large seller obtains the lower unit cost. Large sales volumes serve to offset indivisibilities in the means of reaching, communicating with, and influencing consumers, thereby permitting decreases in the unit cost of carrying out the marketing process and obtaining great total market impact. This is a fact of great importance from the viewpoint of the individual firm and its competitive position.

In the over-all process of putting a finished product finally in the hands of the consumer, volume may be important both directly to the manufacturer and indirectly to him through dealers in his products. Economies of large-scale marketing operations conceivably may occur at the level of the local market, particularly in the operations of dealers, as well as the national market, which is comprised of a network of local markets.

Unit marketing cost advantages arising from larger volume in physically reaching consumers with the product seem similar to the economies of larger scale in manufacturing operations in that both represent actual unit cost reductions; and much the same may be said of communication with consumers in the strict sense of providing information on product quality, price, and availability. Sales promotion, however, may be a somewhat different matter. It is difficult to determine where the provision of information ends and sales promotion begins—advertising, for example, may encompass both. Intense competitive struggles emphasizing sales promotion, which may include both personal and impersonal efforts to stimulate demand for the product of a firm, possibly expand the total demand for the product in question. However, the effort to attract consumers away from competing firms, which counter the move with defensive sales promotion programs of their own, tends to exert an upward push on the unit cost of the marketing process.[2]

Although the tendency may be for sales promotion to raise the unit cost curve of the selling firm, the firm, at least initially and perhaps until its competitors react, often may expect to find a favorable shift in the demand for its products which permits a compensating increase in price or a reduction in manufacturing and other costs per unit, including even promotional costs. The payoff from increased promotional expenditures thus may be derived in a variety of ways. But what happens if the firm is already fully exploiting the technical economies of scale? If sales promotion activities are customary in the industry and even if unit costs of all industry participants are raised by promotional activities, the large volume firm may still secure a relative unit cost advantage over a small firm by making more efficient use of the services of experts and of the mass media, which are available at relatively fixed total costs. Sales promotion though is a complex factor; its outcome is not always readily predictable

[2] Economists, following the reasoning of E. H. Chamberlin through the many editions of his pioneering work *The Theory of Monopolistic Competition*, 6th edition (Cambridge, Mass.: Harvard University Press, 1950), often make distinctions, on the basis of their desirability from the viewpoint of society, between production costs, which include manufacturing and physical distribution costs essential to placing a product in the market, and sales promotion costs, which are intended to stimulate the demand for a particular firm's product and in a sense to tailor the demand to the product. However, from the viewpoint of the survival and prosperity of the individual firm such distinctions are not essential. All costs of doing business in competition with other firms must be borne; and in this respect sales promotion or selling costs are comparable to production costs. Because of the difficulty of distinguishing "information provision" from "sales promotion" in an activity, such as advertising, which encompasses both, it may be sufficient simply to acknowledge that those costs commonly called sales promotion, merchandising, or selling costs contain both elements.

or measurable, so varied are the forms that it may take and so diverse the possible reactions of both customers and competitors. Cost is not the only factor of importance in, for example, an advertising campaign. Location of advertising in media, appeal used, method of presentation, and other factors, in some of which cost is relatively insignificant, may be important. Generally speaking, however, because of the large volume seller's relatively more full and efficient use of the indivisible factors in promotional campaigns—whether the fixed costs of style change, advertising, or direct personal effort—the unit cost advantage may be expected to lie with large volume producers.

Under realistic conditions of imperfect knowledge of market conditions, especially of consumer behavior, importance also may be attached to sales promotion activities as a defensive tactic in protecting a firm's existing market share. If sales promotion activities are customary in a particular industry, the firm must undertake sales promotion activities, or risk the inroads of competitors, although again the advantage in terms of unit cost generally may be expected to rest with the larger volume firm. Volume of output thus may be expected to be an important factor in the unit cost of effective marketing action; but the relevant questions are "How important?" and from the viewpoint of the smaller firm "Can its influence be offset?"

THE MARKET ENVIRONMENT

The automobile was not invented in the United States; but its large-scale production was pioneered in this country.[3] Both the product and its producers exerted great influence on social and economic life, their influence having been so interwoven in the fabric of life in the twentieth century as to be difficult to evaluate. Originated as a luxury item, essentially a toy, the automobile quickly became a necessity, though it also retained its luxury connotations.

Some makes of cars and their manufacturers became well known to most consumers. Many if not most Americans

[3] See Donald A. Moore, "The Automobile Industry," in *The Structure of American Industry*, Walter Adams, editor, revised edition (New York: The Macmillan Company, 1954), pp. 274-86, for a succinct review; or John B. Rae, *American Automobile Manufacturers: The First Forty Years* (Philadelphia: Chilton Company, 1959), for a more detailed review of the early development and growth of the industry.

were fascinated by automobiles and the firms that produced them. The automobile industry, perhaps more than any other single industry, symbolized to many people the mass production, mass consumption orientation of that complex mechanism known as the United States economy. The methods of manufacturing and marketing of automobiles were widely imitated. Firms in other industries became dependent on the automobile industry either as sellers to it or as distributors of its products as well as of other products to keep the automobile operating.

So great was the latent demand for the personal mobility provided by passenger automobiles that tremendous opportunities existed for their production and sale. The automobile industry of the United States, which began in a small way about 1900, quickly grew into a very large industry. Too small to deserve a separate classification in the *Census of Manufactures* at the turn of the century, the industry attained first place in the 1920's in the value of its annual product and has ranked high ever since.[4] Also from the earliest days, a few firms found tremendous success in the industry, initially as assemblers but later also as integrated producers of parts and components in operations undertaken with profits put back into the business.[5] Their rather early dominance of the rapidly growing industry highlighted what became one of the most significant characteristics of the industry and its market: the small number of sellers.

Ford, followed most closely (and eventually overtaken) by General Motors and more remotely by Studebaker, Packard, Nash, Hudson, and later by Chrysler, gained leadership of the industry, while most other participants fell far behind.[6]

[4] U. S., Federal Trade Commission, *Report on Motor Vehicle Industry*, House Document 468, 76th Congress, 1st Session (Washington: U. S. Government Printing Office, 1939), pp. 9-10; and U. S., Department of Commerce, Bureau of the Census, *Census of Manufacturers*, 1947, 1954, and 1958.

[5] Ford Motor Company, for example, incorporated in 1903 with $100,000 in stock subscribed, found its net income after taxes rising from $246,080 for 15 months ended September 30, 1904, to $1,233,772 for 12 months ended September 30, 1907, $7,579,334 for 12 months ended December 31, 1911, and $120,192,643 for 12 months ended December 31, 1922, for a pre-World War II record. In the early years of the firm's growth, Ford's annual rates of return on owner's equity frequently ranged in excess of 100 per cent, despite the reinvestment of most of the firm's earnings. U. S., Federal Trade Commission, *op. cit.*, pp. 634 and 645.

[6] *Ibid.*, p. 29.

Although thousands entered or attempted to enter, the automobile industry never had a truly large number of active competitors. The maximum number of firms participating in the industry on a commercial scale at one time came in 1921 when 88 companies were then actively producing cars.[7] In the same year Ford accounted for more than 55 per cent of passenger car output and General Motors almost 13 per cent, though ten years later their relative positions were to be reversed.[8] The dominance of the few firms continued over the years; and by the end of the depressed 1930's, most other car producers had failed or withdrawn from the industry. In 1946, after the readjustment to peacetime production following World War II, only ten firms were actively engaged in the production and sale of passenger cars.[9] By 1955, following the mergers and the withdrawal from passenger car production of the successor to the industry's newest entrant, Kaiser, only five domestic producers remained selling to the general public through dealer organizations: the Independents—American Motors and Studebaker-Packard—and the Big Three—Chrysler, Ford, and General Motors.[10]

Although other factors, some of which are discussed below, were important, the concentration of industry output in only a few firms, along with the inequalities in their sizes, was a most important influence on the industry participants' choices of market action in the post-World War II years.

[7] Ralph C. Epstein, *The Automobile Industry* (New York: A. W. Shaw Company, 1928), pp. 176-77.

[8] The disparity in the positions of Ford and G. M. generally had been less in other years than it was in 1921. In 1919, for example, Ford accounted for about 40 per cent and G. M. 21 per cent of industry sales. Eight years earlier their shares had been about equal, but thereafter Ford had gained rapidly. U. S., Federal Trade Commission, *op. cit.*, p. 29.

[9] These, as listed by the Automobile Manufacturers Association, included Hudson, Nash, Packard, and Studebaker, the four leading Independents; Chrysler, Ford, and General Motors, the Big Three; and Kaiser-Frazer, Willys-Overland, and Crosley, the other domestic Independents. Checker Motors in 1948 began production of passenger vehicles for sale principally direct to taxicab companies. Production of the Crosley, which was an undersized vehicle, soared to 27,876 units in 1948 but thereafter was cut rapidly; and the car was discontinued in 1952. Automobile Manufacturers Association, *Automobile Facts and Figures*, 1958 edition (Detroit, Michigan), p. 10.

[10] Kaiser production reached a peak of 181,809 units in 1948 and Willys a peak of 35,954 units in 1952; in 1955, the last year of their production, their outputs reached only 1,021 and 4,778 units respectively. *Ibid.*

The earlier enormously successful choices of Ford, General Motors, and later Chrysler gave them powerful voices in determining the market framework. It was in large measure their action which established limits to action of the smaller firms, particularly in the domestic United States market in which most of their sales occurred. Except during the Korean conflict, relatively small proportions of domestically produced passenger cars were exported.[11] The United States car manufacturers, as is well known, participated in worldwide automobile markets; but the domestic and foreign phases of their operations were quite distinct parts of their business, particularly for the Big Three, their foreign sales having stemmed mainly from overseas manufacturing operations. Also, it was a fact of importance that it was a nationwide market in which the high degree of concentration occurred, the relatively standardized cars of the several manufacturers having been identifiable by most consumers and bought, serviced, and used conveniently anywhere within the United States. The influence of the dominant few extended to every corner of the country.

Although the number of manufacturers—domestic and foreign—participating in the United States market increased after 1955 with the upsurge in foreign car sales, major characteristics of this market still appeared to be determined by the five domestic manufacturers, particularly by the Big Three since they generally obtained approximately 80 to 90 per cent of the market. In the ten years prior to 1956, the annual penetration of the market by foreign producers amounted to less than one per cent of total sales. The foreign producers' share of the market expanded spectacularly and reached more than eight per cent of new car registrations in 1958 and ten per cent in 1959 before falling off in later years. But their position, especially before 1958, was relatively limited in relation to the Big Three and generally comparable to that of the domestic Independents.[12] It is not implied that the foreign producers exerted no significant competitive influence in the domestic market. Obviously, as we have seen

[11] In the years 1948-1962, factory sales to foreign markets from plants located in the U. S. ranged between approximately 140,000 and 250,000 units annually compared to total factory sales of approximately 4,000,000 to 7,900,000 units per year. *Ibid.*, 1963 edition, p. 5.

[12] *Supra*, Tables 2 and 10.

previously, they did.[13] Nevertheless, the dominant influences on the supply side of the market stemmed from actions of the Big Three; and both the foreign producers and domestic Independents operated within a market framework largely established by the Big Three.

Under the conditions of an oligopoly market—a situation in which the number of sellers is sufficiently small so that each firm, in determining its own course of action, takes into consideration the probable actions or reactions of its competitors[14]—an intensification of the marketing problem may result:

> Under conditions of imperfect competition or oligopoly some of the commercial activities that make up a large part of the final cost of goods in a freely competitive market tend to be still further intensified. As a substitute for cost reduction and price competition an oligopolist usually finds it expedient to redouble his selling efforts. Even a full monopolist seldom finds it advantageous to trim his advertising outlays; quite the contrary, because his unique position makes the cultivation of consumer good will peculiarly urgent.[15]

If the domestic passenger car market was of this type, which it clearly appears to have been with so small a number of large participants, the Independents, being relatively small firms of the competing industry group, could have been expected to find their problems of survival and prosperity extremely difficult if there were significant advantages of larger size in the marketing of passenger cars.

In this connection, it was a fact of importance that the domestic passenger car industry had physical productive capacity substantially in excess of sales levels generally attained after the period of early postwar shortages came to an end. Since sales had to be sufficient to permit efficient

---

[13] It may be emphasized that foreign competition was of no significance in the postwar decline of the Independents, the upsurge in the sales of foreign cars having occurred several years after the Independents' difficulties. The phenomenon of the foreign car upsurge, as well as the comeback of the Independents, particularly American Motors, seems to have been in part a response to market opportunities created by the actions of the Big Three. *Supra*, chapter vi.

[14] John F. Due, *Intermediate Economic Analysis*, 3rd edition (Homewood, Illinois: Richard D. Irwin, Inc., 1956), p. 49.

[15] George W. Stocking and Myron W. Watkins, *Monopoly and Free Enterprise* (New York: The Twentieth Century Fund, 1951), p. 70. Reprinted by permission of the Twentieth Century Fund, Inc.

utilization of available manufacturing capacity if low unit costs were to be attained, the marketing problem received great emphasis, particularly after 1952. In the 1950's, the total annual capacity of the domestic firms evidently was in excess of 8,000,000 cars. In 1955, total United States production actually amounted to about 7,900,000 cars; and this came at a time of reduced production by the Independents. The four leading Independents had produced approximately 672,-000 cars in 1950 compared with their two successors' total output of about 343,000 units in 1955. Had they actually produced at the 1950 level, the additional production of the Independents would have pushed the 1955 total well above the 8,000,000 mark. After 1955 the Independents reduced their capacity somewhat by elimination of the former Hudson and Packard facilities. In 1959, however, after relatively small additional investment in fixed assets for its remaining automobile plants, American Motors alone produced over 400,000 cars on a multiple-shift basis; and in 1960, the firm's output was more than 485,000 units. In the same period, Studebaker-Packard's physical capacity was of the same general magnitude, although its actual output was much lower. The Independents had had physical capacity in excess of their output levels actually attained, both before and after the mergers, until American Motors' tremendous comeback after 1958. Even without considering any added capacity by the Big Three, the total physical capacity of the domestic plants still would have been substantially in excess of 8,000,000 cars per year.

In the record-breaking sales year of 1963, registrations of all makes totaled approximately 7,560,000 units, of which almost 400,000 were foreign cars.[16] In the earlier peak year of 1955, retail new car sales were less than 7,200,000 units; but in most other postwar years, new car registrations were substantially lower. From 1949 through 1959, with the exception of 1955, actual sales totals ranged from approximately 4,000,000 to 6,000,000 units. In 1958, excess physical capacity evidently was approximately equal to total domestic output of about 4,200,000 units; but thereafter sales and output rose substantially.[17] Thus, it is obvious that the domestic industry had considerable physical capacity in excess of the actual sales and production levels usually attained.

[16] *Supra*, Table 2.
[17] Compare *supra*, Tables 1 and 2.

Optimum economic capacity, of course, may have been at a level other than maximum short-run capacity. The peak output of the industry in 1955, for example, was obtained with considerable costly overtime. Perhaps even greater physical capacity would have been even more profitable to Ford and General Motors in 1955 when their cars were sold in record-breaking volumes. The point remains, however, that excess capacity was costly and, if possible, was to be avoided.

Since fixed charges ran into many millions of dollars for each of the five firms of the domestic industry, large volume was important for obtaining low unit costs. In 1958, for example, the firms' combined total depreciation charges were approximately $700,000,000; their combined amortization of special commercial tooling, an expense item reflecting the writeoff of expenditures sunk prior to a model year in making the model changes, was also more than $700,000,000; and there were undoubtedly other fixed costs which the firms had to bear even to be able to open their doors for business.[18] The individual firms operated under considerable pressure to maintain or expand their sales. Since overhead was a significant component of cost and since the firms of the industry generally had excess production capacity after the end of the early postwar shortages, a large output volume for the individual firm could be expected to result in significantly lower cost per unit than would be possible with a smaller output volume. The lowering of unit cost would improve the firm's competitive market price opportunity and profit position, if the sale of the larger volume could be accomplished with little or no additional promotional cost. Otherwise, the reduction in fixed overhead cost per unit at the larger output would be offset.[19]

[18] General Motors alone accounted for approximately $420,000,000 of the total depreciation and $440,000,000 of the total amortization of special tooling.

[19] In 1957, the average accounting cost and profit per unit of the General Motors' vehicles, including passenger cars and trucks, were reported to be of the following magnitudes:

Hourly-rated labor cost	$ 400
Materials and other direct costs	950
Overhead cost	550
Total cost per unit	$1900
Profit per unit (before taxes)	313
Factory sales value per unit	$2213

Overhead costs, including such items as selling and administrative ex-

Could the individual manufacturer of automobiles indeed increase sales so as to improve the utilization of available productive capacity? Price reductions by a single firm presumably would result in increased sales, possibly at the expense of other firms; but in the oligopolistic condition of the automobile industry, such reductions, at least those by major participants, could be expected to be met by other firms. The probable result would be little or no net gain to the firm first cutting prices unless the total demand for passenger cars was relatively elastic with respect to price changes, in which case the entire industry would enjoy expanded unit sales. This, however, may not have been characteristic of the postwar demand for passenger cars, at least not before 1958, for there may have been other influences which were of overriding importance in the demand for passenger cars. Included among such factors were the large backlog of replacement demand in the early postwar years and widespread consumer preference for innovations in automatic transmissions, refinements in engines, and major style changes, all of which would have been reflected in statistical measures of the degree of price elasticity in the period. The question is not easily answered.

The demand for new passenger cars is an extremely complex item; it may be affected by many factors. Aggregate consumer income, prices of cars relative to other goods and services, quality of cars, significance of innovations, styling and style changes, prices of used cars, existing stocks of cars in the hands of consumers, and other factors may be significant influences on the over-all level of demand for passenger cars. Although price and consumer income factors probably are the most influential, the availability of credit for financing the purchase of cars also appears significant. Restric-

pense, amortization of special tooling, and advertising, and of which some were relatively more fixed than others, thus accounted for approximately 30 per cent of total cost per unit. Assuming no change in average factory sale value or direct material and labor cost per unit, a 25 per cent increase in output would have been accompanied by a reduction in overhead of $110 per unit and a corresponding increase in profits per unit except for additional promotional costs, if any, in obtaining larger volume. On volumes of 3,000,000 or more units per year, the totals could indeed be enormous. See U. S., Senate, Committee on the Judiciary, Subcommittee on Antitrust and Monopoly, *Report, A Study of Administered Prices in the Automobile Industry*, 85th Congress, 2nd Session, Pursuant to S. Res. 231 (Washington: U. S. Government Printing Office, 1958), pp. 125 and 129.

tions on credit, it may be recalled, were considered by the Independents as one of the major reasons for their sales difficulties after the middle of 1953.[20] Easily obtained credit also appeared a significant factor in the great sales expansion of 1955. Passenger cars in these years were complex and expensive consumer goods. Few other consumer goods involved expenditures of magnitudes comparable to those for passenger cars. Next to a home, a car was the most expensive purchase for most consumers. Although many consumers may have strongly desired to purchase a new car, they may have been unable to do so because of the size of the contemplated expenditure in relation to their incomes and other more necessary purchases. Since passenger cars were durable, those consumers who already owned a car could easily postpone their purchase for replacement purposes; and those who owned no car but contemplated the purchase of one could turn to the used car market rather than the new car market.

It appears fairly certain that the over-all demand for new passenger cars, at least since the 1920's, generally has been more responsive to changes in aggregate disposable income or perhaps anticipated income than to changes in price.[21] This conclusion was reached in a pioneering prewar statistical study by Roos and von Szeliski covering the years 1920-1938.[22] A later study by Atkinson covering approximately the same period revealed similar results.[23] Two more recent studies by Chow and Suits, both of which include postwar data and hence seem more relevant for the period studied here, led to essentially the same conclusion.[24] With coefficients of price elasticity ranging in these studies between −1.5 and −0.6

[20] *Supra,* chapter v.

[21] Ford's early growth and dominance of the industry, as has been widely observed, was accomplished by adoption of a standardized vehicle, the famous Model T, and vigorous price cutting, thereby indicating a high degree of price elasticity in the early years of the industry's development; but with the coming of the used car problem, Ford's market position had begun to be eroded by more advanced and higher-priced vehicles in the mid-1920's.

[22] C. F. Roos and Victor von Szeliski, "Factors Governing Changes in Domestic Automobile Demand," *The Dynamics of Automobile Demand* (New York: General Motors Corporation, 1939), p. 20, for a summary of their paper.

[23] L. J. Atkinson, "Demand for Consumer Durable Goods," *Survey of Current Business,* April, 1952, pp. 19-24.

[24] Gregory C. Chow, *Demand for Automobiles in the United States: A Study in Consumer Durables* (Amsterdam: North-Holland Publishing Company, 1957), pp. 4 and 34; and, Daniel B. Suits, "The Demand for

and those of income elasticity ranging between +2.5 and +4.2, the demand for passenger cars evidently was much more sensitive to changes in income than to changes in price, the coefficients indicating the corresponding percentage change in sales for each percentage point change in income or price.[25] It may be noted also that the later the period covered by these studies the lower was the coefficient of price elasticity and the higher the coefficient of income elasticity. Furthermore, the large decline in car sales in 1958 appears to have resulted largely from factors other than price changes. A lack of "consumer confidence" and a "recession psychology" were important influences on sales in 1958.[26] Prices varied little from the 1957 to 1958 models, but sales declined drastically.[27] Consumer attitudes in response to anticipated income changes appeared most significant.

In general, the results of the statistical studies of automobile demand seem consistent. All resulted in coefficients of income elasticity greater than one although the range was relatively broad; and three of the four turned up coefficients of price elasticity greater than one. Only the study by Suits, which extended longer into the postwar period and included the years 1946-1956 in addition to 1929-1941, resulted in a conclusion that the total demand for cars was relatively inelastic with respect to price changes, that is, that the coefficient of price elasticity was less than one.[28] All of these

New Automobiles in the United States, 1929-1956," *The Review of Economics and Statistics*, XL (August, 1958), 273-80. The Chow study covers the years from 1921 through 1953, excluding the years 1942 through 1946. The Suits study covers the period from 1929 through 1956, excluding the years 1942 through 1948.

[25] The chief results of these studies may be summarized as follows:

Study	Years Included	Coefficients of Elasticity of New Car Purchases with Respect to:	
		Price	Income
Roos and von Szeliski	1920-1938	−1.5	+2.5
Atkinson	1925-1940	−1.4	+2.5
Chow	1921-1953	−1.1	+1.7
Suits	1929-1956	−0.6	+4.2

[26] General Motors Corporation, *Annual Report*, 1958, p. 6, indicated that "consumer confidence" apparently as related to a "recession psychology" proved again a major influence on the demand for cars.

[27] *Supra*, Tables 2 and 11.

[28] Roos and von Szeliski took as a fair average estimate of price elasticity -1.5, but they indicated that the results of their study revealed a range probably between -1 and -2. Roos and von Szeliski, *op. cit.*

studies were quite complicated, and the differences among them could easily have resulted from differences in approach, data used, and time periods covered. Unfortunately, there is no particular magic in statistical studies. Their results may apply only to the periods and conditions covered. One never knows with certainty precisely what the coefficients of elasticity are at a particular moment in history or what they will be in the more remote future which is most significant to making the necessary managerial decisions. Nevertheless, if consistent in results, they contribute importantly to the informational basis for action.

The automobile manufacturers themselves seem to have acted as if they believed that in the prevailing price ranges of most of the postwar period the demand for cars was inelastic with respect to price changes, or at least not so elastic as to offset with increased total revenue the increased total costs of larger volume.[29] The fact that they consistently increased prices from 1953, when the shortages of earlier years ended, through 1958 [30] appears consistent with an explanation that the manufacturers considered the total demand for cars to be relatively inelastic or only slightly elastic with respect to price changes. Such action, of course, seems consistent with the conclusions of the statistical studies and particularly the weight given to the consumer income factor.

After about 1958, however, the situation seems to have been somewhat different. Comparison though is not easy. Price and income were not the only variables. Substantial variations in product quality and other features made price

[29] A coefficient of price elasticity of demand substantially in excess of -1 may be required to justify price cutting. The problem is one of relative revenue and cost changes with the changes in price and resulting output. With a coefficient of price elasticity of -1, e.g., a price cut would leave total revenue unchanged, the percentage reduction in price being just offset by an equal percentage increase in units sold; and if the additional units sold cost anything to produce, lower profits would result. With larger output, unit cost might be lower along with the lowered unit revenue, fixed costs being unchanged; but total costs would be increased by the amount of added variable cost for the larger output, thus pressing more closely the unchanged total revenue. Even a coefficient of -1.5 may not be sufficient to offset cost changes, despite the relatively large portion of fixed costs in the automobile industry. See Clare E. Griffin, "When Is Price Reduction Profitable?" *Harvard Business Review*, XXXVIII (September-October, 1960), 125-32.

[30] *Supra*, chapter vi. The two Independents were exceptions to the rising pattern in 1958 and 1959.

comparisons over time difficult. As we saw in Chapter VI, there was a trend toward larger, more luxurious cars by the larger domestic firms through 1958. Relying on a favorable influence of generally rising income, firms emphasized non-price competition: innovation, style change, and the addition of more and more optional features. Widespread price reductions were avoided by the manufacturers. With the introduction of compact cars and the invasion of foreign makes, the situation became even more complicated because of qualitative variations between such cars and the then current full-sized makes. However, it may be observed that the compact car emphasis halted for a lengthy period the upward trend in the average purchase price per passenger car, thereby tending to stabilize the average cost of obtaining passenger car ownership, albeit perhaps with some sacrifice in quality if size of the car was important. Also indicated perhaps was an awareness by the larger manufacturers that further increases in price might place their cars in highly elastic portions of their demand curves so that their unit sales would fall drastically and their total revenues decline, a rather distressing predicament because of their heavy fixed costs. What might have happened if they *had* raised prices, can only be guessed. However, the compact car introduction was eventually followed by considerably larger sales volumes and profits.

The demands for the cars of the individual firm appear to have been considerably more elastic than the demand for all cars. Substantial variations occurred in the shares of the market held by cars of the different manufacturers from year to year. In addition to the influences on the total demand for cars, the demand for a particular car may be affected by its quality, performance, appearance, distinctiveness, price, and other factors in relation to other makes of cars. Styling differentiation may exert a significant influence on the demand for individual makes, and other sales promotion activities also may be important. Yet even these factors were relevant only within the framework of what the other firms were doing.

In this connection it is interesting to note an observation by D. K. Smith in his study of Kaiser-Frazer. Because of a price cut of more than $300 on a certain Kaiser model, Smith concluded that the demand curve for this particular Kaiser model must have been very steeply sloped "since sales increased imperceptibly after the slash."[31] Similar results occurred with other makes. The special promotional price cuts of the leading Independents in 1954 evidently had little influence on their sales. Concurrent with the mergers, sales of their makes fell to very low levels in 1954. Other considerations obviously were far more important than the price cuts.

Thus it seems the demand for cars was relatively inelastic or only slightly elastic with respect to price changes during most of the postwar period but much more sensitive to consumer income changes. In view of these conditions and since the domestic industry was oligopolistic in both structure and behavior, there was little that individual firms could do to stimulate sales of their cars through extensive price cuts. Price cutting by a major manufacturer was likely to be followed by all competing firms in the industry. If all firms in the industry cut prices, their relative market shares would probably remain relatively unchanged; and, unless the total demand for passenger cars was highly elastic with respect to the price reductions, no benefits could be expected to accrue to the industry in the form of higher profits. The market was not known with certainty; and that was part of the problem facing the manufacturers of automobiles.

Accepting as fact the greater sensitivity of automobile sales to income, an alternative course of action emphasizes nonprice competition as a method of maintaining and expanding sales. It appears quite clear that this was a dominant form of competition in the domestic United States car market. The firms all were engaged in struggles to expand and maintain their shares of total domestic sales. Even General Motors, the largest firm in the industry, considered the maintenance of its share of the market as a collateral, though possibly secondary, objective exceeded in importance only by the accomplishment of its target rate of return on investment.[32] Marketing activities, and particularly sales promotion, thus were very important to the automobile industry; and, influenced by the existing market environment, including the unknown and only partly predictable features of that environment, the activities of the firms of the industry tended to follow a rather standardized pattern in which volume of sales

[31] D. K. Smith, "The Problems of a New Firm in an Oligopolistic Industry: Kaiser-Frazer's Experience in the Motor Vehicle Industry," (unpublished Ph.D. dissertation, Harvard University, May, 1950), p. 268.
[32] R. F. Lanzillotti, "Pricing Objectives in Large Companies," *The American Economic Review*, XLVIII (December, 1958), 925, Table 1.

achieved also could be expected to exert significant influence on unit cost and effectiveness.

STYLE AND STYLE CHANGE

"Nonprice" competition has long been customary in the United States automobile market—ever since Ford adopted the practice of other companies and began to emphasize non-price factors in promotion in the 1930's.[33] Strategies emphasizing factors other than price were increasingly stressed in the postwar period and, if anything, became even more powerful weapons of the Big Three, particularly General Motors, in their activities designed to maintain or enlarge market penetration. Among the more potent but complex to evaluate weapons in the sales promotion or merchandising arsenals of the individual firms were their choices of design or style of their passenger cars and optional equipment; and perhaps of even more importance were their frequent changes in style. As a stimulus to sales, change was made for the sake of change. The small as well as the large firms of the industry engaged in the style and style change competition, although with somewhat different strategies because of the differences in their scales of operation.

The "style" of a product is the "distinctive or characteristic mode of presentation or construction of the product."[34] In the case of a passenger car, "style" may be taken as including both appearance and engineering features. Both contributed to the distinctiveness of a particular make; and both could be used to describe the "style" of a car to prospective buyers.

Justification of Styling Emphasis

Officials of the domestic car manufacturing firms considered styling to be of great importance in stimulating and maintaining the sales of their cars. The basis of the industry viewpoint was revealed in the words of Ralph C. Epstein in his classic study of the automobile industry: "Supplying a

[33] Joe S. Bain, *Barriers to New Competition* (Cambridge, Mass.: Harvard University Press, 1956), p. 298. Also see H. B. Vanderblue, "Pricing Policies in the Automobile Industry," *Harvard Business Review*, XVII (Summer, 1939), 385-401 and XVIII (Autumn, 1939), 64-81, esp. 65; and U. S., Federal Trade Commission, *op. cit.*, esp. pp. 1073-74.

[34] *Webster's Collegiate Dictionary*, 5th edition (Springfield, Mass.: G. & C. Merriam Company, 1944), p. 990.

product is but one side of manufacture in its full economic sense; suiting that product to the demands of the mass of its consumers is the complementary necessity without which industrial leadership cannot be long maintained."[35] The early remarks of Arthur Pound in his discussion of the role of research at General Motors also appear relevant:

> There are constants in the automobile business, plenty of them; but, paradoxically, the greatest constant of all is change. He who stands still is lost. The public must be wooed through change as well as quality; science and art provide the material for beneficial change in such abundance that the timing of change becomes an all-important factor; hence the question which management faces is not so much, "Shall we change?" but rather, "How and when shall we change?" . . .
>
> Not all beneficial changes can be introduced drastically as soon as they have been developed. While the public insists on change, it prefers evolution to revolution. Millions can be lost by being too far ahead of the times, just as they can be lost by being too far behind the times.[36]

In addition, a pertinent clue to industry behavior in regard to emphasis on style appears in an observation of C. M. Hewitt that "few consumers want to appear behind the times."[37] If true, this provided a factor on which manufacturers could capitalize to stimulate sales.

The president of American Motors characterized the passenger car industry as a style industry comparable to that of ladies' hats. The latest styles were considered essential to preservation of the market position of the firm. Even large firms were not free of the danger of falling behind in their styling and thereby risking a decline in sales. A financial vice-president of Ford Motor Company, a firm engaged in aggressive efforts to improve its position through style changes, summarized the viewpoint of his firm regarding style and style changes:

> In our own experience we find when the model is

[35] Ralph C. Epstein, *op. cit.*, p. 284.

[36] Arthur Pound, *The Turning Wheel* (Garden City, New York: Doubleday, Doran & Company, Inc., 1934), pp. 285-86.

[37] C. M. Hewitt, Jr., *Automobile Franchise Agreements* (Homewood, Illinois: Richard D. Irwin, Inc., 1956), p. 140.

not changed substantially, that the customers do not buy it.

Now not only we, but our competitors, have had the same experience, . . .

We would like to have lower tooling costs, we would like to have people buy our models, but we find we have to make these changes if we are going to get an increasing share of the business.[38]

The view taken was that consumers would indicate by their purchases which style was most preferred. The most preferred styles would sell best, and the company which provided the preferred styles was in a most fortunate position. The feeling was that style changes significantly influenced the level of demand for the products of the individual firm and that style changes had to be made to enable the firm to expand, or even retain, its market share.

The influence of style changes on the sales of particular makes of passenger cars appears to have been indicated, for example, in the changing market shares of Ford and Chevrolet from 1957 to 1958. In 1957, Ford edged Chevrolet in sales and secured 24.97 per cent of the market compared with 24.34 per cent of the market for Chevrolet.[39] The 1957 Ford cars had been changed substantially from the 1956 models, but the 1956 and 1957 Chevrolets were quite similar. In 1958, Ford continued much the same styling as in 1957 while Chevrolet changed completely from its 1957 model. A drastic slump in Ford car sales occurred during the 1958 recession. While Chevrolet unit sales also fell during the recession, they fell less sharply than Ford sales; and their share of total United States sales expanded. In 1958, Ford's market share fell to 22.11 per cent while Chevrolet captured 26.52 per cent. The apparent major influence slowing the unit sales decline of Chevrolet during the recession was its major style change. Plymouth, which also continued the 1957 styling through 1958, also experienced a slump in its share of sales from 9.95 per cent in 1957 to 8.40 per cent in 1958. There is little wonder then that the domestic manufacturers considered styling changes of great importance in maintaining sales of particular makes, and a boon to the industry in bringing

[38] U. S., Senate, Committee on the Judiciary, Subcommittee on Antitrust and Monopoly, *Hearings, Administered Prices*, 85th Congress, 2nd Session, Pursuant to S. Res. 57 and S. Res. 231 (Washington: U. S. Government Printing Office, 1958), Part 6, p. 2657.

[39] *Automotive Industries*, March 15, 1959, p. 82.

former buyers of cars back into the new car market sooner than would have been the case without style change. Alternative strategies may have been available; but style obviously was important to the competitive struggle in the passenger car market.

Tooling Costs of Style Change

Emphasis upon style and style changes as a major competitive factor in the passenger car market was accompanied by a general and substantial rise in expenditures on tooling required for producing automobiles. Tables 13 and 14 show big increases occurred in the 1950's in the annual total expenses of amortization of the special commercial tools, dies, and equipment used in the automobile industry and in the expenses of amortization per car produced. Rapid amortization of the special tools prevailed since the tools were usable only with the styles for which they were planned. Although not all of the amortization was attributable to passenger car production, most of it evidently was the result of car output.

The figures of the Big Three resulted in part from their truck and other operations; but offsetting these, the Independents also had other operations: appliances for American Motors and trucks for Studebaker. Then, too, relatively speaking, little effort was expended on making styling changes in trucks and other transportation equipment also produced by some of the car manufacturers; and for those firms that were major producers of household appliances, it is probable that only small portions of their total special tooling expenses were attributable to appliances. Tooling for appliances was far less complex in variety and extent than that for cars. Finally, some products of the firms, such as defense goods, were not style goods at all and had no bearing on commercial special tooling. Variations among the firms in degrees of integration of part and component production and hence of inclusiveness of tooling cost tend to limit direct company comparisons of tooling cost per unit produced; however, despite such discrepancies, which perhaps were most important in the case of General Motors because of its many other operations, the figures provide a fair indication of the magnitude and trends in tooling costs for passenger car production. Passenger car output was the item of overwhelming importance to each of the automobile manufacturers. As may be seen, enormous sums were expended on the tooling for passenger car production.

The cost of making style changes and the postwar rise in these costs, shown in Tables 13 and 14, contributed to the difficulties of the small firms as independents. Shortly after the mergers, as we saw previously, officials of both American Motors and Studebaker-Packard singled out rising tooling costs as having been one of the more impelling reasons for the mergers. In essence these increased costs raised the hurdles which had to be met for survival.

With General Motors leading the way (although some of its high tooling cost may be attributed to operations other than passenger car production as well as to its greater degree

TABLE 13

AMORTIZATION OF SPECIAL COMMERCIAL TOOLS, DIES, AND EQUIPMENT BY THE INDEPENDENTS AND THE BIG THREE, 1946-1963 [a]

(Millions of Dollars)

Year	AMC [b]	Hudson	S-P [c]	Stude-baker	Chrysler	Ford	G.M.
1946	$ 2.2	$ 1.3	$ 3.1	$ 3.5	$ 14.4	—	$ 49.9
1947	1.3	1.1	2.6	5.9	2.1	—	80.3
1948	2.1	8.9	3.0	4.1	8.7	—	108.6
1949	7.6	3.9	2.8	4.8	49.4	—	131.7
1950	7.3	3.5	7.9	5.9	10.7	—	141.6
1951	8.3	2.2	7.2	5.3	34.4	$ 19.1	181.9
1952	7.4	2.1	1.4	3.6	30.3	65.9	163.9
1953	10.1	14.0 [d]	3.5	13.1	66.5	57.7	352.5
1954	19.2	—	19.0	—	37.4	71.0	312.6
1955	15.1	—	21.4	—	110.2	122.9	411.5
1956	16.4	—	11.3	—	51.0	128.2	405.0
1957	11.9	—	6.0	—	126.9	208.8	427.3
1958	11.0	—	4.8	—	69.4	215.9	443.8
1959	11.9	—	5.4	—	81.3	188.3	424.6
1960	10.9	—	6.4	—	165.8	143.6	557.5
1961	18.0	—	5.7	—	90.2	184.1	467.0
1962	19.8	—	6.6	—	67.2	170.1	526.9
1963	19.3	—	—	—	93.9	188.9	605.4

[a] Source: Corporation annual reports and *Moody's Industrial Manual*, 1947-1963 editions (New York: Moody's Investors Service).

[b] Figures for AMC are for Nash-Kelvinator for the years 1946-1953; effective with merger on May 1, 1954, Hudson operations are included.

[c] Figures for S-P are for Packard for the years 1946-1953; effective with merger on October 1, 1954, Studebaker operations are included.

[d] Includes accelerated depreciation for writeoff of equipment. A separate figure for depreciation and for amortization of special tools and equipment was not given.

TABLE 14

AMORTIZATION OF SPECIAL COMMERCIAL TOOLS, DIES,
AND EQUIPMENT PER CAR PRODUCED BY THE
INDEPENDENTS AND THE BIG THREE, 1946-1963 [a]

Year	AMC [b]	Hudson	S-P [c]	Stude-baker	Chrysler	Ford	G.M.
1946	$ 31	$ 14	$ 72	$46	$ 27	—	$ 60
1947	11	11	47	48	3	—	56
1948	18	61	31	25	10	—	69
1949	54	27	27	21	44	—	60
1950	41	25	110	22	9	—	46
1951	47	23	95	24	28	$ 16	81
1952	53	27	22	22	32	66	91
1953	61	181	44	70	53	37	126
1954	185	—	169	—	52	42	109
1955	102	—	118	—	80	55	103
1956	138	—	118	—	59	77	132
1957	112	—	82	—	104	111	152
1958	62	—	85	—	119	177	205
1959	32	—	35	—	110	108	166
1960	23	—	61	—	163	76	175
1961	47	—	72	—	139	109	171
1962	44	—	76	—	94	88	141
1963	40	—	—	—	90	96	148

[a] Source: Computations based on amortization of special tools, dies, jigs, and equipment from Table 13 *supra* and passenger car production by manufacturer from *Automobile Facts and Figures* (1958-1964 editions) except for American Motors (Nash-Kelvinator) for which the data were for production before 1954 and factory sales thereafter as reported by the firm for years ended September 30.

[b] Nash-Kelvinator for 1946-1953, American Motors for 1954-1963.

[c] Packard for 1946-1953, Studebaker-Packard for 1954-1962.

of integration of part and component production than was the case for the other firms), total tooling costs and tooling costs per car produced by the industry mounted steadily. Part of the increase in tooling cost may be attributed to the general postwar inflation, the prices of producers goods by the late 1950's having risen on the order of 50 to 70 per cent above their 1947-1949 levels;[40] but since increases in the unit tooling

[40] Using the 1947-1949 base period, the wholesale price index of machinery and motive products stood at 128.4 in 1955, 149.8 in 1958, and 153.0 in 1959; of metalworking machinery and equipment at 142.5, 170.1, and 174.5 in the same years; and of electrical machinery and equipment at 128.2, 152.2, and 154.4 in the same years. Using the same base period, the index for producers' finished goods for manufacturing industries reached 130.9 in 1955, 155.0 in 1958, and 158.1 in 1959. U. S., Department of Commerce, *Statistical Abstract of the United States*, 1961, pp. 331-32.

costs of the industry ranged upward from 200 to 1,000 per cent or more over the same period, much of the rise must be attributed to other factors. Although there was a trend toward more complex vehicles with complicated, often automatic, optional equipment, particularly automatic transmissions, which required added tooling for production, the problem of continued rise in the cost of tooling, especially as evidenced in the historical data for the Big Three, was not so much in the choice of style, but in an acceleration of the frequency of major change in style.[41]

Major style changes came with increasing frequency after the end of World War II, particularly in the 1950's by the Big Three, culminating in a complete annual change by General Motors between the 1958 and 1959 models, introduced in late 1957 and 1958, respectively.[42] Ford followed a similar pattern. In the model years 1946-1954, the Ford basic bodies were each used for three model year intervals. One was used for 1946-1948, another for 1949-1951, and yet another for 1952-1954. The next two basic bodies were used for two model years, one for 1955-1956 and another for 1957-1958.[43] The 1959 model Ford received complete sheet metal restyling although the over-all effect followed the evolutionary pattern

[41] Increased emphasis on the style element and change in style in the 1950's also showed up in increased percentages of the sales dollar required to cover amortization of special tooling. G. M.'s tooling amortization ranged between 1.9 and 2.4 per cent of sales from 1947 through 1952; from 1953 through 1959, the range was between 3.2 per cent and 4.7 per cent, the 4.7 per cent having occurred in 1958 with the second highest figure having been in 1957 at 3.9 per cent. The rates for Chrysler and Ford generally were lower than those for G. M. Chrysler's percentage rose from only 0.2 in 1947 to 3.2 in 1955, 3.6 in 1957, 3.2 in 1958, and 3.1 in 1959. Ford's percentage followed a similar pattern of increase. American Motors' percentage rose from 0.5 per cent in 1947 to 4.0 in 1956 before falling in the late 1950's with its relative stabilizing of Rambler's style and expanding sales volume.

[42] All General Motors makes were changed from 1958 to 1959 models; in the 1959 models they all used the same basic body shell except for the Chevrolet Corvette sports model. *Consumer Reports*, XXIV (April, 1959), 166 and 179; and *Business Week*, June 21, 1958, p. 21.

[43] U. S., Senate, Committee on the Judiciary, Subcommittee on Antitrust and Monopoly, *Report, Administered Prices, op. cit.*, pp. 84-85. Ford's major model changes were speeded up from a three year interval to a two year interval for the 1959 model; in addition, Ford made significant changes from the 1957 to 1958 model with the introduction of a new engine and extensive exterior sheet metal changes although many components of the previous year were used.

of 1957 and 1958.[44] Ford changed extensively again in 1960, adopting a sharply sloping front end design with rather disastrous sales results; but its next basic design for its full-sized cars carried from 1961 through 1963 models. Chrysler also changed styles frequently.[45] With the introduction of compact cars, the Big Three slowed the frequency of change of their cars and retained essentially the same basic styles for three years before their next major changes; but tooling expenses remained large because of the proliferation of new models. (The compact cars had required upon their introductions completely new tooling, distinctive from that of previously existing makes.)

Although the greatest emphasis on style change stemmed from the Big Three, the smaller domestic manufacturers also changed frequently.[46] Studebaker led the postwar style parade with its 1947 model, the first newly designed postwar car, and enjoyed considerable sales success. Unfortunately, the probabilities of repeated success seem to have been against Studebaker, for its later changes seemed far less acceptable to consumers. All the leading Independents had introduced new styles by the time of the 1949 models, which included the first completely new postwar Big Three make, the 1949 Ford; and they followed this with additional major style changes during the 1950's. Their introduction of compact cars, of course, represented major changes.

Despite the competitive pressures imposed by the emphasis of the Big Three on style change as a means of promoting sales—their costs were large but so were their sales volumes—comparison of the historical data of tooling cost per car supports the observation of George Romney that the small firm could obtain as low a unit cost for tooling as a larger volume producer if outputs of 200,000-400,000 units per year could be achieved, since multiple tooling generally was used in the industry for annual outputs above these levels.[47] However, the actual relationships among the large and small

44 *Consumer Reports, loc. cit.*, p. 186.

45 U. S., Senate, Committee on the Judiciary, Subcommittee on Antitrust and Monopoly, *op. cit.*, p. 85. Chrysler followed a two-year interval for major changes from 1953 through 1958 models, changing in 1953, in 1955, and again in 1957.

46 After the Independents merged, there were continued style changes by them. Even American Motors' reintroduction in 1958 of the Rambler first introduced in 1950 may be considered as a style change since the car had been dropped after the 1955 models.

47 *Supra*, chapter viii.

volume producers seem to have been more subtle than those indicated by the historical tooling cost data, for the leading Independents generally had fallen short of such output levels before the substantial comeback of American Motors after 1957. Although they participated in the style competition, apparently to the extent that they were able to generate the cash to do so, the leading Independents followed a practice of making fewer major and less extensive minor style changes than the Big Three, thereby being able to amortize their special tooling over longer periods of time. This was an alternative strategy, but it was also one involving considerable risk in a competitive struggle involving style. That the relationship was more subtle than indicated by the historical cost comparison is reflected in the difficulties of the Independents as separate firms, although several of them prior to the mergers had achieved annual outputs of approximately 200,000 or more units, and, in retrospect, in the eventual withdrawal of Studebaker from the domestic manufacture of automobiles in 1963, a near-record production year for the domestic industry.

With large fixed expenditures, say on the order of $20,-000,000 to $40,000,000 for retooling with a new set of body dies for a single style and even more for a variety of styles, large volumes were required for low tooling cost per unit. Once purchased, the tooling could be expected to last for substantial periods; some of the tooling for stamping lighter sheet metal body components may have been usable through outputs of 1,000,000 or more units before physical deterioration of the dies occurred. Large outputs thus had to be sustained to achieve low unit cost of the fixed investments in tooling. The rise in amortization of special tooling per car produced by General Motors and Ford in 1958, for example, was partly traceable to their sales decline combined with the fixed costs of tooling.

The tooling cost problem of the smaller volume producer resided in the frequency of style change required to provide a sufficiently acceptable and up-to-date product to the consumer. By way of illustration, if all the body tooling for production of a selected style had useful life of 1,500,000 to 2,000,000 units and such volumes were secured on an annual basis from the tooling, Ford or Chevrolet with annual outputs in these ranges for one basic style during much of the 1950's could fully utilize the tooling each year. Tooling would have to be replaced; and it could be replaced with that for an existing style or for a new style at no added cost.[48] There might be added cost for the design and engineering of the new tooling,[49] but the new tooling itself would not involve larger expenditures than replacement of the worn out tools and dies with identical tools and dies. Under such assumed conditions, annual style changes would be feasible for the largest volume makes; and any smaller volume make on which annual style changes were made would be saddled with high tooling costs per unit. At 500,000 units per year, assuming the different manufacturers paid the same for their tooling and that the same conditions held as to the life of the tooling, the costs per unit for annual change would be three times those of the larger volume makes; or the same unit cost could be achieved with a style change after three years. Smaller volume producers would be even more disadvantaged. However, if three sets of tools and dies were used for the larger volume makes by their producers to achieve the large annual outputs, the

[48] Richard Austin Smith, in "Detroit is Flying by the Seat of Its Pants," *Fortune*, LXIII (January, 1961), 190, indicates his belief that General Motors was near the output levels at which its tooling would have to be replaced every two years because of physical deterioration. Since common basic body components were used for several of the firm's makes, the output volumes from much of its tooling were larger than those of its individual makes. The fact that G. M. consistently made large expenditures for new tooling even during the late 1940's and early 1950's, a period of relatively little change in its cars, lends support to this observation, the firm's annual expenditures on new tooling having approximately equalled the annual amortization expense.

[49] Substantial sums also were expended in the design, engineering, and execution, including the removal of old and the installation of new tools and equipment, of annual style changes, primarily for the personnel involved in such activities. At their rates in 1957, the total sums being spent on making style changes were reported to be approximately $500,-000,000 for General Motors, $350,000,000 for Ford, and $200,000,000 for Chrysler. See U. S., Senate, Committee on the Judiciary, Subcommittee on Antitrust and Monopoly, *Hearings, Administered Prices, op. cit.,* Parts 6-7, pp. 2513, 2828, and 4175. It is interesting to note that the General Motors and Chrysler total style change costs each exceeded their respective total amortization of special tooling in 1957 by about $70,000,000. The difference for Ford was greater because of its expenditures for the Edsel which was then in process of introduction. Were these fixed costs of style change? If so, the larger volume producer certainly had a unit cost advantage, especially in the case of General Motors compared with Chrysler. A single line producer, of course, could expect much lower total costs than these; and with a lower rate of major change in style such costs could be spread over longer periods and their annual amount reduced.

cost position of a 500,000 unit producer would equal that of the larger volume producer for changes of equal magnitude and frequency; but any smaller volume producer would still be at a disadvantage.

The actual relationships may not have corresponded precisely with those assumed, because the productive lives of the tools, dies, and equipment may have been longer or shorter in differing proportions, partly because of differences in quality deliberately chosen by designers of the tooling on the basis of anticipated volume requirements, and the production arrangements may have been in varying combinations with multiple tooling for some operations but not for others. Nevertheless, the need for keeping up to date with the latest and most preferred styles was a costly consideration, especially for any producers smaller than the largest. With the pace of style change accelerated in the 1950's, such a conclusion seems consistent with the proportionately greater increases during the 1950's in unit tooling cost for Chrysler and Ford, the two smaller members of the Big Three, compared with General Motors, whose makes generally sold in the greatest volumes. And, any smaller volume producer evidently was even harder pressed in trying to keep up with an increased frequency of style change in the 1950's. Herein lay a necessity for an alternative strategy.[50]

Without question, then, the unit cost advantage in making style changes lay with large volume producers. The question facing a firm was one of how large the volume had to be to achieve competitive tooling costs. In retrospect, the estimate presented by Romney, which was on the order of 200,000 to 400,000 or so units per year for one- to two-shift operation, with modification that the latter was considerably better than the former, seems to have been a fair estimate of the requirements for one line of cars. This was true provided the models

[50] The payoff for General Motors in making frequent sweeping style changes, despite the drawback of an apparently high tooling cost per unit of output, was in a rather persistent increase in its market share. If smaller firms suffered tooling cost disadvantages in making as frequent style changes, they could, and probably found it necessary to, emphasize other promotional strategies, a fact which would have been reflected in lower historical tooling costs per unit with less frequent change of style. The necessity for an alternative strategy is discussed in even stronger terms than here in a penetrating article by John A. Menge, "Style Change Costs as a Market Weapon," *Quarterly Journal of Economics*, LXXVI (November, 1962), 632-47.

in such a line were relatively restricted, and provided consumers found the chosen basic body shell with annual external appearance changes sufficiently acceptable to generate such sales volumes for three or four years, and also provided there was sufficient proliferation in the makes and models of the larger firms to restrain them from making annual style changes of major proportions. The minimum output targets of the Big Three for their compact cars, which was indicated in Chapter VIII, and their reduced frequency of major style change after their introduction of such cars seem to have been consistent with the above observations. Also, tooling in wide variety and often in multiple die sets was used for the largest volume makes for a number of reasons. Geographic dispersion, physical production limits of the tools and equipment used, and diversity of body styles and options within a basic line of cars resulted in the use of multiple tooling. Even in the middle and late 1950's when Chevrolet and Ford were each producing approximately 1,500,000 or more cars per year of essentially one basic style, the total was fragmented into a variety of body styles and equipment options. Six-cylinder and eight-cylinder engines in several displacements and horsepowers were offered in each make. There were two-door and four-door models, conventional sedans, hardtop models, convertibles, and station wagons, for each of which special tooling was required. Hoods, rear deck lids, and some basic body shell components were perhaps produced in annual volumes of 1,-500,000 or more units,[51] in which case the larger producer had an advantage of being able to put into the presses the necessary dies and leave them for an entire annual production run without having to cycle them; but because of the many other components in which variety was offered, the total annual output was built up from the use of tooling in wide variety to produce the diversity of components. Thus, by restricting its variety of body styles and equipment options to a narrow base, the small firm evidently could obtain sufficient utilization of its tooling for competitive costs if it could generate sales of 200,000 to 400,000 units with the upper figure for two-shift operation being the better of the two. For greater

[51] This was the case in the middle 1950's when consumers were willing to buy relatively standardized all-purpose cars in enormous volume. The segmentation of the market and proliferation of models at the end of the decade evidently changed the situation. See the comments on changes in production technique, including a later necessity for "flexible automation," in *Business Week*, October 27, 1962, pp. 150-54.

diversity in body and equipment options, much larger total annual volumes for a given make may have been essential for low tooling costs. There were, however, other volume aspects to the problem of style.

The Risks of Style Change

There were risks involved in not making style changes, but there were also risks in making changes. Indeed, either way the risks connected with decisions regarding style were probably greater than with other merchandising methods, for once a choice was made, the firm was committed for an extended period of time. To try to overcome these risks, consumer surveys were used by the manufacturers to find out what consumers liked and disliked about their products and what they would like in their next car.[52] Consumer demands were recognized as being capricious, but efforts were made to predict them. The firms then directed their efforts toward supplying features which appeared to be widely preferred. Defensive imitation of competitors' innovations was a frequent occurrence.

The firms all maintained large and highly capable staffs to plan and put into production the preferred styling features. Substantial sums were spent on these activities long before the new style models were finally brought to the market. Expenditures had to be made on research, engineering, and planning the style changes. New tools, dies, and equipment had to be purchased and set up for production. Expenditures had to be made for removal of old equipment and its replacement with new equipment. Contracts had to be let for new parts and components for which complete specifications must have been prepared. All these complex activities had to be completed prior to the time of the production of the first of a new style car.

The time required for changes in style was substantial. Ford, for example, ordinarily required about four years for introduction of new models.[53] "Crash programs" could shorten the period to about two years for the introduction of a com-

---

[52] See U. S., Senate, Committee on the Judiciary, Subcommittee on Antitrust and Monopoly, *Hearings, A Study of the Antitrust Laws*, 84th Congress, 1st Session, Pursuant to S. Res. 61 (Washington: U. S. Government Printing Office, 1956), Part 7, pp. 3506-07; and *Hearings, Administered Prices, op. cit.*, Part 6, pp. 2566, 2731, and 2797.

[53] *Ibid.*, p. 2731.

ρ.etely new car; but such programs usually involved substantial added costs. Styling programs of the other manufacturers, including the Independents, covered comparable periods of time. Even after having completed all the basic planning and design work for a new engine, for example, American Motors needed fifteen months from the blueprint stage to get their new V-eight engine into production in 1956 on a "crash program" basis. Ordinarily three to four years were required for such a change by American Motors.[54] With long time periods involved in the planning and introduction of new models, consumer preferences might change substantially. Competitive offerings also could change substantially over such long periods. In combination with the uncertainties of prediction, the result was a high degree of risk related to the choice of style, whether continuation of an existing style or introduction of a new style. The greater the time lag from research to introduction, the greater appears to have been the risk of styling error in the automobile industry. New models could turn out to be what consumers might have wanted at the time they were planned but not at the time of their final introduction to the public.

The risks of error in styling were hazards facing both large and small firms. The introduction and subsequent withdrawal of the ill-fated Edsel by Ford demonstrated the risks inherent in shifting consumer preferences and changing competitive offerings over the time period from the planning stage to final introduction of a car to the public. Similar problems appear to have existed in the early introductions of the 1950 Nash Rambler and the 1953 Hudson Jet, two early compact cars. The two cars were both eventually discontinued; for the Hudson Jet, it was permanent. The original 100-inch wheelbase Nash Rambler was replaced in 1955 by the 108-inch wheelbase Rambler which proved to be the basis for American Motors' comeback. In 1958, the original 100-inch wheelbase Rambler was reintroduced as the Rambler American. Its earlier introduction may have been somewhat ahead of the times; but as things turned out, it was a forerunner of future developments. American Motors may be considered fortunate to have had the tooling for the original Rambler readily available for reintroduction of the

[54] Roy D. Chapin, "The Resurgence of American Motors," A Speech before the Harvard Business School Club of Detroit, April, 1958; and American Motors Corporation, *Annual Report*, 1956, p. 2.

car as evidence of consumer preference for such a car accumulated. The timing of style change was important. It, too, was an element of risk.

Since consumer preferences could not be predicted with absolute certainty, one of the more immediate, but not readily measurable, styling disadvantages of the Independents, particularly before the mergers, appeared in their more limited opportunity for styling diversity. With product diversification in the sense of having several different lines of cars following somewhat different styling patterns, the large firm could spread the risks of styling choices over several makes, using somewhat different approaches for each. Errors on one make might be offset by success on others. Ford's Edsel, for example, may have been a large failure; but Ford's losses from it were more than offset by profits on the firm's other lines. Unfortunate would be the firm that made errors on all its makes. With only one line or at best a narrow product line, the smaller firm lacked as great an opportunity for spreading risk through product diversity. Mistakes by a specialist producer would be relatively more crucial. The acquisition of a diversity of lines in the mergers in 1954 presumably would have reduced the Independents' risk of failure from poor styling choices. Unfortunately, the lack of broader consumer acceptance of the then existing Independent makes, particularly of the full-sized Hudson, Nash, Packard and Studebaker makes whose sales fell sharply after 1953, prevented the accomplishment of this objective of merger. Nevertheless, the advantage of some product diversity was evidenced in a rising sales volume after 1954 for Rambler, which was distinct from the full-sized Nash and Hudson lines. Fortunate was American Motors to have had such diversity. Unfortunate was Studebaker-Packard to have suffered falling sales of both its makes at the same time, a decline which had started before the merger and continued thereafter.

In brief, after the return of more competitive conditions in 1953, even though the economies of large scale may have been sufficiently exhausted at outputs of 200,000 to 400,000 units to permit a firm to obtain on one line of cars tooling costs competitive with most makes, the necessity for a diversity of product styles to spread the costs of error raised substantially the volume requirements for an automobile manufacturer over the long run, perhaps doubling the minimum requirement if diversity and low unit tooling costs on each line or make were sought simultaneously. Faced by the dangers of falling behind with infrequent change or the probability of higher unit costs of frequent style change, the increased tempo of the style race after 1952 raised the hurdles to be met for continued participation of the small producer in the automobile industry.

ADVERTISING

Advertising played an important part in the promotional schemes of automobile manufacturers. With new models being introduced annually, it was desirable for quickly imparting knowledge of the new models to consumers; but much advertising also was used on a continuing basis. Repetition in advertising was essential in establishing and retaining product identity with consumers, the effects of advertising tending to cumulate over time.[55] Although measuring precise effects of specific advertising campaigns confronted industry officials with complex problems, the general nature of the cost relationships to be expected among large and small volume producers seems to have been evident. Covering a national market was costly for automobile manufacturers; and because many advertising media involved fixed commitments for their use, volume of output could be expected to exert important influence on the unit cost and total effectiveness of the advertising phase of the individual manufacturer's promotional activities.

Since prospective purchasers of new cars and their potential choices of a new make could not be identified with certainty—about two out of three car buyers who already owned a car usually bought a new car of the same make as that previously owned,[56] but the timing of their new purchase was not predictable with certainty — the principal advertising media chosen by the manufacturers were those with broad dissemination among large numbers of potential customers. To reach prospective purchasers in the many local markets comprising the national market, the manufacturers used the mass media, magazines, newspapers, radio, television, and

[55] See the comments on the values of repetition in advertising in D. B. Lucas and S. H. Britt, *Advertising Psychology and Research* (New York: McGraw-Hill Book Co., Inc., 1950), pp. 80-90.

[56] See the observation on this relationship by Bedros Peter Pashigian, *The Distribution of Automobiles, An Economic Analysis of the Franchise System*, Ford Foundation Doctoral Dissertation 1960 Award Winner (Englewood Cliffs, N. J.: Prentice-Hall, Inc., 1961), pp. 6-7.

even direct mail broadly distributed. The larger producer, because of the fixed costs of using the mass media in combination with a greater density of coverage of the mass market by the larger producer's product, could be expected to secure lower cost per unit sold in reaching consumers with its advertising. Although specific campaigns or themes may vary in effectiveness, the less expensive sometimes providing the greatest impact, the total market impact of a large volume producer's advertising, in general, could be expected to be greater than that of a smaller producer at the same cost per unit sold, assuming that both the large and small producers paid the same rate for use of comparable time and space in the respective media; or, for the same total impact in terms of time, space, and frequency of coverage, the cost per unit sold for the larger volume producer could be expected to be lower than for a smaller producer.

The use of television as an advertising medium may be used to illustrate the unit cost advantage of a large producer over a small producer. Television had numerous advantages for coverage of large regions and populations. It was timely; it provided a combination of vocal, sight, and motion characteristics which were quite effective; and, depending on the type of coverage desired, it could be used to appeal to a national market or to regional and local markets, all of which possessed characteristics of mass coverage. For a car manufacturer selling in most of the local markets throughout the United States, it was feasible for use in appeals to potential customers throughout the nation. It also could be used on a more selective basis for "spot" commercials, but even such commercials provided a mass coverage, though on a smaller scale. If large and small firms alike attempted to cover the same market using the medium of television, the total cost to each would be the same for comparable time and coverage, for a nationally televised program on a weekly basis perhaps $2,500,000 per year, not including talent costs. Both could even use the same network. Large sales volumes were essential to making use of such a medium at reasonable unit cost. The large producer, because of its larger volume, would have lower costs per car sold than the small producer. For comparable time, space, and coverage, the larger volume producer could be expected to have relatively lower unit costs than the small producer *ad infinitum.* Conversely, the large producer could be expected to secure more saturation in terms of time, space, and frequency at the same unit cost as that of a small producer. For example, Chevrolet might have three television programs to only one for Rambler. Appeals to massive audiences of prospective purchasers through such other media as magazines, newspapers, or radio could be expected to produce similar results because of the fixed costs of using the media, whether for local or national coverage. The small producer thus, in general, could be expected to operate at a relative cost disadvantage in advertising its products.

Fortunately for the smaller volume producer, the total impact or effectiveness of advertising expenditures was not simply a function of time, space, and coverage. Effectiveness of advertising was in part also a function of the appeal or theme used to capture and hold the attention of the audience, the type of program offered, the catchy jingle, the uniqueness of product. Also, to some extent the use of the "shotgun approach," that is, the wasteful scattering of appeal to those not interested, could be avoided. Segments of the market could be reached by careful media selection—perhaps direct mail to owners of selected makes of cars, special types of magazines, or other media. Effective for the smaller firm were special television or radio programming, local presentations, or specialized advertising, for example, American Motors' one-half column advertisements featuring "love letters to Rambler" from their owners. However, this also could be expected to involve both fixed costs and characteristics of mass coverage of the market.

In the use of advertising to reach prospective purchasers of cars the advantage in general could be expected to rest with the largest volume producers. Volume of output was important for spreading the fixed costs of using mass media, whether at the national or local levels. And, the mass media seem to have been essential because of the problem of identifying with certainty those individuals who might be potential buyers of specific makes. It may have been known, for example, that some buyers preferred the specialized features offered by a truly distinctive car such as the compact car; but segregrating these potential buyers from the mass of consumers was difficult, if not impossible.

When attention is turned to the historical advertising expenditures of automobile manufacturers, the expected relationship is found to have been the actual. As may be seen in Tables 15 and 16, the traceable advertising expenditures on

Table 15

PASSENGER CAR ADVERTISING EXPENDITURES BY MANUFACTURER AND PER CAR REGISTERED, 1949-1962 [a]

(Total Expenditure in Thousands of Dollars, Per Car to Nearest Half Dollar)

Manufacturer		1949	1950	1951	1952	1953	1954	1955	1956	1957	1958	1959	1960	1961	1962
AMC (Nash)	Total	2,914	3,383	3,443	2,905	4,412	5,377	6,791	5,626	4,151	4,920	11,648	15,174	10,894	13,556
	Per Car	21.50	19.50	24.50	20.50	32.00	45.50	50.00	49.00	35.50	25.00	30.50	36.00	29.50	32.00
Hudson	Total	3,727	3,256	3,104	2,714	3,612	—	—	—	—	—	—	—	—	—
	Per Car	27.00	24.50	32.00	34.50	54.00	—	—	—	—	—	—	—	—	—
Chrysler	Total	9,829	14,158	16,767	15,769	19,343	23,645	47,585	44,044	47,903	32,927	38,130	36,102	20,304	32,909
	Per Car	11.00	12.50	15.00	18.00	16.50	33.00	39.50	48.00	43.50	50.50	56.00	39.00	32.00	49.50
Ford	Total	13,607	16,981	13,024	15,165	18,354	26,267	48,007	41,043	46,628	44,043	46,533	44,066	28,998	46,244
	Per Car	13.00	11.00	11.50	16.00	12.50	15.50	24.00	24.00	28.00	36.00	27.50	25.00	17.50	25.50
G.M.	Total	28,027	30,245	26,533	23,905	36,879	46,917	81,598	82,166	72,013	63,799	76,324	88,234	64,376	76,652
	Per Car	13.50	10.50	12.00	14.00	14.50	16.50	22.50	27.00	27.00	30.00	30.00	31.00	23.50	21.50
S-P (Packard)	Total	3,052	2,079	3,106	3,617	4,167	6,424	9,940	9,901	4,766	2,130	6,533	8,865	3,005	4,290
	Per Car	31.00	28.50	46.50	54.50	58.50	48.00	67.00	94.50	70.50	42.50	49.00	83.50	41.50	55.00
Studebaker	Total	3,530	3,577	3,274	2,661	3,913	—	—	—	—	—	—	—	—	—
	Per Car	12.50	13.50	16.00	17.00	24.50	—	—	—	—	—	—	—	—	—

[a] Source: Figures for manufacturers based on expenditures by make reprinted with permission from *Advertising Age*, August 9, 1954, pp. 64-65, for the years 1949-1953; November 18, 1957, p. 80, for the years 1954-1956; June 29, 1959, p. 84, for the years 1957-1958; July 4, 1960, pp. 60-61, for the year 1959; December 18, 1961, p. 82, for the year 1960; and October 7, 1963, p. 108, for the years 1961-1962. Copyrights, 1954, 1957, 1959, 1960, 1961 and 1963, Advertising Publications Inc. Figures include traceable expenditures in measured media for each twelve month period for national magazine, newspaper, Sunday supplement, network television, and farm magazine advertising for the years 1949-1954. Figures for 1955-1962 include outdoor advertising in addition to the other expenditures; and in addition to the other, the data for 1957-1962 include spot television advertising. Network radio coverage was discontinued after the first seven months of 1955 and is not included in the figures thereafter.

Table 16

PASSENGER CAR ADVERTISING EXPENDITURES BY MAKE, TOTAL AND PER CAR REGISTERED, 1950, 1956 AND 1962 [a]

(Total Expenditure in Thousands of Dollars,
Per Car to Nearest Half Dollar)

Make		1950	1956	1962
INDEPENDENT:				
Hudson (AMC)	Total	3,256	2,281	— —
	Per Car	24.50	74.50	— —
Nash (AMC)	Total	3,383	3,345	— - -
	Per Car	19.50	39.55	— —
Rambler (AMC)	Total	— —	— —[b]	13,556
	Per Car	— —	— —[b]	32.00
Packard (S-P)	Total	2,079	3,772	— —
	Per Car	28.50	133.00	— —
Studebaker (S-P)	Total	3,577	6,129	4,290
	Per Car	13.50	80.00	55.00
BIG THREE:				
Chevrolet (G.M.)	Total	8,693	30,376	35,617
	Per Car	6.00	19.50	17.00
Ford (Ford)	Total	9,416	29,735	29,698
	Per Car	8.00	21.50	20.00
Plymouth (Chrysler)	Total	4,321	12,416	12,437
	Per Car	8.00	25.50	41.50
Buick (G.M.)	Total	9,888	18,411	11,686
	Per Car	18.50	35.00	29.00
Oldsmobile (G.M.)	Total	4,621	15,134	11,209
	Per Car	12.50	34.50	25.50
Pontiac (G.M.)	Total	4,174	11,429	10,815
	Per Car	9.50	32.00	...20.50
Mercury (Ford)	Total	5,605	10,253	11,197
	Per Car	17.50	37.50	35.00
Dodge (Chrysler)	Total	4,562	12,495	9,626
	Per Car	15.00	56.50	40.50
DeSoto (Chrysler)	Total	2,459	6,621	— —
	Per Car	21.50	65.50	— —
Chrysler (Chrysler)	Total	2,817	11,011	6,964
	Per Car	18.50	103.00	61.00
Cadillac (G.M.)	Total	2,868	6,807	7,326
	Per Car	28.00	51.00	48.50
Lincoln (Ford)[c]	Total	1,961	7,237	5,349
	Per Car	57.00	164.00	169.50
Imperial (Chrysler)	Total	— —	1,502	3,882
	Per Car	— —	143.50	286.50

[a] Source: Data reprinted with permission from *Advertising Age*, September 1, 1958, p. 61, and October 7, 1963, p. 108. Copyrights, 1958 and 1963, Advertising Publications, Inc.

[b] Rambler was not listed separately until 1957. The Rambler expenditure was $2,507,444 in total and $24.28 per car in 1957.

[c] Includes Continental.

passenger cars reveal the advantages of large volume producers. Total advertising expenditures in measured media alone were enormous for the Big Three, and especially so for General Motors, reflecting their tremendous coverage of the national market; but their unit costs of advertising, except for Chrysler in some years after 1953, were below those of American Motors and Studebaker and their predecessors, despite the much smaller total expenditures of the latter. Ford and General Motors generally averaged about the same expenditure per car registered, but General Motors had a substantial advantage in total expenditure. Chrysler's total expenditures generally approached those of Ford, but Chrysler's expenditures per car usually exceeded those of Ford. Along with the Independents, Chrysler suffered a sales slump after 1953; but Chrysler continued large advertising programs in an effort to offset its sales troubles, revealing in the process that advertising was only one among a number of influences on sales. Of course, the question also may be raised as to how far Chrysler's sales would have fallen without the advertising. To achieve the same degree of time, space, and frequency of market coverage as General Motors, Ford and Chrysler would have had to spend two or three times as much per car as General Motors. Such total coverage was completely out of the question for the smaller companies. Even after American Motors' tremendous comeback, its advertising position was most comparable to that of the middle-priced Big Three makes. (See Table 16 for the year 1962.) American Motors' Rambler was still outclassed in advertising saturation and unit cost by the larger volume low-priced Big Three makes. Despite relatively small total expenditures, Studebaker after 1953 was generally far out of line on unit cost. Only the small volume prestige makes—Chrysler, Imperial, and Lincoln—were higher. Obviously, the cost advantages in national market coverage lay with large volume producers, with the largest volume firm in the most favorable position.

Large though the totals were for traceable advertising expenditures on passenger cars, they were far from covering all advertising of the firms. Institutional advertising, separate advertising for parts and accessories, advertising of trucks, appliances or other products, talent costs for television and radio, spot radio advertising, personal sales promotion efforts, and direct mail advertising were not included.

Indications of the manufacturers' total expenditures on passenger car advertising in measured and unmeasured media are shown for 1955 and 1956, for example, in Table 17. Total expenditures were roughly double traceable expenditures for the manufacturers in these years with variation in relative use of measured and unmeasured media. Total expenditures of about $60 to $100 per car probably provide a conservative estimate of the cost of passenger car advertising to the consumer by the late 1950's.[57]

In addition, advertising expenditures for products other than cars and for promoting the firm as an institution may have enhanced passenger car sales in establishing a favorable image of the firm. Repetition of firm name for other products as well as for cars probably contributed to consumer confidence in the firm with the largest and most extensively advertised firm again having the advantage. In any event, total advertising expenditures of the largest firms were indeed staggering, General Motors, for instance, having spent about $239,000,000 in 1960 and $199,000,000 in 1961 and Ford $90,500,000 in 1960 and $132,500,000 in 1961.[58] The smaller companies could not hope to match such great expenditures.

Total advertising impact on potential buyers of new cars was not dependent alone on size of expenditures for time, space, and frequency of coverage in national media. It was highly probable that the marginal dollar expenditure of American Motors or Studebaker or their predecessors provided greater market impact than a marginal dollar of expenditure by one of the Big Three. Diminishing returns very likely resulted as advertising expenditures for a particular make or

[57] Including traceable and nontraceable advertising costs of the manufacturers but excluding dealer advertising done independently. Approximate agreement with these figures appears in a cost breakdown prepared by Ford on the market value added by distribution. For a low-priced (and presumably high volume) $2,500 car, it was estimated that advertising and sales promotion by the manufacturer would average $60 per car. Average dealer advertising and sales promotion was estimated at $45 per car. Figures appeared in an illustrative table used with "The Economic Outlook for 1959 and Its Impact on Auto Sales," A talk before an Educational Round Table, Louisville, Kentucky, December 9, 1958, by R. J. Eggert, Marketing Research Manager, Ford Motor Company. For a high-priced, low volume car, the average unit costs probably are considerably higher. Even so, these costs were relatively small percentages of selling prices.

[58] Advertising Age, May 28, 1962, pp. 1 and 3. The 1960 figure for Ford was estimated by Advertising Age; the others were reported by board chairmen of the two companies at their respective annual meetings.

TABLE 17
ESTIMATED TOTAL ADVERTISING EXPENDITURE BY
PASSENGER CAR MANUFACTURERS IN MEASURED AND
UNMEASURED MEDIA, 1955-56 [a]
(Thousands of Dollars)

Manufacturer	1955	1956
American Motors	$ 18,000	$ 14,500
Chrysler	68,630	60,093
Ford	72,943	88,650
General Motors	170,382	162,499
Studebaker-Packard	13,275	12,842

[a] Source: Data reprinted with permission from *Advertising Age*, August 19, 1957, p. 60. Copyright, 1957, Advertising Publications, Inc.

firm were increased; hence differences in impact may not have been so great as differentials in total expenditure. However, the differentials in total expenditure were so great that the only reasonable conclusion is that the advantages in total market impact rested with the Big Three, and especially General Motors even in comparison with its largest rival, Ford.

A fact of further importance in connection with advertising was that the Big Three were already the large volume sellers in the period under study. They dominated the industry. In one sense, their advertising could be directed toward retaining their market shares, largely through encouraging repeat purchases by previously satisfied buyers of their products. On the other hand, after the close of the exceptional early postwar shortages, the smaller companies, who found themselves operating below profit-making levels from late 1953 through 1957, were in the position of trying to enlarge their market shares. To shove aside the already large Big Three, American Motors and Studebaker and their predecessors undoubtedly could be expected to have to incur larger promotional costs per unit, perhaps through advertising, to divert consumer preference from the Big Three makes previously owned. Thus, the larger volume firms had advantages which probably were not fully reflected in historical cost relationships. Clearly, if one accepts the thesis that advertising does promote and protect the sales of the make advertised, the advantage lay with the larger volume producer, especially to the extent that it had acquired large volume earlier and thereby gained a preferred position with many consumers.

DEALER ORGANIZATIONS

Volume of sales also was important in establishing and maintaining the dealer organizations which played a key role in the promotional schemes of automobile manufacturers. The national market for cars was in effect a network of local markets. Local dealer representation was important in attracting buyers. Final sales of most cars occurred at the level of the local communities in which their purchasers resided, and they were made by dealers to individual consumers. The aggregate of these was the national market. The total market strength of the individual manufacturers depended on their ability to participate in the many local markets which comprised the nationwide market. Such participation, of course, was also essential if national advertising which reached local communities was not to be wasted by lack of local dealer representation.

Dealers played a crucial role. In the words of one dealer evaluating dealer-manufacturer relations, "A well-financed, properly equipped and locally respected dealer body was and is indispensable to a successful automobile manufacturer."[59] Dealers provided manufacturers with representation throughout the country at the level of the local community, a self-financed organization which relieved manufacturers of the responsibility for financing retailing operations,[60] readily available parts and service which substituted for provisions manufacturers otherwise would have had to make, a local identity for the product, and facilities for the trade-in of an old car. In exchange for these contributions by dealers, the manufacturers provided franchises for the sale of particular makes.[61] Exclusive franchise agreements, which gave manufacturers considerable voice in the affairs of their dealers, were used by the industry.[62]

[59] U. S., Senate, Committee on Interstate and Foreign Commerce, *Hearings, on S. 3865, Automobile Distribution*, 85th Congress, 2nd Session (Washington: U. S. Government Printing Office, 1958), p. 43. Statement of Foster W. Talbott, former chairman of N. A. D. A.'s industry-relations committee and a Ford dealer of Baltimore, Maryland.

[60] Car manufacturers often helped finance new dealers, but their assistance was usually directed toward eventually establishing such dealers as financially healthy, locally owned businesses. In a few cases, manufacturers also owned and operated directly a few retail establishments.

[61] See also the comments of Talbott, *op. cit.*, pp. 42-43.

[62] Manufacturers often set sales quotas and specified sales and service facility requirements, too. See C. M. Hewitt, *Automobile Franchise Agreements* (Homewood, Illinois: Richard D. Irwin, Inc., 1956).

Market Coverage

To cover the market adequately, a large number of dealers was required. Roughly speaking, since the nation had 2,936 incorporated and 241 unincorporated places plus 116 towns or townships each of which had a population of 5,000 or more people in 1960 and included a combined population of about 107,000,000 within their limits,[63] a dealer organization large in number was essential in providing manufacturers access to the many local markets.

A comparison of the sizes of the dealer organizations of the Big Three and Independents is shown in Table 18 for the beginning of 1958 and 1959, which covers a crucial turning point in the experiences of the smaller companies, but representative nevertheless of the generally prevailing dealership structures. It may be seen that Big Three dealers were far more numerous than Independent dealers, both in number of franchises and net dealers after allowance for dual franchises held by one dealership.

Substantial change may be noted in the number of dealers during 1958 by comparing the columns. The year was a very poor sales year for the Big Three, and the number of their franchises and net dealers declined.[64] In the same period the two remaining Independents increased their relative dealer strength. In succeeding years, American Motors made further strides reaching a total dealer body of 3,076 on September 30, 1962.[65] Even after the expansion in the size of their dealer organizations, however, the number of franchises of American Motors and Studebaker was still far short of that of the Big Three. Obviously, the market coverage represented by the leading Independents' penetration of local markets was

[63] Reducing the population size to 2,500 increased the total number of places included to 5,445 but added only about 7,500,000 more population within their limits. Some of these, of course, may have been trading centers for extensively populated rural areas. See U. S., Bureau of the Census, *U. S. Census of Population: 1960, Number of Inhabitants, United States Summary*, Final Report PC(1)-1A (Washington: U. S. Government Printing Office, 1961), p. xxiii.

[64] This was a fairly frequent cyclical phenomenon, the weaker, and probably smaller dealers withdrawing in poor sales years and entering with rising car sales; but the long-term trend was also toward fewer dealers. Pashigian, *op. cit.*, chapter iv, esp. pp. 76-102; and Paul H. Banner, "Competition in the Automobile Industry," (Unpublished Ph.D. dissertation, Harvard University, 1954), pp. 218-20. The trend toward fewer dealers continued through 1962. Cf. Table 18 with Table 21 *infra*.

[65] American Motors Corporation, *Annual Report*, 1962, p. 4.

TABLE 18
NUMBER OF FRANCHISES AND DEALERS OF UNITED
STATES PASSENGER CAR MANUFACTURERS AT THE
BEGINNING OF 1958 AND 1959 [a]

Manufacturer	January 1, 1958		January 1, 1959	
	Franchises	Net Dealers	Franchises	Net Dealers
AMERICAN MOTORS	2,200	2,200	2,743	2,743
Rambler	2,200		2,743	
CHRYSLER	17,753	8,673	16,062	8,037
Chrysler	2,754		2,579	
DeSoto	2,256		2,053	
Dodge	3,468		3,229	
Imperial	1,580		1,358	
Plymouth	7,695		6,843	
FORD	12,517	9,743	12,371	8,840
Edsel	1,146		1,561	
Ford	7,020		6,897	
Lincoln-Continental	1,297		1,132	
Mercury	3,054		2,781	
GENERAL MOTORS	20,329	15,513	19,638	14,685
Buick	3,520		3,215	
Cadillac	1,784		1,777	
Chevrolet	7,450		7,246	
Oldsmobile	3,750		3,710	
Pontiac	3,825		3,690	
STUDEBAKER-PACKARD	3,950	2,067	2,479	2,479
Packard	1,969		0	
Studebaker	1,981		2,479	
TOTALS	56,749	38,196	53,293	36,784
Less Intercorporate Dual Franchise Dealers		576		1,245
TOTAL DEALERS		37,620		35,539

[a] Source: Data reprinted by permission from *Automotive News* (*1959 Almanac Issue*), Detroit, Michigan, April 27, 1959, p. 185. Data were estimates by *Automotive News*.

less complete than that of the Big Three, especially for the low-priced, largest volume Big Three makes, although it was close to that of their middle-priced makes.[66] Since the number of local markets was a finite number, the Big Three firms,

[66] The president of Studebaker in 1962 indicated that his company. which then had about 2,000 dealers, covered only about 70 per cent of the U. S. market. Many population centers were without Studebaker dealers. Remarks of Sherwood H. Egbert, President, Studebaker Corporation, to the New York Society of Security Analysts, August 14, 1962.

with their larger numbers of franchises and net dealers after allowance for dual franchises, secured more comprehensive and dense coverage of the nationwide network of local markets than the smaller companies.

The relatively small dealer organizations of the leading Independents in comparison with those of the Big Three had been a characteristic of the industry for many years. Even in the earlier postwar period of easy selling, as may be seen in Table 19, the relative size of the leading Independents' dealer organizations had not been materially different from the pattern prevailing in 1958. Nash-Kelvinator in particular, as noted previously, had followed a conscious policy of restricting franchises during the period of shortages to maintain average dealer volumes. Since market representation could be expanded by providing dealers with dual franchises,

TABLE 19

NUMBER OF FRANCHISES OF UNITED STATES PASSENGER CAR MAUNFACTURERS AT THE BEGINNING OF 1950 [a]

Manufacturer	Franchises
Independents:	
Hudson	2,128
Nash	1,178
Packard	1,363
Studebaker	2,270
Big Three:	
Chrysler	19,930 [b]
Ford	9,084
General Motors	17,989

[a] Source: Totals of number of franchises shown by make of car in *Automotive Industries*, March 15, 1950, p. 89.

[b] The number of dealers for Chrysler was about one half the number of franchises since most Plymouth franchises were coupled with another franchise for a Chrysler make in 1950.

there is little wonder then that dealer organizations figured prominently in the merger discussions. Unfortunately for the Independents, many of the franchises of their combined dealership organizations following the mergers provided duplicating coverage of essentially the same markets; and the number of their dealers was not the whole story.

Sales per Franchise and Dealer

In covering the market satisfactorily, quality as well as

TABLE 20

NEW CAR REGISTRATIONS PER FRANCHISE BY MAKE OF CAR FOR THE UNITED STATES PASSENGER CAR MANUFACTURERS, 1950 AND 1955-1963 [a]

Make		1950	1955	1956	1957	1958	1959	1960	1961	1962	1963
AMERICAN MOTORS:	Hudson	63	33	13	5	—	—	—	—	—	—
	Nash	149	59	19	7	—	—	—	—	—	—
	Rambler [b]	—	—	32	42	68	122	142	125	139	139
CHRYSLER:	Chrysler	46	48	37	39	23	27	33	37	41	38
	DeSoto	41	45	41	46	23	23	14	—	—	—
	Dodge	77	75	61	74	42	59	128	86	96	144
	Imperial	—	4	6	21	11	15	13	9	10	11
	Plymouth	55	72	55	77	57	66	118	88	96	131
FORD:	Edsel	—	—	—	23	25	28	—	—	—	—
	Ford	175	224	195	213	149	215	209	199	223	240
	Lincoln (Continental)	33	25	31	29	23	27	19	30	31	31
	Mercury	232	122	37	85	49	60	118	123	129	114
GENERAL MOTORS:	Buick	189	206	148	112	82	79	86	93	128	145
	Cadillac	81	80	74	79	70	77	85	80	86	91
	Chevrolet	198	216	206	195	170	201	241	231	305	319
	Oldsmobile	121	153	114	99	83	96	97	93	125	135
	Pontiac	122	133	90	84	62	105	111	105	150	173
STUDEBAKER-PACKARD:	Packard	54	41	12	3	2	—	—	—	—	—
	Studebaker	118	45	36	32	19	53	44	34	37	33

[a] Source: For the year 1950: computations based on data provided in *Automotive Industries*, March 15, 1950, p. 89, for the number of dealer franchises at the beginning of 1950, and *ibid*, March 15, 1953, p. 101, for the number of registrations by make of new car; for the years 1955-1963: Data reprinted by permission from *Automotive News* (*Almanac Issues*), April, 1959, 1961, and 1964.

[b] Registered as Nash in 1950 or as Nash or Hudson in 1955.

quantity was essential. Quantity was important in providing access to the many local markets, but quality in the form of financially healthy dealers was essential in assuring continued local representation. In sum, volume was important to both manufacturers and dealers.

As may be seen in Table 20, the leading Independent makes generally sold in smaller volumes per franchise than Big Three makes, at least until American Motors' success with Rambler, although in 1950 their sales per franchise had compared favorably with those of middle-priced Big Three makes. Dealers in the middle-priced Big Three makes, however, achieved actual sales volumes greater than those indicated per franchise, since the franchises for Big Three makes were frequently dualed on an intracorporate basis. The dual franchise pattern is shown for 1962 in Table 21. For many years, Chrysler followed a policy of dualing its Plymouth franchise with one or more of those for its higher-priced makes; but by 1962, many had been set up on an exclusive basis. Lincoln and Mercury franchises were usually dualed, either with one another or with Ford. Cadillac, relatively speaking, was the most extensively dualed General Motors franchise, usually with Buick, Oldsmobile, or Pontiac; but the latter three were also often dualed with another or with Chevrolet. As may be seen in Table 21, or in less detail in Table 18, after allowing for intracorporate dual franchise arrangements, the numbers of net dealers of Big Three makes were significantly below their numbers of franchises. With allowance for intracorporate dual arrangements, the differences in average sales volumes of American Motors and Studebaker dealers and Big Three dealers are shown in Table 22 for selected years representing the situation before and after American Motors' comeback with Rambler. Big Three dealers on the average had the advantage, particularly in consideration of the fact that their large numbers of franchises gave them more representation in the smaller communities in which sales volumes per dealer might be small. Unfortunately, data are not available to allow for intercorporate dualing of franchises which would have provided allowance for Rambler and Studebaker dual arrangements, too, including those with makes of the Big Three, which were fairly numerous after the sales upsurge of Rambler and before the introduction by the Big Three of their own compact cars.

Requirements for Competitive Dealership Organization

To the extent that economies of scale existed at the local dealer level, and they evidently were substantial,[67] volume per

TABLE 21

NUMBER OF FRANCHISES AND DEALERS OF UNITED STATES PASSENGER CAR MANUFACTURERS JANUARY 1, 1962 [a]

Manufacturers	Franchises			Net Dealers
	Exclusives (within corp.)	Multiples (within corp.)	Total	
AMERICAN MOTORS	2,980	0	2,980	2,980
Rambler	2,980	0	2,980	
CHRYSLER CORP.	3,184	6,602	9,786	5,823
Chrysler	18	2,629	2,647	
Dodge	2,067	492	2,559	
Imperial	0	1,315	1,315	
Plymouth	1,099	2,166	3,265	
FORD MOTOR CO.	5,870	6,356	12,226	7,928
Ford	5,442	1,181	6,623	
Lincoln	0	1,021	1,021	
Mercury	428	2,054	2,482	
Comet-Meteor [b]	0	2,100	2,100	
GENERAL MOTORS	9,055	9,853	18,908	13,835
Buick	1,409	1,709	3,118	
Cadillac	173	1,602	1,775	
Chevrolet	4,812	2,158	6,970	
Oldsmobile	1,170	2,351	3,521	
Pontiac	1,491	2,033	3,524	
STUDEBAKER-PACKARD	2,084	0	2,084	2,084
Studebaker	2,084	0	2,084	
TOTALS	23,173	22,811	45,984	32,650
Less intercorporate duals				1,360
TOTAL U. S. DEALERS				31,290

[a] Source: Data reprinted by permission from *Automotive News (1962 Almanac Issue)*, April 30, 1962, p. 95. Data were estimates by *Automotive News*.

[b] Comet and Meteor are listed separately since not all Mercury dealers handled these series.

[67] In his study of franchise systems, Peter Pashigian concluded that dealership distribution cost per unit decreased significantly with increased sales up to outputs of about 800 units annually and then stabilized. Using a base of 100 at annual sales of 800 units, Pashigian estimated that the index of dealership cost per unit was 140 at 100 units, 130 at 200 units, and 110 at 600 units. See Pashigian, *op. cit.*, pp. 222-27. Size of the local market, of course, placed limits on dealer sales potentials.

dealer was important in the ultimate unit cost of putting a car in the hands of the consumer. Considerable advertising, for example, as shown in Table 23 was done at the local dealer level; and while the total costs to a dealer of local newspaper or television advertising were small compared with those of a manufacturer for national circulation, local advertising also involved fixed commitments. As was the case with national advertising, for comparable time, space, and coverage, the larger volume seller gained cost advantages per unit sold.

TABLE 22

NEW CAR REGISTRATIONS PER FRANCHISE AND DEALER OF UNITED STATES PASSENGER CAR MANUFACTURERS, 1957 AND 1960 [a]

Manufacturer	1957		1960	
	Franchise	Dealer	Franchise	Dealer
American Motors	53 [b]	53	142	142
Chrysler	62	126	92	146
Ford	145	187	146	215
General Motors	132	173	151	204
Studebaker-Packard	17	33	47	47

[a] Source: New car registrations for the year divided by the numbers of franchises and net dealers at the end of the year as included in *Automotive News (Annual Almanac Issues)*, April, 1959 and 1961. These data vary slightly from those of Table 20 since only year-ending figures for dealer and franchise numbers are used here rather than an average of beginning and ending numbers.

[b] In 1957 all American Motors dealers sold all three of its cars, and their total is included here.

TABLE 23

DEALER LOCAL ADVERTISING PER CAR, 1956-1963 [a]

Year	Average Expenditure
1956	$41.21
1957	39.78
1958	43.30
1959	39.23
1960	37.17
1961	36.33
1962	34.74
1963	35.36

[a] Source: "Operating Averages for the Automobile Retailing Industry," 1956-1963 annual editions, National Automobile Dealers Association, Washington, D. C.

In the late 1940's and early 1950's, an annual volume of 100,000 to 150,000 units may have been about the minimum to sustain an adequate dealer organization with perhaps 2,500 to 3,000 members, as was estimated by one industry observer;[68] but after that time the required number evidently increased with the intensification of retail competition and narrowed dealer margins of later years. Dealers, of course, could profit from their used car, parts, and service operations; but here volume was also important. Having in the hands of consumers a large number of previously sold cars of the make handled was important in sustaining such operations. In the late 1950's, American Motors officials figured that a market of sufficient size to provide a Rambler dealer sales of 180 cars per year was enough to justify establishing such a dealer.[69] If 3,000 dealers were required to cover the many local markets, this as an average pushed the total for the manufacturer above 500,000 units. This volume, it is interesting to note, was also about the level that could be expected from applying the average dealer sales volumes of the largest volume makes—Chevrolet and Ford, most of whose franchises were exclusive—to the approximate number of franchises found among middle-priced Big Three makes. With sales of roughly 200 units per dealer for 2,500 to 3,500 dealers, the national total would range from 500,000 to 700,-000 units for a manufacturer operating on such a basis. On the basis of the best publicly available information on franchise systems in the distribution of automobiles, a manufacturer with annual sales of 600,000 units would be at a slight cost disadvantage to one with two or three times this total of sales.[70] Companies with volumes much below 600,000 units could expect substantially higher dealership distribution costs per unit and greater difficulty in maintaining adequate dealer organizations.

Considering the scientific approach to locating dealers emphasized by General Motors,[71] whose dealer network was

[68] Joe S. Bain, op. cit., p. 306.

[69] American Motors based its figure on a 6 per cent penetration of a local market in which 3,000 cars per year were anticipated for all makes. See George Melloan, "The Little Two," The Wall Street Journal, March 23, 1959, p. 18.

[70] See the comprehensive analysis by Pashigian, op. cit., pp. 234-38.

[71] Such an attitude at General Motors was described in a statement by its chairman some years before World War II:

To make this [balance between the number of dealers and the potential of the market] effective requires a scientific analysis

the largest of the industry, it is interesting to note that the numbers of General Motors franchises and net dealers were gradually reduced over the postwar years except for Cadillac. Franchises of Ford and Plymouth were reduced, too. The conditions confronting the industry were not static. With population shifts from rural to urban communities, the ease of farm to city highway transportation, the introduction of television as a new and additional method of mass communication, and high-volume low-margin dealer operations encouraged by manufacturers and often resisted by dealers,[72] the number of franchises required for adequate market coverage with aggressive, financially healthy dealers may well have been reduced by the late 1950's. Even so, the requirement of increased sales per dealer demanded large volumes of the manufacturers supplying them.

Substantial volume thus was important in the distribution of automobiles to the nationwide market. Except to the extent that franchises could be dualed with those of other makes, annual sales of 400,000 or so units probably were about the minimum requirement for establishing and maintaining a dealer body sufficiently large in number to participate in the many local markets comprising the national market and sufficiently aggressive and financially healthy to assure continued participation; and sales of 600,000 or

of each community. Out of that there should be developed a 'master' plan for each such community. The master plan should recognize all the essential facts that would lead to placing, in the community under examination, the right number of dealers, each of the right size, each in approximately the right location, and no more. That is the vital thing. No more. And the situation must be reviewed at frequent intervals, so that an adjustment may be made to reflect the changes that are always taking place.
U. S., Senate, Committee on Interstate and Foreign Commerce, Subcommittee on Automobile Marketing Practices, *Hearings, Automobile Marketing Practices*, 84th Congress, 2nd Session, Pursuant to S. Res. 13 continued by S. Res. 163 (Washington: U. S. Government Printing Office, 1956), Part I, p. 82. Reprint of address by Alfred P. Sloan, Jr., chairman, General Motors Corporation, before National Automobile Dealers Association, Detroit, Michigan, April 27, 1938.

[72] See, e.g., *ibid.* pp. 92-127, Testimony of Frederick J. Bell of N.A.D.A.; U. S., Federal Trade Commission, *Report on Motor Vehicle Industry, op. cit.;* and U. S., House of Representatives, Committee of the Judiciary, Subcommittee No. 5 on Antitrust, *Hearings, Automobile Dealer Franchises*, 84th Congress, 2nd Session, Pursuant to H. Res. 11360 (Washington: U. S. Government Printing Office, 1956), esp. p. 288.

more units probably would have been preferable for competition with the largest volume makes of the Big Three.

PRICE POLICIES

Although the apparent merchandising emphasis of United States automobile manufacturers generally was on qualitative product features rather than price as a basis for competition, such emphasis did not mean that price was unimportant. It was a fact of industry behavior that prices of cars of comparable specifications were set at remarkably close levels. Defensive imitation of successful makes and features contributed to the closeness of their comparability. Despite the broadening of market coverage of many makes in the 1950's,[73] price groupings existed in which the various makes and models were closely comparable in quality, size, weight, power, and optional equipment. It was within relatively systematic price classifications that nonprice competition received emphasis.

Price Leadership

In the pricing of passenger cars, volume or size of a firm evidently was an important consideration. Although the largest firm of the industry, General Motors, was not always first to announce prices of its new models, General Motors' prices, either announced or anticipated, evidently set the standard for the industry. Based on statements of officials of the automobile manufacturing firms, this at least was the conclusion of the Senate Subcommittee on Antitrust and Monopoly under the chairmanship of Estes Kefauver. Whether or not General Motors announced its prices first, it appeared to be the price leader.

> In either instance, it is General Motors' actual or expected behavior which is the decisive factor. In one case, the smaller companies simply follow the announced lead of General Motors; in the other, the aim is to guess what the largest company will do and do likewise. . . . There can be little doubt that the key role in the pricing of automobiles in the United States is played by General Motors; it is their de-

[73] *Supra,* chapter vi.

cision which establishes the price level for the whole industry.[74]

George Romney, while then president of American Motors, plainly acknowledged that his firm's pricing policy was strongly influenced by the actions of General Motors: "General Motors being the dominant company in an industry is obviously going to have to be taken into consideration by its competitors."[75] Romney further explained the pricing actions of his company as follows:

> I cannot ignore the prices of my competitors in setting the prices on my cars because I cannot sell my cars if my cars are not priced on the basis where they will sell in relationship to the price of the other fellow's product.
> So one of the things I have to take into consideration in pricing my cars is the price of the competitor.[76]

J. J. Nance had indicated somewhat earlier the emphasis placed by Studebaker-Packard in meeting the larger firms' prices:

> Our prices are determined by competition, the competitive factor, plus an evaluation of the values offered in our products versus competition, and then we arrive at the prices in that way.[77]

Even officials of Chrysler and Ford, the two smaller members of the Big Three, acknowledged their emphasis on General

[74] U. S., Senate, Committee on the Judiciary, Subcommittee on Antitrust and Monopoly, *Report, A Study of Administered Prices in the Automobile Industry, op. cit.*, p. 76. The subcommittee also made much of Ford's "double shift" in pricing its 1957 models: Ford had first offered its new completely redesigned 1957 models with increases ranging from $1 to $104, for an average increase of 2.9 per cent, but later raised them further when Chevrolet, which was introduced two weeks later, came out with prices increased by $50 to $166, for an average increase of 6.1 per cent. Ford had guessed wrong on General Motors' action; but within two weeks, Ford prices had been increased to within $1 to $11 of the nearest comparable Chevrolet models. *Ibid.*, p. 53.

[75] U. S., Senate, Committee on the Judiciary, Subcommittee on Antitrust and Monopoly, *Hearings, Administered Prices, op. cit.*, Part 6, p. 2953.

[76] *Ibid.*, p. 2946.

[77] U. S., Senate, Committee on the Judiciary, Subcommittee on Antitrust and Monopoly, *Hearings, A Study of the Antitrust Laws, op. cit.*, Part 2, p. 876.

Motors' actions in their own processes of setting prices.[78] General Motors, on the other hand, while paying some attention to other firms' actions, emphasized cost factors in setting its prices.

Anticipated costs of production served as the basis for General Motors' prices.[79] Using estimates of standard cost at 80 per cent of capacity, a "profit per car, based on a target rate of return, is added to obtain the provisional manufacturer's price."[80] The target rate of return for General Motors ranged around 15 to 20 per cent of investment on an after tax basis. Since the pricing process usually took about thirty months and market and industry conditions could change substantially within such a period, the cost and price estimates were based on standard volumes below capacity operations. This allowance also provided for averaging out cyclical and seasonal sales fluctuations over the longer run. Prices of current models were related to prices of comparable models in previous years to accommodate a sense of continuity for consumers. The standard cost and price calculations were re-examined before final introduction; last minute adjustments could be made before introduction of new models. Provision could be made for price adjustments on the basis of what General Motors officials thought the market would bear. The objective of General Motors was to achieve a balance between marketability of the passenger car style and other features selected in response to consumer surveys and the cost and price relationships involved in providing the selected product and optional features, while at the same time attempting to secure its target rate of return in the face of competition from other firms.[81]

The prices thus chosen for passenger cars were essentially the manufacturer's prices to dealers. With the addition of allowances for dealer profit margins, suggested advertised

[78] See, e.g., the statements of Theodore Yntema, who was then vice-president in charge of finance at Ford, and of L. L. Colbert, who was president of Chrysler at the time. U. S., Senate, Committee on the Judiciary, Subcommittee on Antitrust and Monopoly, *Hearings, Administered Prices, op. cit.*, esp. pp. 2683-84, 2776-79, and 2784-85.

[79] A. D. H. Kaplan, Joel B. Dirlam, and Robert F. Lanzillotti, *Pricing in Big Business* (Washington: The Brookings Institution, 1958), pp. 48-55. See also U. S., Senate, Committee on the Judiciary, Subcommittee on Antitrust and Monopoly, *op. cit.*, pp. 2518-29. Statement of Harlow Curtice, then president of General Motors.

[80] Kaplan, *op. cit.*, p. 50.

[81] *Ibid.*, pp. 48-55; and Statement of Harlow Curtice, *op. cit.*, p. 2518.

prices to consumers, excluding local taxes and handling charges, were also established. Before the advent of the compact car, dealer margins generally ranged around 24 per cent on General Motors makes, except for 26 per cent on Cadillac.[82] Dealer margins included in the setting of suggested advertised prices of the compacts ranged around 20 per cent.[83] Other manufacturers provided comparable dealer discounts from suggested list prices.[84]

Other firms in the industry besides General Motors also included cost calculations in their deliberations in the pricing process, particularly in determining what product qualities and features could be planned in evolution from existing product qualities, features, and prices. The salient feature in the General Motors' process, however, was its cost-plus emphasis in contrast with the "competitive" price emphasis of smaller firms. Within limits, then, the advertised prices of General Motors cars set the pattern for the industry. Ford usually priced its cars very close to those of General Motors, while Chrysler and the Independents often chose prices somewhat above those of General Motors and Ford cars of comparable specifications, at least before the compact car boom. Alternatively, the smaller companies often entered specific price classes with cars of lesser power, weight, and sometimes over-all dimensions than the Big Three, using such differentiation to appeal to consumer desires for special features, again limiting the observation to an exclusion of the compact car.[85]

Cost Leadership

Consumer acceptance of General Motors cars as "standards of comparison" as well as fear of retaliation by General Motors for "excessively" low prices were possible reasons for other firms' careful attention to General Motors' prices. General Motors cars generally sold in the largest numbers and

[82] Kaplan, Dirlam, and Lanzillotti, *op. cit.*, p. 50.

[83] As shown in comparisons of dealer invoice and suggested list prices of the different makes. Also, see *The Wall Street Journal*, September 22, 1959, pp. 1 and 16, and October 21, 1959, p. 21; and *Business Week*, August 29, 1959, p. 27.

[84] As shown, e.g., in model price lists prepared by Automobile Invoice Service Company, Bakersfield, California.

[85] See, e.g., *Automotive Industries*, "Annual Statistical Issues," for such comparisons of specifications and original advertised delivered prices.

were most familiar to the largest numbers of consumers; and General Motors, as a multiple-line producer, presumably could retaliate especially against a smaller, less diversified manufacturer by price cutting on one or more of its makes or models while maintaining profit margins on its other cars in a market with varied consumer preferences, at least within the limits imposed by antitrust legislation and agencies. The automobile manufacturers' courses of action in setting prices, however, seem to have been based on relationships which were slightly more subtle than these.

It was generally believed by General Motors officials that their company was the low-cost firm of the automobile industry.[86] With the high degree of price conformity of the industry, this belief, of course, was consistent with the General Motors' rates of return, which were generally the highest in the industry, although some of the differences among the firms also may have resulted from variations in degrees of integration of automobile production and of product diversification into other industries. Therefore, if General Motors was the low-cost producer, which the firm appeared to be, the following of General Motors' prices by any smaller companies for comparable car models may well have been about the best they could accomplish. This was the implication of the testimony of Chrysler, Ford, and American Motors officials during the Kefauver investigations. Substantially higher prices than General Motors' prices for comparable cars would have resulted in lost sales. On the other hand, lower prices.of cars of quality comparable to those of General Motors would have pushed more closely on costs, thereby creating a profit squeeze unless the lower prices resulted in a substantial shift of buyers from General Motors cars to those of its competitors, in which case General Motors most likely would retaliate. In the latter case, no firm would have been better off unless, once again, the total demand for cars was highly elastic with regard to price. Whatever the reason for the price leadership by General Motors, however, the following of General Motors' prices for comparable models by any smaller companies involved them in the following of General Motors' costs, too.

While it is unlikely that Chrysler or Ford could have engaged in extensive price cutting without engendering retaliation and thereby a test of comparative manufacturing and

---

[86] Kaplan, Dirlam, and Lanzillotti, *op. cit.*, p. 50.

distribution efficiency among the firms of the industry, American Motors and Studebaker may have had some flexibility in shading their prices below those of Big Three makes without retaliation, as seems to have been evidenced in their early offerings of compact cars at list prices below those of Big Three makes although it should be noted that their lower prices were also accompanied by qualitative differences. The competitive response to the Independents' compact cars was the eventual introduction of the Big Three compacts. Nevertheless, a shading of prices by the smaller firms, perhaps reflecting their willingness to accept lower profit margins than the Big Three in order to gain sales that otherwise would be lost to them, also requires efforts to meet the costs of the low-cost producer, and indeed may make more imperative the necessity for approaching or meeting the costs of the low-cost producer, for profitable sales at low prices per unit also require low costs per unit.

Since economies of large scale were to be found in most phases of manufacturing and marketing automobiles and since General Motors, as the largest volume producer in the industry, was in the best position to obtain the fullest benefits of the economies of scale, the following of General Motors' prices put pressure on any smaller producer to achieve sufficient sales volumes to be able to follow General Motors' costs, or at least to get within profit-making range of them. Thus, in following the low-cost leader who set the price pattern for the industry, volume was extremely important in the competitive pricing of automobiles.

CONSUMER ACCEPTANCE

In the final analysis, although automobile manufacturers may have exerted substantial influence on consumers through their choices of product style, promotion, and prices, consumers in part held the answer to the costs of the manufacturers, at least to the extent that consumer willingness to buy in large volume permitted low unit costs. It was an interaction of choices by and among manufacturers in their product offerings and of consumers in expressing their preferences in purchases that determined the sales volumes and costs of a manufacturer. In the winning of consumer acceptance, however, volume in and of itself was an important factor. The president of American Motors commented on the situation in part as follows:

> Familiarity helps shape styling preferences. . . .
> Styling or product innovations, undertaken by a company doing 50, 30, or 20 per cent of the business, are more certain of public acceptance than equally good or better innovations by smaller firms. . . .
> The smaller company faces a tougher job of building customer familiarity with its product improvements because of its smaller relative volume and lesser advertising, sales, and promotion expenditures.[87]

In a similar vein was an observation by Chrysler officials: "Our best billboard is a car going away from you on the road."[88]

Of great importance in this connection was the fact that some makes of cars, primarily those of the Big Three, had enjoyed enormous sales success in past years. To the extent that buyers of cars had favorable experiences with a make previously purchased, their preferences in new purchases tended to favor their existing make. Loyalty to a make of car and to its manufacturer was important, for about two out of three buyers usually bought the same make as that previously owned,[89] and of the other one out of three, many were buyers who were trading up from lower-priced cars to higher-priced cars but who tended to stay with the makes of the manufacturer of their previous cars.[90] Thus, the fact that a manufacturer had won large sales volumes in the past tended to benefit him in later time periods, to sustain his sales and, by implication, to make it more difficult for other manufacturers to win away large numbers of prior purchasers of a make.

A number of factors evidently served to sustain the importance of past, current, and perhaps anticipated sales volumes in shaping consumer preferences. Passenger cars were large, complex machines. They were so complex that most purchasers of cars were unable to evaluate the many

---

[87] U. S., Senate, Committee on the Judiciary, Subcommittee on Antitrust and Monopoly, *Hearings, A Study of the Antitrust Laws, op. cit.,* Part 1, pp. 455-56.

[88] "Chrysler's New Moves Click—Just in Time," *Business Week,* May 14, 1955, p. 92.

[89] *Supra,* footnote 56.

[90] Ford Motor Company, *Annual Report,* 1956, p. 12.

mechanical features and the over-all levels of quality. Automobiles also were sufficiently expensive and were purchased so infrequently that most buyers had little opportunity or desire to compare the different makes in any systematic fashion. Consumers depended on the "reputation" of the different makes.[91] In determining a car's reputation, the consumer may have relied on the observations and evaluations of his friends and associates, a situation in which large volume was important in providing frequency of contact and therefore inclusion in such observations. In addition, his own experience was important. Once having had a satisfactory experience with a particular make and its sales and service representative—the local dealer—the consumer was likely to purchase the same make again.[92] Other factors also may have been important. In many cases having provided "a sense of power" or "a tonic to the ego of the owner,"[93] becoming almost an extension of the owner's personality, an automobile attracted a hard core of very loyal owners, owners who talked about and often vigorously supported the virtues of the make of car they had so wisely purchased, according to their own way of thinking. Since frequency of contact was important in such word-of-mouth advertising, volume of sales obviously was an important factor. Frequency of contact also was important in the total impact of advertising and in the density of dealer coverage for a make, the advantages again generally having rested with the largest volume sellers of past years. In general, then, the tendency of automobile buyers was "to attribute 'better repute' to the brands with large sales, thus . . . placing the smaller-selling brands at a distinct disadvantage in their ability to expand their market shares."[94] "Bigger means better to many Americans."[95] The idea was that a car selling in large volume must have been good or so many people would not have bought it.

A result of the combined influence of the frequency of

[91] Joe S. Bain, *op. cit.*, p. 300.

[92] The importance of parts and service availability seems to have been reflected in the experience of Volkswagen, the most successful of the foreign producers in penetrating the U. S. market. Volkswagen put emphasis on parts and service availability. See Robert Sheehan, "A Big Year for Small Cars," *Fortune*, LVI (August, 1957), 107.

[93] See E. D. Kennedy, *The Automobile Industry* (New York: Reynal and Hitchcock, 1941), p. 319.

[94] Bain, *op. cit.*, p. 300.

[95] A. D. H. Kaplan, *Small Business: Its Place and Problems* (New York: McGraw-Hill, 1948), p. 77.

consumer contact and familiarity with a car, its promotional activities, its sales and service organization, and its owners was in general an apparently lower degree of relative consumer acceptance of the cars of the small volume manufacturer, that is, of the small volume firm and not the make of passenger car. The automobiles of General Motors, the industry's largest volume firm, in most years depreciated less rapidly than those of Ford and Chrysler; and those of the Big Three depreciated less than those of American Motors and Studebaker and their predecessors.[96] The unique Rambler, however, proved to be an exception. Relative to its original advertised price, Rambler's depreciation rates for several years in a row were lower than those of the nearest comparable Chevrolet, Ford, and Plymouth models until the introduction of compact cars by the latter.[97]

There may have been exceptions, perhaps because of a fortunate combination of product and promotional choices as seems to have been the case with the compact Rambler; but, the general rule seems to have been that the bigger the company, the better its products were likely to be received by consumers. To the extent that this was true, the fact that

[96] See Bain, *op. cit.*, pp. 303-305; and U. S., Senate, Committee on the Judiciary, Subcommittee on Antitrust and Monopoly, *Report, Administered Prices, op. cit.*, pp. 45-51, for earlier observations of this phenomenon. Comparisons by this writer of resale and original values as shown in *N. A. D. A. Used Car Guide Book* and *Red Book National Market Reports* confirm these and indicate that they continued into later periods with the exception noted.

[97] American Motors also called attention to this fact in its annual reports and used it in its advertising. The lower depreciation on some models evidently was in part a function of American Motors' strategy in reducing projected dealer margins on some of its lowest-priced models, principally the Rambler American, somewhat below those of other makes, at least before the introduction of Big Three compacts which also carried reduced dealer margins, as well as the rising consumer acceptance evidenced in increased Rambler sales. Relative to suggested list prices, a smaller dealer margin resulted in relatively higher invoice prices to dealers below which dealers would be reluctant to cut, thereby possibly contributing to a lower depreciation for Rambler compared to full-sized makes. Relative to suggested list prices, the compact makes of the Big Three also generally had lower depreciation rates than their full-sized makes, again apparently in part a result of differing projected margins in setting list prices. Comparisons, e.g., of average retail prices from National Automobile Dealers Used Car Guide Co., *N. A. D. A. Official Used Car Guide*, Southern edition, 1961 and 1962 editions, reveal such relationships between compact and full-sized cars.

the Big Three were already the large firms of the industry gave them preferred positions among consumers. Also, to the extent that this was true, the cars of a smaller firm were more difficult to sell; and, intangible though this influence may have been, it had its effects on cost. For a smaller firm trying to expand its market share in competition with already existing much larger firms, superior effort and judgment, perhaps good luck in choices of product quality and style, or more promotional cost per unit and/or lower price and thus probable sacrifices in profitability were required to win consumers away from the products of the larger volume company.

THE MARKETING PROBLEM AND THE INDEPENDENTS

Despite the heavy odds operating against them, American Motors and Studebaker found a partial answer to sheer volume of sales in the automobile industry; it was the compact car, something new and different, perhaps the last remaining alternative for the two firms in the 1950's. The distinctive product catering to consumer preferences for specialized features not then found in competitive makes offset much of the volume advantage of the Big Three. Product leadership—innovation—was vital in returning American Motors to a profitable position. Over the long run, however, the experiences of the two firms revealed that growth to substantially larger sales volumes than those generally attained by their predecessors was also essential. The return to more "normal" competitive conditions in 1953 had raised substantially the volume requirements for low unit cost operation, especially in the marketing activities of sales promotion and dealership distribution.

With the distinctive Rambler as an opening wedge to a larger market share, American Motors did survive and prosper. American Motors promoted Rambler aggressively using dealer contests in almost unending succession plus, for a while, rebates to consumers with the accomplishment of company sales objectives, boldly advertising Rambler's advantages over competitive makes which were indicated by name, and pointedly picturing American Motors as doing battle with the giants of the automobile industry to save consumers from the woes of the "over-sized gas-guzzling dinosaurs" that monopolists, at least by implication, had thrust upon them.[98] Helped along by a rising wave of criticism of Big Three cars and the evident reluctance of the Big Three to retaliate with price cuts and, because of required lead-times, their inability to offer similar cars quickly, American Motors achieved annual sales volumes on the order of 400,000 units with a relatively narrow line of models or body styles. At these output levels, the firm also generated the funds for a complete change in body style for the 1963 model as well as for substantial changes on an annual basis from the time of first adopting the 108-inch wheelbase 1956 model Rambler as the firm's basic volume car. While stressing stability of style as a promotional device, American Motors did in fact make numerous changes to update it products; and although the broadening of Rambler's models with the intensifying of competition in the compact car field pushed upward American Motors' tooling costs, the firm was able to generate in the years under study at volumes ranging around 400,000 units the funds for style change as well as other promotional activities. Larger outputs might have provided lower unit cost in advertising and dealership distribution; but the position of the Rambler at the 400,000 unit level seems to have been about comparable to that of most makes of the Big Three except for the very largest volume makes. In accomplishing increased sales, largely through innovation in a fortunate set of circumstances for the firm, American Motors clearly made considerable impact on the automobile buying public.

On the other hand, the experience of Studebaker confirmed that small volumes were insufficient to permit survival. Studebaker-Packard's initial efforts to offer a full line of cars, when they failed to win increased consumer acceptance, resulted in the firm's producing and marketing small volumes

[98] American Motors' aggressiveness and boldness showed up in its advertising which often ridiculed other makes of cars in general if not by name. For comment on the consumer rebate promotion, see "Gift to Rambler Buyers — Maybe," *Business Week*, December 24, 1960, p. 59. Buyers of Rambler in certain months of this program were to receive U. S. savings bonds with the amount in proportion to the percentages by which Rambler sales exceeded its sales of the previous year. American Motors' aggressive promotion of Rambler was succinctly described as a "shock treatment" to overcome widespread consumer opinion that Big Three cars were best. See Richard Austin Smith, "Will Success Spoil American Motors?" *Fortune*, LIX (January, 1959), 98.

of separate lines of cars at very high costs. Then subsequently, despite extensive cost reduction efforts, the reworking of Studebaker to produce the Lark, and the reduction of the Studebaker line to only a very few models, Studebaker-Packard found only one profitable year and that was in 1959 with an output of about 150,000 units. However, this evidently was too small and too late to provide a basis for effective marketing action; and after limping along with outputs of approximately 80,000 units per year, Studebaker finally withdrew from the domestic industry. Studebaker's dealer organization, which was considered the weakest in the industry, shared in the blame for Studebaker's failure;[99] and here, of course, volume was an important factor. However, other volume relationships were also important.

Although the relatively small producer had some leeway in avoiding direct price and quality competition with the Big Three because of the opportunity for product differentiation, at least until sales volumes of its successful product choices grew sufficiently to pose a threat to the market position of the larger firm and thereby lead to imitation, substantial volume was important for sustained effective marketing action in the automobile industry. A total of approximately 400,000 units per year was about the minimum for the longer run for a specialist producer and even more was better to permit diversity in automobile styles to spread the risks of error in choices of style and to acquire the benefits of large volume in large-scale advertising and dealership distribution. The minimum volumes required for sustained effective marketing action were substantially larger than the minimum volumes for low unit cost in manufacturing processes. Thus, marketing problems, the winning of consumer acceptance of one's choices of product and the delivering of the product into the hands of the consumer, problems in which both past and current volumes of output were important, seem to have been the key problems in the survival and prosperity of the automobile manufacturer. Confronted by the already large Big Three, the relatively small firms found innovative ability was vital to their continued existence, since growth to larger scales of operation than those from which

[99] See *The Wall Street Journal*, December 10, 1963, p. 4.

the Independents had started as separate firms was also essential.[100]

Because of the general use in the industry of systematic methods of market research and product development, significant innovation became an exceedingly difficult task—particularly the gaining of substantial lead-times on competitors. After the compact car "revolution," the consistent striving by the largest firms to cover most possible market segments, including even specialized consumer demands, reduced the room for maneuver by the individual firms; but opportunities still existed. The problem was to find them.

---

[100] According to Donald A. Moore in his article, "The Automobile Industry," op. cit., p. 303, small firms of the automobile industry in relation to their size "have done more than a proportionate share of pioneering." A record of innovation by itself, however, was not a sufficient condition for survival. Innovations and their timing varied in degrees of importance; and other factors were important, too. Also, see infra, chapter xii.

CHAPTER XI

DIVERSIFICATION AND OTHER PROBLEMS

ALTHOUGH THE PRINCIPAL forces underlying the post-World War II performances of the leading Independents seem to have been related to the scale of their manufacturing and marketing operations, the size of the firms may have been significant in other ways, too. Some suggestions regarding the latter appeared in the anticipated benefits of merger, which served to increase the size of the firms, in financing, purchasing, management, research, and product diversification. Although little comparative information is available regarding these elements, in only one case did the Independents, and then only one of them, clearly seem to have suffered a significant disadvantage related to the size of the firm. The reader is cautioned that the following observations are seemingly reasonable, but tentative propositions, since they are largely untested because of the scarcity of comparative data.

FINANCING

The small firm may experience disadvantages in financing — providing the means of payment for — its operations. The means of payment of a firm's obligations may be generated either internally or externally. Internal sources include those funds generated by retention of earnings and noncash expenses such as depreciation. Externally acquired funds are those provided by original or additional investment in the firm by preferred or common stockholders and by purchasers of debt obligations of the firm. Small firms may find it more difficult than large firms to secure both types of funds.

The highly profitable firm, after its initial financing, may find that it seldom needs additional outside funds from investors or creditors for financing continued operations; and if it does need such funds, the highly profitable firm may find it easy to secure them because of its success. To the extent that manufacturing or marketing operations conducted at a high volume contribute to profitable operations by lowering unit costs, the large firm may be expected to enjoy advantages of large-scale operations in the internal generation of funds. Thus, if the leading Independents were less successful than the Big Three because of size disadvantages in manufacturing and marketing, they were also experiencing some size disadvantages in the internal financing of their operations. Obviously the losses of the leading Independents, especially the heavy losses in the period from 1954 through 1958, curtailed the amounts of internal funds available to them compared with the amounts available from the continued profitable operations of the Big Three. Although internal financial disadvantages may influence a firm's access to external funds, these internal difficulties may be more appropriately analyzed under the headings of manufacturing and marketing, as was done in preceding chapters. This leaves for consideration here the influences of size on external financing of the firms' operations.

Small firms may experience considerable difficulty in securing outside investment funds because of their small size in relation to financial markets. Both the products and the financial performance of the small firm are likely to be less widely known to prospective investors than those of the large firm. "Conservative people are more ready to invest in a concern they already know as a large and presumably a successful one than in some business of which they had never heard before they were invited to buy its securities."[1] In addition, there may be advantages in having quotations available on financial pages of newspapers and in having widespread organized markets for the securities of a firm. If this is the case, small firms may experience greater difficulty and higher costs in obtaining funds than would large firms meeting these requirements. This conception of the conditions under which the small firm may experience financing difficulties, however, does not seem to have applied to the leading Independents.

The leading Independents, like the Big Three, were quite large firms in comparison with most business enterprises. They used the corporate form of business which gave them potentially widespread appeal in financial markets. Their securities were listed on the New York Stock Exchange and were traded frequently. Price quotations for their stocks were readily available in many newspapers; and the companies appeared generally well known to investors, although

---

[1] J. M. Clark, *Studies in the Economics of Overhead Costs* (Chicago: The University of Chicago Press, 1923), p. 131.

perhaps not quite so well known as the Big Three. The widespread recognition that the leading Independents were engaged in a struggle for survival after 1952 appears to have been a far more important influence on their access to external funds than their size in relation to financial markets. And, the same was true of their improved profit performance after 1957. With success in their manufacturing and marketing activities comparable to that of the Big Three, the Independents probably could have sold their publicly offered securities at rates approximating those of the Big Three.[2]

Even during the period after 1953 when their difficulties were very severe, the leading Independents were able to secure borrowed funds in private negotiations at rates approximately equal to those paid by the Big Three. At its founding on May 1, 1954, American Motors Corporation obtained a $73,000,000 line of credit against which the firm had loans outstanding in the amount of $69,600,000 calling for 3.5 per cent interest rate. By the end of September 1954 these loans had been reduced to $29,200,000; and later in the year the firm secured a new five-year $40,000,000 credit agreement at an interest rate equal to the prime commercial rate at the time of borrowing. The initial borrowing under this agreement was at a 3 per cent rate. During this same period American Motors also was paying 3 per cent on a $20,000,000 long-term loan which had been negotiated in 1947 and which called for notes payable of $2,000,000 annually each September 30, 1954 through 1961, with a $4,000,-000 final payment on September 30, 1962. This loan was renegotiated in 1956 to permit deferment of approximately $2,570,000 of the total of $4,000,000 due in 1956 and 1957 installments; but the interest rate was continued at 3 per cent with the final payment still due in 1962. In 1958, American Motors paid off all its short-term bank debt and secured a new agreement for $15,000,000 maximum borrowing to September 30, 1960, at the prime commercial rate at the time each loan was made. In 1960, the amount of available credit was raised to $50,000,000; but American Motors through 1962 had no borrowings against the agree-

[2] Following the improvement in the two remaining leading Independents' profit performances in 1958 and 1959, the prices of their common stocks rose; and the price-earnings ratio for American Motors stock temporarily approximated that for General Motors stock.

ment, its cash balance having been sustained since 1958 by internally generated funds.[3]

Studebaker-Packard began business with a $25,000,000 long-term loan privately negotiated and effective October 1, 1954, at an interest rate of 4 per cent for notes payable annually in the amount of $1,400,000 from October 1, 1957 through 1973, with a final payment of $1,200,000 at maturity on October 1, 1974. The firm also had a $45,000,000 credit agreement effective on the same date and calling for interest payments at a rate of 3.5 per cent. Earlier, in February 1954, Packard — a predecessor of Studebaker-Packard — had secured a $20,000,000 credit agreement with a rate equal to the prime commercial rate at the time of borrowing but not to exceed 3.75 per cent nor fall below 3 per cent. In 1956, $29,700,000 in 3.5 per cent notes under the $45,000,000 credit agreement was converted to 3.5 per cent six-month notes with renewal permitted for additional six-month periods at the option of Studebaker-Packard if no events of default occurred, except that no note could have a maturity date later than July 26, 1959. Also in 1956, the $25,000,000 term loan was renegotiated for the deferment of the first installment payment from October 1, 1957, to October 1, 1959, with final payment still to be made October 1, 1974. The interest rate was continued at 4 per cent. Then, in 1958, the creditors of the firm agreed to a refinancing in which they gave up $54,700,000 in secured notes for $16,500,000 in 5 per cent secured notes and $16,500,000 in $5 convertible preferred stock with a par value of $100.[4]

During 1954, two of the Big Three resorted to borrowed funds. On January 5, 1954, General Motors sold $300,000,000 in 3.25 per cent debentures with final payment due in 1979; these debentures provided net proceeds to the firm of $298,-500,000. In July 1954, Chrysler secured a $250,000,000 loan

[3] The data in this paragraph on the loans obtained by American Motors are based on Nash-Kelvinator Corporation, *Annual Report*, 1947; American Motors Corporation, *Annual Reports*, 1954-1958; *Moody's Industrial Manual*, 1955 edition (New York: Moody's Investors Service), p. 2633, and 1959 edition, p. 2131; and American Motors Corporation, *Annual Report*, 1962.

[4] The data in this paragraph on the loans obtained by Studebaker-Packard and its predecessor — Packard — are based on Studebaker-Packard Corporation, *Annual Reports*, 1954-1958; *Moody's Industrial Manual*, 1955 edition, p. 2720; and Studebaker-Packard Corporation, "Letter to Shareholders," and "Proxy Statement," dated September 24, 1956, pp. 6-8.

agreement with Prudential Insurance Company of America calling for 3.75 per cent promissory notes with the last installment due on July 1, 2054. These notes were convertible to 3.5 per cent notes by either party any time after January 1, 1962, and payable in equal installments over a 20-year period from the time of conversion. (On January 2, 1962, the notes were converted.) In 1956, Ford negotiated a $250,-000,000 long-term loan calling for an interest rate of 4 per cent and repayable over a 20-year period with final payment due November 1, 1976. In 1958, Chrysler secured a bank agreement for a maximum borrowing of $150,000,000 until September 30, 1961, with interest at the prevailing prime commercial rate for 90-day notes.[5]

The rates charged the Independents thus seem to have approximated those of the Big Three. If the rates charged the leading Independents had been higher than those that were charged the Big Three, the higher rates could easily have been attributed to their poorer internal performance. Thus, the leading Independents seem not to have suffered (external) financing disadvantages primarily because of their size in relation to the Big Three and to the financial markets.[6]

PURCHASING

Small firms may experience some disadvantages in purchasing in comparison with large firms. Large firms can buy in large quantities on single orders and secure the maximum discounts for such orders. Purchasing specialists are available to large firms, and their time may be used fully. Orders in bulk may be shipped at lower costs in carload lots, and fixed costs of handling an order may be spread over more units in the larger order.

Again, it may be emphasized that all the domestic passenger car manufacturers, including the leading Independents, were quite large. Specialists in purchasing were available to the leading Independents, and these firms were large

[5] The data in this paragraph on loans obtained by the Big Three are based on General Motors Corporation, *Annual Report*, 1954; Chrysler Corporation, *Annual Reports*, 1954 and 1961; and Ford Motor Company, *Annual Report*, 1956, and *Moody's Industrial Manual*, 1959 edition, p. 1637.

[6] These comparisons unfortunately can not be made with a high degree of precision since the firms under consideration resorted only infrequently to external sources of funds. This observation, admittedly, is tentative.

enough to purchase in carload lots. Presumably, additional discounts were not available for purchases in trainload lots rather than carload lots.

Officials of the leading Independents indicated that, to the best of their knowledge, the small firms paid the same prices as the Big Three for purchases of materials, supplies, and components of comparable specifications. When asked about his firm's purchases of supplies and components, J. J. Nance, then president of Studebaker-Packard, responded that the Big Three probably did not get better prices than the Independents in the open market.[7] He thought that if the Big Three did get a cost advantage on their parts and components, it came on those items produced by integrated operations within the company. George Romney, then president of American Motors, also indicated that, as far as his company was able to determine, American Motors was able to buy parts, components, and materials on a par with the Big Three for comparable specifications.[8] However, he believed that in times of short supply his company did not fare as well as the Big Three in getting scarce materials and supplies. The Big Three, he thought, had an advantage of relatively more assured supplies. He also believed that the Robinson-Patman Act, which was designed to prevent price discrimination among comparable purchasers, was influential in enabling the Independents to buy as cheaply as the Big Three.

Unfortunately, price and quantity data are not generally available for comparison of purchases by the Independents and the Big Three except for limited information on purchases of steel by the Big Three and American Motors in 1956. The data shown in Table 24 appear to support the observations of officials of the leading Independents. Apparently, the larger firms had no advantage in their purchases of steel for automotive uses. Although the quantity purchased was much smaller, American Motors' average cost

[7] U. S., Senate, Interstate and Foreign Commerce Committee, Subcommittee on Automobile Marketing Practices, *Hearings, Automobile Marketing Practices*, 84th Congress, 2nd Session, Pursuant to S. Res. 13 continued by S. Res. 163 (Washington: U. S. Government Printing Office, 1956), Part 1, p. 380.

[8] U. S., Senate, Committee on the Judiciary, Subcommittee on Antitrust and Monopoly, *Hearings, Administered Prices*, 85th Congress, 2nd Session, Pursuant to S. Res. 57 and S. Res. 231 (Washington: U. S. Government Printing Office, 1958), Part 6, p. 2855.

was lower than those of the Big Three. Variations in specifications and timing of purchases may have contributed to
the average cost variations. It is also possible that the differing prices were, in part, a result of bilateral oligopoly
pricing arrangements among the Big Three and the steel
companies whereby price increases in steel were passed along

TABLE 24

TOTAL FINISHED SHEET STEEL PURCHASES, TOTAL
COST OF SUCH STEEL, AND AVERAGE PRICE
PER TON FOR THE BIG THREE AND
AMERICAN MOTORS, 1956 [a]

	Total Purchases (Net Tons)	Total Cost	Average Cost (Per Ton)
American Motors	86,149	$ 10,429,616	$121.00
Chrysler	955,664	130,000,000 [b]	136.00
Ford	1,330,000	180,000,000 [b]	135.50
General Motors	5,299,778	760,604,953	143.50

[a] Data provided in U. S., Senate, Committee on the Judiciary, Subcommittee on Antitrust and Monopoly, *Hearings, Administered Prices*,
85th Congress, 2nd Session, Pursuant to S. Res. 57 and S. Res. 231
(Washington: U. S. Government Printing Office, 1958), Part 7, p. 3792
for American Motors, pp. 3727-28 for Chrysler, p. 3627 for Ford, and
p. 3546 for General Motors.
[b] Estimated by the companies.

to consumers by the Big Three.[9] Finally, although American
Motors' $10,000,000 purchase of steel in 1956 was small in
comparison with the purchases of the Big Three, it was
sufficiently large that a steel producer would be unlikely to
ignore American Motors as a customer. Perhaps American
Motors, losing money in 1956, drove a harder bargain for
steel than the Big Three; and the steel companies were
willing to agree to lower prices to avoid losing the orders
of American Motors if the firm was less able than the Big
Three to pass along higher steel prices to its customers. In
any event, the lower average cost of steel to American Motors
supports the observations that the leading Independents paid
no more, and may have paid less, than the Big Three in
the open market for their purchases.

[9] John F. Due, *Intermediate Economic Analysis* (Homewood, Illinois:
Richard D. Irwin, Inc., 1956), pp. 58-59 and 282, describes this type of
pricing arrangement.

MANAGEMENT AND RESEARCH

Among the ways in which a large firm may gain advantages over a small firm is the quality and performance of its management. Large firms may be better able to use specialists — experts. Also, they may be better able to offer the opportunity needed to attract specialists. The advantage may work in two ways. First, a large firm may permit the specialist to devote his full time and efforts to his particular function. Secondly, devotion to a particular function permits the specialist to increase his knowledge and skill—his expertness — in his particular specialty whether in manufacturing, marketing, financing, or any of the many other business activities. The individual manager, who in performing numerous functions in a small firm would seldom have the opportunity or capacity to become expert in all of them, in the large firm may have an opportunity to specialize in one activity or function and to become an expert in the performance of that in which he specializes.

The improvements to be gained in management performance by means of an increase in the scale of operations of a firm are primarily those related to the opportunity to make a more extensive division of labor, standardization of the processes of management, and the accompanying use of specialists. It appears easier to find or train people to perform specialized jobs than to perform broad-ranging jobs requiring many skills.

Officials of the leading Independents, as we saw previously, expected to gain improved managerial performance as a result of the mergers.[10] After the mergers both firms reported that improvements had been made in managerial activities including administration, research and development, purchasing, and other activities through consolidation. At the time of the mergers, each of the merging firms had considerable excess capacity; and improvement came through elimination of duplicating managerial effort. Even if the leading Independents had been operating at full manufacturing capacity at the time of the mergers, some improvement might have been expected through consolidation of some managerial activities. One research staff for each new firm could have replaced two previously separate staffs to reduce unit overhead cost for this phase of management. One purchasing

[10] *Supra*, chapters ii-iv and vii.

group might have replaced two previously separate groups and handled any added work load with few added staff members. And, even though each of the newly combined firms may have been larger than either of its predecessors, each still needed only one president rather than the two who were replaced. Of course, an additional assistant, possibly a vice-president, may have been needed if the work load of the president greatly increased; but assistants were less expensive than presidents. Similarly, each needed only one team of top managers, a group which probably consisted of fewer members than the total of the two separate groups being combined. Thus, an increase in the size of the leading Independent firms could have been expected to utilize the capacities of management personnel better if some of the previously separate staffs were eliminated.

Some management functions, such as research and development, may require staffs of considerable size for effective accomplishment. However, even in the research and development phase of the planning function of management, the required size did not seem beyond the capabilities of the Independents even before the mergers. The leading Independents appeared able to demonstrate good performance. George Romney was quite emphatic in contending that the Big Three had no special advantages in research and development because of their larger size.[11] Much of the basic research which became applicable in the passenger car industry was done by suppliers of the industry, and the small firms apparently had as much access to this research as the Big Three. The research and development work in the passenger car industry itself appears to have been largely applied research. Even the introduction of automatic transmissions in the United States stemmed largely from the refinement of automatic transmission developments in Europe in the 1920's and 1930's.[12] In addition, refinements in production processes often were stimulated by developments outside of the passenger car industry. Although Ford deserves much credit for the trend to automation — from its earliest history Ford has been a leader in production technology — much work on automation of production in the industry was done by outside

11 U. S., Senate, Committee on the Judiciary, Subcommittee on Antitrust and Monopoly, *op. cit.*, pp. 2873-78.

12 John Jewkes, David Sawers, and Richard Stillerman, *The Sources of Invention* (London: Macmillan & Co., 1958), pp. 263-66.

suppliers engaged in the electronics and machine tool industries. If they had the volumes to permit their use, these developments were also available to the Independents.

That the managerial activities of the Independents in planning for and making innovations compared favorably with those of the Big Three seems demonstrated by the fact that "the small producers have done more than a proportionate share of pioneering."[13] Indeed, innovation may well be a most appropriate role for the small producer. The unit body-frame type of construction, which was later featured on the "compact" cars of the Big Three, was pioneered in the United States by Nash and Hudson. Torsion bar suspension, which was later advertised as a major feature of Chrysler cars, was first featured in a domestic United States car on the Packard in 1955. Furthermore, American Motors and Studebaker-Packard respectively led the way and adapted to the compact car concept more quickly than the Big Three.

While they appear to have done a good job of research and development, the Independents' unit costs of doing so may have been higher than those of the Big Three. That this may have been the situation is evidenced by the elimination of duplicating research groups by the merging companies. In other words, an opportunity to secure unit cost advantages in such management activities as research and development appeared to extend to larger scales than had been attained by the leading Independents prior to the mergers. The larger the output of the one design, of course, the lower would have been the unit cost of its design.

As a specialized staff is developed and as it becomes larger with the growth of the firm, longer channels of communication may develop, red tape may accumulate, and the problems of co-ordination of activities may become more difficult, at least so go the conventional arguments regarding diseconomies of management.[14] However, there is little reason to believe that the leading Independents reached sizes which necessarily would result in diseconomies in management. Even the Big Three may not have been so large as to have suffered diseconomies in management because of their larger size. The range of possible management cost savings probably has been

[13] Donald A. Moore, "The Automobile Industry," in *The Structure of American Industry*, Walter Adams, editor (New York: The Macmillan Company, 1954), p. 303.

[14] See, e.g., G. J. Stigler, *The Theory of Price* (New York: The Macmillan Company, 1946), p. 138.

extended to very large scales of operation by methods of management such as control by the "exception principle" and the decentralization of responsibility and authority to the lowest possible levels combined with the use of rapid communication devices and electronic data-gathering and -processing equipment, all of which were widely used in the automobile industry. Even if there were no further savings in managerial costs through the use of such devices and techniques, there is little reason to believe that their use resulted in higher managerial costs. The electronic and other communication devices may be quite expensive, but their use may substitute for personnel costs that otherwise would be necessary.

On the other hand, the leading Independents may have had an advantage in the flexibility of small firm managements. Some innovations may be so extensive that they are not routine; they upset the normal routine, particularly when there is considerable pressure to change rapidly as in "crash programs" to introduce features already successfully introduced by competitors. With smaller staffs and fewer people to be considered in the process of making major changes, the Independents may have been able to adjust more rapidly to changing conditions. Perhaps this is why the Independents were able to contribute significantly to innovations in the industry.[15]

On balance, for firms that have attained the size of the Independents as compared with the even larger Big Three, the influence of size variations on the costs of effective management, partly because of the difficulty of isolating and evaluating "effectiveness," is so elusive as to preclude more than a very tentative observation. On the basis of cost per unit of output, the Independents probably suffered some slight disadvantage in routine managerial activities but made up for this by a greater degree of flexibility.

DIVERSIFICATION

The emphasis thus far in the study has been on the leading Independents as manufacturers of passenger cars. However, the firms of the automobile industry did produce other products and may have secured advantages from diversification, a factor which added a new dimension of size. Diversifi-

[15] Of course they also may have had a great stimulus to change to avoid, in so far as possible, direct competition with the Big Three.

cation is related not to the scale of operations of the firm, but to the scope of its operations.

When a firm is producing a diversity of products within an industry, a decline in the sales of any one, whether due to errors of the firm in the design, production, and promotion of its products, cyclical variations, or shifts in consumer preferences, may not affect the over-all financial strength of the firm greatly. Similar benefits may be obtained from interindustry diversification. In both types, profit declines on one product may be offset by gains on others. In a diversified firm, risks are spread over many products; and there is a reduction of the possibility of failure of the firm from losses in any one of its product lines.

In the passenger car industry, it was quite clear that one of the factors tending to limit the financial losses of American Motors, particularly in comparison with the much larger losses of Studebaker-Packard, was the greater interindustry product diversification of American Motors. The operations of the Kelvinator and other appliance lines, the plastics business of the Ranco subsidiary, the appliance financing of the Redisco subsidiary, and the foreign subsidiaries of American Motors remained relatively steady earners following the downturn in the sales of Nash and Hudson cars after 1952 and partially offset the losses from passenger car operations. Studebaker and Packard were more dependent on defense and automotive operations, both of which fell off sharply at the same time in 1953 and 1954. They did not have the diversity in appliances or other products which aided American Motors. All of the Big Three also produced products other than cars, although Ford and Chrysler were not so diversified as General Motors.

Diversification also may be achieved to some degree from the offering of several lines of cars, although seasonal and cyclical factors tend to affect all lines but perhaps not to the same degree. In an industry such as the car industry, where style factors and changes were emphasized, the offering of multiple lines apparently provided a substantial advantage to the Big Three. Being able to offer somewhat different styling and features on several lines, the likelihood of extensive losses because of styling errors on any one line was reduced. Ford's experience with Edsel illustrated this situation. Losses attending the introduction and withdrawal of Edsel obviously were offset by gains on other products since

Ford reported substantial earnings in the years covering the Edsel fiasco.

The acquisition of complementary but different lines, it may be recalled, was one of the major objectives of the mergers. Unfortunately, other forces, among which consumer fear of an "orphan" car was important, at the time more than offset the potential advantages to be secured from such a move. And, the firms lacked the sales volumes and resources to maintain separate lines.

The advantage of diversification to the larger firms — and this included American Motors as well as the Big Three but not Studebaker-Packard until after 1959—was a lower risk of failure of the firm from styling errors or shifts in consumer preferences which affected the sales of one or possibly more than one of their products. Indeed, the risks of failure in the passenger car industry may have been so great that only the large firm, large in the sense of producing other products as a means of spreading the risks of error or changing consumer preferences, could be expected to survive. This may be especially important when taxes are minimized by the offsetting of unprofitable operations in some products or lines against profitable operations in other products or lines, a factor which may contribute to continued production of temporarily unprofitable products during periods of adaptation to changed conditions or of recovery from past mistakes.

American Motors had diversification in other than automotive products; but it did not possess as much diversification in multiple car lines as did the Big Three. Until the end of 1959, Studebaker-Packard had little or no product diversification; but subsequently, the firm's push to diversify paid off. The opportunity to use its accumulated tax losses to avoid taxes on profits of acquired companies was one of the factors promoting the continued existence of Studebaker-Packard and enabling it eventually to diversify.

The financial health and survival power of the Independents as automobile manufacturers rather obviously were significantly influenced by their opportunities for diversification. While the influence of larger firm size obtained through diversification may not be readily measurable, it clearly was a significant influence on the financial health of all the passenger car manufacturers and may well have been among the most significant of the influences on the survival and prosperity of the leading Independents.

SUMMARY

Among the other relationships of firm size to the financial health of the leading Independents, diversification appeared to be the most significant influence. In their purchasing and external financing activities, the Independents seemed of sufficient size for effective operation; but they probably obtained some unit cost savings in managerial activities from an increase in firm size as a result of the mergers. Unfortunately, only very tentative observations have been possible.

CHAPTER XII

THE HISTORICAL ELEMENT

THE EXPERIENCES OF THE LEADING Independents in the passenger car industry after World War II also may be placed
in a broader perspective than that which has been emphasized
to this point.

CUMULATIVE INFLUENCES OF HISTORY

Coexisting with and often underlying the technological
considerations, market phenomena, internal organizational
problems, and relationships among the firms of the automobile industry during the years covered in this study was the
influence of developments which, for lack of a more apt
phrase, may be called the cumulative influences of history.
The performances of the leading Independents after World
War II were partly functions of history, both of their own
unique development, the development of competing enterprises, and the evolution of the larger social and economic
environment of which they were a part. Whatever they were,
whether, for example, actions of the management of a firm,
shifts in consumer attitudes toward the firm and its products,
or actions of the firm's competitors—and whether they met
with success or failure—many events of a time period extended their influence to subsequent time periods.

The influence of historical events was illustrated in the
ultimate results of the leading Independents' early post-World
War II laxity in dealing with the unions representing their
employees. High labor cost patterns of the early postwar
years were difficult to break in later years when costs again
became more important to the survival and prosperity of the
firms, for the later efforts to reduce labor costs were met
with opposition from the many employees who had benefited
from liberal contract provisions. Since its labor costs had
been highest in the industry because of unusually liberal
wage standards and seniority rules compared to other car
manufacturers, this was an especially important factor in
the financial performance of Studebaker and later Studebaker-Packard, the influence of which probably extended

even to the time of termination of the firm's South Bend operations.

Although some events of a time period, for example, the introduction and promotion of push-button devices for selecting and shifting gears of automatic transmissions, may have only transitory influence—if any—it is obvious even without trying to trace them in detail that many events of a time period may have long-lasting influence. For instance, the lengthy contest over the Selden patent on the gasoline powered automobile and the defeat in court of its holders by a determined Henry Ford in the early days of the industry's development influenced the subsequent course of events in the industry for many years, including the later development of cross-licensing arrangements whereby conflict over patents was virtually eliminated from the automotive scene, at least among the manufacturers of cars.[1] Production knowledge and most patentable innovations became essentially common property among the manufacturers in exchange for nominal royalty payments.

As an influence on the performances of the leading Independents after World War II, probably the most important events of any time period occurred many years before those selected for our close study. The fact that the leading Independents, or their predecessor companies, were not the ones to enjoy in the early years of the industry's development the tremendous successes of the firms that became the Big Three handicapped them in later time periods. The pioneering work of Henry Ford in mass production coupled with his concept of a mass market for a standardized, low-priced car provided the Ford Motor Company first place in sales in the industry with the famous "Model T" and made Henry Ford a millionaire many times over in the 1910's.[2] The welding together through merger by William C. Durant of a diversity of automotive and other products in the General Motors Cor-

[1] See William Greenleaf, *Monopoly on Wheels: Henry Ford and the Selden Automobile Patent* (Detroit: Wayne State University Press, 1961), esp. chapter x.

[2] See Henry Ford, in collaboration with Samuel Crowther, *My Life and Work* (Garden City, New York: Garden City Publishing Co., Inc., 1922); Allan Nevins, with the collaboration of Frank Ernest Hill, *Ford: The Times, the Man, the Company* (New York: Charles Scribner's Sons, 1954); Allan Nevins and Frank Ernest Hill, *Ford: Expansion and Challenge, 1915-1933* (New York: Charles Scribner's Sons, 1957); and John B. Rae, *American Automobile Manufacturers: The First Forty Years* (Philadelphia: Chilton Co., 1959), esp. chapter vii.

poration, the subsequent reorganization of General Motors under the guiding hand of Alfred P. Sloan, and the firm's emphasis on product evolution at a time of a maturing demand for automobiles enabled General Motors to wrest first place in the industry from Ford in the late 1920's and provided General Motors an enduring strength.[3] In the 1930's, during a period of managerial decay at Ford, Walter Chrysler's product innovations, combined with heavy promotional outlays, catapulted Chrysler Corporation into contention for second place in the industry.[4] Chrysler held this position until the highly successful rebuilding of Ford in the post-World War II period under the forceful leadership of Henry Ford II and Ernest R. Breech.[5] While the predecessors of the firms that became the leading Independents had been fairly profitable in the earlier years of the industry's development, they were, relatively speaking, far less successful than the Big Three, a fact which left them at a distinct disadvantage in later time periods, particularly in terms of their influence in the market and their accumulated resources. Probing and responding to the market and changes in it, each of the firms that became the Big Three had found keys to enormous growth at different intervals in the industry's development and had gained thereby advantages which extended into subsequent periods.

Also of importance in this connection was an apparent tendency for the events of a time period to be cumulative in their effects. Each time period provided a basis out of which the events of the future evolved. Change and adaptation to change created new conditions out of which came further change. The process was unending. To the extent that consumer loyalty in repeat purchases was a determinant of new car sales, the past successes of the Big Three, the large market shares won by them, provided them preferred market positions in later periods, especially after the early

[3] See Arthur Pound, *The Turning Wheel* (Garden City, New York: Doubleday, Doran & Co., Inc., 1934); Rae, *op. cit.*; and Alfred P. Sloan, "My Years with General Motors," *Fortune*, in five parts beginning in Vol. LXVIII (September, 1963).

[4] Leonard W. Weiss, *Economics and American Industry* (New York: John Wiley & Sons, Inc., 1961), p. 338.

[5] See "Rebirth of Ford," *Fortune*, XXXV (May, 1947), 81-89 ff.; "Ford's New Managers," *Fortune*, XLVII (May, 1953), 142-43 ff.; and Allan Nevins and Frank Ernest Hill, *Ford: Decline and Rebirth, 1933-1962* (New York: Charles Scribner's Sons, 1963).

1920's when replacement demand became an important component of the total demand for automobiles. This is not to say that early gains in the market could not be lost to superior action by competitors or thrown away by inaction or careless action of the firm. Nevertheless, the firm or firms which first became large obtained influence in the market which strengthened their positions relative to smaller competitors in later periods.

In addition, success or failure in a time period had financial effects which tended to cumulate in succeeding time periods. Success in the market, such as those choices that provided the early growth of the Big Three or much later American Motors' success with the compact car, provided profits for further activity. Failure had an opposite but also long-lasting effect. For example, having chosen a full-line approach but meeting only failure for its efforts to expand or even sustain its sales, Studebaker-Packard found the drains on its cash to be enormous. The influence of this choice was long-lasting, and it severely reduced Studebaker-Packard's resources available for further activity. The key idea here is contained in the statement: "It takes money to make money." With variations in degrees of market success among the participants in the industry in various time periods, further variations also could be expected in later time periods because of the variations among the firms in accumulated resources.

Thus, degrees of success or failure were important. Reflected imperfectly though they may have been in the financial statements of the firm, many events of past periods made their mark. Among them were the evolution of a mass market for cars and the development of a production technology in which substantial economies of scale were found. The Big Three capitalized upon the great opportunities existing in these earlier years of the industry's evolution, a time of nonexistent or low corporate income taxes, which was therefore a more favorable juncture for internal financing of growth than was the case in later years. Historical events and their cumulative effects in large measure determined the opportunities and limitations of opportunity confronting the firms of the automobile industry, including the resources available for their subsequent action, the relationships among them, and especially the inequalities in their scales of operation and over-all size during the immediate postwar and succeeding years.

THE CORPORATION

In fostering the cumulation of the effects of history, the use of the corporate form of business, the invention and importance of which has been documented by others,[6] was an important underlying influence on the firms of the automobile industry. The corporation provided a powerful instrument for the bringing together and keeping together of the men and material resources required for productive purposes. The great successes of the Big Three in the earlier years of the automobile industry's development and their growth to very large scales of enterprise may have been possible without the use of the corporate form of business; but the continuance of the enterprise so developed scarcely seems conceivable without the use, at least in the United States, of the corporate form of business as a means of acquiring and retaining private capital.

The corporation, an entity created under the laws of the individual states by the granting of a charter to its organizers, is a collection of persons brought together for the purposes indicated in the charter. But the corporation is also an entity independent of its human membership; it is a "legal person," the equivalent under the law of a human being. It can sue and be sued in court; it can hold and sell property; and in accordance with the wishes of those who control it, rules and regulations can be established for its internal conduct subject to the restraints imposed by the constitution and laws of the state and the charter granted to it.

Unlike the unincorporated forms of business, the proprietorship and the partnership, whose obligations if necessary may be settled out of the personal assets of their owners, the corporation is responsible for the obligations incurred in its name. The use of the corporate form of business provides a limitation of liability to its owners. But more significantly, the use of the corporate form of business adds a new

[6] See, e.g., the pioneering work of Adolf A. Berle, Jr., and Gardiner C. Means, *The Modern Corporation and Private Property* (New York: The Macmillan Co., 1932); or the later work of Edward S. Mason, editor, *The Corporation in Modern Society* (Cambridge, Mass.: Harvard University Press, 1959).

dimension to life. Under the laws of some states the corporation acquires perpetual life; and in those states with limits to the life of charters, the renewal of corporate charters generally has been an easy matter. With perpetual life possible, so long as its operations are conducted successfully and a majority of its owners do not desire termination of their affairs in a collective enterprise, the corporation is not subjected to an inevitable dissolution of its business with the withdrawal or incapacity of its owners and is unlike the less sophisticated forms of business which terminate with the withdrawal or death of their owners.

The Big Three, having grown large as a result of successful action, particularly their innovations, whether in products or production processes, in earlier time periods of the industry's development, though not the same time period, gained advantages of large size which were perpetuated in later time periods by their organization as corporations. They became institutions of economic activity. People entered and left the companies over the years; but in a sense the organizations continued, building in each succeeding time period on the basis left from earlier periods. In this way, the potentially cumulative benefits of the corporate form of business, effectively exploited, helped sustain the early leads which the Big Three had obtained and thus contributed to the difficulties of any existing or newly established smaller competing firm in later time periods.

THE ANTITRUST DILEMMA

The firms of the automobile industry, corporations, creations of men, operated within a framework of legislation and judicial interpretation, also a creation of men. In the United States, direct public control in the form of specifying prices, costs, or output levels of business has been avoided, with the exception of that economic activity endowed with characteristics of the public utility, and except for periods of wartime stress.[7] Rather, placing faith in the institutions of private property and the profit motive, the people of the United States have relied upon the force of competition, presumably in free and open markets, to regulate business activity in the public interest. But this has not been without some doubts.

[7] See, e.g., the comments of Vernon A. Mund, *Government and Business*, second edition (New York: Harper & Bros., 1955), pp. 67-104.

One can scarcely observe the size and financial strength of firms like the Big Three of the automobile industry without feeling simultaneously admiration for the accomplishments that their extensive operations represent and fear of potentially disruptive effects of their economic power. The Big Three over the years demonstrated great feats of productivity which obviously contributed to the well-being of the American people; but as focal points for enormous flows of goods and money, they also possessed tremendous market power which posed a threat, real or imagined, of less effective economic performance than might have seemed assured with a large number of competing firms in the automobile industry. Obviously the structural and behavioral conditions of the United States automobile industry did not correspond to those of the classical theoretical model of a society organized on a purely or perfectly competitive basis. The individual firms of the automobile industry, the leading Independents as well as the Big Three, did have market power; the number of firms in the competing industry group was not large; the size of the firms in relation to the extent of the market was not insignificant, although the Independents may have been in positions not unlike those of minuscule competitors responding to forces largely beyond their control or influence; and the firms of the industry did not ignore the actions of competing firms, in fact, could not ignore the actions of competitors without running a risk of loss in market penetration and probably declining profits.

Obviously the market powers of the Big Three were greater than those of the Independents; and this was an influence which worked to the disadvantage of the smaller firms. Were the market powers of the Big Three also detrimental to the public? One may well question whether the difficulties of the Independents and their decline in number should have been taken as evidence of a public need for antitrust remedies against the dominance of the industry by the Big Three. A tentative answer follows.

The productive contributions of the Big Three to the well-being of American consumers may be seen in the vast array of their cars on the highways; but the social desirability of the competitive stimulus was evidenced in the impact of the Independents, and that of the foreign producers, in stimulating the industry's shift to the compact car, thus indicating the importance of a variety of alternative sources of supply. In their discovery and exploitation of the market potential for the compact car, American Motors, Studebaker, and the foreign producers helped satisfy desires of consumers who might otherwise have been ignored by the Big Three in the race for the mass consumption dollar; but in retrospect, considering the availability of information in their market studies, in which of course occasional mistakes were possible, and acknowledging the need for long lead-times for significant product changes, the Big Three did not seem laggard in their market responses.

To a degree, the problems of the Independents were also problems of the Big Three, although much of their influence may have been submerged in the financial strength and diversity of operations of the Big Three. Through their product offerings and promotional programs, in which the largest firm occupied an enviable position because of the potential unit cost advantages of large-scale sales promotion, the Big Three exerted influence in shaping consumer preferences; but they did not control the consumer. Although the Big Three may have had the advantage in their volume influence and diversity of automobile lines, the Independents also exerted influence on consumer preferences but did not control them.

The benefits of large-scale advertising can hardly be overestimated, especially for General Motors in relation even to Chrysler and Ford and for these three in relation to the smaller firms. Yet, advertising alone was not enough to gain sales; a product capable of winning and keeping consumer acceptance was also essential. No one of the automobile manufacturers was so large as to be completely immune to the test of the market, a fact which was reflected in shifts in market shares among the several producers of the industry, although one may question the long-term significance of General Motors' repeated ability not only to recover after each of its slumps in market share but also gradually to enlarge its position. Also, like the Independents, the Big Three faced problems of organizing production; but unlike the Independents until the comeback of American Motors, the Big Three had successfully attained output levels at which they could exploit most if not all of the economies of scale in the manufacture and physical distribution of cars, thus making efficient use of productive resources. Indeed, even disregarding the interrelated and hard to evaluate influence of sales promotion advantages of large volume, the existence of economies of scale in the manufacture and physical distribution of cars goes far toward explaining not only the variations in performance between the Independents and the Big Three but also the historical existence of so high a degree of concentration in the automobile industry.

Until the comeback of American Motors with its compact Rambler, the Independents generally failed to meet even the lowest of the output volume requirements estimated as essential to low unit cost in the manufacture of cars. Increased mechanization and automation in the postwar years raised these estimated requirements to approximately 200,000-400,-000 units per year of one basic body shell on one-two shift operation, about double what they had been before the war. Furthermore, until the "piggyback" innovation in the transport of completed automobiles in the late 1950's, the Independents' output levels were far below the 1,000,000 and more units per year estimated as required for physical distribution costs competitive with those of the most widely dispersed regional assembly operations. Among the Big Three, only General Motors enjoyed volumes sufficient to permit the operation of more than one extensive regional assembly system. Excluding its prestige Cadillac car which was assembled in one plant, General Motors operated two essentially parallel regional assembly systems: the Chevrolet and the Buick-Oldsmobile-Pontiac systems. Ford's assembly arrangements for Mercury involved a much smaller number of plants than did those for its Ford division; and Chrysler's assembly plants were the least numerous among the Big Three. The opportunities to use such arrangements were based in large measure upon consumer willingness, perhaps influenced by manufacturer sales promotion, to buy relatively standardized cars of essentially one make or of closely related makes. Although the "piggyback" innovation improved the relative physical distribution cost position of the centralized producer, it was a fact of history that it came too late to be of much value to any of the Independents except American Motors. Large output volumes obviously were required for efficient use of resources in the automobile industry. However, the evaluation of such factors as the above for their social and economic significance is not an easy task, partly because of the difficulties in making precise measure of the nature and extent of economies of scale as well as of the competitive action essential to assuring that their benefits are passed on to the public.

The automobile industry was an oligopoly, a type of industrial structure which economists and antitrust agencies have found difficult to evaluate for social and economic significance—so much so, in fact, that expert economists and lawyers have often found themselves entangled in controversy in measuring and evaluating the economic data of antitrust cases.[8] Elements of monopoly and competition have been found to exist simultaneously.[9] Measuring their relative importance in specific cases has not been easy. The difficulty rests in the complexity of the concepts of competition and monopoly and the problems involved in their incorporation into the law as a basis for public action. Theories of "workable" or "effective" competition perhaps have been most useful not in defining adequate standards for antitrust action but in indicating how very difficult it is to derive such standards for incorporation into the law.[10] Certain specific actions such as, for example, collusion in setting prices, conspiracy in dividing markets, or agreements to exclude competitors have been successfully described in the law and its judicial application as socially unacceptable actions to acquire monopoly

[8] One has only to review the records of antitrust actions to observe conflicting interpretations of the economic data of such cases. See also the summary comments on the processes of litigation and negotiation and uses of economic data in antitrust cases by Mark S. Massel, *Competition and Monopoly: Legal and Economic Issues* (Washington: The Brookings Institution, 1962), chapters v and vi, esp. pp. 167-69.

[9] Kaysen and Turner, e.g., say: "We do not attempt to classify individual markets as competitive or monopolistic. Individual markets show varying mixtures of competitive and monopolistic elements; they are more or less competitive rather than all or not-at-all competitive." Carl Kaysen and Donald F. Turner, *Antitrust Policy: An Economic and Legal Analysis* (Cambridge, Mass.: Harvard University Press, 1959), p. 24.

[10] See, e.g., the critical reviews of the problem by Edward S. Mason, "The Current Status of the Monopoly Problem in the United States," *Harvard Law Review*, LXII (1949), 1265-85; Alfred E. Kahn, "Standards for Antitrust Policy," *Harvard Law Review*, LXVII (1953), 28-54; and Massel, *op. cit.*, chapter vii. Acknowledging the difficulties of developing standards for antitrust action, Jesse W. Markham, e.g., in "An Alternative Approach to the Concept of Workable Competition," *The American Economic Review*, XL (June, 1950), 361, suggested: "An industry may be judged to be workably competitive when, after the structural characteristics of its market and the dynamic forces that shaped them have been thoroughly examined, there is no clearly indicated change that can be effected through public policy measures that would result in greater social gains than social losses." As a standard this is certainly vague, but it is also a reflection of the complexity of the problem. Such a standard would seem to invite controversy in application to antitrust cases.

power and therefore illegal;[11] but structural standards for antitrust action have been very difficult to derive.[12]

Despite a presumption of monopolistic tendencies or conditions in the dominance of industries by single or several firms, officials of antitrust agencies and courts of law generally have been reluctant to impose restraints on the growth of firms "fairly won" by means of forthright rivalry or competition and not by collusion or conspiracy to monopolize. The public problems involved in establishing limits on the size or market share of business enterprise, in the words of two close observers of the problem, "include the difficulty of defining products and markets in a way that will be generally acceptable and will stay put (what about the substitutability of one product for another?) ; the unmeasurable economies of scale, including the economies of experience, technical skill, and research; the possible damping effect on business enterprise of such upper limits; the possible compatibility of oligopoly and forthright rivalry (particularly in innovation) ; and finally the tendencies of giant business units constantly to change their product 'mixes' and thereby to intensify interproduct and interindustry competition."[13]

As an industry in which the economies of large-scale operation obviously are substantial, though perhaps difficult to measure with precision, the automobile industry is of a type which poses a dilemma for those concerned with the encouragement of competition. This state exists because efficiency in the use of productive resources in such an industry may be expected to lead to reductions in the number of participants in the competing industry group if benefits of the economies of scale are passed on to consumers, thereby providing economic efficiency in resource utilization to the benefit of the public. To those who reason from economic models of industry structure and performance in which the adequacy of competition in protecting the interests of the public is

11 Massel, op. cit., pp. 89-90.

12 E.g., in the case of United States v. Aluminum Company of America, 2d Circuit, 1945, 148 F. 2d 416, 424, Judge Hand indicated that 90 per cent of the market was enough to constitute a monopoly but that it was doubtful whether 60 per cent or 64 per cent would be enough. See also Andreas Papandreou and John T. Wheeler, Competition and Its Regulation (New York: Prentice-Hall, 1954), chapter xvii, esp. pp. 304-05, and 330-32.

13 Joel B. Dirlam and Alfred E. Kahn, Fair Competition: The Law and Economics of Antitrust Policy (Ithaca, New York: Cornell University Press, 1954), p. 33.

identified with "large" or even "appreciable" numbers of competitors, the reduction of an industry to a small number of competing enterprises raises threats of diminished competition; but if economies of scale are in fact substantial, such a reduction may well be inevitable and possibly desirable if benefits of economies of scale are passed on to the public.

If the producers who attain large volumes actually pass on to consumers benefits of the economies of scale in the form of lower prices and improved products, an expected outcome will be the elimination of producers who are too small to acquire the economies of scale and thereby achieve profitably product prices and improvements competitive with those of the larger producers. An exception may occur when the small enterprise successfully avoids direct competition with the large producers with appeals to consumer desires for specialized features, including possibly distinctive style or differentiation, not found for one reason or another in products of its large competitors. Since a small number of large producers in an industry in which the economies of scale are substantial can meet the entire market demand at lower prices than can be accomplished by small producers, the net result expected is the elimination of the small enterprise and a reduction in the number of competitors. Indeed, the continued existence of very small participants in industries in which the economies of scale are substantial may well be cause for greater public concern than their elimination, since their continued survival may be evidence of excessive, possibly protective pricing by large firms of the industry.

On the other hand, harsh though the outcome may be for those who have direct interests in the small firm's operations, its elimination may lead one to believe that its large competitors are passing on to consumers the benefits of the economies of scale, although not constituting positive proof that this is the case. Elimination of the small producer, for example, might also result from its own ineffectiveness on bases other than the scale of its operations, from the provision to consumers by the large producers of not all but enough of the benefits of economies of scale to drive out small producers, or from the allocation by large producers of the unit cost savings of large scale to increased sales promotion. In the last case, the large producer might maintain the same total cost and price as would have resulted without acquisition of the economies of scale. Such sales promotion aids in attracting consumer demand to products of the large firms and away from those of firms too small to engage profitably in similar sales promotion activities. This "expensive" promotion may also provide consumers benefits of economies of scale in the form of support of television programs, magazines and other media for which consumers would otherwise have to pay more. Thus, if economies of scale are in fact substantial and if their benefits are passed in some form to the consuming public, there may exist an inherent conflict between efforts to obtain simultaneously efficiency in resource utilization at the industry level and the continued existence of a sufficient number of competitors to assure continued passage of benefits of industrial efficiency to the public. If economies of scale are substantial, an "appreciable" number of competitors may be small indeed. Easily applied measures of economic data are lacking, which poses a dilemma.

Perhaps most significantly for those concerned with problems of industrial organization and public policy, we can see in the existence of this dilemma a need for further work. If the elimination of all but a small number of competitors is an expected outcome of providing to the consuming public benefits of the economies of scale, of which the desirability may be accepted but also of which the difficulty of measurement and evaluation may be acknowledged, how can competition adequate to protect the interests of the public be assured? Despite the difficulties involved, if we are to continue reliance upon the force of competition as a regulator of economic activity, means must be found to resolve the dilemma. Perhaps the only solution is the watchful eye of the public or its agencies; but it may also yet be possible to define rules of economic action or structure which, if met, will assure efficiency of resource utilization to the best advantage of the public, despite a condition in which a small number of competitors seems inevitable and perhaps economically desirable because of the economies of scale. A dilemma did exist and it still exists as a feature of the environment in which business is conducted. Much work toward resolution of this problem has been done by proponents of "workable" or "effective" competition in their efforts to develop standards for the measurement and evaluation of the adequacy of competition, but much remains to be done.

Whether, however, such competition as existed among

the firms of the automobile industry—and it seems to have been of relatively high degree—was or is "workable" or "effective" in fully protecting the public cannot receive a final answer here, since the question is yet to be tested in the courts. The Big Three have not been free of criticism and antitrust attack for some activities, most significantly those alleged to have been harmful to dealers, independent finance companies, and parts manufacturers;[14] but there have been no direct antitrust attacks upon, although there has been some criticism by independent observers of, the dominance of automobile manufacturing by the Big Three. The use of laws of incorporation facilitated the growth of large firms of the automobile industry; the existence of laws of antitrust obviously did not prevent corporate growth or the perpetuation of its results in later time periods, which perhaps was as it should have been if the economies of scale in the automobile industry were so great as seems to have been the case. A traditional sentiment for antitrust was a feature of the environment within which the automobile business was conducted, but the difficulties of formulation and application of antitrust policy were also features; and these were facts of considerable importance to the leading Independents in their struggles for survival and prosperity in the 1950's.

In essence, the existence of economies of scale in the manufacture and sale of automobiles raised obstacles to the survival of the small firms of the industry; and the small firms stood or fell by themselves in meeting these obstacles.

[14] Robert F. Lanzillotti, "The Automobile Industry," in *The Structure of American Industry*, third edition, Walter Adams, editor (New York: The Macmillan Company, 1961), p. 349.

THE TASK OF MANAGEMENT

A STUDY OF THE experiences of the American Motors and Studebaker Corporations and their predecessor companies provides considerable insight into the nature of the influences at work within and upon the United States automobile industry in the decades following World War II. There were similarities in the experiences of American Motors and Studebaker, as there had been in the experiences of their predecessors; but there were also differences. Being the small firms of the automobile industry and having to respond to influences largely beyond their control, they had positions in the industry which were very similar; but the outcomes of their participation in the industry differed. American Motors, after a series of lean years, staged a tremendous comeback. Studebaker survived, but not as a domestic manufacturer of cars. American Motors had found success in its automotive ventures; Studebaker had found failure. But this was only a part of the picture.

IN REVIEW

Caught by a shift in market conditions in 1953, after an exceptional postwar boom in the sales of all types of durable goods, and suffering, according to their managers, numerous disadvantages relative to the larger firms of the industry, the leading Independents — Hudson, Nash-Kelvinator, Packard, and Studebaker — sought to improve their potential for survival and prosperity by means of merger in 1954. Different courses of action were followed by the newly formed companies. American Motors, largely continuing its predecessors' roles as specialist producers, promptly consolidated the production of its cars around the basic body shells of Nash, concentrated on its Rambler series which had evidenced an expanding market potential, and found that the combination of price, quality, and style of its Rambler, which became the "original" compact car, provided it a tremendous comeback after 1957. Studebaker-Packard, having gained through merger a full line of cars for entry into each of the major price classes then current, continued the separate operations of its predecessors but met only failure for its efforts to participate as a full-line producer. The firm's continued survival was related to its eventual return in late 1958 to a specialist role in the industry, a change which was belatedly reflected in the dropping of Packard from the corporate name in 1962, and to the success of its diversification program which began only after Studebaker-Packard's return to profitable operations with the Lark, temporary though the profitable condition was.

Technological considerations weighed heavily in the performances of firms of the automobile industry. While obviously not the only factor, the desire to acquire and retain the economies of large-scale operation was an important stimulus to action in the automobile industry. The mergers among the leading Independents were attributable in large measure to anticipations of savings in the unit cost of manufacturing and selling automobiles in larger volumes, thereby permitting profitable sales of their cars at lower, more competitive prices. Although the precise extent of their influence was difficult to determine — the variety of productive arrangements and the willingness of consumers to purchase standardized cars in large numbers were interrelated and complicating factors — economies of scale clearly existed in virtually every activity related to the design, manufacture, and physical distribution of cars. In addition, there were unit cost advantages of large volume in national advertising, dealership distribution and local advertising, and the sales-spurring device of frequent style change, all of which became relatively more important after the beginning in 1953 of a race between Ford and Chevrolet for first place in industry sales. The requirements for operation at low unit cost, particularly in marketing activities to meet the competitive thrusts of the larger firms of the industry, were generally beyond the levels of output accomplished by the leading Independents as separate companies and by their successor companies until the sales comeback of American Motors after 1957. The leading Independents faced strenuous battles in the market place with the already large Big Three: Chrysler, Ford, and General Motors, who earlier had attained successfully the scales of operation for exploitation of the economies of scale and who enjoyed promotional advantages of large market shares in encouraging further sales, especially repeat sales to previously satisfied owners of their makes.

The Independents also were confronted with problems not directly related to the scales of their operations, that is, problems which were not based directly on output volume considerations. Changes in market conditions, including, for example, the over-all relationship of the demand for and supply of automobiles, shifts in consumer preferences and attitudes, particularly the "orphan car" attitude toward Independent makes, changes in credit restrictions on the financing of cars at wholesale and/or retail, variations in the style, quality, and promotion of the cars of the Independents and those of their competitors, and changes in prices and price differentials among the different makes offered by the industry, presented the firms with difficult problems, including the necessity for frequent readjustment in courses of action. Internal organizational problems, including such factors as the efficiency and effectiveness of labor and management, wage and other cost differentials among the firms of the industry, especially the high labor cost problems which officials of the Independents considered to be a major disadvantage, were also vital considerations. And, for the leading Independents as the relatively small participants in the automobile industry, an oligopoly selling differentiated products, the difficulty and importance of being different, of providing distinctive products, was of great importance in the automobile industry of the middle and late 1950's. Many factors thus were significant influences on the performances of American Motors and Studebaker and their predecessors in the years 1946 through 1963. These influences might have been and some, in fact, eventually were alleviated by determined action of management or the elapse of time without the necessity of fundamental changes in the scale of operations or size of the firms.

The problem and value of being different, a difficult thing to evaluate since it is in part subjectively determined, may be ranked along with technological considerations as a most important underlying influence on the survival and prosperity of the smaller manufacturer of cars, particularly after the middle of 1953 with the return of more competitive conditions in the new car market. So great was the productive capacity of Chrysler, Ford, and General Motors and so outstanding their ability to predict and satisfy, indeed in large measure to shape and determine, the needs and desires of most purchasers of passenger cars, that the opportunity to offer distinctive products to those consumers who wanted something other than the sameness of a Big Three product was a most important factor in providing the smaller firm access to consumer dollars and a place in the market. Although many factors obviously were contributing influences, the unique Rambler was perhaps the single most important factor in the tremendous comeback of American Motors. It provided the firm an opening wedge for an expanding market share; and with its unique unit body-frame construction, it was a car which the Big Three, having chosen to emphasize the large, luxurious, all-purpose car, could not closely imitate quickly. Studebaker, following Rambler's acknowledged success in 1957-1958, jumped into the compact car parade in late 1958 with its 1959 model compact Lark. The Lark returned the company to a profit position and was a key element in the continued survival of the firm as a corporate entity by providing funds and encouragement for investors to facilitate its diversification into other industries. Unfortunately, the Lark provided only a temporary respite for Studebaker as a participant in the domestic car industry. The Big Three introduced their compact cars in the next year after Studebaker's entry; and Studebaker, not having enjoyed the longer lead of American Motors with its Rambler, found that the Lark was a case of being too late with too little.

The new and the different were important elements for the Big Three, too. This was evidenced in their frequent style changes and other product refinements, including the offering of optional equipment in wide variety. The Big Three's swing to automatic transmissions and high-powered V-8 engines in the early 1950's, their introduction of such cars as Chevrolet's Corvette sports car and Ford's Thunderbird, their initial introduction of compact cars and later proliferation of compact and other models, Chrysler's experimental work with gas turbine engines for passenger cars, and still later Ford's introduction of Mustang, a sports-type car for popular price ranges, were of this character. The Big Three could not prosper solely on the merits of their past successes. Creators of change, they also had to keep pace with the changes of their competitors.

Given the conditions imposed by the existence of substantial economies of scale in the manufacture and sale of passenger cars, the then existing inequalities in the sizes of the firms participating in the automobile industry, and the imponderables of a market in which many factors influenced the supply of and demand for cars, the difficulties of the leading Independents following the shift from a sellers' to a buyers' market in 1953 were, if not inevitable, at least highly probable. American Motors and Studebaker-Packard, in brief, were faced with alternatives of attaining sufficient sales volumes to secure the economies of scale vitally necessary to obtain unit costs comparable to those of the Big Three and resulting prices competitive with the Big Three, a difficult task, or of producing for selective market segments with limited sales potentials. By keeping a step ahead of the Big Three in catering to consumer desires for specialized features or qualities in cars, including the new and the different, no easy task, direct competition might be avoided.

The two sets of problems were not unrelated. American Motors was successful in discovering and satisfying consumer desires for what came to be known as the compact car, and Studebaker soon followed with its compact Lark; but, having found an expanding market as product leaders, they faced imitation and direct competition from the Big Three, who had advantages, particularly in their marketing activities and the loyalty of prior purchasers of their cars. The Big Three quite reasonably could be expected to respond to evidence of an expanding market potential. Alternatively, if the Independents then abandoned the expanding market segment and moved on to something again new and different, remaining small and attempting to participate as product leaders catering to small market segments, they faced problems of insufficient volumes to take advantage of the economies of scale. Either course was hazardous. Clearly, the leading Independents faced uphill battles in their struggles for survival and prosperity in the automobile industry.

IN CONCLUSION

The experiences in the automobile industry of the American Motors and Studebaker Corporations and their predecessors also underscored the importance of management, for within the existing environment, the variations in firm performance were also partly functions of managerial effectiveness. Although decisions and action were taken in the names of the several enterprises of the industry, the firms were not the active agents. Men, the human element of economic activity, were the source of decision and action; it was their individual and collective action which was the action of the firm. The problems of doing business—the discovery, evaluation, and response to the opportunities and restrictions of opportunity, whatever they were, whether technological phenomena, market conditions, the cumulative effects of history, or other influences—were problems of management in both uses of the word. They were problems of the men who were the managers; and they were problems involved in the process through which the managers planned, organized, directed, and controlled the affairs of their respective firms.

Under conditions such as the peak postwar boom with an expanding market for cars and a short supply, the capability of management may have counted for little in the profit performance of the firm, at least in the short run; but with the return of more competitive conditions after the shift in 1953 from a sellers' to a buyers' market, the effectiveness of managerial performance became a more important influence on the financial performance of the business enterprise.

To a degree, the hands of the managers of the leading Independent firms were tied by the events of the past. The outcome of past choices of their predecessors, their competitors, and the larger society in which they operated established limits to the scope of managerial action in the period under study. Managers of past years shared responsibility for the performances of their successors. Nevertheless, acknowledging the influence of the past, the managers of each period had decisions to make and actions to take.

Starting from a base of existing or anticipated resources and estimates of market potentials for various product price, quality, and style combinations, competitive activity in the automobile industry was determined in large measure by the investments that officials of the firms of the industry were willing and able to make in the changes that they introduced in their products and production processes. Choices of product prices, qualities, and styles could be neither too far out of line with those of competing firms nor beyond the limits of acceptability to consumers without risking either retaliation and/or imitation by competing firms or loss of consumer confidence and sales. A range of choices obviously existed; but its limits were not easily discovered. An appropriate balance, whatever it was, as for example that combination of product qualities which became the compact car, had to be achieved. But more than this, the appropriate choices had to be accomplished in confrontation with an unknown and only partly predictable future.

From the earliest days of the automobile industry's development, change was one of its most important features. Ford, for instance, capitalized on a change from previous practices in the industry in introducing mass production techniques and standardizing on the one model offered at a low price. Change was a part of the competitive struggle among the firms of the industry; but the outcome of change could not be known with certainty until after the fact, and then not always with precision because of the diversity of influences on the performance of the firms of the industry. The managers of the firms faced difficult tasks. Decisions had to be made with incomplete information. Neither consumer demand nor behavior of competing firms, or changes in either, could be predicted with certainty. In the search for correct courses of action, mistakes as well as successes were inevitable. Ingenuity, initiative, and determination, but also flexibility, the ability and willingness to recognize and respond to changed conditions or to the inevitable mistakes, were important aspects of management. Broadly speaking, management was a trial-and-error process of action and reaction in a changing environment which was established in part by the firm itself.

The officials of American Motors guessed, "gambled," and won increasing consumer acceptance of the distinctive Rambler by boldly and aggressively promoting that which they had chosen at a time of a quite different market approach by the Big Three, undertaking what had the appearance of a crusade against the "oversized, gas-guzzling dinosaurs" of the Big Three and outspokenly picturing their firm as doing battle with giant monopolists. The emphasis on the compact car was a strategy that worked. Credit must be given to American Motors officials, along with those of the foreign producers, for the discovery and exploitation of the market potential for the compact car. Having gained a larger market share but faced with more direct competition, American Motors found new choices were essential. In the late 1950's, however, the choice of that combination of price, quality, and style that became the compact car was, if not most important, one of the most important factors in American Motors' survival and prosperity. In contrast, Studebaker-Packard officials guessed, "gambled," and lost with their product choices. The head-on clash with the Big Three inherent in its full-line approach did not work. This did not mean that the basic principle underlying this approach was wrong. Rather, burdened by the accumulated results of many shortcomings, including poor choices of product style as well as high-cost operations, Studebaker-Packard was evidently wrong to have believed it had the financial and other resources to acquire its benefits. In retrospect, the prolonged continuation of the full-line approach at a time of sharply reduced sales was a crucial error. Spending money in 1955 and 1956 like a billion dollar company at a time when its sales were less than one half this amount, Studebaker-Packard suffered enormous losses; and officials of the company found their subsequent choices of courses of action severely restricted. In more sophisticated language it might be said that American Motors officials had "correctly" estimated the market potential of the compact car and that Studebaker-Packard officials had "incorrectly" estimated that for their company's products.

Numerous and diverse were the influences on the leading Independents, their owners, and their managers, as collective-entity Davids doing battle with Goliaths. The combination of the mass market and modern technology, including the organizational superiority of the corporate form of business, coupled with the historical fact that competing firms had acquired dominant positions in the automobile industry in earlier years of its development, imposed heavy burdens on the managers of American Motors and Studebaker as it had on their predecessor firms. Product leadership was vital to the continued survival and prosperity of the small firm, provided such an innovator could avoid serious and frequent errors; but in the long run, growth, perhaps as a result of innovation, to a substantially larger scale than that from which the small firms had started was also essential. American Motors met these requirements at a crucial time; Studebaker and its predecessors did not. The rewards for success in the passenger car industry were great; but also great were the risks.

Since the automobile industry's methods of manufacturing and merchandising have been widely adopted, the course of events in the industry may hold lessons for those in other industries. Success requires the meeting of many influences simultaneously, though not necessarily in precisely the same fashion by each industry participant. Big business seems not only inevitable in many industries but also highly desirable for reasons of efficiency. If the automobile industry is in fact a trend setter, small enterprises in other industries facing similar conditions may find existence increasingly difficult. When industrial capacity outstrips demand, however, the relatively small producer may find among its most important assets the ability to discover and move quickly to provide in the market unique or distinctive products or services, perhaps gaining in the process the growth to larger sales volumes so necessary in industries oriented toward mass production for large markets. Style variation may help; but significant product leadership is of greater value, as indicated by the fact that a restless search for the new and the different is a source of strength for the largest firms, too. Luck may play a role, but an energetic management keenly aware of these conditions and striving constantly to meet them is essential to business success. Such conditions pose major challenges, for the decisions of the few men at the top are vital to the many who have interests in the enterprises: the consumers, suppliers, creditors, distributors, employees, owners, and finally, the managers themselves.

SELECTED BIBLIOGRAPHY

Books

Adams, Walter (editor). *The Structure of American Industry.* Revised edition. New York: The Macmillan Company, 1954.

————. *The Structure of American Industry.* Third edition. New York: The Macmillan Company, 1961.

Bain, Joe S. *Barriers to New Competition.* Cambridge, Mass.: Harvard University Press, 1956.

Borden, Neil H. *The Economic Effects of Advertising.* Chicago: Richard D. Irwin, Inc., 1942.

Chamberlin, E. H. *The Theory of Monopolistic Competition.* Sixth edition. Cambridge, Mass.: Harvard University Press, 1950.

Chow, Gregory C. *Demand for Automobiles in the United States: A Study in Consumer Durables.* Amsterdam: North-Holland Publishing Company, 1957.

Clark, J. M. *Studies in the Economics of Overhead Costs.* Chicago: The University of Chicago Press, 1923.

Drucker, Peter F. *Concept of the Corporation.* New York: The John Day Company, 1946.

Edwards, Corwin D. *Maintaining Competition.* New York: McGraw-Hill Book Company, 1949.

Epstein, Ralph C. *The Automobile Industry.* New York: A. W. Shaw Company, 1928.

Florence, P. Sargant. *The Logic of Industrial Organization.* London: Kegan Paul, Trench, Trubner, and Company, 1933.

General Motors Corporation. *The Dynamics of Automobile Demand.* New York: General Motors Corporation, 1939.

Greenleaf, William. *Monopoly on Wheels: Henry Ford and the Selden Automobile Patent.* Detroit: Wayne State University Press, 1961.

Hewitt, Charles M., Jr. *Automobile Franchise Agreements.* Homewood, Ill.: Richard D. Irwin, Inc., 1956.

Kaplan, A. D. H., Dirlam, Joel B., and Lanzillotti, Robert F. *Pricing in Big Business.* Washington: The Brookings Institution, 1958.

Keats, John. *The Insolent Chariots.* Philadelphia and New York: J. B. Lippincott Company, 1958.

Kennedy, E. D. *The Automobile Industry.* New York: Reynal and Hitchcock, 1941.

Macdonald, Robert M. *Collective Bargaining in the Automobile Industry.* New Haven, Conn., and London, Eng.: Yale University Press, 1963.

Mahoney, Tom. *The Story of George Romney.* New York: Harper and Brothers, 1960.

Maxcy, George, and Silberston, Aubrey. *The Motor Industry.* London: George Allen and Unwin, Ltd., 1959.

Nevins, Allan, with the collaboration of Frank Ernest Hill. *Ford: The*

Times, the Man, the Company. New York: Charles Scribner's Sons, 1954.

————, and Hill, Frank Ernest. *Ford: Expansion and Challenge, 1915-1933.* New York: Charles Scribner's Sons, 1957.

————. *Ford: Decline and Rebirth, 1933-1962.* New York: Charles Scribner's Sons, 1963.

Pashigian, Bedros Peter. *The Distribution of Automobiles, An Economic Analysis of the Franchise System.* Ford Foundation Doctoral Dissertation 1960 Award Winner. Englewood Cliffs, N. J.: Prentice-Hall, Inc., 1961.

Pound, Arthur. *The Turning Wheel.* New York: Doubleday, Doran, and Company, 1934.

Rae, John B. *American Automobile Manufacturers: The First Forty Years.* Philadelphia and New York: Chilton Company, 1959.

Robinson, E. A. G. *The Structure of Competitive Industry.* London: Nisbet and Company, 1950.

Seltzer, L. H. *A Financial History of the American Automobile Industry.* New York: Houghton Mifflin Company, 1928.

Stigler, George J. *The Theory of Price.* New York: The Macmillan Company, 1946.

Stocking, George W., and Watkins, Myron W. *Monopoly and Free Enterprise.* New York: The Twentieth Century Fund, 1951.

Vatter, Harold G. *Small Enterprise and Oligopoly: A Study of the Butter, Flour, Automobile, and Glass Container Industries.* Corvallis, Ore.: Oregon State College Press, 1955.

Weiss, Leonard W. *Economics and American Industry.* New York: John Wiley and Sons, Inc., 1961.

Whitney, Simon N. *Antitrust Policies: American Experience in Twenty Industries.* Volumes I and II. New York: The Twentieth Century Fund, 1958.

Government Publications

U. S., Federal Trade Commission. *Report on Motor Vehicle Industry.* House Document 468, 76th Congress, 1st Session. Washington: U. S. Government Printing Office, 1939.

————. *Report on Corporate Mergers and Acquisitions.* House Document 169, 84th Congress, 1st Session. Washington: U. S. Government Printing Office, 1955.

————. *Industrial Concentration and Product Diversification in the 1,000 Largest Manufacturing Companies: 1950.* Washington: U. S. Government Printing Office, 1957.

U. S., House of Representatives, Committee on Interstate and Foreign Commerce. *Hearings, Automobile Marketing Legislation.* 84th Congress, 2nd Session, Pursuant to H. Res. 528, 2688, and 6544. Washington: U. S. Government Printing Office, 1956.

U. S., House of Representatives, Committee of the Judiciary, Subcommittee No. 5 on Antitrust. *Hearings, Automobile Dealer Franchises.* 84th Congress, 2nd Session, Pursuant to H. Res. 11360 and

S. Res. 3879. Washington: U. S. Government Printing Office, 1956.

U. S., Senate, Committee on Interstate and Foreign Commerce, Subcommittee on Automobile Marketing Practices. *Hearings, Automobile Marketing Practices.* Parts 1 and 2. 84th Congress, 2nd Session, Part 1: Pursuant to S. Res. 13 continued by S. Res. 163; Part 2: On S. 2929, 3110, 3494, 3543, and 3946. Washington: U. S. Government Printing Office, 1956.

————. *Hearings, Automobile Marketing Practices — Finance and Insurance.* 85th Congress, 1st Session, Pursuant to S. Res. 26. Washington: U. S. Government Printing Office, Part 1: 1957, Part 2: 1958.

————. *Hearings, Automobile Price Labeling.* 85th Congress, 2nd Session, On S. 3500. Washington: U. S. Government Printing Office, 1958.

U. S., Senate, Committee on the Judiciary, Subcommittee on Antitrust and Monopoly. *Hearings, A Study of the Antitrust Laws.* 84th Congress, 1st Session, Pursuant to S. Res. 61. Washington: U. S. Government Printing Office, Parts 1, 2, and 3: 1955, Parts 6, 7, and 8: 1956.

————. *Hearings, Administered Prices.* Parts 6 and 7. 85th Congress, 2nd Session, Pursuant to S. Res. 57 and 231. Washington: U. S. Government Printing Office, 1958.

————. *Report, A Study of Administered Prices in the Automobile Industry.* 85th Congress, 2nd Session, Pursuant to S. Res. 231. Washington: U. S. Government Printing Office, 1958.

Articles

Blair, John M. "Technology and Size," *The American Economic Review,* XXXVIII (May, 1948, Proceedings), 121-52.

Clark, J. M. "Toward a Concept of Workable Competition," *The American Economic Review,* XXX (June, 1940), 241-56.

Griffin, Clare E. "When Is Price Reduction Profitable?" *Harvard Business Review,* XXXVIII (September-October, 1960), 125-32.

Lanzillotti, Robert F. "Pricing Objectives in Large Companies," *The American Economic Review,* XLVIII (December, 1958), 921-40.

Mason, Edward S. "The Current Status of the Monopoly Problem in the United States," *Harvard Law Review,* LXII (1949), 1265-85.

Menge, John A. "Style Change Costs as a Market Weapon," *Quarterly Journal of Economics,* LXXVI (November, 1962), 632-47.

Suits, Daniel B. "The Demand for New Automobiles in the United States, 1929-1956," *The Review of Economics and Statistics,* XL (August, 1958), 273-80.

Vanderblue, Homer B. "Pricing Policies in the Automobile Industry," *Harvard Business Review,* XVII (Summer, 1939), 385-401, and XVIII (Autumn, 1939), 64-81.

Industry, Trade, and Other Materials

Advertising Age. Chicago: Advertising Publications, Inc., 1950-1964.
American Motors Corporation. *Annual Report.* 1954-1963.

Automobile Manufacturers Association. *Automobile Facts and Figures.* Detroit, Michigan: 1947-1964.

————. *Motor Truck Facts.* Detroit, Michigan: 1959-1963.

Automotive Industries. Philadelphia: Chilton Company, 1947-1964.

Automotive News. Detroit: Slocum Publishing Company, 1950-1964.

Banner, Paul H. "Competition in the Automobile Industry." Unpublished Ph.D. dissertation, Harvard University, 1954.

Business Week. New York: McGraw-Hill, Inc., 1946-1964.

Chrysler Corporation. *Annual Report.* 1946-1963.

Consumer Bulletin. Washington, N. J.: Consumers' Research, Inc., 1946-1963.

Consumer Reports. Mount Vernon, N. Y.: Consumers Union of United States, Inc., 1946-1963.

Ford Motor Company. *Annual Report.* 1955-1963.

Fortune. Chicago and New York: Time Inc., 1946-1964.

General Motors Corporation. *Annual Report.* 1946-1963.

Hudson Motor Car Company. *Annual Report.* 1946-1953.

Moody's Industrial Manual. New York: Moody's Investors Service, 1947-1964.

Nash-Kelvinator Corporation. *Annual Report.* 1946-1953.

————. "Letter to Stockholders and Notice of Special Meeting of Stockholders," dated February 8, 1954; and "Proxy Statement," dated March 24, 1954. (Hudson issued an almost identical letter and statement.)

National Automobile Dealers Association. "Operating Averages for the Automobile Retailing Industry." Washington: 1955-1963.

National Automobile Dealers Used Car Guide Company. *N. A. D. A. Official Used Car Guide.* Washington: 1958-1964.

National Market Reports, Inc. *Red Book National Market Reports.* Chicago: 1952-1962.

New York Times, The. 1946-1964.

Packard Motor Car Company. *Annual Report.* 1946-1953.

————. "Letter to Shareholders and Notice of Special Meeting of Shareholders," dated July 9, 1954; and "Proxy Statement," dated August 17, 1954. (Studebaker issued an almost identical letter and statement.)

Smith, David K. "The Problems of a New Firm in an Oligopolistic Industry: Kaiser-Frazer's Experience in the Motor Vehicle Industry." Unpublished Ph.D. dissertation, Harvard University, 1950.

Studebaker Corporation. *Annual Report.* 1946-1953.

Studebaker-Packard Corporation. "Letter to Shareholders," "Notice of Special Meeting of Shareholders to be Held October 31, 1956," and "Proxy Statement," dated September 24, 1956.

————. "Notice of Special Meeting of Shareholders to be Held October 15, 1958," and "Proxy Statement," dated September 4, 1958.

Studebaker (Studebaker-Packard) Corporation. *Annual Report.* 1954-1963.

Wall Street Journal, The. 1953-1964.

INDEX

A. B. C. appliances, 62

Abernethy, Roy, 47, 66, 68

Adams, Walter, 9n, 188n, 256n, 274n

Administered Prices,
Hearings, 1n, 9n, 117n, 121n, 155n, 156n, 160n, 161n, 203n, 210n, 235n, 236n, 252n, 253n,
Report, 7n, 195n, 207n, 235n, 242n

Advantages of size, 36-7, 43-4, 104, 142-274 (see also economies of scale)

Advertising, 65, 186-8, 187n, 216-23, 241, 245, 268, 276

Aerophysics Development Corporation, 81, 84

Age of cars in use, 26-7, 27n

Aircraft industry, 83

Alexander, R. S., 185n

Altofer Brothers Company, 20, 20n

American Motors Corporation, 1, 2, 4, 8, 25n, 31n, 34n, 36, 37n, 38, 38n, 47-69, 47n, 48n, 54n, 67n, 70, 73-4, 80, 90, 117, 117n, 123-5, 127-8, 137, 137n, 139-41, 143-4, 143n, 147, 154, 155n, 159, 164, 166, 168, 169n, 174-6, 180, 180n, 190, 192n, 193, 202, 204-206, 207n, 208n, 209, 214-15, 218-23, 225-6, 225n, 228-32, 235, 238-40, 242-4, 242n, 244n, 249, 249n, 250n, 252-3, 256, 258-9, 264, 268-9, 275, 277-9, 281-2
Decline, 48-63
Formed by merger, 34-8
Proxy fight threat, 60
Resurgence, 63-9
Separate divisions planned, 36 (see also Nash, Nash-Kelvinator, and Hudson)

Amortization of special tooling, 205-206

Andrews, E. C., 105n

Antimerger Act of 1950, 8

Antitrust and Monopoly, Subcommittee on, (see Senate, Committee on the Judiciary, and House, Committee of the Judiciary)

Antitrust Laws, A study of the,

Hearings, 8n, 9n, 25n, 34n, 65n, 108, 142, 154n, 155n, 157n, 213n, 235n, 240n

Antitrust problems, 266-74

Appliance Division, American Motors, 62
(see also Kelvinator Division)

Assembly operations, 156, 156n, 163, 171-4, 176-9, 181-4, 269

Assets, operating, definition of, 22n

Atkinson, L. J., 196, 196n, 197n

Associates Investment Company, 99

Atomic Energy Commission, 88

Attorney General, U. S., 8

Automated engine line(s), 158-9, 164
Packard's, 49-51

Automation, 157n, 158-9, 158n, Flexible, 212n

Automobile Manufacturers Association, 4n, 7n, 13n, 14n, 26n, 28n, 131n, 140n, 157n, 166n, 172n, 190n

Bain, Joe S., 7, 7n, 154n, 161n, 162-4, 162n, 166-9, 201n, 232n, 241n, 242n

Banner, Paul H., 225n

Barit, A. E., 32, 35, 35n, 37n, 38, 143n

Barnes, Stanley N., 8n, 10n

Behnke, A. H., 87

Bell, Frederick J., 233n

Berle, Adolf A., Jr., 265n

Big Three, the, 2, 5, 7-8, 12, 14-18, 22-4, 39, 65-7, 69, 69n, 72, 90, 94, 97, 102, 104-107, 108n, 109, 111, 113-19, 115n, 117n, 121-2, 126-9, 127n, 131n, 133, 137-41, 147, 156, 159-61, 165-6, 171, 175, 177-9, 182-3, 190-3, 190n, 192n, 201, 204, 207-209, 211-12, 220-23, 225-6, 229, 232, 235, 237, 239-40, 242-5, 248-53, 251n, 255-9, 257n, 262-9, 274, 276, 278-9, 281-2 (see also Chrysler, Ford, and General Motors)

Body-frame, unit, 37, 122, 144, 256, 278

"Bootlegging" of cars, 30
Botany Mills, Inc., 97
Brady, Robert A., 10n
Break-even point, 51, 58
Breech, Ernest R., 263
Bremer, R. E., 87
Bright, James R., 158n
Briggs body plants, 72, 78, 167
Briggs, C. E., 87-8
Britt, S. H., 216n
Brodie, G. H., 87
Brown, J. L., Jr., 47
Buick, 133n, 138n, 179, 220, 226, 228-30, 269
    Electra, 132
    Le Sabre, 132
    Special, 112, 130n, 132, 138n, 139-40
    Super, 112
Bunting, C. G., 100
Burlingame, Byers A., 94, 100-101

Cadillac, 112-13, 132-3, 134n, 156n, 178, 220, 226, 228-30, 233, 237, 269
Cannan, Edwin, 149
Census of Manufactures, 189
Chamberlin, E. H., 187n
Chapin, Roy D., 45
Chapin, Roy D., Jr., 38, 48, 63n, 67n, 68n, 108n, 117n, 123-4, 123n, 124n, 214n
Chapman, Bernard A., 48, 62, 155n
Checker Motors Corporation, 7, 190
Chemical Compounds Division, Studebaker Corporation, 100
Chemical Compounds, Inc., 98
Chevrolet, 29, 111-12, 114, 120, 120n, 127, 132-6, 134n, 136n, 139, 156, 156n, 176-7, 176n, 179, 203, 209, 212, 218, 220, 226, 228-30, 232, 235n, 242, 269, 276
    Chevelle, 128, 128n, 130n, 140
    Chevy II, 128, 130n, 132, 140
    Corvair, 128, 130n, 132, 140, 159
    Corvair Monza, 137
    Corvette, 133, 207n, 278
Chicago, Milwaukee, St. Paul, and Pacific Railroad Company, 180n
Chippewa plant, Studebaker-Packard Corporation, 84-5, 95
Chow, Gregory C., 196, 196n, 197n
Chrysler (car), 112-13, 134n, 220-

1, 226, 228-30
Chrysler Corporation, 7, 16, 16n, 23, 72, 72n, 78, 86, 88, 107-108, 108n, 112-13, 120-1, 128, 133, 142, 142n, 147, 167, 174-5, 174n, 178, 189-91, 190n, 205-206, 207n, 208, 208n, 210n, 211, 219-21, 223, 226-31, 235, 236n, 237-8, 240, 242, 250-1, 251n, 253, 258, 263, 268-9, 276-8
    100-day strike, 16n, 28, 107-108
    (see also Chrysler, DeSoto, Dodge, Imperial, and Plymouth)
Chrysler, Walter, 263
Churchill, Harold E., 87-8, 94, 98-9
Clark, J. M., 9, 9n, 248n
Clark, Paul M., 88
Clarke Floor Machine Company, 98
Clarke Floor Machine Company Division, Studebaker Corporation, 100
Colbert, L. L., 142, 236n
Compact car(s), 63, 66, 94, 97, 102, 104, 115, 123, 127-41, 181, 199, 208, 212, 229, 237, 239, 242-3, 242n, 246, 256, 264, 268, 275, 278-80
Competition, 7, 9-10
    And antitrust, 266-74
    Difficulty of new entry, 7, 190
    Effectiveness and promotion of, 9-10
    In automobile market, 25, 29, 147
    "Pure," 267
Concentration in industry, 3, 4n, 6, 8, 10
    In automobile industry, 189-91, 190n, 269-74
Conner plant, 72, 78, 86
Consumer Reports, 69, 69n, 102, 102n
    Lark "best buy," 102
    Rambler "best buy," 69
Consumers Union of America, 69
Cooper, Ernest, 100
Corporate form of business, the, 265-6
Cost,
    Complications in using data, 11
    Differentials and profits, 152-3
    "Leadership," 237-9

Cox, William W., 100
Credit, reliance on, 27, 28n, 196
Credit restrictions, 25, 110-11, 126, 277
Crosley Corporation, 190n
Cross, Richard E., 66
Crowther, Samuel, 262n
Crusoe, Lewis D., 153, 158
C. T. L. Division, Studebaker Corporation, 100
C. T. L., Inc., 98
Curtice, Harlow, 155-6, 236n
Curtiss-Wright Agreement with Studebaker-Packard, 83-5
Curtiss-Wright Corporation, 2, 81n, 83-7, 89-94, 89n, 159
Cushman, Edward L., 48, 66, 117

Daimler-Benz A. G., 89, 92
Davis, D. J., 158n
Dealer(s), 29, 110-11, 115, 126, 131, 136, 143, 145, 176n, 224-34, 236-7, 245, 274
  American Motors' integration of Nash-Hudson, 51-2, 68
  Dual franchises, 68, 69n, 70, 78, 96
  Failures, 30, 30n, 111
  Packard's distribution to, 38-9
  Profits,
    Of General Motors', 29-30
    Of Studebaker's, 30
    Of Studebaker-Packard's, 30n
  Role in merger plans, 36-7, 39
  Studebaker - Packard's dual plans, 78, 96
  "Supermarket," 30
Defense production, 18, 20-1, 20n, 101, 103, 124-5
  Contracts of Packard for, 40
  Curtiss-Wright's, 83-4
  Cutback hits Studebaker-Packard, 75, 79-81
De Groat, George, 158n
Demand for cars, the, 13, 25-6, 29, 109, 186-7, 195-7, 196n, 203, 212, 264, 277, 279
Department of Commerce, Business Services Administration, 27, 105
Department of Defense, "Narrow Base" production policy, 41
Department of Justice, U. S., 8

DeSoto, 112, 134, 158, 220, 226, 228
"Dinosaur in the Driveway, The," 50, 65
Dirlam, Joel B., 236n, 237n, 238n, 271n
Diversification, 62, 97-103, 257-60
Dodge, 112-13, 132, 134n, 175, 220, 226, 228, 230
  Dart, 128, 130n, 132, 140
  Lancer, 132, 140
Donner, Frederic G., 172n
Dreyfuss, Henry, 127n
Due, John F., 192n, 253n
Dun and Bradstreet, Inc., 30n
Durant, William C., 262
Dynamics, Definition of, 3

Economies of scale, 9, 54-5, 142-8, 239, 268, 271-4, 276, 278
  Advertising, 216-23
  Dealership distribution, 224-34
  Financing, 247-51
  Management, 254-7
  Manufacturing, 142, 149-69
  Marketing, 142, 169, 185-215
  Physical distribution, 170-84
  Purchasing, 251-3
Edsel, 134, 134n, 210n, 214-15, 226, 228, 258-9
Edwards, Corwin D., 9, 10n
Egbert, Sherwood H., 99-103, 103n, 226n
Eggert, R. J., 177n, 222n
Ellis, Howard S., 10n
Else, Donald P., 48
El Segundo plant, American Motors Corporation, 58, 62
Epstein, Ralph C., 190n, 201, 202n
Ernst and Ernst, Accountants, 82
Eskridge, Joseph W., 48
Everitt - Metzger - Flanders Company, 45
Exports of cars, 26n, 191, 191n

Federal Trade Commission, 4n, 5n, 8, 8n, 44n, 148, 148n, 156n, 189n, 190n, 201n, 233n
Ferry, Hugh, 39, 42, 99-100
Financing, 247-51
Fisher, Franklin M., 131
Fleener, L. A., 100
Ford (car), 106, 112-14, 120, 127, 132-6, 134n, 136n, 139, 156, 156n,

158, 177, 179, 203, 209, 212, 220, 226, 228-30, 232-3, 235n, 242, 269, 276
Fairlane, 128, 128n, 130n, 132, 139-40, 181, 182n
Falcon, 128, 130n, 132, 137, 140, 159, 182n
Galaxie, 182n
Model T, 196n, 262
Mustang, 278
Thunderbird, 278
Ford, Henry, 47, 262, 262n
Ford, Henry II, 263
Ford Motor Company, 7, 16, 23, 99, 107, 110, 112-13, 119-21, 121n, 128, 133, 147, 153, 158-9, 158n, 159n, 161n, 164, 174, 176n, 177n, 178-9, 182n, 189-91, 189n, 190n, 194, 196n, 201-202, 205-209, 207n, 210n, 211, 213-15, 219-23, 222n, 226-31, 235, 235n, 236n, 237-8, 240n, 242, 251, 251n, 253, 255, 258-9, 262-3, 268-9, 276-8, 281
Top goal to outsell Chevrolet, 29, 29n
(see also Edsel, Ford, Lincoln, and Mercury)
Foreign cars, 15, 17, 65, 128-30, 129n, 135-6, 135n, 138, 138n, 191
Foreign producers, 5, 15, 140, 191-2, 268, 281
Francis, Clarence, 99-101
Franklin D i v i s i o n , Studebaker Corporation, 100
Franklin Manufacturing Company, 99
Freight costs, 170-84

Galbraith, J. K., 10n
Gale, A. R., 100
General Electric Company, 39
General Foods Corporation, 99
General Motors Corporation, 7, 16, 23, 25, 25n, 28, 28n, 44, 106-108, 106n, 107n, 108n, 112-13, 115, 120-1, 128, 133, 147, 155, 165, 172n, 173, 178-9, 182n, 189-91, 190n, 194, 194n, 197n, 200-207, 207n, 209, 210n, 211, 211n, 219-23, 226-38, 232n, 233n, 242, 249n, 250, 251n, 253, 258, 262-3, 268-9, 276-7
(see also Buick, Cadillac, Chev-

rolet, Oldsmobile, and Pontiac)
Gering Products, Inc., 97-8
Glore, Forgan and Company, 42
Gotsch, Arthur, 88, 94
Granatelli, Anthony, 100
Grant, Walter R., 87-8, 116
Gravely Tractors Division, Studebaker Corporation, 100
Gravely Tractors, Inc., 98
Graves, W. H., 87
Greenleaf, William, 262n
Griffin, Clare E., 198n
Griliches, Zvi, 131
Grundy, Gordon E., 100-101
Guthrie, Randolph H., 101

Hallas, Howard, 65
Hammer, Richard, 103
Hammond, J. C., 100
Hand, Judge Learned, 271n
Hanson, B. W., 100
Harder, Del S., 158
Harper Hospital, 47
Harris, W. B., 5n, 29n, 32n, 102n, 106n, 107n, 108n, 113n, 115n, 116n, 117n, 118-19, 118n, 119n, 121
Hayakawa, S. I., 127
Heller and Associates, Robert, 82
Herzog, Paul, 176n
Hess, John L., 69n
Hewitt, C. M., 202, 202n, 224n
Hill, Frank Ernest, 262n, 263n
Historical influences, 261-5
Hoffman, Paul G., 40-2, 87-8
House, Committee of the Judiciary, Subcommittee No. 5 on Antitrust, 233n
Hudson, J. L., 44
Hudson (car), 48, 50-1, 53, 58-9, 112-13, 134, 147, 220, 228, 258
Elimination of full-sized car, 51, 55, 60, 63
Hornet, 49
Jet, 55, 111-14, 122, 132, 136, 214
Hudson Motor Car Company, 1, 4n, 8, 13, 18, 20n, 21-3, 22n, 25, 25n, 32, 34-8, 34n, 40, 42, 44, 48, 52, 54-5, 61, 64, 71, 106-107, 110-11, 111n, 119, 121-5, 122n, 143-4, 167-9, 169n, 189, 190n, 193, 205-206, 215, 219, 227, 275
Dealer organization, 52, 68, 70

Merger agreed to, 35
Purchases steel plant, 26n, 107
Hudson Special Products Division, American Motors Corporation, 36, 48-9, 51-2, 55, 59, 125
Plant disposals, 49, 52, 62
Separate Hudson car operations ended, 49
Hurley, N. P., 183n
Hurley, Roy T., 83, 89
Hutchinson, R. A., 87-8, 94

Imperial, 112, 134n, 178, 220-1, 226, 228, 230
Independents, the, 2-5, 7-8, 10-18, 20-4, 30-3, 37, 40, 45-6, 67, 104-26, 137, 140-2, 144-7, 149, 156, 160-1, 166-9, 171, 173, 175-80, 183, 191-3, 192n, 200, 208-209, 214-15, 220-2, 225, 229, 237, 239, 246-9, 251-7, 260-3, 267, 269, 274-7, 279-80
(see also Hudson, Kaiser-Frazer, Nash-Kelvinator, Packard, Studebaker, and Willys)
Innovation(s), 121-2, 121n, 144, 151, 195, 202, 243, 246, 246n, 255-7, 262, 271, 282-3
Body-frame, unit, 37, 122, 144, 256, 278
Electronic push-button driving, 72-3
Non-slip differential, 72
"Piggyback," 179-84
Torsion bar suspension, 71, 256
(see also compact car)
Investment, long-term, definition of, 22n

Jeffery Company, Thomas B., 44
Jewkes, John, 255n
Joint Committee on the Economic Report, 157n, 158n
Jung, Allen F., 136n, 138n

Kahn, Alfred E., 270n, 271n
Kaiser, Edgar F., 157
Kaiser - Frazer Corporation, 4n, 7-8, 7n, 34, 42, 124, 190n, 199, 200n
Kaiser, Henry, 7n
Kaiser Motors Corporation, 157
Kaiser-Willys, 8, 47, 68
Merger of, 42

Kaplan, A. D. H., 236n, 237n, 238n, 241n
Kaysen, Carl, 131, 270
Keats, John, 127
Kefauver committee, 155, 238
(see also Senate, Committee on the Judiciary, Subcommittee on Antitrust and Monopoly)
Kefauver, Estes, 234
Kelvinator Corporation, 44
Kelvinator Division, American Motors Corporation, 36, 48, 55, 59, 258
Detroit plant, 66
Labor costs, 66-7, 117
Products, 62
Kennedy, E. D., 241n
Kenosha plant, American Motors Corporation, 49-50, 58, 63
Kerkorian, Kirk, 100
Kidder, Donald E., 100
Korean War, 16, 28, 78-9, 108, 131, 191
Market effects of its ending, 29
Kuhn, Loeb and Company, 42

Labor costs, 66-7, 79, 108, 115-18, 125, 261-2
Labor difficulties, 79, 106-107 (see also strikes)
Lanzillotti, Robert F., 9n, 200n, 236n, 237n, 238n, 274n
Laughna, R. P., 88
Lawrence and Sons, Cyrus J., 42
LeGrand, Rupert, 158n
Lehman Brothers, 42
Leonard appliances, 62
Liggett, C. D., 100
Lincoln, 112-13, 134n, 156n, 178, 220-1, 226, 228-30
Continental, 220, 226
Loewy, Raymond, 103
Lucas, D. B., 216n

McCulloch Corporation, 99
Macdonald, Robert M., 116n
McGaughey, William, 48
MacMillan, C. M., 100
Mahoney, Tom, 35n, 36n, 60n
Management,
Advantages of large-scale, 254-7
Complacency of Independents', 118-22
"Exception principle," 257

General problems of, 279-83
Manufacturing, 149-69
Market conditions, 105-10, 119, 188-201
Buyers' market, 25, 28-9, 31-2, 54, 120, 168
Change in, 23, 25, 28, 30-1, 145
"Normal" competitive, 31, 243
Sellers' market, 29, 105
Marketing, 170-246
Advertising, 216-24
And the consumer, 239-43
And the Independents, 243-6
Dealership distribution, 224-34
Environment, 188-201
Physical distribution, 170-84
Pricing policies, 234-9
Style promotion, 201-216
Marketing Practices, Automobile, Hearings, 172n, 173n, 175n, 233n, 252n
Markham, Jesse W., 270n
Mason, Edward S., 265n, 270n
Mason, George, 31-2, 34-6, 37n, 38-9, 44, 47, 65, 143n
Massel, Mark S., 270n, 271n
Materials restrictions, 16, 16n, 26, 29, 105, 107-108, 111
Maxcy, George, 163-8, 163n, 164n
Means, Gardiner, C., 10n, 265n
Mechanics Educational Society of America, 66-7
Melloan, George, 69n, 232n
Mendler, E. C., 87
Menge, John A., 211n
Mercedes-Benz, 89, 92, 94
Mercedes-Benz Sales, Incorporated, 93, 100
Mercury, 112-13, 132-3, 134n, 179, 220, 226, 228-30, 269
Comet, 130n, 132, 140
Meteor, 128, 128n, 130n, 132, 139-40
Merger(s), 1, 4, 8, 8n, 31-2, 34-46, 64, 82, 122-3
Advantages expected from, 36-7, 43-5, 143-7, 168, 254, 256, 260
Alternatives to, 46
Considered and discussed, 31-2
Denial of merger intention, 40
Dissent by Hudson stockholders, 37
Nash-Kelvinator-Hudson agree-

ment of, 35
Rumors, 34n, 42
Stage set for, 31-3
Studebaker - Packard agreement of, 42
Metropolitan, 53
Mewhort, W. D., 98
Milligan, Melvin L. II, 30n, 80, 94, 100
Milwaukee plant, American Motors, 49-50
Milwaukee Road, 180n
Minkel, Lewis E., 100
Monopolistic practices vs. fair competition, 6, 271
Monsanto Chemical Company, 98
Moody, Clark, 29n
Moore, Donald A., 9n, 188n, 246n, 256n
Moore, Meade F., 48, 65
Mund, Vernon A., 266n

Nance, James J., 25, 25n, 32, 35, 35n, 38-42, 70, 87-8, 87n, 111n, 113, 117-21, 118n, 119n, 120n, 124n, 145-6, 145n, 148n, 157, 175n, 176n, 235, 252
Nash (car), 48, 50-1, 53, 58-9, 112-13, 177, 214, 220, 228, 258, 275
Ambassador, 49
Elimination of full-sized car, 51, 60, 63
Statesman, 49
Nash, Charles W., 44
Nash Division, American Motors Corporation, 36, 47, 52
Dealers, 68, 70
Plants, 49
Nash-Kelvinator Corporation, 1, 4n, 5n, 8, 13, 18, 18n, 20-1, 20n, 21n, 23, 25, 25n, 28, 28n, 31-2, 31n, 34-40, 34n, 42, 47-8, 52, 54-5, 61, 64, 66, 71, 106-107, 107n, 110-11, 114, 121-5, 122n, 143-4, 146, 166-7, 169, 169n, 171, 189, 190n, 205-206, 215, 219, 227, 250n, 275
Merger agreed to, 34-38
Nash Motors Company, 44
National Automobile Dealers Association, 29, 29n, 176n, 224n, 231n, 233n
National Production Authority, 16n
Nevins, Allan, 262n, 263n

New Brunswick plant, Studebaker Corporation, 78
New York Central Railroad, 88
New York Stock Exchange, 248
Nonscalar problems, 104-26
Definition of, 104

Ohio Automobile Company, 45
Oldsmobile, 112, 133n, 134n, 158, 179, 220, 226, 228-30, 269
Olds F-85, 130n, 132, 140
Oligopoly, 10, 192, 195, 200, 253, 270, 277
Onan, C. Warren, 100
Onan and Sons, Inc., D. W., 98
Onan Division, Studebaker Corporation, 100
Oppenheim, S. Chesterfield, 10n
Organization for European Economic Co-operation, 158n, 164n
"Orphan car," 81, 123-5, 259, 277
Overhead costs, 194-5

Packard (car), 38, 70-1, 73-5, 89-91, 94-5, 94n, 102, 112-13, 134, 147, 220, 226, 228
Clipper, 39, 71, 75, 86, 89, 112-13, 119
Separate car discontinued, 86-7, 89
Packard Division, Studebaker-Packard Corporation, 43, 72, 100
Detroit facilities set aside, 86-7
Packard, J. W. and W. D., 45
Packard Motor Car Company, 1, 4n, 8, 13, 18, 20-1, 20n, 21n, 23, 25, 25n, 28, 28n, 31n, 32, 34-6, 38-43, 38n, 39n, 45, 72n, 75, 80-1, 87-8, 91, 99-100, 102, 102n, 107-108, 107n, 108n, 111, 114, 116, 118-21, 120n, 124, 124n, 144, 145n, 146, 157n, 158-9, 167-9, 169n, 189, 190n, 193, 205-206, 215, 219, 227, 250, 250n, 258, 275-6
Denial of interest in merger, 40
Need to revitalize, 38-9
New Utica plant, 40
Papandreou, Andreas, 271n
Pashigian, Bedros Peter, 216n, 225n, 230n, 232n
Paxton Products, 98, 100
"Phantom freight," 176n
"Piggyback," 179-84, 269

Definition of, 180n
Plymouth, 112-14, 120, 120n, 127, 132-6, 134n, 136n, 139, 156n, 158, 179, 203, 220, 226-30, 233, 242
Valiant, 128, 130n, 132, 137, 140, 159
Pontiac, 112, 120, 132, 133n, 134n, 179, 220, 226, 228-30, 269
Tempest, 130n, 132, 140
Porta, Armando J., 88, 94, 99
Pound, Arthur, 123, 123n, 202, 202n, 263n
Powers, R. P., 87
Price(s), 11, 28, 60, 71, 105, 111-15, 119, 122-3, 129, 131-9, 134n, 146, 195-201, 197n, 198n, 234-9, 242n, 262
Production of cars, 13-14, 16-18, 26, 28, 95n, 109, 140, 166-9
Big Three makes, 14-17, 140
Independent makes, 13-18, 140
Restrictions on, 16-17
Tables of, 14, 140
Profit(s), 18-23, 31, 40-1
Of dealers, 29-30, 29n, 30n
Operating, definition of, 20
Rate(s), 22-4
Progress Sharing Plan, American Motors Corporation, 67-8
Prudential Insurance Company of America, 59, 251
Public policy, 6, 8-10, 267-74
Purchasing, 251-4
"Pure competition," 267

Quasi-reorganization, 85-92

Rack car, 179-81, 180n, 181n
Rae, John B., 188n, 262n, 263n
Rambler, 44, 49-54, 58-60, 64-6, 68-9, 94, 112-15, 122, 124, 127-9, 129n, 130n, 132, 135-7, 135n, 136n, 140, 179, 180n, 181, 207n, 208n, 214-15, 218, 220-1, 226, 228-30, 232, 242-4, 242n, 244n, 269, 275, 278
Ambassador, 52
American, 51-2, 65, 132, 135n, 136n, 214, 242n
Classic, 180
Earlier car reintroduced, 52
New "basic volume car," 50, 65
Selected "car of the year," 69
Upgraded with new names, 51-2

Ranco Incorporated, 36, 62, 258
Reciprocity Agreement of American Motors and Studebaker-Packard, 50
Redisco, Incorporated, 55, 62, 258
Refinancing, Studebaker-Packard Corporation, 92-5
Refrigeration Discount Corporation, 59-60, 62
Registrations of new cars, 13, 15-18, 26, 40-1, 49, 53-4, 74, 95, 106, 130, 147, 178, 192
Regulation W, 110n
Renault, 129n, 132, 135
Reuther, Walter, 117n
Revlon, Inc., 98
R. L. Polk & Co., 15n, 53n, 74n, 130n
Robert Heller and Associates, 82
Robinson-Patman Act, 252
Romney, George, 1n, 7, 34n, 35n, 36, 38, 47, 47n, 49-50, 50n, 59-60, 59n, 65-6, 67n, 108n, 110n, 117, 122n, 143n, 144, 144n, 154-69, 155n, 175n, 208, 211, 235, 252, 255
Roos, C. F., 196, 196n, 197n

Sales, dollar, 18-21, 40-1, 54, 100
Sales promotion, 65-6, 186-8, 187n, 276
Sawers, David, 255n
Schaefer, Inc., 98
Schmidt, W. M., 88
Scribner, C. D., 87
Selden patent, 262
Senate, Committee on Interstate and Foreign Commerce, 224n
Subcommittee on Automobile Marketing Practices, 172n, 173n, 175n, 233n, 252n
Subcommittee on Surface Transportation, 180n
Senate, Committee on the Judiciary, Subcommittee on Antitrust and Monopoly, 1n, 7n, 8n, 9n, 25n, 30n, 34n, 65n, 108n, 111n, 117n, 121n, 142n, 143n, 145n, 154n, 155, 155n, 156n, 157, 157n, 160n, 161n, 195n, 203n, 207n, 208n, 210n, 213n, 234, 235n, 236n, 240n, 242n, 252n, 253n, 255n
Sheehan, Robert, 135n, 241n

Shortages, 13, 26, 105-108
Overcome, 108
Steel, 107
Silberston, Aubrey, 163-8, 163n, 164n
Size problems, general discussion of, 142-8
Skillman, Sydney A., 88, 94, 99
Sloan, Alfred P., Jr., 233n, 263, 263n
Small firm, position of the, 6
Smith, Adam, 149n
Smith, D. K., 7, 7n, 199, 200n
Smith, Richard Austin, 210n, 244n
Soelch, John, 100
Sonnabend, A. M., 97-9, 97n
Specialist producer,
American Motors' role as, 50, 65-6, 69, 275
Studebaker-Packard's return to role as, 94, 102-103, 276
Stigler, George J., 149n, 151n, 256n
Stillerman, Richard, 255n
Stocking, George W., 9, 9n, 192n
Stock, large price rise in common, of American Motors, 64
of Studebaker-Packard, 96
Stock split, reverse, 41, 43
Strikes and other labor difficulties, 13, 26, 105-109
Studebaker (car), 70-1, 73-4, 89-91, 94-5, 94n, 101, 112-13, 115, 136, 175-6, 176n, 179, 180n, 220, 226, 228, 230
Avanti, 103, 140n
Champion, 114
First new postwar car, 106
Hawk, 94, 140n
Lark, 94-7, 99, 101-102, 129, 129n, 130n, 132, 136-7, 136n, 140, 180-1, 245, 276, 278-9
Scotsman, 90, 92, 102, 112
Studebaker Corporation, 1-2, 4n, 8, 13, 18, 20-3, 20n, 22n, 25, 25n, 30, 32, 34, 36, 38n, 40-3, 45, 75, 80-1, 87-8, 91, 102, 106-107, 111, 115-16, 118-21, 120n, 124, 144, 145n, 146, 157n, 158, 162, 166-9, 171, 189, 190n, 205-206, 208, 215, 219, 221, 227, 258, 261, 275
Denial of interest in merger, 40
Merger agreed to, 38-44

Purchases steel plant, 26n, 107
Studebaker Brothers Manufacturing Company, 45
Studebaker Division, Studebaker-Packard Corporation, 43, 72
Los Angeles assembly ended, 86
Packard operations consolidated with, 87
Studebaker International S. A., 100
Studebaker of Canada, Limited, 100
Studebaker-Packard (Studebaker) Corporation, 1-2, 2n, 8, 25, 30n, 38, 38n, 41n, 42-4, 42n, 44n, 50, 70-103, 70n, 71n, 73n, 81n, 87n, 92n, 94n, 95n, 103n, 115-18, 123-5, 123n, 125n, 127-8, 137, 139-41, 145, 147, 157, 157n, 158n, 168, 174-6, 180, 190, 204-206, 209, 215, 219-23, 225-6, 226n, 228-31, 235, 239, 242-5, 250, 250n, 252, 256, 258-9, 261, 264, 268, 275-9, 281-2
Formed by merger, 38-44
Full-line approach, 70-92
Quasi-reorganization, 85-92
Refinancing, 92-5
Renamed Studebaker, 2, 99-100
Separate divisions continued, 43
Transfer to Canada, 2, 101
Utica plant, 40, 72, 78, 84-6, 94-5, 157n, 158
Studebaker Universal S. A., 100
Style, 73, 90, 188, 201-16, 240
Subcommittee on Antitrust and Monopoly (see House, Committee of the Judiciary, and Senate, Committee on the Judiciary)
Suits, Daniel B., 196-7, 196n, 197n
"Supermarket" dealers, 30
Szeliski, Victor von, 196, 196n, 197n

Talbott, Foster W., 224n
Tax(es), 264
Loss to carry back or carry

forward, 97
Credits, 21, 37, 41, 58, 61-2, 75
Thomas B. Jeffery Company, 44
Thomas, Kenneth, 100
Tooling costs, 55, 60, 71, 143-5, 159-62, 165, 167, 194, 204-16, 244
Torsion bar suspension, 71, 256
"Trade-ins," used car, 27-8, 28n
Trans International Airlines, Inc., 98, 100
Turner, Donald F., 270n

United Automobile Workers of America, 67, 67n, 116, 117n, 18
United States v. Aluminum Company of America, 271n
Used car sales, 27
Utica-Bend Corporation, 85, 94
Utica plant (see Studebaker-Packard)

Vance, Harold S., 32, 42, 87-8
Vanderblue, Homer B., 201n
V-8 engine, 50-1, 59-60, 71, 73, 86, 102, 119-20, 120n, 158, 214, 278
Volkswagen, 128-9, 129n, 132, 135-6, 241n
Volume leadership, struggle for, 29
von Szeliski (see Szeliski)

Warner Gear, 22
Warnken, E. P., 100
Watkins, Myron W., 9, 9n, 192n
Weiss, Leonard W., 9n, 263n
Wheeler, John T., 271n
Whitmer, A. D., 100
Williams, John D., 145
Willys Motors Division, Kaiser Industries, Inc., 7n
Willys-Overland Motors, Incorporated, 8, 34, 42, 190
Wilson, Charles E. ("Engine Charlie"), 41
Wolfson, Louis E., 60

Yntema, Theodore, 121n, 161n, 236n